D1119635

From Script To Production

From Script to Production

By Jonathan Saville
University of California
San Diego

Educational Associates
Little, Brown and Company, Boston

Project Manager: Sheridan Hughes
Design and Production: Henry Ratz

Copyright © 1975 by The Regents of the University of
California and the Coast Community College District.
All rights reserved. No part of this book may be
reproduced in any form by any electronic or
mechanical means including information storage and
retrieval systems without permission in writing from
the publisher, except by a reviewer who may quote
brief passages in a review.

Published simultaneously in Canada by Little, Brown
and Company (Canada) Limited.

Library of Congress Catalog Card Number 75-13443

Manufactured in the United States of America

First Printing

Contents

Preface

The first uses of educational television were simply developments of earlier habits. In other words, when it was perceived that the learning process might be enhanced through this medium, the academic world merely converted lectures into speeches and expanded the classroom setting by replicating it on the television screen. The consequence was an overall reduction in the effectiveness of education. It was a misuse of the medium to use the TV set as a kind of sophisticated microphone, with the only advantage being that it enabled the lecturer to drone on before an audience of 1,000 instead of 100. The result was a more complete alienation of students and a failure to utilize the unique properties of an important medium. But finally we are beginning to understand and to take advantage of the full potential of television as a teaching device. If it is at its worst when used to mass-produce speeches or lectures, it is at its best when introduced as another kind of resource. When drama is adapted inventively, when the technical details of perspective, focus, and emphasis are handled with skill, then it becomes possible for television to offer what is at once an aesthetic and an educational experience. And with the advent of public television there has been a resurrection of dramatic performance among other kinds of humanistic enterprise.

One great advantage of putting drama on public television has of course been freedom from those restrictions that hamper commercial television; emphatic commercial triviality has been a barrier to full utilization and enjoyment of the medium. A second advantage has been the development of ways in which action, dialogue, and stage presence have been adapted for the home screen. Public programming of series such as Classic Theatre: The Humanities in Drama, used (as in this book) in conjunction with formal and informal courses in schools and colleges, can afford the viewer a unique combination of entertainment and edification. This is not such a bad thing—we ought to recall that Chaucer's audience and the poet himself had no more sublime end than that in mind.

The dramas analyzed, discussed, and reviewed in this volume constitute what is really a new scholarly resource, an archive of dramatic production. I have always felt it essential to match simple literary acquaintance with a living production, for the real test of a drama is the way it goes over on stage. Nothing can be of more use and pleasure to the reader of plays than to be informed and contradicted by an intelligent and lively stage interpretation. As productions, these plays are immensely distinguished, involving some of the finest actors and companies now at work. They bespeak the justifiable pride of those repertory groups, schools, and training centers that have given us a viable modern stage. But it would not be to the point to view all this or to read it without remembering that these plays are documents of humanism. It did not seem contradictory to those who created our intellectual tradition to have that tradition affirm or criticize itself in dramatic dialogue. My own sense of drama has always been that of philosophy in action. I hope the reader will find these texts and commentaries to be as relevant to his own life as they are to the more immediate purpose they serve.

Ronald Berman

Chairman
National Endowment for the Humanities
Washington, D.C.

Introduction

The student whose experience of the theatre is confined to reading the printed texts of plays (and this is the case in most drama courses) sees only the skeleton of this art. The atmosphere created by a set, the characterization suggested by costumes, the sound of voices, the feelings expressed through gesture, the inflection given to a line or phrase—all these the reader must supply from his own imagination. Often enough his perceptions of these elements are vague and inconsistent, and sometimes he may forget about them altogether.

The playgoer, on the other hand, has a full experience of the play—staged, spoken, acted, converted into the living image of reality that only the theatre, of all the arts, can give us. But unless he knows the script on which the production is based, he will not be aware of the ways in which this particular production is only one of a large number of possible stagings of the same play. He will not be conscious of that immense series of decisive choices by means of which the director, the scenic and costume designers, and the actors have transformed the script into a particular and unique embodiment of its words, different from all other productions, past and future.

The Classic Theatre and the texts that accompany it attempt to give the student both perspectives—that of the playgoer, who sees a particular production, and that of the reader, who silently absorbs into his imagination the script on which all productions of the play must be based. It is the special aim of *From Script to Production* to sharpen the student's awareness of the differences between the printed and the staged play, and of the radical transformation a play undergoes when a particular group of theatre people set out to make it their own. In the thirteen chapters of this collection—one for each drama in The Classic Theatre—the main emphasis is therefore on the relationship between script and production, and the articles chosen for inclusion all, in one way or another, focus on this issue.

Among the commentaries collected here, the reader will find literary analyses of the plays, discussions of problems of interpretation and staging, accounts of the circumstances under which the plays were first produced, and reviews of various productions ancient and modern. Thus, for example, there is an analysis of *The Playboy of the Western World* based purely on the printed text but with implications as to how the play ought to be directed and acted; an interview with the director of The Classic Theatre's *Edward II;* a description of theatres and theatre-going in the eighteenth century that throws light on the early production problems of *The Rivals;* a detailed account of the Moscow Art Theatre's production of *The Three Sisters,* under the direction of Stanislavsky and Nemirovich-Danchenko; a discussion of three films based on *Macbeth;* and nine reviews of various productions of *Hedda Gabler* and of various actresses—great and not so great—in the title role. Having read these articles and reviews—and having seen and read the plays themselves—the student will probably abandon forever any illusions he may have had as to the possibility of a definitive production of *Macbeth* or *Hedda;* and I think it likely he will also give up the notion that the script alone provides an answer to all questions one may bring to it. You cannot have theatre without playwrights—but at the same time you cannot have theatre without directors, designers, and actors; and the play itself takes on its full (and ever changing) reality only with the participation of all of these.

The selections that follow are reproduced unchanged in format and spelling from the original sources, all of which are specified in footnotes; omissions are indicated by ellipses. Titles and section headings in brackets have been added by the editor.

From Script to Production forms part of a course devised by University of California Extension, San Diego, and it was written with their administrative support. Mary Lindenstein Walshok, Marjorie Schneider, and—especially—Cathy Todd played important roles in the preparation of the book. Special thanks are due to Larry Kramer for his tireless aid in researching the subject and locating the selections, and to Sheridan Hughes for her exceptionally skillful administration of the entire project, carried out with impeccable efficiency under conditions of great pressure. The book is respectfully dedicated to F., D., and L. P.

Jonathan Saville

La Jolla, California

Macbeth

William Charles Macready (1793–1873) was a famous English actor who played the role of Macbeth many times between 1820 and 1851. The following article, based on a prompt book of a Macready production and on contemporary reviews, describes his performance. We give three excerpts from the description: Macbeth's first encounter with the witches (Act I, Scene iii), the sequence of events from the dagger soliloquy to the knocking at the gate (Act II, Scenes i and ii), and the scene of Macbeth's final defeat (Act V, Scene vii).

MACREADY'S PRODUCTION OF *MACBETH*
Alan S. Downer

The martial music ceases. The three witches are by this time lined up on the left side of the stage, awaiting the entrance of Macbeth.

He comes in, from the back at right, crossing a rustic bridge in the center, and walking towards the footlights like a warrior returning homeward flushed with victory, glancing at the sky as he says, "So fair and foul a day I have not seen." He is average height, something under six feet, and he speaks with a quiet voice which suggests subdued power. His wig is short and black, and a clipped beard and moustache outline his face. He is wearing a knee-length garment which suggests a kilt, a beret with badge and feather, and a plaid scarf thrown over his left shoulder. In his right hand he bears his baton, on his left arm a small round shield.

Banquo is with him, on his left, as he sees the witches. When he asks, "Are you aught that man may question?" each witch lays the forefinger of her right hand on her lips and with her left hand points at Macbeth. Macbeth turns to the witches, his right hand raised in surprise, his left clutching his scarf, his eyes wide and his mouth slightly open. The witches then address the hero after each "Hail" pointing with a crooked finger. After their predictions, they start to withdraw, and Macbeth crosses to them with, "Stay you imperfect speakers," in a curt and fretful manner.

The King's messengers arrive, convey their information, and are thanked for their pains. They bow and confer on the left, moving upstage to center as Banquo goes up to speak with them (l. 127), leaving Macbeth alone, on the apron, for his soliloquy. This is spoken with an air of brooding revery and he exclaims, as if endeavouring to deceive himself, "This supernatural soliciting cannot be ill"; and then continues, in a startled and hurried manner, as if a thought of indefinable evil shot through his mind, "Cannot be good." From this moment on, Macbeth is an altered man, shaken by dark emotions, the slave of fate: "If chance will have me king, why chance may crown me." He is in fact so wrapped in his horrible imaginings, that unconscious of his companions he works across the stage to the right before they break in upon him. Recalled to his senses, he speaks to his friends with overdone warmth, as Banquo goes once more up stage across the bridge and pantomimes orders to the army waiting off right. The martial music resumes as Macbeth orders them towards the King, and the curtain falls on the general exit. . . .

Excerpted from Alan S. Downer, "Macready's Production of *Macbeth,*" *Quarterly Journal of Speech,* vol. 33, no. 2 (April 1947), 172–181. Reprinted by permission of the Speech Communication Association.

. . . The whole soliloquy is delivered with a ghastly expression of imaginative terror, the earlier portion at once majestic and awful, with one of Macready's typical elisions: "There's no such *thingitisthe* bloody business. . . ." As he comes to the end, the bell strikes twice, off left; in an almost imploring voice he cries,

> Hea-hear it not Duncan, for it is a knell,
> That summons thee to heaven or to hell,

pointing upward and downward. He disappears into the King's chamber, with a crouching form and a stealthy, felon-like step, pausing when part way through the door so that his left leg and foot remain tremblingly in sight for a moment.

The sounds of rain and thunder roll forth loud and long as Lady Macbeth comes on stage, and continue until she is firmly established in the center of the scene. Thunder punctuates her speech, after "stern'st good night," after "Whether they live or die." At this point the storm breaks out afresh, and Macbeth's offstage cry and his Lady's speech are muffled by it. Suddenly, Macbeth rushes on stage, two daggers clicking like castanets in his hands; he stops, bent backwards as if shot through the breast with an arrow. His face is white, his hands and daggers stained with gore. In a broken and terrifying whisper, he says, "I have done the deed. Didst thou not hear a noise?" He infuses additional pathos into his need of blessing by repetition:

> "Amen"
> Stuck—stuck in my throat.

Lady Macbeth takes the daggers and goes into the King's chamber, shutting the door behind her. The knocking commences; Macbeth's lamentations for his lost innocence become fearfully bitter. As the Lady returns, he buries his head in his arms, and the knocking continues until his savage howl,

> Wake Duncan with thy knocking. I would thou couldst!

He stands with his face turned from his wife and his arms outstretched to the irrecoverable past. As she drags him from the stage to their chambers, nothing remains but darkness and the sound of knocking. . . .

. . . All, however, is but preparation for the climactic moment of the play: the death duel between Macduff and Macbeth. Once more the scene is on the ramparts of the castle, with a great iron gate in the background. Macbeth enters, determining not to commit suicide. The gates are burst open with a tremendous shout and Macduff rushes on, crying, "Turn, hellhound, turn!" Macbeth warns him off, but Macduff engages him with his sword. After a few passes, Macbeth throws him back, his countenance flushed with conscious security, with an expression of ineffable contempt. Holding his sword with careless ease, he announces that he bears a charmed life. Macduff counters with the story of his nativity, and the effect upon Macbeth is wondrous. Like a man about to be devoured by a wild beast, he stands gazing upon his enemy in breathless horror as if all the sinews of his frame had relaxed at one moment. "I'll not fight with thee!" he cries, and retreats towards the castle.

Macduff's taunts of "Coward" and "Show and gaze o' th' time" awaken in him his martial ardor. He turns upon his fate, and stands at bay. His eye kindles, his bosom swells, his head is upreared in defiance, and "deserted by fate and metaphysical aid," he summons up his honest power to fight and die like a hero. The swordsmen rush upon each other and after a few desperate passes, Macbeth receives his death wound and staggers back. He catches himself, and with a momentary suggestion of his regal stride returns, only to fall on Macduff's sword in yielding weakness. The spirit fights, but the body sinks in mortal faintness. Thrusting his sword into the ground, he raises himself by its help to his knees where he stares full in the face of his vanquisher with a resolute and defiant gaze of concentrated Majesty, Hate, and Knowledge, and falls dead, as Malcolm and his thanes enter. To the general cry of "Hail, King of Scotland," the curtain falls.

Charles John Kean (1811–1868) was another English tragedian well known for his Shakespearian roles. In a quite negative review of Kean's Macbeth, G. H. Lewes presents his own views of the role and describes what he considers Kean's failures in interpretation.

CHARLES KEAN AS MACBETH
G. H. Lewes

. . . Macbeth himself admits of two different conceptions. He may be represented as "bloody, bold, and resolute"—a border chieftain in a turbulent and incult period—a man of the dark ages, rushing onwards with reckless impetuosity—murdering his royal host, seizing the crown, and accomplishing his *coup d'état* without respect to persons. In this view, all the metaphysical meshes which entangle him would be but the excuses of his conscience, or the instruments used to serve his purpose; they would be to him what "Socialism" and "saving society" were to that more ignoble usurper who snatched a crown in 1852. I do not think this the Shakespearian Macbeth; but I think it is a conception of the character which might be very dramatic and effective. The other and the truer conception would represent a wild, rude, heroic nature, hurried by his passions into crime, but great even in crime—severed from the rectilinear path of honour by the horrible suggestions of the Witches coming upon him in the flush and exaltation of victory, and playing on his active imaginations, making him its slave. For Macbeth is distinctively a bold soldier, and a man of most impressible imagination. He is intensely superstitious: in those days all men were, but the imaginative were so to an inordinate degree. He *sees* a dagger in the air; he *hears* the sleeper say, "Macbeth doth murder sleep; Macbeth shall sleep no more." He tells us how Macbeth is represented as more imaginative than the common run of men. He is good, too; full of the milk of human kindness. He would be great, is not without ambition, but is without the ill-

From G. H. Lewes, "Charles Kean as Macbeth," reprinted in George Rowell, ed., *Victorian Dramatic Criticism* (London: Methuen, 1971), pp. 93–97. (Originally in *The Leader,* February 19, 1853.)

ness which should attend it. He desires highly, but would win holily. He has a moral conscience. And here lies the tragedy. He is no common murderer; he is criminal because great temptations overcome great struggles; the tragic collision of antagonistic principles—Ambition and Conscience—take him from the records of vulgar crime, and raise him into a character fitly employed by Art. One might enlarge here upon the manner in which Shakespeare's own intense reflectiveness is allowed to shine through his varied creations. He cannot even take this wild, feudal chief, without making him nearly as metaphysical as Hamlet. I hint this view, and pass on.

All through the play we see him as one made irresolute by conscience, but resolute and terrible in act—when roused to action—because his nature is that of a brave onrushing soldier. His hands once reddened by murder, he pursues with vigour the murderer's career. He is bold, even in the very face of his superstition. What though Birnam wood *be* come to Dunsinane, and what though Macduff be not of woman born, the soldier fights like a desperate man, defiant of the metaphysical terrors that shake him.

Does Charles Kean represent either of these characters? He does not. He cannot be said to take any view of the *character* at all; he tries to embody the various feelings of each situation; taking, however, the literal and unintelligent interpretation, so that almost every phase of the character is falsified. We see neither the gallant soldier, nor the imaginative man. His bearing is neither warrior-like nor reflective. The wondrous touches with which Shakespeare illuminates the character are all slurred over by him. When the witches accost him, his only expression of "metaphysical influence" is to stand still with his eyes fixed and his mouth open, in the way you know. The *fluctuating* emotions which Macbeth must be undergoing all that time are expressed by a *fixed* stare. And the profound art of Shakespeare, shown in Macbeth's *tentative* appeals to Banquo—avoiding all mention of what the witches promised him, yet trying to get at Banquo's thoughts by alluding to Banquo's children—these touches, which an actor of intelligence could not, one would think, fail to make impressive, are passed over by Charles Kean, as if they were ordinary lines of the text. As a palpable illustration of his unintelligent reading of the character, let me refer to what I have before called his *literal* interpretation (it is of that kind which always supposes that the word "tears" must be uttered in a tearful voice). In that famous dagger soliloquy, will it be credited that he does not rise to a crescendo of horrible amazement at the words

Thou marshall'st me the way that I was going!

but at the superfluous fact that

Such an instrument I was to use;

and again he flies into a paroxysm of horror at seeing "on its blade and dudgeon gouts of blood." Now, considering that he has already determined on murdering Duncan, and the dagger has marshalled him the way, the horror at gouts of blood is ludicrous; the horror is the parent, not the child of his blood; it precedes, it does not succeed it. Let me call attention to one egregious and constant mistake Charles Kean commits in this as in other parts—viz., the alternation of explosive rant with calmness. One moment he is ranting till his voice is hoarse, and the next he is as quiet as a melancholy recluse. Now every one knows that even in the subsidence of rage there is peculiar agitation; and although the voice may be low, its tones are tremulous.

In Charles Kean's Macbeth all the tragedy has vanished; sympathy is impossible, because the mind of the criminal is hidden from us. He makes Macbeth ignoble—one whose crime is that of a common murderer, with perhaps a tendency towards Methodism.

Richard David's detailed review of two modern British productions of Macbeth *shows the enormous number of complex choices (in acting, direction, sets, costumes, casting) that go into the staging of this play, and how radically different two productions based on the same text may be. The two productions are: Michael Benthall's at the Old Vic (winter, 1954–55), with Paul Rogers in the title role, and Glen Byam Shaw's at the Shakespeare Memorial Theatre, Stratford-upon-Avon (summer, 1955), with the Macbeth of Sir Laurence Olivier.*

THE TRAGIC CURVE
Richard David

. . . During the season 1954–5 the Shakespeare theatres of both London and Stratford confined themselves to a single—and the same—tragedy: *Macbeth.* The two productions were diametrically opposed in intention and method. A comparison between the two is therefore interesting in itself. I hope it may also demonstrate the nature of the tragic curve, how it runs in *Macbeth,* and in what ways actors and producers may sustain or suppress it.

The producer's problem in *Macbeth* is a particularly hard one, for three reasons. In the first place the play, like so many of Shakespeare's tragedies but more so than most, exists on several levels at once. Like *Hamlet* it is a first-rate thriller as well as a tragedy; but whereas in *Hamlet* the tragic burden is so much wrought into the fabric that the work does not make sense when presented as a straight "Revenge play," the Grand Guignol *Macbeth* can stand on its own legs. There are, then, the two equal and opposite errors, of playing the piece as melodrama without poetry and sacrificing dramatic grip for the tragic overtones. Secondly, in taking the butcher Macbeth as his tragic hero Shakespeare was sailing as near the wind as it is possible to go; he risked alienating the sympathy and cooperation of the audience, which is essential if the tragic progress is to have significance. As Aristotle said, the fall of a plain bad man is plain uninteresting. Thirdly, the tragic curve in *Macbeth* is of a peculiar foreshortened variety. The hero is tempted in the third scene, falls in the seventh, and by the eighth is damned beyond redemption. Shakespeare uses some subtlety in making the process appear more extended than it is, and a corresponding subtlety is required of actor and producer.

Excerpted from Richard David, "The Tragic Curve," *Shakespeare Survey* (Cambridge: Cambridge University Press, 1956), Volume 9, pp. 122–131. Reprinted by permission of Cambridge University Press.

Michael Benthall's production at the Old Vic, with Paul Rogers in the name part, leant very much towards the melodramatic. It must have been the noisiest *Macbeth* ever. The play opened with a wild and raucous cry, as a battle-casualty, leaving the field where Macbeth and the rebels could still be heard "memorizing another Golgotha," staggered on to the stage and fell, to be ghoulishly seized upon by the witches in the guise of ragged camp-scavengers. Every entry was clamorously accompanied by trumpet and drum, or by the pipes at full blow. At every opportunity the rough and eager thanes spurred on the action by their interjections of scorn or cheers of approval. The set (by Audrey Cruddas) was no more than a rough-hewn square arch, on either side of which appeared, as necessary for the indoor scenes, doorways, recesses, the lower treads of a sharply ramped and angled staircase. Through the opening of the arch was seen, dimly, the bleak heath or the dark inward of the castle and, suddenly, for the English scene, a dazzling rain-washed sky, pure and pitiful—the most moving visual effect in the play. In this spare setting the actors moved with exemplary speed and urgency. Such scenes as that of Duncan's murder gained enormously from all this; the racing terror of the interchange between murderer and accomplice—

> Did not you speak?
> > When?
> > > Now.
> > > > As I descended?
> Ay.

could hardly have been bettered. But there was seldom any variation in this hurdling pace, never a let-up or breather; even the English scene, after the initial effect of the heavens opening, was conducted at a brisk and worldly trot. This is not of course a matter just of words-per-second. The "Tomorrow" speech (of which more hereafter) was, by metronome, exceedingly slow; but because it was interpreted at plot-level, as an illustration of rather than as a comment upon the action, the audience's reaction-clock continued to tick brightly through it, keeping perfect time.

As Macbeth, Rogers accepted his part in the thriller. The play might as well have been called "Manhunt" as "Macbeth," for the audience was never called upon to agonize for a tragic hero but only to witness with excitement and approval the cornering of a dangerous killer by the forces of the law. This Macbeth, at his very first entry, was already clearly cut off from human help and human contact. He had that whickering look in the eye of a horse about to shy or a Faustus expecting the Devil at any moment to present his bill. He could not be drawn inexorably into the web of evil, for he was already in it and could only thresh about in the meshes. In other words the tragic curve had been cut down to its last, declining section, and this had then to be spun out over five acts. At this stage of his progress the hero is reduced to only two reactions, frenzy and exhaustion. These, exaggerated in the very conception of the production, became, by the usual debasing process of a long run, in the end almost ludicrous. At each performance the later speeches became more frothily unintelligible, the pauses between the "Tomorrows" were longer drawn out, the contrast between the black hair of Act one and the white of Act five was heightened, and the panting in the final duel sounded more like a wheezy steam-engine. It is only fair to add that these extravagances were as tumultuously clapped on the last night as on the first. . . .

The Stratford production, directed by Glen Byam Shaw, was anything but gang-sterly. David King's bloody sergeant and Geoffrey Bayldon's Duncan gave the play a rousing send-off, and the final battle-scenes, with the assailants tumbling up the battle-ments from the back of the stage, went with a swing; but with Macbeth's presence the movement became slow, quiet, withdrawn. The critics complained that Olivier seemed almost indifferent whether he killed Duncan or not. The effect, as we shall see, was de-liberate, but in attaining it the producer was compelled to forgo precisely that kind of suspense and plot-tension that was the mainspring of the Benthall version. Against this loss must be set two overwhelming gains: a Macbeth who held the full sympathy of the audience to the bitter end, and a true conveying of that atmosphere of mystery that is peculiar to the play.

Here a digression is needed—a digression, because this mystery is not the essence of the tragedy, does not shape the tragic curve, but is an incidental colouring only, without which, it must be admitted, *Macbeth* would not be *Macbeth*. It is generated, in large part, by the witches. Can the witches, in this twentieth century, be presented as anything but figures of fun?

The tendency has been to make them human in the hope of making them credi-ble, and to bring out in each a distinguishing "character" to give them solidity. Of the Stratford witches a gossip-writer objected: "Must they always be so *unanimous,* always give—like occult prototypes of the Beverley Sisters—an object-lesson in coordination and *esprit de corps?* Surely their scenes might gain from a suggestion of disharmony or at least variety between the three, from a little bumping and boring round the cauldron-mouth? They are unnatural enough in other ways without being, for old women, unna-turally cooperative." This surely is the most wrong-headed nonsense. The purpose, the effect of the witches are single. The three are collectively a manifestation of evil. There is more than one witch because antiphony is dramatically more effective than mono-logue; they are three, because that is a handy number and has magical associations.

The Old Vic followed the gossip-writer's recipe. There was one fishwife, one female impersonator haggish and falsetto, one ditto in *ottava bassa* and made up as the Ugly Duchess. Not for one moment did they suggest that they were to be feared, or create any atmosphere beyond that of the music-hall. The Stratford witches were all alike, in rags certainly, but rags of a silvery grey that seemed part of the early mist, and with lank grey locks unbound about their faces. Whereas the Old Vic witches kept up a per-petual hurly-burly, these were predominantly still (save for an unnecessary weaving of the hands), now in a huddle mid-stage, now, with a start, sliding three ways into its corners. Though their performance had not quite the concentration required to per-suade us that evil was here personified, at least they never broke the mystery or fell out into the full daylight of ridicule.

The other ingredient of this mystery is of course provided by Macbeth himself in his more reflective speeches. Rogers, carried along post-haste by the action of the play, could never afford for a minute to relinquish the role of man of action and paint the scene. Such speeches as "Now o'er the one half-world Nature seems dead," or "Come, seeling night," were spurs to action, not reflections on the ghastly implications of ac-tion; each word was pressed to give, vehemently, its full and active meaning. Olivier, on the other hand, was able, without breaking the thread of the play, to step for a moment outside it and project an authentic spell over the auditorium. What a chill was in his rooky wood! The secret of his power was that the whole action was presented as, in a sense, outside time; it was not, as at the Vic, a crisp series of events, consequentially interlocked and reported by an outside observer, but Macbeth's nightmare vision of his own predicament. The hideous deeds presented to his will seemed, like the air-drawn dagger, unreal; his intellect rejects them, and yet he remains under a terrible and inescapable compulsion to do them. He is a man possessed, but by no petty devil capable of no more than fits and froth. It was Olivier's achievement to make the audience share this possession, to bring them under the same spell, so that they experienced Macbeth's progress from the inside and themselves travelled the tragic curve.

This sympathy, in the literal sense, was maintained until the very end of the play. Even when intellectually the audience has long changed sides and stands with the heaven-blest justicers from England, it could still be drawn to feel and to share the ache of the mind diseased, the rooted sorrow. Rogers, in this speech to the doctor, had been a Hitler rating an incompetent subordinate: there was no distinction between "Canst thou not minister" and "Throw physic to the dogs." Olivier's Macbeth, with a tender flexibility of phrasing, not only showed us the bond of affection between husband and wife but also (the hands gesturing dumbly and half-unconsciously towards his own breast) included himself in the plea for mercy. Or take the "Tomorrow" speech. In such set-pieces Olivier often appears to be unconventional, wilful even, for the sake of being different. There seemed no particular reason for any one of his intonations, pauses, emphases here. Paul Rogers had used the speech to portray utter spiritual exhaustion: the words issued one by one, with great silences between, as if from parched lips, in an almost monotonous whisper. Yet if you strained your ears through the pianissimo and the pauses you could detect that fundamentally every tone and stress was natural and logical. There was no obvious logic in Olivier's version; but as a whole—and with the mazed head-shake of the final "nothing"—it perfectly conveyed the hurt bewilderment of Fate's victim. Almost one said "a man more sinned against than sinning."

With the whole action of the play as it were absorbed into Macbeth the other characters and the accessories were automatically reduced in importance. Yet the meditative pace of the production allowed the designer, Roger Furse, to elaborate his scenery and devise some happy effects of atmosphere. The sets were for the most part realistic (except that the pointed arches were obstinately asymmetrical); the heath was authentically heathery, the castle had indeed a pleasant seat overlooking a loch-filled glen, and for the last scenes of the play we were on the very battlements with a distant view of snow-covered Grampians. Particularly effective was the narrow, cloister-like corridor at the far end of which suddenly appeared the spark of the sleep-walker's taper; while the only blunder was the setting of the English scene. Here what is needed is the strongest possible contrast to shag-haired Scotland, and this poor poster of Cumberland hills was not sufficiently distinct to become the rival symbol and to stand for sanity, piety and civilization. If we must have realism here, only Windsor Castle or the Tower of London will do. But for the most part the naturalism of the sets succeeded in underlining the supernatural strangeness of the scenes they framed. (The clothes were not so happy. Whereas Audrey Cruddas at the Vic dressed the characters in neat, dark kilts, workmanlike leather jerkins, and rough bear-skins, Furse chose the more treacherous kirtles and cloaks. Poor Banquo, in a carroty bob and knee-length greeny-blue nightie, was cruelly served.) . . .

It was Macbeth's play. And yet Sir Laurence's success was fed by the brilliant direction of Glen Byam Shaw. Scene after scene was lit by touches of genius: sometimes the merest details in aid of continuity and plausibility, as when the attendant, who is later to usher in Banquo's murderers, at Macbeth's state entry takes a step forward but checks at the look in the King's eye warning him not to broach the business at so public a moment; or Macbeth's overhearing of the young princes' plan to flee the country; or his threatening of Macduff, in the witches' cavern, interrupted by the sound of the galloping messengers who (we learn later) bring the news that Macduff has escaped him. Others added touches of vitality: the murderer, greeted by Macbeth with "There's blood upon thy face," claps a guilty hand to his cheek before resuming sufficient boldness to retort " 'Tis Banquo's then." Others again, no less simple and direct, were of greater import. Let me take a few of the key scenes and, comparing them with the Old Vic versions, support my view that Byam Shaw gave us Shakespeare's tragedy in all its balanced perfection, Benthall another play of the same name.

The Old Vic opening has already been described. Stratford began with a conjuring trick. The witches were discovered, in a close group, apparently floating in mid air; as the scene proceeded they slowly came to earth. It was apparently because there was only one such stunt that the first-night reporters decided that on the whole the production was dull. At the risk of appearing merely contrary I say that this opening was Byam Shaw's one serious blunder. The audience was bound to be so curious as to how the trick was worked (was that a gauze sliding up to the flies?) that they could have no eyes or ears for the witches themselves, or for Shakespeare's purpose in bringing them on at all.

Skip to their meeting with Macbeth. At the Vic the day was more foul than fair. The witches, excited and garrulous, ranged over the whole stage before retreating right as Macbeth and Banquo entered from the left. The encounter was face to face across the width of the stage, factual, impartial. At Stratford there was a boulder mid-stage on which the witches huddled side by side to exchange their sinister confidences. At the sound of Macbeth's drum they shrank into the prompt corner, their greyness blending with the nondescript colour of wings and proscenium. Macbeth, entering up-stage right, advanced to the centre and stepped up onto the boulder, where he stood bathed in strong light as of the setting sun (here it was more fair than foul). Thus all attention was concentrated on the face of Macbeth as he stiffened at sight of the witches and as, guarded still, he listened to their prophecies. All the tension was gained by this device of focusing. Whereas at the Vic Banquo was made fiercely suspicious, Macbeth shaken to pieces by the apparition, at Stratford the commonsensical Banquo rather doubted his senses, while Macbeth, when he finally stepped forward to debate the "imperial theme," showed no more than head-shaking puzzlement till a sudden tremor on "unfix my hair and make my seated heart knock at my ribs" betrayed the hidden disturbance. Note also how Byam Shaw got the witches off the stage. At the Vic they had retired, under the persistent questioning, to the central arch, and thence slipped away together while the stage temporarily darkened. At Stratford the bland daylight remained undisturbed over all. As Macbeth fixed on the second witch the first slid like a lizard from the scene; when attention shifted to the third the second was gone; and as Macbeth and Banquo turned on each other in eager surmise the third too vanished. This was genuine producer's sleight of hand, worth all the flying-ballet apparatus in the theatre workshop.

Turn now to the long sequence leading up to Duncan's murder and its discovery. "If the assassination Could trammel up the consequence, and catch With his surcease success": again the opening speech, examined in isolation, did not convince. The hissing sibilants, the lines tumbling one into another, surely suggest breathless excitement, near hysteria, and so Paul Rogers rendered it, though perhaps with too much emphasis to catch the authentic note of panic. Olivier, on the other hand, was merely petulant— with the object maybe of avoiding a too early disintegration into hysteria. There could, however, be no doubts about the succeeding interchange with Lady Macbeth, a perfectly modulated "movement," in which Macbeth's fate is sealed. To her first taunts he remained obstinately impervious, his back turned. She drew closer, and launched into the horrible boast of her own callousness that is to shock him into compliance. At this Macbeth swung round to her, his back now to the audience, and laid his hand on her elbow in a gesture at once deeply affectionate and protesting. As she persisted in her self-torture, he tore himself away and moved across the stage, but his rejoinder, over his shoulder, the last weak objection of "If we should fail," showed that his defences were shaken. Lady Macbeth again moved to him and seizing him by the shoulders from behind murmured in his ear the final temptation—how easy is it then. He turned to her with "Bring forth men children only," but it was said wryly, in almost mocking praise of her lack of scruple, and he still did not take her hand. There needed a further pause for reflection, the growing confidence of "Will it not be received . . . ?" before with "I am settled" he was her own again.

Not long after came another imaginative stroke. Lady Macbeth has gone to drug the grooms, Macbeth is giving last instructions to the servant. The man is still beside him when he sees the spectral dagger and checks at it like a pointer. With a terrible effort he withdraws his gaze for a moment and dismisses the servant; then with a swift and horrid compulsion swings round again. The first part of the dagger speech was spoken with a sort of broken quiet, only the sudden shrillness of "Mine eyes are made the fools o' th' other senses" and "There's no such thing" revealing the intolerable tension that strains the speaker. Rogers at the Old Vic used more voice, and carried on in this more openly rhetorical style to the end of the speech. "Tarquin's ravishing strides" he illustrated by taking three paces, tramp, tramp, tramp, across the stage; and kneeling at the foot of the stone steps to Duncan's room he adjured them not to betray his further advance. Olivier dismissed the influence of evil in its physical manifestation only to be more strongly seized by it in his mind. The second part of the speech sank to a drugged whisper and, speaking, Macbeth moved, as in a dream, towards Duncan's room, but with his face turned away from it. Tarquin's strides were only dimly reflected in the dragging pace, and it was the already trodden stones behind him that Macbeth, with deprecating hand, implored to silence. It was this scene above all that brought the audience under the enchantment.

About the murder itself little need be said. The Old Vic had the lead here, for Stratford allowed too much of the urgency to leak away. Yet there were great moments. Vivien Leigh was at her searing best, and I shall long remember the despairing, fumbling abhorrence with which Olivier sought to ward off the multitudinous seas of blood that seemed to be swirling about his very knees.

At the Old Vic the admirable thread of the scene was rudely broken by the most stupendous knocking—the same error that in *Lear* accompanies the King's distracted exit from Gloucester's castle with the father and mother of all thunderclaps. At Stratford the knocking was peremptory but distant—a summons, not instant execution. The flow of the scene was checked by it and diverted in a new direction, not permanently interrupted. Nor was the porter allowed to be more than an interlude. At the Vic the contrast between the racing murder-scene and Laurence Hardy's expansive jesting was too great, and the whole scene fell into incompatible sections of melodrama and farce. At Stratford Patrick Wymark, though funny, was briskly funny, with all the time a backward glance for the master and mistress whose stage he was conscious of usurping—an impression reinforced by the guilty speed with which he made himself scarce on Macbeth's re-entry.

Paul Rogers reappeared in a long ashen robe and, all the time that Macduff was in Duncan's room, remained leaning against the wall at the foot of the staircase, gazing up it as if almost fainting in anticipation. Small wonder that Lennox became immediately suspicious, or that suspicion grew by leaps and bounds at Lady Macbeth's patently false "What, in our house?", at her feigned swoon, and at Macbeth's extravagant rhetoric, so that at the end of the scene the murderer stood ringed by angry and accusing faces. Olivier, in a black monkish cassock, paced the stage uneasily, by fits and starts, during the conversation with Lennox, his guilty hands closely folded in his long sleeves except when, with a gesture at once furtive and half-automatic, he withdrew them for a moment and hurriedly inspected them front and back. The flurry of the alarm was well done, the stage filling confusedly and yet without confusion. In the hurlyburly "What, in our house?" was no more than faintly off-key, but Lady Macbeth, anxiously aware of the slip, was fain to feel her way to the support of the proscenium arch. Macbeth re-entered from Duncan's room at the opposite side and at the back, and began his act, glancing uneasily for support to his wife, now divided from him by the whole diagonal of the stage. She instinctively took a step forward to assist him and, as Macbeth's web of deception grew more and more tangled, slowly, inexorably, the two were drawn together by the compulsion of their common guilt to the centre of the stage. Just before she reached her husband Lady Macbeth fainted. Genuine? Feigned? No need even to ask the question. Her collapse was as inevitable a result of the dramatic process as is the spark when two charged wires are brought together. Here was first-rate theatre.

In these earlier scenes Benthall and Rogers, by speeding up the deterioration in the hero's character, had further foreshortened Shakespeare's already foreshortened process. Now even the action was concertina'd, for the scene of the murder led into a dumb-show of the coronation (the old man submerged) and this into the reception of Banquo. There was thus literally no time for the Macbeths to grow disillusioned with their gains and to realize that "Nought's had, all's spent." The duel between killer and cops was on, and nothing else mattered. Macbeth did not hide the malignancy of his questions about Banquo's ride, a scene played by Olivier in an enchantingly easy banter. The colloquy with the murderers, because it is long, because it is commonly considered dull, because it is not directly concerned with forwarding the plot, was heavily cut. After that it might be truly said of the Old Vic *Macbeth* that all was over bar the shouting.

At Stratford nothing was shirked. The scene of the old man, played with gentle pathos by John MacGregor, made a fitting end to the first movement of the play. His final couplet

> God's benison go with you; and with those
> That would make good of bad, and friends of foes!

has been denounced as a meaningless interpolation. Whatever its meaning, it is evidently authentic Shakespeare, for, like "All may yet be well," it conveys exactly the sense of uneasy pause that regularly occurs at this point in a Shakespearian tragedy. The interview with the murderers was given in full, and became one of the most dramatic and revealing scenes in the play. The murderers, half-scared, half-fascinated by the now evil magnetism of the King, shrank back each time he approached them in a swirl of robes, while he, pacing the stage between and around them, continuously spun a web of bewildering words about their understandings, about his own conscience, about the crime that between them they were to commit. Nor was there any loss of brilliance in the ghost scene; indeed it was here that Olivier's full power, wisely confined till now, was at last unleashed to range magnificently. It may be noted, too, that here again, and in the cauldron scene, the attention at Stratford was characteristically focused on the face of Macbeth, while at the Vic Rogers had his back to the audience, the "thing he looked on" taking the centre of the stage. The Vic incidentally used a vast cauldron from which speaking apparitions could emerge effectively. At Stratford the cauldron was small, and the witches, leaning over it, plucked horrible emblems from it—a severed head transfixed on a pike, a bloody foetus, a waxen crowned child— while the voices came, not altogether satisfactorily, from elsewhere. The severed head was a replica of Macbeth's. Having entered from up stage he stood behind it, echoing with his own head its agonized pose, and the message came as in a trance from his living lips. I expected this severed head to reappear at the end of the play—a fine irony if it could have been brought off, but the producer did not risk it. Not only was Macbeth killed off stage (as in the text) but the "usurper's cursed head" was merely pointed at on an unseen battlement. This I feel is weak. *Macbeth* is the one tragedy of Shakespeare in which the hero does not die before the eyes of the audience, the author having deliberately substituted the more violent alternative of bringing on the head. No doubt the Elizabethans could take this better than we, and in addition were experts in such effects. Still, I should like to see it tried again.

One more scene requires analysis: the murder of Lady Macduff. This again is usually regarded as unimportant or unplayable or both, and is hurried over perfunctorily. The Old Vic made little of it, for Gwen Cherrell could not persuade us that the Lady was real (like the blinding of Gloucester in *Lear* this is essentially a realistic scene) and the killing of the boy was a dagger-of-lath affair. At Stratford Maxine Audley's noble bearing, her passionate resentment at her husband's flight, and her scarce-hidden pride in his honourableness established at once a great lady and a woman of character. The murderers entered to a startled hush; they paused, and then the boy made his ungainly run across the stage, a puny, unplanned, forlorn attempt at defence. A blow with the hilts, a thrust. The murderer hung back, as if himself aghast at what he had done, leaving the boy standing isolated in mid stage, with both hands huddled over his wound. For a long moment he hung, wavering, then crumpled slowly to the ground. There was still silence, a long, shocked silence, before the first animal scream broke from his mother.

This was hitting below the belt, but that is precisely what Shakespeare intended to do. It was not until this moment that the full horror of Macbeth's actions bursts upon the audience. Duncan's murder takes place off stage, and out of sight out of mind; Banquo's we see, but it is a huddled affair in the dark. The third murder is in broad daylight, cold, deliberate, wanton, without any shadow of disguise or palliation. And immediately we are switched from this savage, bestial, devil-possessed Scotland to England, humane, civilized England, the England of Edward the Confessor. Sanity is here to redress the balance; the audience changes sides, and the tragic curve begins to dip towards its setting. . . .

The English director Peter Hall has been much concerned with the problems of transferring Shakespeare to the film. In the following brief excerpts from an interview and a newspaper article, he comments on three of these problems: the greater intimacy of acting style required by the film; the relationship between the speaking of Shakespeare's verses, with the particular rhythm they impose, and the rhythm created by the film director as he cuts and edits what is produced by the cameras; and, finally, the essential difference between writing for the stage and writing for the screen.

[COMMENTS ON FILMING SHAKESPEARE]
Peter Hall

. . . If you boom Shakespeare you lose him. You end up with vocal varnish. It's true there are areas in Shakespeare when mere rhetoric does occur, and then indulgence of this sort is necessary. And there is deliberate rhetoric like the Player King. But in his case, of course, Shakespeare is showing up the kind of rhetoric he believed to be out of date in the theatre, his theatre. The trouble is that the theatre in the nineteenth century went in for rhetoric, the set-piece recitation. I believe in the other school of acting, that of powerful restraint—what Anna Magnani, for example, was doing here the other week in *La Lupa*. Or what Duse, one imagines from the accounts of her and her film

Excerpts from an interview with Roger Manvell (1969) and an article in the *Sunday Times* (January 26, 1969), both reprinted in Roger Manvell, *Shakespeare and the Film* (New York: Praeger, 1971), pp. 122–126. © 1971 by Roger Manvell. Reprinted by permission of Praeger Publishers, Inc., New York, and J. M. Dent & Sons, London.

clips, must have done as distinct from Bernhardt. So when one is filming, the closeness of the camera is no embarrassment. It is, in fact, a support. It insists on thoughtful speech! My company working in the [*Midsummer Night's*] *Dream* already appreciated this because of the work they had done with me in the theatre. All we had to do was make sure the faces did nothing excessive in expression during the close shots. . . .

. . . I believe in editing to the rhythm of the text. Most Shakespearean films, those using the English text, drive me mad because the visual rhythm contradicts the verbal. The verbal rhythm derives, of course, from Shakespeare's use of beat in verse. The important thing in Shakespeare, as in a Mozart aria, is phrasing. There must be some awareness of the end of the line even in Shakespeare's mature verse with its run-on lines; the end of the line still needs marking. Actors tend to meet this requirement in different ways—Peggy Ashcroft, for example, hits the last word in the line percussively; John Gielgud elongates it. But everyone has to do something. The modern generation from the acting schools, I've found, have never even heard of the iambic pentameter. But it's the basic unit of Shakespearean phrasing. Shakespeare has all the formal strength of the great French dramatists, without their rigidity. So the speaking of Shakespeare must conform to this rhythmic pattern. But the traditional Shakespeare film in English has ignored any kind of reflection of the aural pattern in the visual pattern. They should surely match. In the *Dream* my aim was to create a picture rhythm by cutting to the verbal pattern—that is, on the caesura, or at the end of the line. . . .

. . . It's true that Shakespeare's structural rhythms, the counterpoint between scenes, often work in the same way as good film editing. But, in a more important respect, Shakespeare is no screen writer. He is a verbal dramatist, relying on the associative and metaphorical power of words. Action is secondary. What is meant, is said. Even his stage action is verbalised before or after the event.

This is bad screen writing. A good film-script relies on contrasting visual images. What is spoken is of secondary importance. And so potent is the camera in convincing us that we are peering at reality, that dialogue is best under-written or elliptical. . . .

The verbal essence of Shakespeare is inescapably non-cinematic. In spite of this—indeed, in contradiction to it—I have tended to use the advantage of the cinema not to make a film in the accepted sense, but to communicate his words. . . .

The particular advantages and problems of producing Shakespeare for television are the subject of an article about The Classic Theatre's Macbeth. *The following excerpt begins by describing a scene from a rehearsal for the television production, and this is followed by brief interviews with Eric Porter and Janet Suzman (Macbeth and Lady Macbeth).*

LEWIS NKOSI TALKS TO THE TWO LEADING ACTORS IN A NEW PRODUCTION OF *MACBETH*

. . . Then silence. A moment of great emotional stress in the play. Looking pale, fragile and rather insubstantial under the studio make-up, Janet Suzman as Lady Macbeth stretched out her hand to place it reassuringly on a doubting Macbeth. Eric Porter, now magically transformed from the hollow, stooping Soames of *The Forsyte Saga* into a bewildered, massively doomed hero, was holding on to a dagger. Then his hand quietly slipped away, leaving Janet holding the dagger instead.

Janet Suzman, sitting on the floor of her Hampstead house a week later, recalled the incident. "He had never done that before because the dagger wasn't there during the rehearsal. But it was terrific." It is moments like these, perhaps, which suddenly make great television drama.

"I find that the greatest compensation in working in television," said Eric Porter, "is the fact that the camera can work six inches away from the face so that during all these intimate soliloquies—'if it were done, when 'tis done, then 'twere well it were done quickly'—you can look straight into the viewer's eyes."

However, transferring Shakespeare to television is naturally not without headaches. "In television there's this terrible danger," Eric Porter was explaining, "that because they need to change a bit of scenery or that bit of light, they can stop and suddenly: phew!!! It's like a cushion letting the air out. Rather like running a four-minute mile and after about two-and-a-half minutes somebody tells you your shoes have fallen off or your trousers are falling down. You then stop, pull them up quickly and try to get back into the same speed that'll get you into the four-minute class. It's difficult."

Nevertheless, according to Janet Suzman, *"Macbeth is one of the very few Shakespeare plays that, God willing, will work on TV because it's enormously conspiratorial, and sort of urgent. And the scenes are, on the whole, largely between two people or three people. The play has a tremendous pressure on it right from the beginning. There's very little exposition. From that point of view it might be televisionic."*

Lewis Nkosi, "Lewis Nkosi Talks to the Two Leading Actors in a New Production of *Macbeth,*" *Radio Times,* September 17, 1970. Reprinted by permission of *Radio Times,* BBC Publications.

Any production of a Shakespeare play (or of any play) demands that the director and actors find an interpretation that will unify plot, dialogue and action and make them meaningful. The director of a film version must, in addition, decide how far and in what way he will exploit the expressive possibilities of the new medium, and how far he will range from Shakespeare's text and the conventions of stage production. In a discussion of three filmed versions of Macbeth, *Roger Manvell explores three ways of dealing with these various problems: the fairly "straight" production and superficial interpretation of director George Schaefer; the idiosyncratic exploitation of the medium by Orson Welles; and the masterly version of* Macbeth *by the Japanese director Akira Kurosawa, who discards Shakespeare's text, yet at the same time brilliantly recreates on the screen the emotional effects of Shakespeare's tragedy.*

[GEORGE SCHAEFER'S *MACBETH* (1960)]
Roger Manvell

. . . An obvious possibility in filming Shakespeare has always been to provide screen versions of established stars performing characters they have been accustomed to project from the stage. . . . George Schaefer's production of *Macbeth* in 1960, with Maurice Evans and Judith Anderson, was a film in its own right, but with Judith Anderson in particular in one of her established stage parts. . . . George Schaefer's *Macbeth* was directed on a relatively modest scale. Shot in colour on location in the Scottish sunshine, or on the unpretentious castle sets designed by Edward Carrick (Edward Craig, the son of Gordon Craig), this film lacked any feeling for the haunted ferocity of Shakespeare's most fatalistic tragedy, and it should surely have been photographed in black and white. The film has, rather, the respectful earnestness of a routine, academic production in some conventional, well-established theatre. Judith Anderson's over-theatrical Lady Macbeth showed no recognition that to play this woman as a mere virago is to miss the whole point of her over-strained and essentially feminine nature, which leads to her eventual collapse. Maurice Evans's blusteringly masculine Macbeth reveals nothing of the flawed conscience and inner weakness of this man, which make him lose his nerve when driven by his wife to commit the one murder most necessary to the fulfillment of their ambitions, though he is only too ready to consolidate his power, once he has achieved it, by using agents to commit his further crimes for him. It is a major miscalculation in the film to let Macbeth merely dream of his final, and fatal, encounter with the witches instead of facing them out of sheer necessity. Reliance on the occult is an essential part of Macbeth's weakness, and his ever-increasing commitment to witchcraft central to the play's theme. Macbeth's bombast is mere noise to cover over his secret fears and his growing realization that "naught's had, all's spent," a fatalism which finally overcomes him.

Macbeth is one of Shakespeare's more difficult plays; its proper interpretation on the stage has been the subject of debate by actors and actresses at least since the

From Roger Manvell, *Shakespeare and the Film* (New York: Praeger, 1971), pp. 114–116. © 1971 by Roger Manvell. Reprinted by permission of Praeger Publishers, Inc., New York, and J. M. Dent & Sons, London.

eighteenth century, and turns, among other things, on the changing relationship, and balance of power, between Macbeth and his wife. The over traditional performances played on one note by Maurice Evans and Judith Anderson ineffectually mask the great opportunities which the sheer closeness of the film to both character and action makes possible. . . .

SHAKESPEARE BY ORSON WELLES
[FILM VERSION OF *MACBETH* (1948)]
Roger Manvell

. . . Welles's approach to *Macbeth* was bound to be unusual. First of all, he imposed upon it a theme which has no parallel in the text, and announced it himself at the beginning of the film—much as Laurence Olivier was to do at the beginning of *Hamlet.* The words were spoken over shots of the witches seen amid a swirl of mists at work over their cauldron, shaping the clay image of a baby, which was to be a symbol used throughout the film. *Macbeth,* Welles said, was a story which involves "plotting against Christian law and order"; the hostile forces were "agents of chaos, priests of hell and magic" making use of "ambitious men" to achieve their dark and primal purpose. In order to provide a Christian symbol in the film he created a new character, a priest, to whom he gave lines taken over from other, suppressed characters. Welles cut the play extensively (the film runs only eighty-six minutes); he re-arranged scenes; he even introduced lines from other plays. . . .

The action is not only changed, but incredibly speeded up. The friar intervenes after the witches' prophecies; indeed, the prophecies are fulfilled immediately after their announcement; the Thane of Cawdor is dragged on, a prisoner, and his insignia handed over to Macbeth, who at once dictates the letter to his wife, whom we then see reading it. Macbeth, riding through the mist, arrives to join her as Cawdor is executed, the axe descending to the beat of a drum. His head is later put on display, spiked on a lofty cross. Macbeth, in fact, embraces his wife while a corpse swings in the background. Here is speed, but there is more to come. King Duncan, a slow, fat man, arrives as Macbeth and Lady Macbeth are still talking, and while Duncan is praising the beauty and peace of the castle, which is little more than a rugged cavern, Lady Macbeth is presenting Macbeth with the drugged drink for the guards. Banquo arrives, and as soon as he is disposed of, Macbeth plunges into his speech of the "air-drawn" dagger at the line, "Now o'er the one half-world/ Nature seems dead." As he speaks the line, "moves like a ghost" there is a quick dissolve to Lady Macbeth bending over the king. There is recurrent thunder throughout the scene in which she drives him to Duncan's room, where his shadow is seen looming over the sleeping man. An owl shrieks, and he starts in fright. While the murder takes place, off-screen, the cam-

From Roger Manvell, *Shakespeare and the Film* (New York: Praeger, 1971), pp. 56–59. © 1971 by Roger Manvell. Reprinted by permission of Praeger Publishers, Inc., New York, and J. M. Dent & Sons, London.

era holds on to a scene of the castle cliffs. When Macbeth returns to his wife, his hands ("This is a sorry sight") appear to be suddenly enlarged by being held close to the camera.

Welles frequently uses striking compositions, with violent contrast between foreground and background figures. The influence of Eisenstein (who uses these patterns or groupings with greater aesthetic restraint) is evident not only in the deployment of lines of men with their tall and slender lances, but also in the juxtaposition of the characters in twos or threes, often with a vast head-and-shoulders looming in the foreground of the shot, with the complementary character or characters placed (in near profile, or in full figure at a distance) in the background. A composition such as this follows now, with Macbeth in the foreground and Lady Macbeth in full-figure profile posed behind him. The effect is too beautiful, too self-consciously photogenic, destroying the powerful atmosphere of the moment. As she grasps the dagger from him, the knocking at the gate is heard. Water drips down into the courtyard where Macbeth waits, with great play of his hands in the foreground. After the castle has been roused, we go straight over to the establishment of Macbeth and Lady Macbeth as King and Queen with the line: "Thou hast it now: King, Cawdor, Glamis, all." The camera is sharply tilted, the composition becoming again over selfconscious. "You lack the season of all natures, sleep," she says, and adds seductively, "To bed. To bed." But Macbeth draws the curtain between himself and his wife, and his voice rises to a scream on the words, "Methought I heard a voice cry 'Sleep no more'," taken from the scene after Duncan's murder.

The courtyard of Macbeth's royal castle is a purely stylized structure, an open area all but surrounded by towering crags; steps lead down into it. Macbeth, wearing a huge, square-shaped, Mongolian-looking crown cornered with spikes, sits enthroned like a god, the silhouette of his head and shoulders filling the foreground of the frame, while all those who speak to him stand dwarfed below in the courtyard. He summons the murderers destined to kill Banquo; the close-ups develop as he dominates them, and over-stylized two-shots, mostly in profile, are used when Macbeth warns his wife of the impending "deed of dreadful note." When the murderers bring back their news, the camera is tilted up to show Macbeth either flanked by these agents or alone. As his doubts crowd in on him because Fleance has escaped, he wanders through the dripping caverns of the castle, and finally bathes his sweating face in water streaming down the wall. His voice echoes, repeating his words. He comes to a great butt of wine, which leads him straight into the banquet scene, one of the most effective sequences in the film. His face blenches at the sight of the ghost, and the scene cuts to the astonished, staring faces of the guests. Back in close-shot on the face of Macbeth ("Never say I did it"), he raises his finger, the shadow of which, pointing, takes the camera round until we see the table empty except for Banquo's ghost seated at the far end. Macbeth's drunken face sweats. Finally he breaks up the banquet by upsetting the contents of the table. Then he sits, leaning back against the table—"The time has been, my senses would have cooled/ To hear a night-shriek," he says, from later in the play. Lady Macbeth, almost a cypher in this scene, manages to dismiss the guests. This is followed by an impressionistic scene of Macbeth's resort once again to the prophecies of the witches.

The scene with Macduff in England is played symbolically under a great Iona cross, and it is the friar, not Ross, who warns Lady Macduff of her danger and later brings the news of her death to her husband. These are the forces of goodness gathering to overcome evil, and the music of the English scene emphasizes this. Immediately these forces begin to mass in Scotland, carrying their tall, spindly crosses. Macbeth's supporters are few in number; a prolonged shot, which tracks with Macbeth, finally brings him to Lady Macbeth's bedroom. While the armies of Malcolm and Macduff cut down the trees of Birnam Wood, the scene is intercut with those of the army, advancing with their branches through the mist. The sleep-walking scene follows: Macbeth joins his wife again as she says, with an echo of her early seductiveness, "To bed. To bed. To bed." He wakes her with a kiss, and she runs screaming from him through a dream-like perspective of pagan monoliths, finally throwing herself over a cliff to her death. Her end is announced as from a great distance against this same vista of monolithic stones. Macbeth utters the speech, "Tomorrow and tomorrow and tomorrow," against a cloud-scape, with a big close-up as climax. He looks down, a towering profile, on a small figure in the courtyard below, reduced to a pinhead. Seyton, his servant, becomes a dwarf swinging on the rope of the alarum-bell. It is a scene from hell, a hell assaulted now by the battering-rams of the invading armies. After his final struggle and death, Macbeth's severed head is tossed away like garbage.

Welles has described this elaborate re-visualization of the play as a "violently sketched charcoal drawing of a great play." He wanted it to be a "Stonehenge-powerful, unrelieved tragedy." It was to this end, therefore, that the sets created an artificial world of caves, rock-enclosed areas like the core of an extinct volcano, catacombs and cells with fiercely barbed window frames; it is a world of moving mist and falling water; swine wallow in mud at the castle entrance. Shots are distorted in mirrors to reflect the bent mind of Macbeth. The costumes are part Asiatic, part barbaric, made up alike of skins, cloth and metallic armour. Special effects are used to make the scenes of witchcraft macabre and unearthly. . . .

AKIRA KUROSAWA'S
MACBETH, THE CASTLE OF THE SPIDER'S WEB (1957)
Roger Manvell

. . . Here is an extract from the script of the film, part of the sequence of the murder of the Lord (Duncan):

The scene in the Unopened Chamber—Taketoki Washizu is sitting alone in the centre of the room. Each time the flame of the candle stirs, the shadow of Taketoki moves. There is an air of gloom—Taketoki's glaring, bloodshot eyes stare.

The dark-coloured traces of bloodshed upon the wainscot—Taketoki turns his eyes away, yet on the very wood of the floor from which he averted his eyes the outline

From Roger Manvell, *Shakespeare and the Film* (New York: Praeger, 1971), pp. 105–107. © 1971 by Roger Manvell. Reprinted by permission of Praeger Publishers, Inc., New York, and J. M. Dent & Sons, London.

is suggested of a strange figure which the blood has drawn. Suddenly Taketoki rises impatiently to his feet; but he remains standing motionless, looking to the side. Asaji, with a spear in her hands, enters quietly. Taketoki is staring at Asaji lost in a trance. Asaji, approaching Taketoki, forces him to take hold of the spear. At the same time, the two stare at each other, pale.

The sky—an owl with its sharp cry flies across the crescent moon, which looks like a sickle.

In the Unopened Chamber—Taketoki looks up to the sky, and staring for an instant at Asaji with a strange smile, walks from the room uncertainly.

Asaji—seeing him go, sits down quietly, and keeps quite still in the same pose.

—A long interval—

Taketoki comes back with a ghastly look; splashed with blood, he stands with the spear like a stick, and sits down. Asaji wrests the spear from Taketoki's hands and goes out.

In front of the Chamber—Asaji appears and eases the blood-smeared spear into the hands of the sleeping warrior.

In an outstanding article on the film contributed to *Sight and Sound* (Autumn 1965), J. Blumenthal comes to the heart of the problem of Shakespearean adaptations. This is arguably the best essay yet written on the subject. He sees *The Castle of the Spider's Web* as a film masterpiece in its own right precisely because it does not attempt to adapt Shakespeare's play to the screen through its *text*. He acknowledges that incidental beauties may occur in the adaptations by such masters of the theatre as Laurence Olivier, or even in the visual theatricalities of Orson Welles, but in Welles's *Othello* (which he prefers to Welles's *Macbeth*) he thinks "the cinematic flourishes are gratuitous," providing a sugar-coating of striking photographic compositions or dramatic cutting which do nothing to deepen the experience of Shakespeare's play, because they do not represent any real, filmic expression of it. Kurosawa's transmutation of *Macbeth* is a radical one; he "relies on Shakespeare only as a scenarist whose vision is consonant with his aim, and never as a master of pentameter," which can only too easily become ludicrous on the screen.

Kurosawa's characters speak "only when they can't communicate in any other way." Washizu, in fact, is barely articulate, but this does not prevent him from undergoing the same broad experiences as Macbeth, a character who communicates through poetic speech. Washizu "thinks in another medium." And so does Kurosawa, who conveys meaning "by the manipulation of material reality." The woodlands, the forests, the horses, so immediately responsive to the same supernatural terrors as Macbeth, become the central imagery through which the theme of the film is expressed. "The forest is Washizu's mind," a "labyrinth" (Kurosawa's word) in which Washizu is constantly lost. "I must paint the forest with blood." This forest, with its demon witch, takes charge of the action, imbues it with meaning in a manner which makes the sets in *Henry V* appear mere backdrops. In the action, the men and their horses become a violent tumult, time and again returning to the fatal woodlands in which they are always lost and terrified. "Film narrative depends on the material components of the world being depicted"; the theatre depends on the power of what is uttered by the actors. . . .

Edward the Second

J. B. Steane, in the following excerpts from his book on Christopher Marlowe, writes vividly of the particular tone of Edward II: *the pettiness of its world, the unpleasantness of its people, its lack of tragic grandeur or of any wider reference than the mean desires and ambitions of its characters. It is in this general nastiness and smallness that Mr. Steane finds the unifying feeling of the play.*

EDWARD II
J. B. Steane

Chaucer's Monk provides a reminder of the classic idea of tragedy:

> Tragedie is to seyn a certeyn storie,
> As olde bokes maken us memorie,
> Of him that stood in greet prosperitee
> And is y-fallen out of heigh degree
> Into miserie, and endeth wrecchedly.

Superficially, *Edward II* tells such a story. . . . But the initial prosperity and high-degree of the tragic hero are normally real and habitual: the high ground is also firm ground except in that place where is the tragic circumstance. Oedipus treads the solid, reliable ground of his kingdom until it dissolves beneath him revealing the abyss into which he must fall. Greatness, power and security have been there in the beginning, and the ending accomplishes a reversal. In *Edward* the secondary tragedies of Gaveston and Mortimer follow this pattern; but the final tragedy of the king himself is only a worsening of the situation in which he was found at the beginning of the play. Instead of greatness, power and security, we were presented from the start with pettiness, impotence and confusion. These are the norms of the play. It is a mean, petty world that is exhibited, and when Edward "endeth wrecchedly," his death is all of a piece with his miserable life. Nevertheless, he does fall from the height of his momentary triumph: "*Edward* this day hath crownd him king a new." At that central point in the drama, he stood "in greet prosperitee" on a peak of success and confidence which is, however, isolated in a context of frustration and dread. Man is seen as a pathetic creature, bickering or suffering; and he is still more pathetic for having been dressed in a little brief authority. . . .

   The people of the play are on the whole most unlikeable. The historian Stubbs, quoted by Charlton and Waller, writes of the actual reign words which could well have been written of the play: "outside of the dramatic crises it may be described as exceedingly dreary. There is a miserable level of political selfishness, which marks without exception every public man; there is an absence of sincere feeling except in the shape

Excerpted from J. B. Steane, "Edward II," *Marlowe: A Critical Study* (Cambridge: Cambridge University Press, 1964), pp. 205–206, 213, 225–227, 231. © 1964, Cambridge University Press. Reprinted by permission of Cambridge University Press.

of hatred and revenge . . . and there is no great triumph of good or evil to add a moral or inspire a sympathy."

. . . In this play [Shakespeare's *Henry VI, Part Three*], written before *Edward II,* the personal wills, honours and ambitions, like the individual violences and sufferings, all take their place in a larger setting. All life is involved, and the application of the then-and-there is extended as the scene is magnified beyond what it visibly presents.

But in Marlowe's play there is nothing of this. Life beyond the passionate yet petty play of personal will is barely glimpsed, and the realm seems to be only of nominal importance. The dominant attitude implied in the play is that the realm is a counter: one of the factors in the working of personal desires. To Edward it is a poor thing: let it float away, be divided up, let the nobles have the treasury: one nook in which to play with Gaveston would be worth more. Edward is not Marlowe, nor is Mortimer; but Marlowe despises, I think, *and* sympathises with both, and this not with a normal detachment, for he seems to know of nothing better. Obviously in a theoretical way he does: there is the prince and Kent. But no inner knowledge, dramatised or rendered in the poetry, nothing "beyond" which comes from any depth or speaks with any passion makes itself felt in this play. If it were there, "moral history" must have emerged: some positive, or some feeling for the values of stability and restraint. But Marlowe appears to see nothing beyond his men. To that extent there is a personal involvement as with Tamburlaine and Faustus. The aspiring mind, which may be a term ennobling the selfish go-getter, whether sated like Tamburlaine or thwarted like Faustus, has none of that altruistic interest and sympathy by which the mind grows. Fewer and fewer things outside the self really matter. But the selfishness does survive: the personal condition is the one thing that is important. And because Edward's self-love is reflected by Gaveston, he is the only thing in the world with real significance:

> *Mort.* Why should you loue him, whome the world hates so?
> *Edw.* Because he loues me more then all the world. (371–2)

There has always been in Marlowe the sense that the world is less than man (Tamburlaine offers himself to Zenocrate as the last and best gift; and Faustus' ambitions stretch "as farre as doth the minde of man," creation's crown). The world is the setting for man: man is the stone in the ring. But the setting cheapens with the jewel. Tamburlaine is great (subjectively) and so is his world; Edward is a poor creature, and the world's worth has decreased proportionately. . . .

But the play speaks with its own harsh voice and has its own bitter flavour. Edward weakly protesting to his barons ("Was euer king thus ouerrulde as I?"), weakly, impotently raging or abjectly and wretchedly submitting. Gaveston's pathetic strutting before the lords who not only hate but despise him; learning of his banishment, frustrated of his last sight of the king. Mortimer's petty motivation: his resentful pride, laughed at by the dapper jack, nobility humbled by the upstart. The pricking of the bubble of Isabella's eloquence; the humiliating violence offered to the bishop of Coventry; the enforced removal of the protesting queen; and above all the king subject to every indignity, crownless and washed in puddle water. There is surely a unity of tone and feeling here. . . .

In the comments below, Robert Fricker is less concerned with the moral or personal atmosphere of the play than with how it is put together as a drama. He concerns himself with the shape of the plot, the "dramatic rhythm" of the actions, and the way the scenic units function in giving the work structure and impetus.

THE DRAMATIC STRUCTURE OF *EDWARD II*
Robert Fricker

. . . Most readers will find it difficult to get a clear idea of the plot of the other plays, whereas it is comparatively easy to sum up the action of *Edward II:* it is the struggle between a king and his peers about a minion, which leads to the latter's death and is followed, first, by the king's revenge and, secondly, by the struggle for power carried on by his antagonist which ends with the death of both the hero and his adversary. This clear outline of the plot is the result of the envisagement and subsequent handling of the material not as a series of episodes but as a whole. Marlowe did not merely condense the material which he found in Holinshed and other chroniclers with a view to reducing the events of twenty-three years to the "two hours traffic of the stage," but he selected only those episodes which fitted into the pattern of the play as he conceived it, bound them together and gave prominence to certain minor characters, while he rejected other events which would have made excellent theatre. He eliminated all that would have spoilt his design, namely the prolonged conflict lifting up now the king and now the barons, while it inevitably draws to its tragical conclusion. . . .

In the final scene of the play, which follows hard upon the hero's death, Mortimer feels he has reached the goal of his aspiration:

> As for myself, I stand as Jove's huge tree,
> And others are but shrubs compar'd to me.
> All tremble at my name, and I fear none.

From this zenith of his power he is pushed down by the young King who, supported by the nobles, confronts him and the Queen with a determination which is not to be shaken, though it is distinguished by its humanity.

Thus the play ends with the rapid rise to triumph of the forces which represent poetic justice. Looked at from a distance, *Edward II* shows—in the first two acts or, more exactly, until III, 2—the struggle for Gaveston with the culminating points for the hero in I, 1 and at the end of I, 4, and the lowest points in the middle of scenes I, 4 and III, 2. In the latter scene the struggle for Gaveston is ended and immediately followed by Edward's revenge which is achieved at the end of act III where, as in a classical tragedy, the hero seems to have secured the victory over his antagonists. The play about Gaveston now changes into the struggle for power which is caused, directly,

Excerpted from Robert Fricker, "The Dramatic Structure of *Edward II*," *English Studies,* vol. 34 (1953), pp. 206, 213–216. Reprinted by permission of *English Studies,* Swets en Zeitlinger.

by this very vengeance (itself rooted in Edward's love of Gaveston) and indirectly by the change of Mortimer's character. During act IV the counter-action gathers force and approaches its climax at the beginning of the last scene of the play where Mortimer exults in his absolute power. This gradual rise is accompanied by the slow decline of the hero's fortunes which, after many oscillations, reach their lowest point in the death scene. Then we witness the swift rise to power of the hero's son which is accompanied, again in a contrasted sense, by the sudden fall of the antagonists.

In spite of a certain weakness of the link between the two movements of the action, the play forms an organic whole. Its structure is characterized by what may be called dramatic rhythm. It would be easy to represent this movement, which I have tried to express in the terms of the drama and—tentatively—of music, graphically by lines tracing, by their varying inclination, the speed with which the actions led by the hero and his antagonist proceed. The result would be, roughly speaking, the rapid fall and rise of the hero's line in the first act, the much slower decline in act II which ends in III, 2 and is followed by a vigorous rise in the second half of this act. The last two acts show the undulating falling line of the hero's fate, to which is attached, in the last scene, a steep rise. The line thus described would be accompanied, but in a contrasted sense, by that of the antagonist. The play conceived in this manner would consist of three successive waves and counterwaves which differ from one another only by their growing size. Translating the dramatic structure into terms of music, we may say that the first act gives the tragic theme, which is followed by two variations in each of which the theme is brought nearer to its tragic conclusion.

Thus *Edward II* forms a strongly and closely knit whole from which no part, however loosely joined to the body of the play it may seem, can be separated without either changing the rhythm of the action or weakening its logical structure. It is true that Marlowe might have used a different technique altogether to obtain this result, and given it more outward unity by using, for instance, the messenger's report of classical drama. But the effect would have been entirely different and *Edward II* would not have been acted on the Elizabethan stage for which it was written. Marlowe knew what was expected of him and represented all the episodes of the play on the stage, i.e. he adopted the *ab ovo* technique of the popular drama. Although he selected from the vast body of material offered to him by the sources only those incidents which had a direct bearing on the gradual unfolding of Edward's tragedy, the amount he used is nevertheless enormous when we consider the length of the play. He conquered the difficulties by speed and concentration.

The structural unit of *Edward II* is neither the act nor the scene, but what may be called the scenic section. . . . The main functions of the scenic units in *Edward II* are the regulation of the rhythm of the action and the reception of a vast material. The action passes swiftly from one unit to the next, and often the impression of speed is heightened by the abrupt opening of scenes which suggests that the action represented has been going on for some time before. The beginning of the play shows Gaveston reading the King's letter. He limits himself to picking out the two most significant lines and proceeds straight to the heart of the matter. Without turning back to what has passed he looks ahead to what is to come. The next section presents the king in the full course of a hot dispute with the barons.

K. Edw. Lancaster!
Lan.   My lord?
Gav.   That Earl of Lancaster do I abhor. *(Aside.*
K. Edw. Will you not grant me this? In spite of them
          I'll have my will; and these two Mortimers,
          That cross me thus, shall know I am displeas'd. *(Aside.*

The essence of the dispute which has taken place before they enter, is contained in these few lines which introduce the hero. We do not not know what his will is—but that is of secondary importance: he is crossed in his will by Lancaster and the Mortimers, and Gaveston by his asides shows that he hates them. It is his will the king will have, and it is one of the men he names that will block it. The dramatic conflict is foreshadowed in this breathless passage, the beginning of the drama properly speaking.

It has been noticed that Marlowe, true to his classical training and contrary to the stage customs of his time, does not represent the traffic of the battles on the stage. Thus, of the battle of Boroughbridge he only gives a breathing-space filled in with the defiant speeches of the leaders, and the result: the condemnation of the rebels. The second armed conflict between the King and Mortimer he omits completely and proceeds straight to the moment when Edward and his favourites "shape [their] course to Ireland." What he gains by this technique is again speed and concentration: the attention of the audience is not diverted by noisy "alarums and excursions" but remains fixed on the intellectual conflict.

Marlowe's grip on the attention of the audience is further tightened by the reduction to a minimum of the elements creating relief from the forward urge of the action. He gives us neither comic scenes nor descriptions but concise soliloquies which contain a lyrical element, and short scenic sections which do not allow for a lengthy breathing-space. The dynamic force of the play is intensified by the almost complete lack of retrospective passages and descriptions. Rarely do the characters look back on their past experience: their attention—and with it that of the audience—is bent on the immediate future, and when they remember the past it is only in short snatches like Edward's

Tell Isabel, the queen, I look'd not thus,
When for her sake I ran at tilt in France,
And there unhors'd the Duke of Cleremont.

Here, of course, the reminiscence has a dramatic function: by its associations with glorious deeds of chivalry it creates a sharp contrast to the miserable situation in which the King now lives who is timorously facing his murderer.

It is the powerful rhythm of the action which captures the mind of the modern reader perhaps more than the rational exposition of causes and motives. The sacrifice of the earlier heroes' aspiring minds and of the poetry depending on it is compensated for by this dramatic element, and what the characters lack in that respect they gain in outline and impetuosity. The cosmic element gives way to the dynamic; lyrical poetry is transformed into the dramatic poetry of action. . . .

The tone, atmosphere, characters, structure, dramatic rhythm—and many other characteristics—of
Edward II *constituted immediate, practical problems for Toby Robertson, who directed the play for*
the theatre in 1958 and more recently for television—in fact, for the BBC production included in The
Classic Theatre. *Mr. Robertson explores the theatrical problems in an interview with John Russell*
Brown, and in a later article discusses the specific problems of directing Marlowe's play for
television.

DIRECTING *EDWARD II*
Toby Robertson, in an interview with John Russell Brown

BROWN: I thought your 1958 production of *Edward II* had an athletic forcefulness
to it. Was this what you were aiming for?

ROBERTSON: That was my first impression when I read the play. When I first of
all proposed doing it there was considerable opposition to it, largely because it was
considered to be a rather inferior chronicle. What struck me was the extraordinary
speed of events, the way the play leaps from event to event—it is like hurdle jumping.
For example in the first part where the action moves at a terrific pace there is actually
one scene of only four lines length.

BROWN: This is one of the things that led you to such a bare set. Did you regret
this bareness?

ROBERTSON: No, no. Not at all. The absolute bareness of the set gave us the
chance to push the focus completely and totally onto the actors. For two years before
I did the play I was an actor at Stratford—and there was an enormous number of
plays we did there with very heavy sets and rich costumes. Often I found this getting
in the way—almost running against the play, against its speed and pace. I may have
stripped everything bare for my production as a protest against two years of acting at
Stratford. The production I admired most while I was there—and one which I was able
to see on many occasions—was Michael Langham's production of *Hamlet,* and this had
a great influence on me. I tried to find a way of doing *Edward II* where I could bring
even the most minor character on stage and give him the absolute focus that was necessary and that he needed to support him. Even a messenger is of real importance; he
must come on and take center stage and look down at the people he's talking to and
thus communicate to the audience as well. I think this is one of the reasons why the
production seemed to have great clarity: every character who came on took an absolutely dominant place. Like in television: once an actor is there, you give him a close-
up as soon as possible. I wanted to give even the smallest part his close-up.

BROWN: But the price you paid for it was large at times. One wasn't sure whether
Edward and his nobles were at court or in the country. For example, the meeting with
Gaveston at Tynemouth involves a movement away from Court and the center of
power for Gaveston's sake, and this calls for representation. Or the scene with the

Toby Robertson, in an interview with John Russell Brown, "Directing *Edward II*," *Tulane Drama Review*, vol.
8, no. 4 (T24) (Summer 1964), 174–183. Reprinted by permission of John Russell Brown and *The Drama
Review*.

abbot, when Edward is disguised as a holy man—this scene can bring a kind of peace into the play at the end, and possibly your bare stage and your emphatic placing of characters sometimes lost that kind of modulation.

ROBERTSON: Yes, I think you may be right. I'm thinking of doing the play again. I don't want any more sets, perhaps even less. But I would like to achieve more quality—to catch the emotional feeling of a scene more by lighting. This is something that that stage wasn't able to do. I would like to use lighting more and scenery even less.

BROWN: And more music?

ROBERTSON: Possibly, but used with great discretion. The music is the words—in the "mighty line." This play needs orchestration. That was the exciting thing about doing it.

BROWN: Related to this is the over-all structure. Did you find the reiterated themes and the repetitive business of the early scenes difficult? Did you cut at all?

ROBERTSON: We cut extraordinarily little. I think that repetition is necessary—is part of the whole play's development. The development of Edward's character—he starts as a very young king unable to cope with an attack by the people around him, unable to cope with the nobles. He shouts; he screams; he loses his temper. He's obstinate, sulky. And then, gradually, in a series of related scenes, the iron enters into his being and he grows from the cockerel into the lion. I find that the shape and structure of the play is brought out mainly through the development of Edward: as he matures and becomes mellower, the play slows up.

BROWN: Do you think the play is centered on the hero?

ROBERTSON: Yes I do, because the central idea in the play, that of the relationship between power and suffering, is developed most strongly in the character of Edward. Although it is Edward's fascination with Gaveston that is the mainspring, and Edward himself is centered on Gaveston, the play itself centers on Edward. I didn't make Gaveston enough of a Renaissance Machiavellian figure who dominates Edward physically and intellectually. I overstressed the physical and made Gaveston too much Edward's dependent creature. When Gaveston dies, it is his memory that keeps Edward going, together with those pale shadows of Gaveston—Spencer and Baldock.

BROWN: Surely, they haven't the intellectual dominance of Gaveston, who is capable of making quicker intellectual turns than anybody else in the play.

ROBERTSON: And one feels that they are dispensable: as their first scene points out, they will serve the strongest party, that is, their own interests.

BROWN: I think you do your production an injustice to say that you made it Edward's play. Clifford Leech has said, in *Critical Quarterly,* that your production was characterized by "neutrality"; that it was a performance in which we felt the "diffused vitality of human spectacle." The play seemed more variously alive than it had been before. A number of minor characters stay in my mind: Edmund, Isabella, and the younger Mortimer.

ROBERTSON: When I say Edward is the hero I don't want to belittle the importance of Mortimer, Isabella, Kent, etc. It is one of the strengths of the play that the supporting parts are so eminently actable—Lightborn, the young Prince, Baldock. In fact, for the critics in 1958 the actability of the play seemed a surprise—that and the strength and uncompromising honesty of its emotional relationships. The homosexuality in the play is treated without the reserve, almost hesitancy, found in Tennessee Williams or in Anderson's *Tea and Sympathy*. The lack of shame about homosexuality in *Edward II* perhaps partly created the enormous interest. When you say the other characters emerged clearly, I think that is largely because of the staging—the sense of focus—and partly because in fact it was extremely well acted. A number of the cast have gone on to play important roles with the Royal Shakespeare and National Theatre companies. But I did concentrate on telling the story through the characters and perhaps not worrying about "interpretation." But certainly *Edward II* is a play of great passion and great love. Homosexual love is treated here as love in the classical sense. There is, in the imagery, a feeling of going back perpetually to the classical precedents. From this, a strength is drawn. They see themselves as a part of a great tradition. It is nothing to be ashamed of—or afraid of.

BROWN: And Kent, who seems to be a vacillator on the page, in your production became a most useful representative for common affection and feeling: a very important standard.

ROBERTSON: Kent is, if you like, the Common Man of the play. First he supports Edward against the barons over the question of Gaveston, but as soon as Edward begins to overload Gaveston with political powers and honors, he has to move against Edward. But when the barons over-reach themselves he swings back. He tries to keep a common sense balance in the play, but among the forces which are at work—the ambition, the struggle for power, and the passionate loves and hates—he simply has no place. Unable to commit himself to either party for long, trusted by no one, his failure is that of the good man submerged by forces which he cannot control or understand.

BROWN: So in fact *Edward II* is much more than a homosexual play. It's a play about emotions, affections, loyalties, and power.

ROBERTSON: Definitely. There is no condemnation of the homosexual relationship at all. This is not what the barons mind about it. There's that long speech by the elder Mortimer: "The mightiest kings have had their minions/ Great Alexander loved Hephaestion. . . ." The real issue is: have your favorite but keep him as your favorite and don't let him get involved with the politics of the realm. A distinction is made between public behavior and private morals. The play is not concerned with morals.

BROWN: It has something to do with the individual's confidence, doesn't it? I mean the changes in Edward: when he is victorious, his new ruthlessness suggests an interaction between the affections and confidence. But perhaps this is just another aspect of the treatment of power.

ROBERTSON: Yes, I agree with you about the hardening in Edward, but one of the most horrifying aspects of power in the play is Gaveston's hold over Edward. From his avowed intention in his opening soliloquy "to draw the pliant king which way I please," their relationship is like that of weasel and rabbit. When Edward realizes that he really will be deposed, he says, all right, I give in now. He lets Gaveston go, and Gaveston returns, saying "I hear it whispered everywhere,/ That I am banished, and must fly the land." Then the horrifying power that Gaveston has over him is shown, and Edward becomes like a crawling sycophant; one realizes what is particularly horrifying: Edward is totally in love with Gaveston—is dotty about him—but Gaveston is just using Edward. Very early in the play: "I must have wanton Poets, pleasant wits,/

Musicians, that with touching of a string/ May draw the pliant king which way
I please." I think this is all of it for him; he does it for his own aggrandizement.

BROWN: And, in contrast, Edward's desire for Gaveston is shown as a permanent
part of his nature; after Spencer and Baldock, there is Lightborn, to whom Edward
gives a "jewel" in his very last scene. It seemed to me that you pointed up in your production this permanence in Edward's nature.

ROBERTSON: Yes, this has to emerge. It wasn't entirely deliberate when I began,
but once we were in rehearsal it became clear that this was almost the last "love scene"
in the play.

BROWN: And Lightborn is Marlowe's own invention; he's not in the source.

ROBERTSON: He is the most Machiavellian figure—specifically, an Italian figure,
perhaps Marlowe drawing on his experience in Walsingham's secret service.

BROWN: And Edward knows he must not trust him, yet he does trust him and as-
tonishingly goes to sleep.

ROBERTSON: We played this with Edward almost lying in Lightborn's lap and sort
of crooning to him. He's very gently stroking him and it became like a child asking for
love, wanting love, affection. And, of course, this is the trouble—this is what Edward
needs. You feel it in the beginning of the play. Even the barons, who aren't sympathetic to him, recognize his need.

BROWN: Did you make a visual distinction between Edward's party and the
barons?

ROBERTSON: We tried to emphasize this in the costuming, to give Edward and
Gaveston Italianate Renaissance clothes, whereas the barons were dressed more medie-
vally, more Gothic, with fur and steel. And they were very provincial, great magnates
from Warwick or Lancaster. Some critics disapproved of our giving them modern-day
accents of their particular region; one of the critics said that it was a pity that the
actors couldn't speak the king's English. But this idea of the king's English is something that must have come in within the last fifty years or so; and it's a concept that
has been killing English speech.

BROWN: Surely the critics all praised the verse speaking—

ROBERTSON: Oh, yes—and it was very clearly spoken. But I was lucky in doing
Edward II for the Marlowe Society because there's a tradition of verse speaking there
under the tutelage of George Rylands.

BROWN: This is Shakespearian verse speaking, isn't it?

ROBERTSON: Chiefly. But if you take a group of people who have worked with the
Marlowe Society, under Rylands, they are, from the first opportunity, very conscious
of what the rhythm of the verse should be—how it should go. I was working with people who were already very responsive to this approach. And we worked on the play
simply through the movements and climaxes and rhythms suggested in the speeches
themselves.

BROWN: Did you use any special rehearsal techniques to make sure that this part
of the play was mastered?

ROBERTSON: We used to have a lot of private sessions working over the emotional
background: Edward and Gaveston, Isabella and Mortimer. At first the uninhibited
display of affection that Edward has for Gaveston was a problem for the actor but, by

working alone without other actors watching, this gradually changed as the actor's confidence increased. This is a young man's play—particularly in the beginning—and we
had a young company who attacked the play with enormous gut and bite—there was
no holding back. They weren't afraid of being called hams. There was none of this
coolness about the play that one finds a good deal of the time with professional actors
who think it bad taste to throw themselves too vigorously into something.

BROWN: There is a clarity and forcefulness in Marlowe's writing.

ROBERTSON: It is extremely easy to listen to—the images aren't complex. The same
images tend to come through again and again and the language is beautifully simple.
Compared with Shakespeare, Marlowe has a coarse, vigorous vulgarity that comes
straight to the point. Everybody really says exactly what he means. And the images are
usually hard images: "But when the imperial Lion's flesh is gored/ He rends and tears
it with his wrathful paw." There's a great, growling strength to it and the lines never
get prettified. This is something for young actors to hold onto, good strength for them
to anchor with. Marlowe always wants the audience to know fully and quickly. Somebody can come into the middle of a scene and say, "We've heard . . ." For example,
Gaveston is captured by the barons and they're about to haul him off and the next
moment Arundel enters and says, "His majesty,/ Hearing that you have taken Gaveston,/ Entreateth you by me, yet but he may/ See him before he dies." In a twink Edward knows about Gaveston's imminent death; it was impossible for Edward to have
heard or for any messages to have passed, but that doesn't matter. As far as the drama
is concerned, Gaveston's death must be prevented: this is all-important and must be
made clear with no unnecessary fuss. Edward asks for him, the barons say yes, and
then they act treacherously and kill Gaveston on his way to Edward so that Edward
really has a reason for beating the barons in battle and acting without mercy towards
them. This kind of foreshortening—this kind of theatrical reasoning—comes up again
and again in the play, especially in the first part. These are short cuts through to the
next development in the action. Marlowe doesn't bother to play the intervening bits.

One of the things about the play which is fascinating is that it moves at such an
extraordinary pace all the way through that it's very difficult to know where to break.
There really aren't act divisions at all, just scene breaks. And, of course, it's possible
that Marlowe wrote it to be played all the way through continuously. We broke twice.
The first time was after the barons go away finally to raise their troops and Edward
says, "Poor Gaveston, thou hast no friend but me." This was rather a marvellous ending because both Mortimers had gone and Edward is alone when Gaveston appears out
of the darkness; Edward speaks his line and they both turn and go. We began the next
scene almost as if it were a few years later, and the scene begins with "And so we live
here and walk about the walls." And then later we broke it before the scene where Edward says, "Thus after many threats of wrathful war,/ Triumpheth England's Edward
with his friends." The Queen has gone over to France and Mortimer and Edmund
have joined her. But it doesn't look as if they are going to have any luck in France.
And the scene begins with Edward as the full despot surrounded by his favorites. Then
comes the news that the Queen is arriving and that Mortimer has escaped. There is
a year's gap in this break. So Edward is able to start the play as a young man of
about eighteen or twenty and finish as a broken man of about fifty. There is tragedy

even in the physical alteration from the young god to the filthy, degraded, disgusting old man who's suffered every form of physical indignity.

BROWN: You are scheduled to do an *Edward II* in the West End this year. Have you any aims for this production?

ROBERTSON: In 1958 I emphasized the emotional side of it. Now I'd like to bring out more of the play between intellect and power. It's difficult. I've not thought about the play much since 1958, yet I find that every time I come back to it it's hard to look from a fresh viewpoint. So much of what I did in '58 seems right. The bare platform put everything into the correct focus; the development and relationship of characters was all there. But I want to show Edward as a more deluded character than I did before. Doing it with young people had one disadvantage—it was almost impossible to bring out the irony. Irony is a more mature quality, and I was young, too. But, then, the whole sweep of the play, its momentum, may be difficult to get with older, more professional actors. That sweep is there in the image, "There is a point, to which when men aspire,/ They tumble headlong down." The first two parts of the play show each character moving very fast up to the point to which he aspires, and then it's the tumble.

BROWN: Have you begun to think about casting?

ROBERTSON: The great thing is having the right voice, the right organ to play this stuff. Edward needs extraordinary range—from the young man to the mature soldier to the old man. This is where Edward is so different from Richard II, who always remains a reflective poet. He never becomes involved. Edward is totally involved as a full physical being. The steel enters him and he fights. At the end, when things go wrong and he tastes defeat, there is a passionate strength in his despair, things like "Let Pluto's bells ring out my fatal knell,/ And hags howl for my death at Charon's shore," when Spencer and Baldock are both taken from him. The emotions are minutely and completely expressed, and this needs voice to express. That's why I was so happy about the bare setting and costumes: the whole thing came back to the words. That is not to say that there wasn't characterization, but it's the language that precisely defines character here.

PUTTING ELIZABETHAN DRAMA ON THE BOX
Toby Robertson

My own involvement with *Edward* and *Richard* is very personal. Not only did I direct *Edward II* for the theatre, and both productions for television, but was closely involved in all stages of Richard Cottrell's stage production of *Richard II*. Despite the Royal Shakespeare Company and the National Theatre having had their productions adapted for television, this is the first time that there has been a continuity of director

Toby Robertson, "Toby Robertson, Who Directed Ian McKellen in *Richard II* and in this week's *Edward II,* Discusses: Putting Elizabethan Drama on the Box," *Radio Times,* July 30, 1970. Reprinted by permission of *Radio Times,* BBC Publications.

with the same company (in this case the Prospect Theatre) working on the same play in an Elizabethan context.

Such a continuity is invaluable for the actor who has been playing in the theatre and needs to adjust to the scale of the box; but the advantage of an actor playing in the theatre before coming to TV is incalculable.

There is one great difference between theatre and television: in the theatre there is a physical relationship of the audience to the stage and the actor. The modern revolution in staging Elizabethan plays springs from the realisation that it is essential to remind each member of the audience that he is part of a corporate act.

This is very different from viewing in one's own living-room. Just as an audience's response to a performance is influenced by the colour and size of an auditorium, so a viewer is affected by the circumstances in which he watches a television programme. The embracing of Edward and his male favourite, the death by red-hot poker of the homosexual king, tenderly washed, kissed, and then murdered by his destroyer can seem as much an intrusion into the living-room as can pictures of the Congo or Vietnam. Incidents which in the theatre become part of the whole design, on the box can often be gratuitously shocking.

But the Elizabethan theatre was working in a popular tradition in the same way as television is today. Blood and thunder, a ferocious story, and love interest are all ingredients of a popular tradition, whether on television or on the stage. The Elizabethan playwright gave his audience what they wanted, and he worked within his limitations. He wanted his audience "to see," but to see through the imagination—in complete contradiction to most television productions which hope to win an audience with naturalism.

So how are the ingredients of the Elizabethan play to be adapted for TV? Can the viewer accept a degree of stylisation to remind him it is *a performance?* Can the appeal be to the imagination rather than to illusion? Most Shakespeare television productions I have seen aim at and often achieve great naturalism. For example, there is a different set for each scene, and the actor thinks his soliloquy with "voice over" and lips closed. The director too often strives against the limitations of the TV studio and wishes he was making a film.

But Elizabethan plays were written to be performed on a bare stage with no settings and few props. Shakespeare himself was conscious of his theatre's limitations and apologised for them.

In the two productions of *Richard II* and *Edward II* I have tried to a limited degree to eschew naturalism. *Richard II* came first with a semi-naturalistic set on a permanent platform and tower which were added to by variously shaped arches used in different positions. The continual use of the same set gave a unity to the play and, I would like to think, was a continual reminder of the importance of the imaginative element. *Edward II* is even more austere than *Richard II*. I made a deliberate choice to use the stage set because I thought it the best setting for the play. Marlowe's writing is quite different from Shakespeare's: it is rougher, more direct and immediate. Though recorded at the Piccadilly Theatre, I have not treated the performance as if it were an outside broadcast; there's no audience to soften the impact. It may be too uncompromising— you must judge for yourself.

The Duchess of Malfi

In her introduction to the New Mermaid edition of this play, Elizabeth Brennan recounts the true story from which Webster took his plot, shows how he transformed his material, and surveys some of the basic elements of the drama: characters, imagery, themes. She concludes by alluding to some of the puzzles of meaning and motivation The Duchess of Malfi *presents.*

INTRODUCTION [TO *THE DUCHESS OF MALFI*]
Elizabeth M. Brennan

[The sources of the play]

*W*ebster found the material for *The Duchess of Malfi,* as he had done that of *The White Devil,* in a true story of life in Italy in the century previous to his own. Giovanna d'Aragona had been married in 1490, when she was about twelve years old, to Alfonso Piccolomini, son and heir to the first Duke of Amalfi. Three years later he succeeded to the dukedom, but ruled only for five years before dying of gout. The Duchess, a girl of nineteen or twenty, was left with a daughter, Caterina. Her son was born posthumously in 1499 and succeeded to the dukedom which she ruled for him as regent. Despite French and Spanish invasions the state flourished, and the Duchess was able to pay off debts which had been incurred by her husband.

The Duchess of Amalfi had lived prosperously for some years before meeting Antonio Bologna who came of a reputable family and had been brought up at the court of Naples. As major-domo to Federico, the last Aragonian King of Naples, Antonio had followed his master into exile in France. Upon Federico's death in 1504 Antonio returned to Naples where he was offered the post of major-domo in the household of the young widowed Duchess, who was herself a member of the house of Aragon. The Duchess fell quickly and passionately in love with Antonio. Fearing the wrath of her brothers—Lodovico, who had resigned his title to become a Cardinal, and Carlo (Webster's Ferdinand) who had succeeded to his brother's title of Marquis of Gerace—the Duchess married her major-domo in secret, with her waiting-woman as sole witness of the ceremony.

Incredible as it may seem in life as in Webster's play, the marriage was successfully concealed for some years. The birth of the first child was undetected; but the birth of a second caused rumours which at last reached the ears of the Duchess' brothers, who set spies to watch her. Antonio took his two children to Ancona, leaving the Duchess, who was again pregnant, in her palace. Unbearably lonely, she soon found an excuse to set out with a great retinue for a pilgrimage to Loretto from whence she proceeded to join Antonio. Upon her arrival in Ancona she revealed her marriage to her household and declared that she would renounce her rank and title to live privately with her husband and their children. One of the astonished servants set out to inform the Cardinal what had happened; the rest deserted her and returned to Amalfi.

Excerpted from the New Mermaid edition of John Webster, *The Duchess of Malfi,* ed. Elizabeth M. Brennan (New York: Hill & Wang, 1966-6th impression, 1975), pp. vii-xxx. © Ernest Benn Limited 1964. Reprinted by permission of Ernest Benn Ltd., London, and Farrar, Straus & Giroux, Inc., New York.

At Ancona, where their third child was born, the Duchess and Antonio were allowed only a few months' peace before the Cardinal of Aragon put pressure on Cardinal Gonzaga, Legate of Ancona, to banish Antonio. Fortunately, Antonio had foreseen this, and had made preparations to take refuge with a friend in Siena. As soon as the decree of his banishment was issued—in the summer of 1511—Antonio set out with the Duchess and their children and so they escaped any possible attempts that might have been made to capture or murder them. The Cardinal continued to exert his influence against them and the head of the Signiory of Siena was persuaded by his brother, Cardinal Petrucci, to expel them from that city. This time Antonio and his family did not depart so quickly and on their way to Venice armed horsemen overtook them. By asserting that her brothers would not harm her in person the Duchess was able to persuade Antonio to escape with their eldest child, a boy of six or seven years of age, to Milan, where they arrived safely, probably in the later summer of 1512. There is no evidence to connect the Aragonian brothers with the death of the Duchess, but after being taken to her palace in Amalfi neither the Duchess nor her two youngest children nor her waiting-woman were ever seen again.

Antonio did not know what had happened to them. For over a year he lived in Milan, first under the protection of Silvio Savelli, and later in the households of the Marchese di Bitonto and Alfonso Visconti. Though his wife's brothers had confiscated his property in Naples, Antonio still hoped to appease them. Perhaps they held out promises of restoring the Duchess to him. Yet Antonio was continually being warned that his life was in danger. One person who gave him a warning was a man called Delio who had been told of Antonio's story by a Neapolitan friend. One day in October, 1513 Delio and a friend passed Antonio, who looked dismayed, with two servants on their way to mass at the church of S. Francesco. A few minutes later an uproar was heard, and, looking back, Delio and his friend saw that Antonio had been stabbed to death by a Lombard captain called Daniele da Bozolo and three accomplices. All four escaped.

The diary of Giacomo the Notary, of Naples, records the stir caused by the Duchess' leaving her duchy to go on the pilgrimage to Loretto and by her subsequent revelation of the marriage to her major-domo. The Corona group of manuscripts in the Biblioteca Nazionale in Naples contains accounts of the Duchess' life which were originally collected in the sixteenth century but which were subsequently copied out and augmented by later writers up to the eighteenth century. Behind these manuscripts lies the story narrated as the twenty-sixth of the first part of Matteo Bandello's *Novelle*, published in 1554. Though these accounts contain more details of Neapolitan interest than Bandello's novella, only one version is obviously independent of his.

The novella includes both material based on hearsay and some imagined dialogue, but it is sufficiently accurate in outline to warrant the assumption that, since Bandello wrote sonnets under the name of Delio, he himself was the Delio who had known Antonio Bologna and heard his story in Milan; the Delio who had been a witness of Antonio's murder.

Bandello relates the tragic story without moral comment, but since his introduction decried murders which are motivated by a desire to avenge wounded honour, a condemnation of the Aragonian brothers is implicit. The French writer François de Belleforest is more outspoken. At the end of his account of the Duchess, the first story in his second tome of *Histoires Tragiques,* the reader's sympathy is with the murdered Duchess, the victim of her brothers' cruelty; but in the course of his narration Belleforest exclaims continually against her. He presents her as a lascivious widow who is unable to live without a man and who forgets her noble blood to run after a man far beneath her station. Her feigned pilgrimage to Loretto is an execrable impiety. This version, with its moral comment was given to English readers by William Painter in the *Second Tome of the Palace of Pleasure* (1567). . . . Painter's version of Bandello was probably Webster's main source for the outline of *The Duchess of Malfi.* . . .

[Webster's transformation of the characters and of their motivation]

The most important difference between Webster's story of the Duchess of Malfi and that given by other writers lies in the attitude to the heroine. Webster's Duchess is not the wanton widow of Belleforest and Painter. Within the play itself the dramatist considers the possible charges against her and demonstrates how her life and death refute them, stressing her purity and integrity. Though Antonio's praise of her in the opening scene underlines her purity and her piety, these qualities are questioned by others because she lives in a society that is both corrupt and corrupting. Only in the fact that it is her own court which breeds corruption may any ambivalence of attitude to the Duchess be implicit; though the evidence of their characters almost certainly suggests that the Aragonian brothers constitute the "curs'd example" which poisons their sister's court near the head. Moreover, if their influence is sufficiently strong to limit the Duchess' freedom in marriage, there would not appear to be any possibility of her being able to exercise her ducal authority to rid the court of their unhealthy presence.

The evil with which the Duchess is supposed to be possessed is a projection of the evil in the minds of her brothers. Thus, when Ferdinand accuses her, both to her face and in her absence, of lust and wantonness, his words reveal the state of his own mind. His salaciousness is observed both in his conversation with courtiers (I,ii, 31–34) and in the obscene allusion to women's preferences which his sister cannot mistake, though he tries to excuse it. Ferdinand questions whether her children—beggarly brats he calls them—were ever christened; but it is seen that one of the Duchess' last earthly concerns is that her daughter be brought up to pray. In the face of danger the Duchess is able to think and speak of Heaven; she accepts persecution as a necessary means of divine guidance (III,v, 73–78); she meets death kneeling, in an attitude of Christian humility. When life briefly revives in her strangled body Bosola sees her as a fair soul capable of leading him to salvation; when she is dead at last she epitomizes the

> . . . sacred innocence, that sweetly sleeps
> On turtles' feathers: . . . (IV,ii, 349–50)

The Cardinal who complains that the Duchess makes religion her riding hood to keep her from the sun and tempest is the man who jokes obscenely with a mistress kept in his own household; the man who resigns his religious vestments for the accoutrements of war. The animality of Ferdinand's nature forces itself to the surface in the horrible form of lycanthropy. In contrast to the Duchess' last hours, those of her brothers reveal their consciousness of the hell that awaits them. Ferdinand declares in his madness that when he goes to hell he will take a bribe with him. The Cardinal is puzzled in a question about hell fire; troubled by the thing armed with a rake which seems to strike at him, threatening death and, at the same time, recalling the devils of the mystery plays who, armed with pitchforks, herded the bad souls into hell. Despite his military reputation, the Cardinal's death wants courage as much as it wants the kind of Christian stoicism displayed by his sister. His attitude in the face of death is no more dignified, no braver than Cariola's. . . .

It is Bosola's personal tragedy that, having sold his services to the evil brothers, he is forced to be a destroyer of goodness that is personified in their sister. For Bosola is sensible of the qualities of the Duchess and he tries, in his own fashion, to bring her comfort. He has no physical comfort to offer her but, when she has lost all that means most in this world, Bosola prevents her from losing eternity. Mental affliction brings her to despair; to die in despair is to die denying the grace of God. Bosola's appearances in a variety of disguises are not further acts of torment; they are sympathetic attempts to make the Duchess rise from despair. As the tomb-maker he stresses the importance of the soul by reminding her of the frailty of the body. His message—of the life of the soul—is one of Christian comfort; and it is to this message that the Duchess responds with an assertion of her own integrity:

> I am Duchess of Malfi still. (IV,ii, 139)

She is afraid neither of death nor of the manner of her death. She can say, sincerely,

> . . . Tell my brothers
> That I perceive death, now I am well awake,
> Best gift is, they can give, or I can take. (IV,ii, 219–21)

At the moment of death her soul is prepared for Heaven. . . .

[Imagery and themes]

The imagery of *The Duchess of Malfi* constantly suggests a series of contrasts and parallels: between light and darkness; health and sickness; sanity and insanity; life and death. Webster presents other contrasts by different means. Antonio is skilled in the tilt-yard and speaks in praise of good horsemanship; Bosola becomes provisor of the Duchess' horse. Thus an ironic parallel between them is implied. The jesting of the Duchess and Antonio as they prepare for bed is echoed in some of the words Bosola speaks to her before her murder. Similarly, the Duchess' first wooing of Antonio is paralleled to and contrasted with Julia's wooing of Bosola; the Duchess' secret, but fruitful marriage to Antonio contrasts with the openly scorned, sterile, "conventional" union of Julia with the old courtier Castruchio.

Such contrasts are related to a conflict at the heart of the play: the conflict between appearance and reality. This is epitomized in the Duchess from the moment when, having told her brothers that she will never marry, she immediately turns to complete her plan of marrying Antonio; but, indeed, this conflict is present in each of the major characters. The brothers who should love the Duchess are her most cruel enemies; the husband who should give her strength has to take courage from her example. The most complicated presentation is found in Bosola, in whom it is made visible through the use of disguises, though they are in fact less important than the invisible disguising of his true nature at the beginning of the play, and his conversion, after the death of the Duchess, at the end.

The death of the Duchess suggests a paradox: the darkness of evil extinguishes the light of good, but only to liberate the good, fair soul from its paper prison and its cage into the light of eternity. It is Bosola who is left in "this sensible hell" where, despite conversion, he is unable to prevent himself from murdering goodness. . . .

[Problems of interpretation]

An examination of themes and images in *The Duchess of Malfi* provides one method of interpreting its meaning; a study of the characters' philosophy constitutes another. Yet neither method provides a means of answering the question which the story itself so forcibly presents: *Why* was the Duchess of Malfi murdered? Many answers to the question have been given, both in the play itself and by modern commentators on it, no less than by the early narrators of her history. She has been accused of a variety of misdemeanours: marrying outside the church; jesting with religion; marrying beneath her station; succumbing to lust. It must be admitted that she does literally marry outside the church; that she calls Cariola a "superstitious fool" for objecting to a feigned pilgrimage; and that the Duchess herself recognizes that simple virtue should not be forced into devious paths; only unjust actions should wear the masks and curtains which she and her husband have to adopt. It is the evil will of her brothers—one of them a Cardinal—that forces her to a secret marriage which is not illegal. The Duchess later speaks of it as a sacrament of the church. Cariola tries to fend off death with the cry that she has not been to confession for two years; if she dies now she is damned. In the Duchess' calm preparation for the next world there is the implication that—by contrast—she is in a state of grace. So she appears to Bosola as "sacred innocence"; and yet it is after this that Webster shows how Julia's wooing of Bosola echoes the Duchess' swift wooing of Antonio.

To some critics the power of the threat of evil to the goodness of the Duchess lies in its unspecified horror. The Aragonian brothers have no valid reason for killing her. Within the play they both produce reasons for their deeds, but these need to be carefully examined. Webster's characterization of Ferdinand suggests that incestuous love of the Duchess explains his behaviour, but there is no such explanation for the Cardinal's share in her death. Other questions which deserve attention concern whether the brothers are realistically or symbolically represented; why Ferdinand appears to be the Cardinal's twin; what significance there is in Webster's making Ferdinand the Duchess' twin, and her junior. . . .

The problem of what The Duchess of Malfi *means, and of how we are to react to the actions of its characters, has vexed critics of the play. The following rapid survey of various interpretations suggests that there is a deep ambiguity in Webster's drama, both morally and in terms of character motivation. For John Russell Brown, what holds the play together and gives it its meaning and effect as a theatrical work is its atmosphere and its dramatic structure.*

[THE "MEANING" OF *THE DUCHESS OF MALFI*]
John Russell Brown

. . . Although Webster chose a simple, affecting story, his dramatization has perplexed and divided opinion. "The most serious error that critics of Webster have committed," say Professor Ribner in his *Jacobean Tragedy* (1962), "has been to regard him as a dramatist lacking in moral vision" (p. 99). But a concern with such matters has not brought agreement. According to Ribner, Antonio's death proves "the nobility of his endurance" (p. 121), and according to Professor Ornstein, in *The Moral Vision of Jacobean Tragedy* (1960), his death is "contemptible" (p. 144). Una Ellis-Fermor thought that the cardinal "redeems himself at the last" (*Jacobean Drama* [1936], p. 180), but Dr Gunnar Boklund sees him revealed then as a "coward," without "even the redeeming feature of bravado" (pp. 133–4). To some critics the courtship of Antonio by the duchess is "a charming idyll" (Ribner, p. 116), but others say that "the more we consider the Duchess, the more hints seem to appear" (C. Leech, *John Webster* [1951], p. 75). Bosola is said to be more a chorus than a character; or, on the other hand, to show a development from illusion to self-knowledge. Ferdinand's madness is "convincing" and "unconvincing"; his motivation "sexual," "emblematic," "routine," "muddled." Whether critics look for a "moral vision" or consistent characterization, they do not often agree. Not all would subscribe to Professor Leech's temperate judgement:

> in *The Duchess* we are pulled successively in different directions, and on the completion of our reading are likely to feel we have the task of constructing a whole of which Webster has given us the separate parts.

Some believe that the play would always "ingeniously acquit itself." This disagreement should be expected. The main source offers conflicting judgements. The action is subtly planned. The dialogue is delicate and vexed. The play was intended for skilled performance in an intimate theatre, before a sophisticated audience. And we know that Webster worked arduously and persistently, and sought intractable issues: at the centre of his earlier tragedy was the dazzling incongruity of the "White Devil." From the beginning of *The Duchess* the audience is taught to look for contradictions, and to expect subtle resolutions:

> if 't chance
> Some curs'd example poison 't near the head . . .

From the Introduction to John Webster, *The Duchess of Malfi*, ed. John Russell Brown (Cambridge, Mass.: Harvard University Press, 1964), pp. xlvii–xliv, liv–lv. Copyright © 1964 John Russell Brown. Reprinted by permission of Methuen & Co. Ltd., London, and Harvard University Press, Cambridge, Mass.

Some such flashes superficially hang on him, for form; but
observe his inward character . . .

What appears in him mirth, is merely outside; . . .

   . . . will seem to sleep o' th' bench
Only to entrap offenders in their answers; . . .

     As I have seen some
Feed in a lord's dish, half asleep, not seeming
To listen to any talk; and yet these rogues
Have cut his throat in a dream . . .

Your darkest actions—nay, your privat'st thoughts—
Will come to light. (I.i. 13–316)

The cardinal at one moment turns Bosola away and then, in private, recommends his preferment. Antonio is the duchess' steward who is sent a brief message by his mistress, and then her beloved. Contradictions span the whole play: Ferdinand tells his sister that it is a sin to remarry, and in Act IV calls her innocent; she doubts and then affirms a renewal of love in "another world;" the cardinal seems "fearless" and then falls helplessly, like a young hare.

What "principle of unity" is there in this view of men and actions? First, an "atmosphere," developing in the course of the tragedy: a dark sensationalism and menace, contrasted with softness, intrigue, madness, moral sayings. Around 1920 this was Webster's chief appeal; for Rupert Brooke, F. L. Lucas, and T. S. Eliot:

He knew that thought clings round dead limbs
Tightening its lusts and luxuries.

(T.S. Eliot, "Whispers of Immortality")

Since then critics have searched rigorously for a unified "moral vision," and have divided opinion; and this division points to the play's other unity. So does the play's style and structure. It is a unity of empirical, responsible, sceptical, unsurprised, and deeply perceptive concern for the characters and society portrayed. . . .

. . . Many details have to be held in the mind in order to discuss Webster's characters. And, indeed, there is a careful ingenuity in every element of the writing—all except one, which is not verbal: the large and sweeping impression of the play in performance.

In the first three Acts, crowded court scenes alternate with private scenes. The focus moves incessantly, illuminating briefly a whole court, groups, couples, individuals; no one person holds the stage for long. The birth of the first child in Act II is attended by alarms and followed by a still darkness. In Act III the flight from Malfi leads the duchess and her husband to the open country where they separate and the duchess becomes a prisoner. In Act IV, the prison provides the one consistent setting and a steady dramatic focus: it is dark, and alternately frighteningly still and frighteningly wild. The duchess dies separated from everyone she loves or knows. Then the last Act is a mixture of slow cunning and sudden moves. Entries seem timed by some manipulating

fate: there is a sharp decisiveness ("O, my fate moves swift!"), an elaborate involvement ("You'll find it impossible To fly your fate"), and a contrivance ("Such a mistake as I have often seen In a play"). In a tragedy where appearances and judgements
change like quicksilver, and the plot has many by-paths and hesitations, and some irre-
ducible contradictions (the neglect of the son of the first marriage and, perhaps, Bosola's long failure to find the duchess' husband), the simple eloquence of the shape of
the action is especially impressive. The dramatist's silent handling seems to have something like a "meaning": a suggestion that the duchess had to die, and her imperma-
nent world to be destroyed.

And, briefly, in the last silent homage to the son of the duchess, there is a hint
that men may, perhaps, wish for some renewal and order. . . .

*The distinguished American poet and critic Kenneth Rexroth expands on the notion that the "mean-
ing" of* The Duchess of Malfi *lies in its atmosphere, and he suggests that the play is great because of its peculiar psychological effect on an audience.*

THE DUCHESS OF MALFI
Kenneth Rexroth

The drama of Shakespeare is distinguished, even in the plays where he is still
learning his craft, by an extraordinary coherence of all the artistic processes, of creation,
of structure of the work itself, of response in audience or reader. Subjective-objective,
classical-romantic, expressionistic-architectural, realism-symbolism—such antitheses
are subsumed in a synthesis of completely integrated communication. It is this massive
integrity which has led innumerable critics to postulate a man, Shakespeare, who is far
better organized than most humans, let alone most writers or people of the theater.
Even the plays that seem to reflect a period of personal tragedy and disillusion, such
as *Hamlet* or *Troilus and Cressida*, show few signs of any fragmentation of personality in
their author—whatever may be the case with their heros and heroines.

Few contemporary artists in any medium could be found to show forth better
the schism in the most fundamental nature—the very sources—of creativity, which has
become so characteristic of all the arts since the early years of the nineteenth century,
than Ben Jonson and John Webster, writing three centuries ago. The difference is so
great that we seem to be dealing with two distinct operations of the mind. The plays
of Jonson are classic in structure and objective in their delineation of motives and behavior, but also they are conceived of as taking place "out there." The esthetic process,
from creator to spectator, occurs in material which is independent of either of them
once it has been formed.

Kenneth Rexroth, *"The Duchess of Malfi," Saturday Review*, March 4, 1967, p. 21. Reprinted by permission of
the author.

Webster is not the least interested in what happens "out there." He uses poetry, drama, acting, stage effects solely to work inside the spectator. The material of Webster is the collective nervous system of his audience. This is beyond romanticism and its subjectivity. Nothing would appear quite like it until, following Poe, Mallarmé 300 years later would make the method explicit. Yet how explicit? We have no name for it, and that in a field ever fertile with jargon—criticism and esthetics. And few critics watching *The Duchess of Malfi* or reading *L'Après-midi d'un Faune* are aware of what is happening to them.

The Duchess of Malfi is a fashionable play, a revival of the tragedy of blood so popular at the beginning of Elizabethan drama. So are *Macbeth* and *Hamlet.* Webster is a conscious, deliberate disciple of Shakespeare. So are Beaumont and Fletcher. It is one of the first tragedies that can be called decadent, both in its verse structure and in its somewhat phosphorescent dramaturgy—the greatest of a class that includes Tourneur, Ford, and Shirley and would be imitated, carefully but with only limited success, by Shelley in *The Cenci.* Yet it really isn't like any of these plays.

In the very first scene of *Duchess,* Webster, wasting no time, starts out to do something quite different from Shakespeare in *Macbeth* or Shelley in *The Cenci.* Shakespeare is building a character, setting a scene, creating a psychological environment that will define the character and the tragedy of Macbeth himself—out there. Shelley does that, too, but he is more interested in himself, in expressing himself, perhaps in scaring himself a little. We call it romantic subjectivism.

In the opening scene of *Duchess,* Antonio and Delio carry on a dialogue which seems objective enough. They describe, as they appear, all the important characters, their interrelations, and hint at the potentialities for tragedy these relationships embody. But in what an extraordinary fashion! Webster uses a standard device, the opening dialogue, "Hello, old friend, what's been going on while I've been gone?" to string together a series of carefully concealed assaults on the nerves of his audience:

> If it chance some cursed example poison it near the head, death and diseases through the whole land spread. . . .

> I do haunt you still. . . .

> They are like plum trees that grow crooked over standing pools. They are rich and over laden with fruit but none but crows, pies and caterpillars feed on them. . . .

> Places in court are like beds in hospital, where this man's head lies at that man's foot, and so lower and lower.

Corruption—the idea echoes with the word throughout the first act in what purports to be the ordinary conversation of a court. It is a court where the head sickens and the members rot, but over and above the careful setting of a situation. Webster is striving to affect the audience directly. This play is going to take place inside the heads—in each individual brain—of the audience.

Is this melodrama? The play is certainly a melodrama by conventional definition, but this is more like hypnotism. As the play goes on, horror seeps into the most commonplace statements until language loses its informative role and becomes a kind of argot whose aim always is not communication between the characters but manipulation of the minds of the audience. Meanwhile, the action goes on, bodies move in space with uncanny haste and glow with foxfire. The stage is lit with decay.

Melodrama is supposed to be bad art. Is *The Duchess of Malfi* great art? It certainly is great melodrama, probably the greatest ever written, and in addition—and more importantly—it adds an entirely new dimension to drama, or even to art as a whole. If great art makes us confront the profoundest meanings of life, *Duchess* is hardly art at all, because it literally doesn't mean much. When we leave the play our nerves have been rubbed raw and tortured. Does this make them more acute receptors? It may just as well dull our sensitivity as sharpen it. We are left nervously exhausted by a novel such as *Les Liaisons Dangereuses,* but we are also left prostrate by a long look into the abysm of deliberate evil, and our valuations of human conduct and our responses to those valuations have been subtly reorganized. The good and evil that struggle in *The Duchess of Malfi,* once the play is over, vanish. The Duchess changes her costume and is just an actress, impatient to be gone to a late supper.

In recent years the estheticians and critics who try to establish a moral ground of justification for the arts have shifted their position to a kind of physiological esthetic: "The arts work upon us through abstract, purely artistic qualities. They do not teach or even communicate. The experience of the subtle architectonics of a great work of art makes us more refined, more efficient organisms, and the cumulative effects of such experiences through life make us better men." There is not an iota of empirical evidence for this notion. On the contrary, society has always been suspicious of "esthetes" as secret rascals given to shocking depravities. This is not true, either; Oscar Wilde's Dorian Grey and the heroes of Huysmans' novels are excessively rare types. Although it follows the conventions of tragedy and deals, with great psychological penetration, with the slow corruption of consciously chosen evil, *The Duchess of Malfi* is not a nerve tonic or a moral stimulant. It is simply very great entertainment and its own excuse for being.

Aside from its problems of interpretation, The Duchess of Malfi *has had considerable difficulty in convincing playgoers that it can be a successful theatre piece. The following survey of modern productions and their critics indicates the sorts of things actors and directors are up against when they attempt to put Webster on the stage.*

[*THE DUCHESS OF MALFI* IN THE THEATRE]
John Russell Brown

. . . In the present century there have been more productions and a greater reliance on Webster's text, although always cut. . . . At first directors were shy of the horrors. The critic of *The Times* in 1919 excused the audience's "tittering . . . towards the close" and the next production of 1935 played safe: "horror was absent altogether. The masque of madmen was turned into a sort of ballet" *(Daily Telegraph);* "The dead-hand scene is produced in a pleasant amber light and the pallor of human flesh is hidden by a glove" *(New Statesman);* the director "cannot put Elizabethan ferocity into the hearts of his actors" *(Times).* Peggy Ashcroft has twice played the duchess, and now Ferdinand and Bosola have returned to Restoration prominence. Even in the tame 1935 production, "John Laurie's . . . epileptic frenzy" as Ferdinand was "genuinely terrible and his ranting [had] a ghastly perverse sincerity." In this part the chief laurels are Gielgud's: fifteen years after his performance, Mr Tynan remembered the "thrill of finality" he gave to "I will never see thee more" *(Observer,* 18 Dec. 1960) and Mr Hobson his "torment of spirit that still excites the imagination" *(Sunday Times,* 18 Dec. 1960). Gielgud had accepted the indications of incestuous desire; and they seemed so up-to-date that he was praised for an originality that is partly Webster's. William Rea's Bosola of 1919 exploited the character's isolation, playing him "with an air of melancholy reverie and aloofness which gave him immense distinction" *(Times).* Cecil Trouncer, in 1945, risked consistency to give a full interpretation: in *The Sunday Times,* James Agate called it "a grand exhibition. I am not persuaded that the actor knew quite what to do with this mixture of Enobarbus and Thersites; to watch him do it was nevertheless a rich experience." *The Times* called his "vital study, of . . . a murderer of fortune prematurely aged in the galleys," the "supreme attraction of the revival."

The constant problem has been the shape and effect of the play as a whole. The fifth Act has often been called "irredeemable." According to *The Hartford Courant* (10 Jan. 1946), Auden's adaptation was chiefly confined to Acts IV and V, but:

> Early in the play an interpolated passage . . . establishes the Duke's concern for his sister as born of affection, if perhaps a little incestuous, while the Duke's original confession that he merely sought to secure her estates is saddled on the Cardinal.

But still Rosamund Gilder, in *Theatre Arts* (Dec. 1946), called the production laboured, lacking "intensity and lurid beauty." Productions have often been praised for isolated

From the Introduction to John Webster, *The Duchess of Malfi,* ed. John Russell Brown (Cambridge, Mass.: Harvard University Press, 1964), pp. lvii–lix. Copyright © 1964 John Russell Brown. Reprinted by permission of Methuen & Co. Ltd., London, and Harvard University Press, Cambridge, Mass.

"moments": *Theatre Arts* said that the play at the Phoenix was "curiously episodic, and the episodes are somehow not cumulative"; and Mr Hobson said that the Aldwych *Duchess* had "no drive, no force, no continuity," as if the director had decided that "it is in single lines that the genius of Webster lies." The rôles of the duchess, Bosola, and Ferdinand have been variously and effectively realized in performance, but the structure of the play has yet to be vindicated. This may not be Webster's fault. The records suggest that no production has been interested in manifestations of guilt, judgement, and responsibility, or in the workings of fate or the presentation of society. At the Aldwych, the Five-Act structure was ignored; there was no presence-chamber; and among the lines cut were Bosola's concluding:

> Let worthy minds ne'er stagger in distrust
> To suffer death, or shame for what is just.

While such neglect is possible, the tragedy cannot be said to have had a fair chance in the theatre.

A review of the 1946 New York production expresses the rather widespread opinion among theatre critics that The Duchess of Malfi *is a bad play and not stage worthy.*

[REVIEW OF *THE DUCHESS OF MALFI*]
Wolcott Gibbs

"The Duchess of Malfi," John Webster's sixteenth-century Neapolitan tragedy, somewhat rearranged by W. H. Auden, stars Elisabeth Bergner, who, it seems, has long dreamed of resurrecting this lady of multiple sorrows. The reasons for her choice presumably lie in the fact that almost no heroine on the stage has a more complex or a bloodier history, or one offering more opportunities to a versatile actress. From the tender opening scene with the man whom she marries somewhat against his better judgment, she goes on to low comedy in a pregnancy of really notable Elizabethan frankness; to tragic bewilderment in her interviews with her brothers, one ruthlessly driven by greed, the other half-mad and incestuous; to noble renunciation when she parts from her husband and her little boy; to horror when she is a prisoner guarded by gibbering madmen; to unendurable grief when the bodies of her husband and son are delivered to her by a smirking cutthroat; and finally to a mood of exalted resignation when her own executioners appear with an open coffin and a noose. It is a part that calls for an impressive range of emotion, and it is easy to understand why Miss Bergner coveted it.

In spite of the real passion and eloquence of some of its scenes, however, I suspect that *The Duchess of Malfi* is not much of a play for the modern stage. Unlike Shakespeare,

From Wolcott Gibbs, "The Theatre," *The New Yorker,* October 26, 1946, pp. 47–48. Reprinted by permission; © 1946, 1974 The New Yorker Magazine, Inc.

Webster hadn't much use for tidy construction, and his plot, rather than being an orderly march to its inevitable tragedy, seems to be little more than a collection of violently melodramatic and barely connected episodes, shifting wildly in time and space. His characterization, too, is almost comically simplified by present standards. The wicked brothers and their oily henchman are monsters from the pit, whose long careers of bribery, seduction, perversion, and murder reach a fitting climax when somehow they all manage to stab one another simultaneously and die together in a gaudy atmosphere of brimstone and mortuary rhetoric. The Duchess and her mate, on the other hand, are such dreams of persecuted beauty and virility, such shapely vessels of love on the lam, that they seem more than mortal and consequently, I'm afraid, rather less than fascinating. Now and then, lines of great poetry come through the confusion on the stage, but for the most part the play has the air of a burlesque of Shakespeare, almost as damaging as any done by Beerbohm. . . .

In a review of The Classic Theatre's television production of The Duchess of Malfi, *Raymond Williams writes critically of the various fashions in interpreting and producing the play, many of which are exemplified or alluded to in the preceding essays. He suggests that* The Duchess *should be taken seriously, as a real vision of human experience conditioned by real social and moral disintegration, and he goes on to assert that the BBC production successfully embodies this vision.*

VERSIONS OF WEBSTER
Raymond Williams

. . . It was interesting to see a relatively straight production of Webster's *The Duchess of Malfi* (BBC 2). When I was a student we used to read Webster and Tourneur and Ford as what, following Eliot, we called "savage farce." The extremity of some of the horrors—a brother giving his sister a dead man's hand; the dance of the madmen; the final chain of killings, like a court ritual gone wrong—was ordinarily seen in a dimension of absurdity. What happened was too bizarre to be taken quite seriously, but when it was joined to the desperate intensity of some of the verse it could be seen as a particular mode: farcical but savage, the two apparently opposite feelings conjoined in a specific emotion which had the attractive quality of distance.

That interpretation seems to me now a product of its period: not so much the period in which we inherited it, and certainly not Webster's early 17th century, but the years, say, from Wilde's *Salomé* to Eliot's "Sweeney Agonistes": the specific period of a specific social group, from the 1890s to the 1920s. The arbitrariness of the violence, the exhibited distortions of the sexual feelings, the conscious playing with the bizarre and

Raymond Williams, "Versions of Webster," *The Listener,* vol. 88 (October 19, 1972), p. 515. Reprinted by permission of the author.

the insane: these composed a mode, and it is easy to understand how it could be projected onto Webster and his contemporaries. Moreover, though in my own case assent to any such interpretation had long been withdrawn, there was the subsequent and very comparable fashion of what was called, in the late Fifties and Sixties, the "theatre of the absurd" and the associated "theatre of cruelty." Was not Webster ready-made for this? I remember a lively Cambridge production in which the chain of killings at the end was performed by the actors standing in a ring, each with a knife in the next man's back. It was a comment of a kind, on the arbitrariness and on the absurdity. The lively cynicism of a young man's response to this kind of world communicated very easily: the outrage modulated to a laugh. But while this was possible in a student production, what was normally happening, in the professional theatre, was an extension of arbitrary and insane horror to a practised convention.

Who then would have expected, from a contemporary television production of *The Duchess of Malfi*, anything like what we got? Think of the mad scene or the waxwork corpses or the final slaughter: would not any of twenty highly-praised directors have seen them and loved them as production numbers? There were in fact a few survivals from the past: notably a stress on incest—a frustrated incestuous love—as the Duke's motive for revenge on his sister's marriage. That kind of Freudianism is so deep in contemporary ideology that there is a certain inevitability in its abstraction from the ambiguous intensity and confusion of the responses Webster wrote for the Duke: the physical and sexual ferocity of Act II, Scene v; the calculating power and acquisitiveness of Act IV, Scene ii. It is interesting that in a world like our own, which is no stranger to every kind of cruelty and confusion, habitual interpretations pick up the sexual but not the economic and political drives; or, in dividing them, fail to recognise the ways in which, in a particular social and sexual structure, they become fused or displace one another. Among the other survivals, but in a very minor way, we had Julia and the Cardinal rather self-consciously in bed, but done as if from stock, with Julia sliding out at a now practised angle, as if going for a shower. But these moments from a different sensibility stood out because the tone of James MacTaggart's production was so different.

Perhaps the main reason for the straightness with which it was played was that it was set in a great house, so that the realism of a social location was persistently stressed. Also, the text, with less cuts than is usual, was respected in the speaking, and there were several finely considered performances of this spoken kind. And then, as in the original, this spoken action created an active dimension within which the spectacular horrors were significant rather than instrumental or isolated. What I found myself considering, as in no other production I have seen, was the full human experience which this extraordinary play embodies. For it seems, looking back, that the fashionable revival of the Jacobean plays as savage farce, like the later period of the theatre of the absurd and the cruel, was a product of relative security and of the kinds of indifference which that breeds. Everyone says that it was a product of insecurity—wars and the break-up of values—but much of that was in the head, and in a later generation some responses have changed: the disintegration and the suffering have gone so deep, become so internal, that they are capable of resuming their ordinary human dimensions: not savage farce but the sober recognition of anger, confusion and violence.

At any rate, this is how *The Duchess of Malfi* was played, and it came through, as such, very strongly. On reflection, one could see that its specific social dimension, though stressed, had been diminished. The play ends with a moral reflection which is to ratify the bringing to power of the young Duke of Malfi. The production ended with the child staring at the intolerable ruin and turning and being led away. For my own part, I have read Webster and the others differently since I realised that Hobbes was their contemporary: what they wrote as young men, in a dramatic action, he wrote as an old man in a philosophical argument. The connections are specific: the sense of the war of all against all, the murderously destructive isolated appetites. This is redeemed in the dramatists by the conventional restoration of an innocent prince; redeemed in Hobbes, more realistically, by an absolute sovereign: in fact, redeemed by the ending of that system of absolute and irresponsible power which created both a Duke and a Bosola and victims beyond counting. But the confidence of that kind of analysis has been shaken in its turn: the child simply looking and turning away is now a more widely shared emotion, and the production underwrote it.

Given the relative cultural prestige, among the highly educated, of television and the theatre, it seems possible that the production will get less notice than it deserves. But this is not the only occasion on which television, even with material ordinarily thought of as high culture, has shown itself significantly ahead of the theatre and other similar received institutions.

Paradise Restored

Paradise Restored is an original television play by Don Taylor based on events in the life of the great seventeenth-century English poet, John Milton. When a playwright uses real history or biography as the basis of his drama, he has at his disposal a certain amount of more or less true information, found in documents of the period he is writing about or derived from them. Out of this material, often very limited in quantity and quality, he must develop living characters, create a dramatic structure, and invent actions and dialogue that will reveal character and theme. The following two excerpts from early memoirs or biographies constitute virtually all the "authentic" information we have about Milton's first marriage, to Mary Powell; everything else about Mary in Paradise Restored is dramatic invention or interpretation on the part of the author, Don Taylor.

[MILTON'S FIRST MARRIAGE]
Edward Phillips

About Whitsuntide it was, or a little after, that he took a journey into the country; nobody about him certainly knowing the reason, or that it was any more than a journey of recreation; after a month's stay, home he returns a married man, that went out a bachelor; his wife being Mary, the eldest daughter of Mr. Richard Powell, then a justice of the peace, of Forest Hill, near Shotover in Oxfordshire; some few of her nearest relations accompanying the bride to her new habitation; which by reason the father nor any body else were yet come, was able to receive them; where the feasting held for some days in celebration of the nuptials, and for entertainment of the bride's friends. At length they took their leave, and returning to Forest Hill, left the sister behind; probably not much to her satisfaction, as appeared by the sequel. By that time she had for a month or thereabout led a philosophical life (after having been used to a great house, and much company and joviality). Her friends, possibly incited by her own desire, made earnest suit by letter, to have her company the remaining part of the summer, which was granted, on condition of her return at the time appointed, Michaelmas, or thereabout. In the meantime came his father, and some of the forementioned disciples. . . .

Michaelmas being come, and no news of his wife's return, he sent for her by letter; and receiving no answer, sent several other letters, which were also unanswered; so that at last he dispatched down a foot messenger with a letter, desiring her return. But the messenger came back not only without an answer, at least a satisfactory one, but to the best of my remembrance, reported that he was dismissed with some sort of contempt. This proceeding, in all probability, was grounded upon no other cause but this, namely, that the family being generally addicted to the cavalier party, as they called it, and some of them possibly engaged in the King's service, who by this time had his headquarters at Oxford, and was in some prospect of success, they began to repent them of having matched the eldest daughter of the family to a person so contrary to them in opinion; and thought it would be a blot in their escutcheon, whenever that court should come to flourish again.

Excerpts from Edward Phillips' account of Milton's marriage, reprinted in James Holly Hanford and James G. Taaffe, *A Milton Handbook*, 5th ed. (New York: Appleton-Century-Crofts, 1970), pp. 28–30. (Excerpts originally appeared in *The Early Lives of Milton*, ed. Helen Darbishire, 1932. Reprinted by permission of Constable and Co., Ltd., and Barnes & Noble, Inc.)

However, it so incensed our author, that he thought it would be dishonorable ever to receive her again, after such a repulse; so that he forthwith prepared to fortify himself with arguments for such a resolution, and accordingly wrote two treatises, by which he undertook to maintain, that it was against reason, and the enjoinment of it not provable by Scripture, for any married couple disagreeable in humor and temper, or having an aversion to each other, to be forced to live yoked together all their days. The first was, his *Doctrine and Discipline of Divorce;* of which there was printed a second edition, with some additions. The other, in prosecution of the first, was styled *Tetrachordon.* . . .

[MILTON'S FIRST MARRIAGE]
Anonymous

. . . In this while, his manner of settlement fitting him for the reception of a wife, he in a month's time (according to his practice of not wasting that precious talent) courted, married, and brought home from Forresthall [i. e., Forest Hill], near Oxford, a daughter of Mr. Powell. But she, that was very young, and had been bred in a family of plenty and freedom, being not well pleased with his reserved manner of life, within a few days left him, and went back into the country with her mother. Nor though he sent several pressing invitations could he prevail with her to return, till about four years after, when Oxford was surrendered (the nighness of her father's house to that garrison having for the most part of the meantime hindered any communication between them), she of her own accord came, and submitted to him, pleading that her mother had been the inciter of her to that frowardness. He, in this interval, who had entered into that state for the end designed by God and nature, and was then in the full vigor of his manhood, could ill bear the disappointment he met with by her obstinate absenting; and, therefore, thought upon a divorce, that he might be free to marry another; concerning which he was also in treaty. . . .

Excerpts from an anonymous biography of Milton, reprinted in James Holly Hanford and James G. Taaffe, *A Milton Handbook,* 5th ed. (New York: Appleton-Century-Crofts, 1970), pp. 31–32. (Excerpts originally appeared in *The Early Lives of Milton,* ed. Helen Darbishire, 1932. Reprinted by permission of Constable and Co., Ltd., and Barnes & Noble, Inc.)

This biographical information about Milton and his first wife has been used for literary purposes by authors other than Don Taylor. The English poet, Robert Graves, wrote a novel on the subject, narrated in the first person by Mary Powell herself. Like Mr. Taylor, Mr. Graves added a great deal of invented material to the historical "facts" (which themselves do not seem to be thoroughly reliable). But Mr. Taylor's additions and interpretations had to be done through the medium of dialogue, gesture, and camera work, whereas Robert Graves had at his disposal the quite different techniques of narrative prose fiction. The excerpts that follow are from the chapter in which Mary describes the unpleasantness of the early days of her marriage, and the reasons for her leaving Milton's home.

WIFE TO MR. MILTON: THE STORY OF MARIE POWELL
Robert Graves

The more pertinaciously I tried to make my husband understand how he hindered his own end by an impatience and severity towards me, the more impatient and severe he grew. He is a man who never graciously acknowledges himself at fault, fearing by any such admission to impugn his own authority and judgment. For though he has often changed his mind and turned cat in pan even upon matters of religious principle, yet (this I write without irony or reproach, but as a mere matter of fact) he is constant and loyal to one thing at least, which is a humble faith in his own infallibility: no man in the world was ever so sincere and modest in his self-devotion. Now, as a punishment for what he called my foolish glozing and deceit, he banished me from his chamber altogether for the space of three weeks, giving me a bed in a cramped back closet that opened from it; and by day kept me a close prisoner in the house and garden. I had no work to employ me, because my clothes and his were all in good repair, and at broidery I have no skill, and we kept no poultry nor brewed our own beer. Kitchen work I love, but my husband told me that Jane and Trunco needed no third pair of hands in the kitchen, and that I would but delay their necessary work by gossiping with them. Since also he would not suffer me to play and sing on my guitar, which he said distracted him from his studies, and since there was no one to play at cards with me, I could find little to do besides reading; yet every time I wished to take a book from his shelves I must first ask his leave, and if he considered the book to be improper for my reading he would forbid it me. When I asked whether I might sit and listen while he taught our nephews Latin, forasmuch as I had not yet forgotten the rudiments learned from our curate, the Reverend Fulker, he answered that my presence would distract the boys and be a great inconvenience to himself. "And besides," said he, humorously, "one tongue is enough for a woman. . . ."

This was the tenth day of my captivity, just before supper, and going to my coffer in the closet I took out my vellum book, and unlocked it and began to write. I was trembling with rage and could hardly shape the letters as I set down: "Marie Powell was married to John Melton, alias Milton, Junior, and he altered her name to Mary Milton. Thus she exchanged the honourable arms of Powell (which her father blazoned

From Chapter Fifteen of Robert Graves, *Wife to Mr. Milton: The Story of Marie Powell* (New York: Creative Age Press, 1944), pp. 197, 200–202, 202–203, 204. Copyright 1944 by Robert Graves, copyright renewed 1972 by Robert Graves. Reprinted by permission of Farrar, Straus & Giroux, Inc., New York, and A. P. Watt & Son, London.

for her on the title page of this book) for the arms of Mitton, which were in error bestowed upon his father, a scrivener, by the Garter King-at-Arms, who thereby endowed the said ungenteel John Melton Junior, with the fraudulent titles of Armiger and Gentleman."

Then I left off writing and began to read and dream of Mun. My husband came to the door and pushed it open without knocking, as was his custom. He saw me with the book and asked me what I read.

"Nothing," I replied.

"Were an answer of that nature given me by a pupil of mine I should beat him severely," said he.

"I do not doubt it, Husband," I answered, my rage rising again. "You seem to be more generous with the ferule than with the fruit pastry."

"What book do you read without my permission?" he asked again, threateningly.

"My own book," I answered, and locking the clasp hastily, I put it underneath me where I sat upon the coffer.

"Give it to me," said he, "or I will pluck it out from under you."

"Not I!" was my answer. "It is my book, and was given to me by my Godmother Moulton, with advice never to show it to any person living."

"Wife," he said, "beware to remember your bridal vow: you have now no worldly chattels that are not mine."

"Very, very true," said I. "You also made the same endowment of your chattels to me; but since you have withheld several of your books from me, you cannot complain if I withhold this single one from you."

"You disobey my plain command to yield up this book?" he asked. "You dare to oppose me in a point of house-rule?"

"I do," said I, beside myself with wrath, "and if you lay a finger upon me you must beware, you leather-sided villain! I will not cry out for pity in the Latin tongue as your miserable pupils do, but defend myself, tooth and nail, as once you defended yourself against your tutor, Mr. Chappell; and, s'blood! I warrant I will leave my mark upon you."

"So!" he said, breathing heavily. "So it has come to this! My fire, my spirit, my blood!—your earth and phlegm, your cold, muddy, scolding nastiness! Well did Solomon write that a bad wife is to her husband as rottenness to his bones, as continual dropping!"

"Do not provoke me to bandy the rhetoric of Turnbull Street and Billingsgate with you, Stinkard, Base Slubberdegullion, Cheesy Plagiarist, Immortal Whip-Arse, Eater of Stinking Beef!" I cried; for, by God, when I was angered beyond endurance, I was my mother's eldest daughter. "Do you take me for Issachar's ass that I should bear all your scandalous revilements and submit to them in patience?"

He looked incredulous loathing, and with no more farewell than, "I shall speak with you again to-morrow morning," he went out again, locking the door after him. I laid me soberly down upon me bed, pulled off my gown, drew the quilted coverlet over me and with no more ado fell asleep. . . .

I remember no more, but I awoke laughing and there was my husband in coat and hat and shoes standing over me. The dawn had come, but it was as yet too early for me to rise, so I wished him good-morning and asked him why he was already astir.

When he made no answer, I told him that I was heartily sorry for the quarrel between us, and was resolved to be a good wife to him; but that being confined strictly in his house all day, like a prisoner, with no employment nor any means of exercising my body, the gross humours were naturally pent up and worked upon my mind like a poison, so that I had said I knew not what.

He answered shortly: "Nay, Mary, we did not quarrel; for there can be no such thing as a quarrel between master and servant. You were rebellious and impudent and disobedient; and all this night I have watched and pondered upon my trial, and at last with the dawn I have been granted illumination. To correct you corporeally as you deserve I cannot, or not without scandal—and, as wise Virgil says, no man can win a memorable name by conquest of a woman; to prolong your confinement would be neither convenient nor healthy; I cannot mulct you of money, for you receive no wages; you are insensible to gentle chiding; to forgive you would be weakness. I am determined to put you to public shame, by sending you back to your father's house at Forest Hill; nor will I receive you to my bosom again until I be assured of your hearty repentance. Moreover, at Michaelmas-tide, when I expect your return, Esquire Powell must pay me your promised marriage portion of one thousand pounds, as also the other money owed me, five hundred pounds; without the money you will not be welcome, as he must understand plainly. . . ."

He glowered magisterially at me, griping at the air with his hands, until I drove him out of my chamber with these words: "Since I am your wife in name only, and since you are determined to pack me off home again, a virgin yet, it ill becomes you to stand there gaping at me, with offence to my modesty. Mercy guard me! Remember how the chaste Lady in your Ludlow Masque answered the lascivious wizard when he held her prisoner in his castle and lusted after her with his rolling eye. . . ."

Much of Paradise Restored *is devoted to Milton's relations with his three daughters. Here, too, Mr. Taylor has based his dramatic portrayal of the relationship on a few fundamental documents, and has invented all the rest in order to interpret the information the documents give us. Here are the documents.*

[MILTON'S DAUGHTERS]
Edward Phillips

. . . And those children he had by the first [wife] he made serviceable to him in that very particular in which he most wanted their service, and supplied his want of eyesight by their eyes and tongue. For though he had daily about him one or other

Excerpted from Edward Phillips' narrative of Milton's life, reprinted in James Holly Hanford and James G. Taaffe, *A Milton Handbook,* 5th ed. (New York: Appleton-Century-Crofts, 1970), pp. 46–47. (Excerpt originally appeared in *The Early Lives of Milton,* ed. Helen Darbishire, 1932. Reprinted by permission of Constable and Co., Ltd., and Barnes & Noble, Inc.)

to read to him; some persons of man's estate, who of their own accord greedily catched at the opportunity of being his readers, that they might as well reap the benefit of what they read to him, as oblige him by the benefit of their reading; others of younger years sent by their parents to the same end; yet, excusing only the eldest daughter by reason of her bodily infirmity and difficult utterances of speech (which to say truth I doubt was the principal cause of excusing her), the other two were condemned to the performance of reading, and exactly pronouncing of all the languages of whatever book he should at one time or other think fit to peruse; *viz.* the Hebrew (and I think the Syriac), the Greek, the Latin, the Italian, Spanish, and French. All which sorts of books to be confined to read, without understanding one word, must needs be a trial of patience almost beyond endurance; yet it was endured by both for a long time. Yet the irksomeness of this employment could not always be concealed, but broke out more and more into expressions of uneasiness; so that at length they were all (even the eldest also) sent out to learn some curious and ingenious sorts of manufacture, that are proper for women to learn, particularly embroideries in gold or silver. It had been happily indeed, if the daughters of such a person had been made in some measure inheritrixes of their father's learning; but since fate otherwise decreed, the greatest honor that can be ascribed to this now living (and so would have been to the others, had they lived) is to be daughter to a man of his extraordinary character. . . .

FROM THE COURT PROCEEDINGS
RELATIVE TO MILTON'S WILL

Milton's nuncupative or verbal will leaving all his property to his wife was contested by his daughters, Mary, Anne, and Deborah. The citations are from the sworn testimony of Milton's brother and servant, who appeared as witnesses for the widow. The will was held invalid on technical grounds.

That on or about the twentieth day of July, 1674, the day certain he now remembereth not, this deponent being a practicer in the law, and a Bencher in the Inner Temple, but living in vacations at Ipswich, did usually at the end of the term visit John Milton, his this deponent's brother the testator articulate, deceased, before his going home; and so at the end of Midsummer Term last past, he this deponent went to visit his said brother and then found him in his chamber within his own house situated on Bunhill within the parish of St. Giles, Cripplegate, London. And at that time, he the said testator being not well (and this deponent being then going into the country), in a serious manner, with an intent (as he believes), that what he then spoke should then be his will, if he died before his this deponent's coming the next time to

Reprinted in James Holly Hanford and James G. Taaffe, *A Milton Handbook,* 5th ed. (New York: Appleton-Century-Crofts, 1970), pp. 52–54. The explanatory note is by Messrs. Hanford and Taaffe. (Proceedings originally reprinted in *The Early Lives of Milton,* ed. Helen Darbishire, 1932. Reprinted by permission of Constable and Co., Ltd., and Barnes & Noble, Inc.)

London, declared his will in these very words as near as this deponent can now call to mind. *Viz.* "Brother, the portion due to me from Mr. Powell, my former [first] wife's father, I leave to the unkind children I had by her; but I have received no part of it, and my will and meaning is they shall have no other benefit of my estate, than the said portion and what I have besides done for them; they having been very undutiful to me. And all the residue of my estate I leave to the disposal of Elizabeth my loving wife" [testimony of Christopher Milton].

That this deponent was servant unto Mr. John Milton, the testator in this case, deceased, for about a year before his death, who died upon a Sunday the fifteenth of November last at night, and saith that on a day happening in the month of July last, the time more certainly she remembereth not, this deponent being then in the deceased's lodging chamber, he the said deceased, and the party producent in this cause his wife, being then also in the said chamber at dinner together, and the said Elizabeth Milton the party producent having provided something for the deceased's dinner which he very well liked, he the said deceased then spoke to his said wife these or the like words as near as this deponent can remember, *viz.* "God have mercy Betty, I see thou wilt perform according to thy promise in providing me such dishes as I think fit whilst I live, and when I die thou knowest that I have left thee all," there being nobody present in the said chamber with the said deceased and his wife but this deponent. And the said testator at that time was of perfect mind and memory, and talked and discoursed sensibly and well, but was then indisposed in his body by reason of the distemper of the gout, which he had then upon him. Further this deponent saith that she hath several times heard the said deceased, since the time above deposed of, declare and say that he had made provision for his children in his lifetime and had spent the greatest part of his estate in providing for them, and that he was resolved he would do no more for them living or dying. . . .

That this respondent hath heard the deceased declare his displeasure against the parties ministrant his children, and particularly the deceased declared to this respondent that a little before he was married to Elizabeth Milton his now relict, a former maid servant of his told Mary one of the deceased's daughters and one of his ministrants, that she heard the deceased was to be married, to which the said Mary replied to the said maid servant, that that was no news to hear of his wedding, but if she could hear of his death that was something; and further told this respondent that all his said children did combine together and counsel his maid servant to cheat him the deceased in her marketings, and that his said children had made away some of his books and would have sold the rest of his books to the dunghill women [testimony of Elizabeth Fisher]. . . .

[MILTON'S DAUGHTER DEBORAH]
Jonathan Richardson

. . . As we are at a loss as to the particulars of the affair, what I have suggested will, I hope, be sufficient—only let me add, that that daughter [Deborah], who was certainly one (if there was really more than one) that was thus serviceable to her excellent father in his distress, expressed no uneasiness that I ever heard of when she gave accounts of Milton's affairs to the many inquirers lately; but, on the contrary, spoke of him with great tenderness. Particularly, I have been told, she said he was delightful company, the life of the conversation—and *that* on account of a flow of subject and an unaffected cheerfulness and civility. One instance of her tender remembrance of him I cannot forbear relating. The picture in crayons I have of him was shown her after several others, or which were pretended to be his. When those were shown and she was asked if she could recollect if she had ever seen such a face: "No, no." But when this was produced, in a transport: " 'Tis my father! 'Tis my dear father! I see him! 'Tis him!" And then she put her hands to several parts of her face: " 'Tis the very man! Here, here."

It is not only the dramatist or the novelist who must add various kinds of speculative interpretation to the documents in order to make human sense out of them. The modern historian or biographer must do the same thing, even though he does not allow himself (as the dramatist and novelist do) the poetic license of inventing scenes and dialogue. In the following passages, two Milton scholars attempt to understand Milton's relationship with his daughters.

[MILTON AND HIS DAUGHTERS]
Edward Wagenknecht

. . . The daughters, of course, lived on. The eldest, Anne, though attractive to see, was apparently "retarded" and not quite ablebodied. None of them seem to have had much gift for letters, and Milton, apparently despairing of anything better for them, finally spent a good deal of money to have them learn a "gentlewomanly" trade. Anne signed the receipt for her share of his estate with a mark, and Mary spelled Milton with a small *m* and two *l*'s. Yet Richardson says that Milton would call his daughters at any hour of the night to take down what came to him! Even a girl who understood the value of what her father was creating would have had to be something close to a saint to be willing to make such sacrifices for it—and him—and there is no indication

Reprinted in James Holly Hanford and James G. Taaffe, *A Milton Handbook*, 5th ed. (New York: Appleton-Century-Crofts, 1970), p. 51. (Material originally printed in *The Early Lives of Milton*, ed. Helen Darbishire, 1932. Reprinted by permission of Constable and Co., Ltd., and Barnes & Noble, Inc.)

From Edward Wagenknecht, *The Personality of Milton* (Norman: University of Oklahoma Press, 1970), pp. 120–122. Copyright 1970 by the University of Oklahoma Press; reprinted by their permission.

that Milton's daughters did understand; they were no part of that "fit audience though few" for which he labored. Edward Phillips adds that his uncle required both the younger girls to read to him in his blindness in "Hebrew (and I think the Syriac), the Greek, the Latin, Spanish, and French," and one does not know whether to marvel more at his ability to understand what to them must have been so much gibberish or at their patience to go through with it. Patience, according to the legend, had little to do with the matter, and Munkácsy's immense canvas of Milton dictating *Paradise Lost* to his daughters, which hangs over the staircase in the New York Public Library, fairly crackles with hatred and resentment, never remotely suggesting that anybody pictured in it has the remotest concern with spiritual matters. Nor do the daughters seem to have taken kindly to the third wife.

Like most men of means in his time, Milton was accustomed to personal services from his youth. Aubrey says that, as a child, when he studied until midnight or after, "his father ordered the maid to sit up for him," and it does not seem to have occurred to either of these males that this was an unreasonable imposition upon a woman who had probably been working all day and who must get up early in the morning to begin her work again.

Yet Milton's relations with his daughters may not have been quite so uncomfortable as we have sometimes assumed. We have, to be sure, the shocking story that when Mary heard he was to marry Elizabeth Minshull, she remarked that the news of his wedding could not interest her much, but that if she could hear that he was dead, that would be worth hearing, and the same servant who testifies to this adds that Milton's children conspired with tradespersons to cheat him and tried to sell his books away from him for waste paper. But the testimony of servants is not always reliable, and over against this we must place the account of Deborah's emotion when Jonathan Richardson showed her the Faithorne crayon of Milton: " 'Tis my father! 'Tis my dear father! I see him! 'Tis him!" Richardson says too that Deborah spoke of her father

> with great tenderness: particularly I have been told she said he was delightful company, the life of the conversation, and that on account of a flow of subject and an unaffected cheerfulness and civility.

Perhaps Deborah, being the "baby," had felt Milton's severity less than her sisters. She was the only one of the girls who wanted any mementoes—or anything else than money—from his estate. We hear of his having tried to teach her Latin, and in her later years she herself did some teaching. Perhaps she left home when she did against his will, and it may be that by the time the estate was settled, her resentment had been softened by time or even replaced by remorse. . . .

[MILTON'S THIRD MARRIAGE]
William Riley Parker

. . . It was about this time that he himself was considering the desirability of a third marriage. His three motherless daughters needed someone besides a servant to supervise their various activities. He could not do it; both his blindness and the demands of his work made it impossible. Anne was sixteen and a half, Mary was fourteen—each of them old enough to manage a household—yet the household was not being managed to Milton's satisfaction. His means had been painfully reduced by the Restoration; perhaps he could not afford a wife, even if he could persuade some gentlewoman to marry him. He had lost all of the £2,000 which he had saved out of his salary as Latin secretary; he had put it for security and improvement into the Excise bank, which failed with the collapse of the Commonwealth. Having neglected to recall the sum in time (how costly his political optimism!), he had since been unsuccessful in his attempts to recover it, despite, as his nephew said, "all the power and interest he had in the great ones of those times." An estate of about £60 a year, which belonged to the Dean and chapter of Westminster, had also been taken away from him. And that was not all: he had lost, we are told, "another great sum, by mismanagement and for want of good advice." The scrivener's son was not good at handling money. He was fifty-four, and blind, and frugality in living had become a necessity instead of a principle. His daughters, however, seemed not to have grasped these facts. They needed a mother, and he needed a wife and good housekeeper. Yet he had little to offer except straitened security, and a good name, and affection if she were the right person.

His friend Dr. Paget evidently helped Milton to a decision. He introduced the poet to Miss Elizabeth Minshull, his own first cousin once removed. She was a woman of twenty-four, with red or golden hair, and with a quiet and agreeable disposition, capable no doubt of managing a home with firm efficiency. We do not know on what grounds Dr. Paget recommended her to Milton, and we do not know whether the marriage was a businesslike agreement between two mature people or an emotional product of considerable association and genuine liking. However, on 11 February 1663 Milton filed his formal intention of marriage, even venturing to sign the allegation with his own hand—a brave, sprawling signature. The wedding took place at St. Mary Aldermary on 24 February. The officiating minister was almost certainly Dr. Robert Gell, who had been a Fellow at Christ's College, Cambridge, when Milton was a student there.

The new Mrs. Milton was evidently a sensible woman, with no fancy or extravagant notions. (The critical John Aubrey thought her "a gentle person," of "a peaceful and agreeable humour." Of yeoman stock, she had been born and reared in Wistaston, Cheshire, where her mother still lived and her brother Richard was a framework knitter. She was old enough to know what she was doing when she decided to become the wife of a blind scholar and the stepmother of three children. It is clear from subsequent events that she tried intelligently to make the marriage a success and that she learned quickly the peculiar likes and dislikes of her unusual husband. She discovered,

Excerpted from William Riley Parker, *Milton: A Biography* (Oxford: Oxford University Press, 1968), Volume I, pp. 583–586, 639–640. © Oxford University Press 1968, reprinted by permission of the Oxford University Press, Oxford.

for example, that he was very temperate in his eating and drinking, rarely taking wine between meals. Strong liquor he eschewed altogether. He preferred food most in season or easiest procured, and required little, "but what he had, he always loved to have of the best." It is likely that he early explained his tastes to her, for we know that she promised to provide him with "such dishes" as he enjoyed as long as he lived. In later years, after a satisfying meal, he used to remind her, jokingly, of this promise, and praise her faithfulness to the contract.

He called her "Betty." "God have mercy, Betty!" he would exclaim when feeling particularly jovial. She was very kind, very thoughtful of him, and he learned to lean on her for many things. Waking in the morning he would sometimes ask her to write down perhaps twenty or thirty lines of poetry which had come to him. He would talk to her about his favourite English poets—Cowley, Shakespeare, Spenser, she later remembered—and about the authors who were becoming famous in the new world of Restoration literature. Thomas Hobbes, for instance, he acknowledged "to be a man of great parts, a learned man," and yet he did not like him at all. "Their interests and tenets were diametrically opposite." Sir Robert Howard, the dramatist, he liked; and John Dryden, although Dryden was no poet—"a good rimist, but no poet."

Becoming acquainted with the house in Jewin Street of which she now was mistress, Elizabeth Milton observed many things which might have helped her to understand the man she had married. There were more books, probably, than she had ever seen before in her life. Her husband was not wealthy; he preached frugality as a virtue; yet there were two exceptions to his rule of economy: "he was not sparing to buy good books" and he "was generous in relieving the wants of his friends." She noticed his organ and other musical instruments, his swing, his favourite chair, his writing case and tobacco box, both of tortoise-shell. She stood before the two portraits of him and studied them; she liked the one painted when he was a Cambridge scholar; it still resembled him, she thought. She examined the coats of arms of his father and mother, and his personal seal, both of which had a spread eagle with two heads; and eventually she learned that he was born in a place in Bread Street called the Spread Eagle. All about her were many relics of the past in which she had not shared.

Still in the house, of course, were three lively relics of that past; and from subsequent events we infer that the daughters of Mary Powell Milton did not take kindly to their second stepmother. Anne was already as old as her own mother had been when she married Milton; and her sister Mary was probably beginning to think of herself as no longer a child. Except for the brief time of their father's second marriage, the three girls had been motherless for almost eleven years, and their remaining parent had been too preoccupied with other matters to pay much attention to them. There were visits, perhaps, with their grandmother Powell; but most of their training had been entrusted to servants. None of them was ever sent to school; instead they were taught at home by a mistress kept for that purpose. Since their father's own education had begun in this way, doubtless he considered it appropriate for his daughters. It was expensive, however. Later, when he was disgusted with the results, and hurt by the unkindness of his children, he used to say that he "had spent the greatest part of his estate in providing for them." According to his lights, he unquestionably provided for them; but the story of Milton and his three daughters is a sad story, vague in its chronology, sordid in some of its details, fragmentary and elusive in its essential facts. We do not know enough to assess blame. But we know enough to recognize familiar factors in human misunderstandings—selfishness, pettiness, resentment, and pride. Elizabeth Minshull aggravated a tension which had been growing for years, and she could not have been long in realizing her predicament.

What were the facts of the situation? Let us begin with one which Milton himself may have been slow in comprehending: the three daughters inherited neither the talents nor the intellectual aptitude of their father. They had the benefits of private tuition, but they seem to have profited little. Perhaps they were incapable of learning much; perhaps they were rebellious. In any case, Anne, the crippled one, seems not even to have learned to write her name. Her speech difficulty may have been regarded as an insuperable barrier to education; we do not know. The other two daughters learned to read and write, and Deborah, late in her life, became a schoolmistress herself. What they were taught, we do not know. Remembering Milton's own theories of education, his emphasis in actual practice upon rapid learning of many languages, and his natural eagerness to have his daughters serviceable to him in his blindness, we may reasonably infer that any tutor whom he employed to teach the girls was instructed to prepare them quickly in Latin, Greek, Hebrew, and some modern foreign languages—just as John and Edward Phillips had been prepared. If such was the fact, we know that it resulted in failure—and some would add, "of course." Mary and Deborah were never able to understand books in foreign languages; this we hear from Deborah herself and from an independent source, although Milton himself seems to have tried to teach Deborah Latin. It is also a fact, however—an often recorded fact which has puzzled some biographers and outraged others—that Mary and Deborah were able to read aloud from books in foreign languages and be intelligible to their father. They learned to pronounce words, not only in Latin, French, Italian, and Spanish, but also in Greek and Hebrew, with their vastly different alphabets. This extraordinary skill a blind man, no matter how patient or how anxious, could hardly have taught them. Moreover, the man whose need was so great that he suffered them to read to him thus blankly was the same man who in 1662 taught Ellwood Latin by stopping him whenever his voice betrayed a lack of comprehension.

Let it be said, simply and without censure, that this sort of reading demanded great patience on both sides. We can be sure that Milton would not have endured it if more learned eyes had been at his disposal. Mary and Deborah endured it, we are told, "for a long time." We do not know when they started, but unless they were trained at different periods, it could hardly have been long before the third marriage, when Deborah was ten. There is evidence that by this time Mary had conceived a violent dislike for her father, and an unwelcome linguistic education in progress may have had much to do with it. We are told that when a maidservant informed Mary she had heard of Milton's approaching marriage, the daughter replied that it "was no news, to hear of his wedding; but if she could hear of his death, *that* was something!" We are also told (in a context which refers the events to this same period) that "all his said children did combine together and counsel his maidservant to cheat him in her marketings," and that "his said children had made away with some of his books and would have sold the rest of his books to the dunghill women." Milton, hard at work on his epic "of man's first disobedience," heard these stories of spite and hatred, for his maid-servant felt obliged to tell him.

Eventually the new wife heard the stories too. We do not know what she did to remedy the situation, but it is a fact that the daughters continued to live under the parental roof for approximately six more years. It also seems to be a fact that, from time to time during this period, Milton found it necessary to ask Mary or Deborah to read to him in some foreign language. He must have realized their growing irritation at the task, but his need was desperate, and obedience to parents was ever a virtue. Alas for his later reputation and the understanding of posterity, he even had a little joke which he repeated whenever visitors remarked on the strangeness of reading so many languages without comprehending any. "One tongue," he would say, "is enough for a woman." It was a masculine jest, with centuries of satirical laughter behind it; but later ages, more conscious of woman's emancipation than of her traditional garru-lity, have sometimes heard it with a literal mind. The cream of the jest is, of course, that Milton's facetious reply should have been remembered and recorded for posterity, and all his serious comments upon his daughters' education quickly forgotten. To com-pensate for this irony, let me make one observation and make it dogmatically: if either Mary or Deborah Milton had evidenced the slightest aptitude for languages and the slightest desire to learn, their father would have taught them. The admirer of Queen Christina, the friend of Lady Ranelagh and Lady Margaret Ley, was no advocate of ignorance in women. . . .

Christopher Milton, bencher of the Inner Temple, made it a point to visit his elder brother at intervals. On or about 20 July 1674, after the end of the Trinity term, he made one of these calls; he was planning to leave London and return to Ipswich for the summer vacation. His coach left about noon, and so he went that morning to the little house in Artillery Walk. Climbing the familiar stairs, he found his brother in his own chamber, obviously "not well," but perfectly lucid and calm. Betty Milton was there with her husband, and the maidservant, Elizabeth Fisher, was occasionally in and out of the room. Later, Christopher had sad reason to recall the scene clearly.

As nearly as he could recollect, John at some point in their conversation said to him, "Brother, the portion due to me from Mr. Powell, my former wife's father, I leave to the unkind children I had by her; but I have received no part of it, and my will and meaning is they shall have no other benefit of my estate than the said portion and what I have besides done for them, they have been very undutiful to me. And all the residue of my estate I leave to the disposal of Elizabeth, my loving wife.

A stiffly formal statement this, as remembered later by a lawyer. But legal lan-guage aside, the sentiment does not sound like that of a Christian poet who has preached charity and forgiveness to others, and had tried to practise these virtues; nor does it sound like the serene Milton pictured for us by his earliest biographers. It is clear that he had made no such statement when his brother had visited him before, and his three daughters had lived away from home for four or five years. Had some-thing happened recently to upset him? The month was July, and on 1 June, in far-away Dublin, Deborah Milton had married a weaver named Abraham Clarke. Did she perhaps, in a proud letter, present her father with a *fait accompli,* flaunting the independ-ence she had come by so naturally? We shall never know. We do not even know whether Milton learned of this marriage before his death; from subsequent events it is certain that Deborah's two sisters had not heard. A bond that Milton received on 27 July from one Richard Hayley of Elstree, Hertfordshire, may or may not have some bearing on the case; the nature of this business transaction is unclear.

As a lawyer, Christopher should have done one of two things if he had thought his brother in any real danger of dying soon. He should have told him to commit his will to paper, or he should have called for proper witnesses to this oral, nuncupative will. He did neither. We shall never know why. Perhaps he took the whole matter lightly, and feared to miss the Ipswich coach. Milton, on the other hand, seems to have regarded the business as settled. He was the son of a scrivener, the brother of an attorney; he had argued points of law with the great Salmasius; but in the managing of his own last will and testament he acted like a complete innocent. Soon after his conversation with Christopher, perhaps at noon the same day, he and his wife were having dinner together in his lodging-chamber and the maidservant heard him talk very gaily, saying "God have mercy, Betty! I see thou wilt perform according to thy promise in providing me such dishes as I think fit whilst I live; and, when I die, thou knowest that I have left thee all." (So he believed; but in this, as in many other things during his life, Milton's wishes were eventually to be frustrated.)

The dramatic clashes between Milton and his wife and daughters, as shown us in Paradise Restored, *are not only matters of personality but are also involved with the particular culture in which
Milton lived. Edward Wagenknecht attempts to understand Milton's difficult relations with women
in terms of general seventeenth-century Christian ideas about the sexes.*

"MILTON AND EVE"
Edward Wagenknecht

. . . Richard Garnett declared that Milton's "he for God only, she for God in him"
embodied "every fallacy concerning woman's relation to her husband and to her
Maker." So it must seem to a feminist age. Says Eve,

> "I chiefly who enjoy
> So far the happier lot, enjoying thee
> Pre-eminent by so much odds, while thou
> Like consort to thyself canst nowhere find,"

and again,

> "My author and disposer, what thou bidd'st
> Unargued I obey; so God ordains.
> God is thy law, thou mine; to know no more
> Is woman's happiest knowledge and her praise."

Adam stands as a kind of high priest between her and God, and though she does not
lack intelligence, she would rather learn from him at second hand than from Raphael
directly. Douglas Bush has rightly observed that she thinks about her husband much
more than she thinks about God, and when they are expelled from the Garden together, Adam laments the loss of divine communion while she mourns the loss of her
flowers and her home. But if Milton thought this made her inferior to Adam (and, by
implication, women inferior to men), he did not blame her for it. This was the way
God made it and the way it ought to be, and whatever was, was right. There was
nothing about any of this that was peculiar to Milton. He shared these notions with
the whole tradition of Hebrew-Christian civilization, and he could not have denied
them without flying in the face of that tradition, violating the principle of order, and
breaking the Great Chain of Being. Nobody who knows him will need to be told that
he would have done just that had such action seemed to him to be called for. He did
not so conceive it. But where he does depart from conventional ideas, it is always because he sympathizes more with women than other men did, not less.

Milton's condemnation of Adam for the sin of idolatry in choosing Eve before
God shows that he never accepted the extreme romantic view that love is the supreme
good of life. . . .

From Edward Wagenknecht, *The Personality of Milton* (Norman: University of Oklahoma Press, 1970), pp.
122–123. Copyright 1970 by the University of Oklahoma Press; reprinted by their permission.

In spite of the interest attached to his personality and his political activities, it is as a poet—one of the greatest of English poets—that Milton is chiefly remembered. The following examples of Milton's poetry illustrate two aspects of his art. The sonnet is autobiographical; it probably dates from 1652, the year in which Milton's blindness became total. The extract from Milton's great epic, Paradise Lost, *comes at the very end of the poem, when Adam and Eve, banished from Paradise because of their disobedience, set out into the fallen world of suffering and achievement.*

SONNET XIX ["ON HIS BLINDNESS"]
John Milton

When I consider how my light is spent,
    Ere half my days, in this dark world and wide,
    And that one talent which is death to hide
    Lodged with me useless, though my soul more bent
To serve therewith my Maker, and present
    My true account, lest he returning chide,
    "Doth God exact day-labor, light denied?"
    I fondly ask. But Patience, to prevent
That murmur, soon replies: "God doth not need
    Either man's work or his own gifts; who best
    Bear his mild yoke, they serve him best. His state
Is kingly: thousands at his bidding speed,
    And post o'er land and ocean without rest;
    They also serve who only stand and wait."

From Douglas Bush (ed.), *The Complete Poetical Works of John Milton* (Boston: Houghton Mifflin, 1965), p. 190. Copyright © 1965 Houghton Mifflin Company.

FROM *PARADISE LOST*
John Milton

". . . This further consolation yet secure
I carry hence; though all by me is lost,
Such favor I unworthy am vouchsafed,
By me the Promised Seed shall all restore."
So spake our mother Eve, and Adam heard
Well pleased, but answered not; for now too nigh
Th' Archangel stood, and from the other hill
To their fixed station, all in bright array
The Cherubim descended; on the ground
Gliding metéorous, as ev'ning mist
Ris'n from a river o'er the marish glides,
And gathers ground fast at the laborer's heel
Homeward returning. High in front advanced,
The brandished sword of God before them blazed
Fierce as a comet; which with torrid heat,
And vapor as the Libyan air adust,
Began to parch that temperate clime; whereat
In either hand the hast'ning Angel caught
Our ling'ring parents, and to th' eastern gate
Led them direct, and down the cliff as fast
To the subjected plain; then disappeared.
They, looking back, all th' eastern side beheld
Of Paradise, so late their happy seat,
Waved over by that flaming brand, the gate
With dreadful faces thronged and fiery arms.
Some natural tears they dropped, but wiped them soon;
The world was all before them, where to choose
Their place of rest, and Providence their guide:
They hand in hand, with wand'ring steps and slow,
Through Eden took their solitary way.

Paradise Lost, Book XII, lines 620–649, in Douglas Bush (ed.), *The Complete Poetical Works of John Milton.*
(Boston: Houghton Mifflin, 1965), p. 459. Copyright © 1965 Houghton Mifflin Company.

She Stoops to Conquer

In early January, 1773, the Westminster Magazine *published an article—author unidentified—on two types of comedy, the "laughing" and the "sentimental." The article constitutes an attack on the current fashion for sentimental comedy, and it urges a return to the kind of comedy that makes us laugh at the follies of mankind; the latter, for the anonymous author, is "true" comedy. When Goldsmith's* She Stoops to Conquer *was first acted, two and a half months later, it seemed in large part to be obeying the criteria set down in the* Westminster Magazine—*and no wonder, for the author of the article was Goldsmith himself.*

AN ESSAY ON THE THEATRE; OR, A COMPARISON BETWEEN LAUGHING AND SENTIMENTAL COMEDY
Oliver Goldsmith

The Theatre, like all other amusements, has its Fashions and its Prejudices; and when satiated with its excellence, Mankind begin to mistake Change for Improvement. For some years, Tragedy was the reigning entertainment; but of late it has entirely given way to Comedy, and our best efforts are now exerted in these lighter kinds of composition. The pompous Train, the swelling Phrase, and the unnatural Rant, are displaced for that natural portrait of Human Folly and Frailty, of which all are judges, because all have sat for the picture.

But as in describing Nature it is presented with a double face, either of mirth or sadness, our modern Writers find themselves at a loss which chiefly to copy from; and it is now debated, Whether the Exhibition of Human Distress is likely to afford the mind more Entertainment than that of Human Absurdity?

Comedy is defined by Aristotle to be a picture of the Frailties of the lower part of Mankind, to distinguish it from Tragedy, which is an exhibition of the Misfortunes of the Great. When Comedy therefore ascends to produce the Characters of Princes or Generals upon the Stage, it is out of its walk, since Low Life and Middle Life are entirely its object. The principal question therefore is, Whether in describing Low or Middle Life, an exhibition of its Follies be not preferable to a detail of its Calamities? Or, in other words, Which deserves the preference? The Weeping Sentimental Comedy, so much in fashion at present, or the Laughing and even Low Comedy, which seems to have been last exhibited by Vanburgh and Cibber.

If we apply to authorities, all the Great Masters in the Dramatic Art have but one opinion. Their rule is, that as Tragedy displays the Calamities of the Great; so Comedy should excite our laughter by ridiculously exhibiting the Follies of the Lower Part of Mankind. Boileau, one of the best modern Critics, asserts, that Comedy will not admit of Tragic Distress. . . . Nor is this rule without the strongest foundation in Nature, as the distresses of the Mean by no means affect us so strongly as the Calamities of the Great. When Tragedy exhibits to us some Great Man fallen from his height, and struggling with want and adversity, we feel his situation in the same manner as we suppose

Reprinted from Arthur Friedman, ed., *Collected Works of Oliver Goldsmith* (Oxford: Oxford University Press, 1966), Volume 3, pp. 209–213. © Oxford University Press 1966, reprinted by permission of the Oxford University Press, Oxford.

he himself must feel, and our pity is increased in proportion to the height from whence he fell. On the contrary, we do not so strongly sympathize with one born in humbler circumstances, and encountering accidental distress: so that while we melt for Belisarius, we scarce give halfpence to the Beggar who accosts us in the street. The one has our pity; the other our contempt. Distress, therefore, is the proper object of Tragedy, since the Great excite our pity by their fall; but not equally so of Comedy, since the Actors employed in it are originally so mean, that they sink but little by their fall.

Since the first origin of the Stage, Tragedy and Comedy have run in different channels, and never till of late encroached upon the provinces of each other. Terence, who seems to have made the nearest approaches, yet always judiciously stops short before he comes to the downright pathetic; and yet he is even reproached by Caesar for wanting the *vis comica*. All the other Comic Writers of antiquity aim only at rendering Folly or Vice ridiculous, but never exalt their characters into buskined pomp, or make what Voltaire humourously calls a *Tradesman's Tragedy*.

Yet, notwithstanding this weight of authority, and the universal practice of former ages, a new species of Dramatic Composition has been introduced under the name of *Sentimental* Comedy, in which the virtues of Private Life are exhibited, rather than the Vices exposed; and the Distresses, rather than the Faults of Mankind, make our interest in the piece. These Comedies have had of late great success, perhaps from their novelty, and also from their flattering every man in his favourite foible. In these Plays almost all the Characters are good, and exceedingly generous; they are lavish enough of their *Tin* Money on the Stage, and though they want Humour, have abundance of Sentiment and Feeling. If they happen to have Faults or Foibles, the Spectator is taught not only to pardon, but to applaud them, in consideration of the goodness of their hearts; so that Folly, instead of being ridiculed, is commended, and the Comedy aims at touching our Passions without the power of being truly pathetic: in this manner we are likely to lose one great source of Entertainment on the Stage; for while the Comic Poet is invading the province of the Tragic Muse, he leaves her lovely Sister quite neglected. Of this, however, he is noway solicitous, as he measures his fame by his profits.

But it will be said, that the Theatre is formed to amuse Mankind, and that it matters little, if this end be answered, by what means it is obtained. If Mankind find delight in weeping at Comedy, it would be cruel to abridge them in that or any other innocent pleasure. If those Pieces are denied the name of Comedies; yet call them by any other name, and if they are delightful, they are good. Their success, it will be said, is a mark of their merit, and it is only abridging our happiness to deny us an inlet to Amusement.

These objections, however, are rather specious than solid. It is true, that Amusement is a great object of the Theatre; and it will be allowed, that these Sentimental Pieces do often amuse us: but the question is, Whether the True Comedy would not amuse us more? The question is, Whether a Character supported throughout a Piece with its Ridicule still attending, would not give us more delight than this species of Bastard Tragedy, which only is applauded because it is new?

A friend of mine who was sitting unmoved at one of these Sentimental Pieces, was asked, how he could be so indifferent. "Why, truly," says he, "as the Hero is but a Tradesman, it is indifferent to me whether he be turned out of his Counting-house on Fish-street Hill, since he will still have enough left to open shop in St. Giles's."

The other objection is as ill-grounded; for though we should give these Pieces another name, it will not mend their efficacy. It will continue a kind of *mulish* production, with all the defects of its opposite parents, and marked with sterility. If we are permitted to make Comedy weep, we have an equal right to make Tragedy laugh, and to set down in Blank Verse the Jests and Repartees of all the Attendants in a Funeral Procession.

But there is one Argument in favour of Sentimental Comedy which will keep it on the Stage in spite of all that can be said against it. It is, of all others, the most easily written. Those abilities that can hammer out a Novel, are fully sufficient for the production of a Sentimental Comedy. It is only sufficient to raise the Characters a little, to deck out the Hero with a Ribband, or give the Heroine a Title; then to put an Insipid Dialogue, without Character or Humour, into their mouths, give them mighty good hearts, very fine cloaths, furnish a new sett of Scenes, make a Pathetic Scene or two, with a sprinkling of tender melancholy Conversation through the whole, and there is no doubt but all the Ladies will cry, and all the Gentlemen applaud.

Humour at present seems to be departing from the Stage, and it will soon happen, that our Comic Players will have nothing left for it but a fine Coat and a Song. It depends upon the Audience whether they will actually drive those poor Merry Creatures from the Stage, or sit at a Play as gloomy as at the Tabernacle. It is not easy to recover an art when once lost; and it would be but a just punishment that when, by our being too fastidious, we have banished Humour from the Stage, we should ourselves be deprived of the art of Laughing.

The play was received well by both critics and audience, although not everyone approved of it. The following brief surveys of early critical opinion indicate why the play was such a success, and at the same time raise a number of interesting issues connected with Goldsmith's idea of comedy.

[THE RECEPTION OF *SHE STOOPS TO CONQUER*]
Clara M. Kirk

Goldsmith's second Laughing Comedy was a complete success, and it has remained one of the few eighteenth-century plays that has been persistently and successfully revived. Performed for twelve nights at Covent Garden before the theater closed for the season, it was resumed again at the Haymarket during the summer. The critics praised it and were soon lampooning Colman for his hesitation in putting on a play which had met with such popular approval. Command performances were given before the king and queen on May 5, and again on November 10. Horace Walpole, after seeing the comedy, admitted that "it makes you laugh very much"; on sober afterthought, however, Walpole decided that he did not approve of his own laughter, for he considered the play "wretched" and "low." " 'Stoops,' indeed!" he wrote to his friend, John Monck Mason, "So she does—that is, the Muse. She is draggled up to her knees, and has trudged, I believe, from Southwark Fair." In a letter to the same friend on May 27, 1773, his remarks on *She Stoops to Conquer* were still more critical:

> Dr. Goldsmith has written a comedy—no, it is the lowest of all farces. It is not the subject I condemn, though vulgar, but the execution. The drift tends to no moral, no edification, of any kind. . . . What disgusts me most is, that though the characters are very low, and aim at low humour, not one of them says a sentence that is natural or marks any character at all. . . . Garrick would not act it but bought himself off by a poor prologue.

A convincing reply to Walpole's comment is to be found in a brief exchange between Goldsmith and Reynolds' pupil and friend, James Northcote, after the opening night. "Did it make you laugh?" Goldsmith asked. "Exceedingly," was the reply. "Then," said Goldsmith, "that is all I require," giving him a handful of tickets for the benefit night. Johnson's praise, which he pronounced in Goldsmith's presence a few days after the opening of the play, was to the same effect: "I know of no comedy for many years that has so much exhilarated an audience, that has answered so much the great end of comedy—making an audience merry." Johnson's words were corroborated by *The Evening Post* which reported on March 16, 1773, that "the audience is kept in a continual roar." Since the aim of Laughing Comedy, as Goldsmith had pointed out in his *Essay on the Theatre,* was laughter rather than tears or morals, *She Stoops to Conquer* was a perfect fulfillment of the playwright's intention "to hunt after *nature* and *humour* in whatever walks of life they were most conspicuous."

From Clara M. Kirk, *Oliver Goldsmith* (New York: Twayne, 1967), pp. 136–138. Copyright © 1967 by Twayne Publishers, Inc. Reprinted by permission of Twayne Publishers, Inc.

[THE RECEPTION OF *SHE STOOPS TO CONQUER*]
Arthur Friedman

Colman had no confidence in Goldsmith's play, but, in Dr. Johnson's words, he "was prevailed on at last by much solicitation, nay, a kind of force, to bring it on." The manager apparently wished to delay the production until the next theatrical season, but Goldsmith, pressed by a creditor for "a large sum of money," could stand no further delay. By 4 March 1773 the play was in rehearsal, and it was first performed at Covent Garden on 15 March.

The difficulties that *She Stoops to Conquer* faced on its first night are stated in a review in the *Morning Chronicle* for 16 March:

> It is brought out at the fag end of the season, when it is barely possible for the author to have his three nights. The chief actor of the house [Smith] has thrown up his part [as young Marlow], his example is followed by a very contemptible performer [Woodward], but who was nevertheless wanted in the piece; a singer is given somewhat more than a third-rate character; and a young actress, who, in her walk, is by no means deficient in merit, is put into a consequential part, which she is not in any degree equal to. . . . To crown all, a report is industriously circulated, that the piece is exceedingly low, the humour fit only for St. Giles's, and that the comedy will certainly be damned.

As opposed to all these difficulties faced by the new play, there was one important circumstance in its favour. Just a month before Goldsmith's first night Samuel Foote had presented his Primitive Puppet Shew at the Haymarket, in which he ridiculed genteel and sententious comedy in a piece called *The Handsome Housemaid, or Piety in Pattens;* and the popularity of this production helped prepare the town for Goldsmith's "laughing comedy."

On the night of the first performance a number of Goldsmith's friends—Dr. Johnson, Sir Joshua Reynolds, the Burkes, Cumberland, and others—attended the theatre to support the play, but their aid was not needed: ". . . no attempt is made by the author," the *Morning Chronicle* reported the following day, "to avail himself of the vitiated taste of the times; he has offered the public a true comic picture, and altho' it differed most essentially in manner, stile, and finishing from those which have of late years been received, and encouraged almost to adoration, its own excellence prevailed, laughter sat on every face, mirth, and extatic joy, the proper effects of comedy, universally prevailed, and the most impartial, and repeated plaudits were showered down on the author." And a correspondent in the *Public Advertiser* two days later observes:

> . . . the Applause given to a new Piece on the first Evening of its Representation is sometimes supposed to be the Tribute of partial Friendship. The Approbation on the second Exhibition of Dr. Goldsmith's new Comedy exceeded that with which its first Appearance was attended. Uninterrupted

Excerpted from the Introduction to *She Stoops to Conquer* in Arthur Friedman, ed., *Collected Works of Oliver Goldsmith* (Oxford: Oxford University Press, 1966), Volume 5, pp. 89–95. © Oxford University Press 1966, reprinted by permission of the Oxford University Press, Oxford.

Laughter or clamorous Plaudits accompanied his Muse to the last Line of his Play; and when it was given out for the Author's Benefit the Theatre was filled with the loudest Acclamations that ever rung within its Walls.

The *Morning Chronicle* for 26 March reports further, "Dr. Goldsmith's new Comedy was performed last night, for the fourth time, and received with greater applause than even on the first night of its representation." Goldsmith could well write to Cradock, "The Play has met with a success much beyond your expectations or mine."

Several of the newspapers summarized the plot and carried paragraphs and verses mostly in praise of the play but sometimes condemning it as "low." The only detailed criticism of the production appeared in the *Morning Chronicle* for 16 March, and parts of it are of sufficient interest to quote at length.

> This Comedy is written by the ingenious Dr. Goldsmith; it is founded on a plot exceedingly probable and fertile; each act contains a great deal of natural business and incident; the characters are, for the most part, entirely original; they are well drawn, highly finished, and admirably supported from the 1st to the last scene of the piece. It abounds with genuine wit and humour; without the aid of Irish bulls, forced witticisms or absurd conceits, the audience are kept in a continual roar; occasionally a sentiment is delivered, but then it arises naturally from the fable and character, is well expressed, and has its full weight with those that hear it. Considered generally, this piece has more real merit than any performance which has borne the name of comedy since the Clandestine Marriage [by Colman and Garrick, first acted in 1766]. . . . Hardcastle is a good-natured particular old fellow, fond of telling a story, and ridiculous, without offending.—Mr. Marlow, a man of sense, education, and breeding; but, as many men are, exceedingly timid in the presence of modest women of accomplished education, impudently familiar in company with those of low degree. This character is, as far as we can recollect, an original one. The success with which it was received is a proof that it is by no means an unnatural one.—The Squire is a compound of whim and good-natured mischief; the engine of the plot, and the source of infinite mirth and a variety of very laughable mistakes, which arise in a simple, artless manner, and which the author has taken an admirable advantage of, and produced a very comic effect from, without exceeding the line of probability. . . .

Then, after designating some "parts of the comedy which would bear pruning," the reviewer turns to the performers:

> Mr. Lewes gave most perfect satisfaction to the audience in Mr. Marlow. He played the part with ease, with spirit and with characteristic humour. . . . Mrs. Bulkeley deserved no small share of applause. The Author could hardly have wished for a better representative of Miss Hardcastle. Mr. Shuter was tolerable perfect, perfectly *sober,* and extremely pleasing [as Hardcastle]. . . . He last night was universally well received. Mrs. Green [as Mrs. Hardcastle] was lively and characteristic. Mr. Quick [as Tony], exceedingly well, but had rather too much grimace.

. . . The play was published by F. Newbery at four o'clock on 25 March, and a notice of the performance that same evening in the *Morning Chronicle* for the next day comments: "It is very remarkable, that almost every one present had the play in their hands, insomuch that the Orange-women acknowledged they never sold so many of any new piece during its whole run, as they disposed of yesterday evening in less than half an hour." On 27 March "A New Edition" was advertised, and on 1 April the *Morning Chronicle* reports: "No piece was ever honoured with so rapid a sale as Dr. Goldsmith's new comedy. In three days time the publisher had disposed of four thousand."

The critics of the published play in the monthly publications, unlike the newspaper writers, were less interested in considering the elements in the play which made it successful on the stage than in determining whether the kind of comedy Goldsmith wrote was a proper kind. Concerning this question the reviewer in the *London Magazine* for March 1773 (xlii. 144–6) takes a middle position:

> This comedy is not ill calculated to give pleasure in the representation; but when we regard it with a critical eye, we find it to abound with numerous inaccuracies. The fable . . . is twisted into incidents not naturally arising from the subject, in order *to make things meet;* and consistency is repeatedly violated for the sake of humour. But perhaps we ought to sign a general pardon to the author, for taking the field against that monster called Sentimental Comedy, to oppose which his comedy was avowedly written. Indeed, the attempt was bold, considering the strength of the enemy; and we are glad to observe that our author still keeps the field with flying colours.—But, (metaphor apart) it appears that the Doctor was too ardent. Well considering that the public were long accustomed to cry, he resolved to make them laugh at any rate. In aiming at this point, he seems to have stepped too far; and in lieu of comedy he has sometimes presented us with farce.

The writer in the *Critical Review* for March (xxxv. 229–30) judges the play by principles very similar to those used by Goldsmith three months earlier in his "Essay on the Theatre":

> The public have for some years submitted to be imposed on by a species of comedy very different from what the ancients conceived, or the moderns, upon the revival of literature, adopted. Aristotle, who defined comedy to be an exhibition of human manners in low life, gave the law to every comic writer, and the *Dramatis Personae* never rose above the private gentleman or the respectable merchant.

Among the moderns the Italians succeeded poorly in comedy, the French "followed a better track," and the English made further improvements:

> The English seem to us to have excelled other nations in the strength of their characters, the warmth and bustle of their plots, and the variety of their incidents. An English comedy upon the great stile of the ancients, is a very difficult undertaking. Being twice as long as that of either the ancients or the French, it requires the utmost exertion of skill, to vary the humour in such a manner as to keep up the spectator's pleasure, and still

never lose sight of the plot. This end, however, Vanbrugh, Farquhar, and Steele have very happily attained.

After such excellent examples, comedy, both in France and England, has been seen entirely to languish. La Chaussè first set the fashion of the *Comedie Larmoyant,* or the *Tradesman's Tragedy,* as Voltaire expresses it; and it has since prevailed in France to the utter extinction of all other comic representations. As we often imitate not only the dress of that people, but also their manner of thinking, we have followed them in their dramatic declension; and it was supposed, by the lovers of the old comedy, that she was extinct among us. The present play is an attempt to revive the dying art; and the author's well-deserved and unprecedented success, has shewn how ready mankind are to welcome back a favourite mistress, even after she had been guilty of a long elopement. . . .

To conclude; the utmost severity of criticism could detract but little from the uncommon merit of this performance; and the most laboured encomiums could add as little to the general and judicious applause with which it still continues to be received.

William Woodfall, writing in the *Monthly Review* for April (xlviii. 309–14), is able, by including the phrase "of the prevailing manners" in his definition of comedy, to arrive at directly opposite conclusions from those of the preceding critic:

Comedy has been defined by all theatrical Critics, from Aristotle down to the correspondents of a News-paper. We do not, however, remember a definition exactly in the following terms: Comedy is a dramatic representation of the prevailing manners of people not in very high or very low life. It must therefore vary, as those manners vary; and be wholly regulated by them. Hence the difference between . . . all those original writers, who at different periods of time have written immediately from the manners passing in review before them. Few of our English writers of Comedy have aimed at being originals. Some exception may be made in favour of Vanbrugh, Congreve, and Farquhar; the great merit of whose Comedies is, that they represent the manners of the times. . . . Our customs and manners have undergone a gradual alteration. A general correspondence arising from trade, and the progress of the arts, has brought the nation, as it were, together, and worn off those prepossessions and habits which made every little neighbourhood a separate community, and marked every community with its peculiar character. The business of comedy is therefore changed. . . . Some of our late writers have therefore very judiciously had recourse to what is called *Sentimental Comedy,* as better suited to the principles and manners of the age. A general politeness has given a sameness to our external appearances; and great degrees of knowledge are every where diffused. An author, therefore, has not that variety of character, and that simplicity and ignorance to describe, which were the capital ingredients in the old Comedy. Modern writers may indeed have carried the matter too far, and perhaps kept their eyes too much on French models. . . . They have erred however only in the execution: they are right in their general principle. . . .

But Dr. Goldsmith does not seem to have been of this opinion. Having read more about even his own countrymen than he had ever seen of them, and recollecting that the comedies he had perused were very different from those which now prevailed, he imagined the Comic Muse had fled the land. He determined to call her back, and employ her first in introducing the Good-natured Man, and afterwards the present Comedy.

The fable of *She Stoops to Conquer* is a series of blunders, which the Author calls the *Mistakes of a Night;* but they are such mistakes as never were made, and, we believe, never could have been committed. . . .

In this light we are obliged to consider Dr. Goldsmith's play, as most of its incidents are offences against nature and probability. We are sorry for it, because he certainly has a great share of the *vis comica;* and when he has thrust his people into a situation, he makes them talk very *funnily*. His merit is that sort of dialogue which lies on a level with the most common under-standings; and in that low mischief and mirth which we laugh at, while we are ready to despise ourselves for so doing. This is the reason why the Reader must peruse the present Comedy without pleasure, while the repre-sentation of it may make him laugh. . . . We wish, however, that the in-genious Author could employ his talents, so as to divert the galleries, with-out offending others who have a right to his attention. This he might do, by taking some story of a distant date, when the manners were generally such as he chuses to represent. He would then find characters and circum-stances to his hand; and his language and dialogue would have all their ef-fect: we should put outselves back in imagination, and have the same kind of pleasure which is now given us by the best of our old comedies.

She Stoops to Conquer remains a successful stage work, two hundred years after its first performance. In reviews of two recent productions, Michael Billington and the author of this anthology point out the strengths of the play when it is well acted.

SHE STOOPS TO CONQUER [IN A 1969 PRODUCTION]
Michael Billington

This brisk and lively revival is eminently welcome for a number of reasons. Firstly, it's nearly a decade since the play got a major London production and periodically it's good to be reminded that Goldsmith gave us our first modern comedy of class distinctions. With this production, London also gets its first glimpse of the work being done in Manchester by the 69 Theatre Company: an enterprising group that operates in the north for six months of the year and that has so far given local theatregoers a mixture of Ibsen, Shakespeare, a George Eliot adaptation, a musical documentary and a new play by Gerard McLarnon. But, most important of all, London audiences can now see for themselves how Tom Courtenay has for some time been quietly nurturing his talent in the north and astutely widening his range. . . .

The key to his interpretation—and to the whole production—can be found in Marlow's first confrontation with Hardcastle, whose house he has mistaken for an inn. Technically, this scene is the mainspring of the whole plot but here it becomes something more. We realise just how much this initial gaffe brings out the worst in both parties. As a house-guest Marlow would be obliged to listen politely to his host's tedious military anecdotes but, relieved from any social obligation, he can show them up for what they are. On the other hand, Courtenay makes one aware of the fact that there is something intolerably arrogant and high-handed about Marlow's behaviour ("And now to see that our beds are aired and properly taken care of"), even supposing him to be in an inn. His subsequent discomfiture, for the first time in my experience, seems well-earned: a man who so lords it over his social inferiors obviously deserves to be taken down a peg or two.

Apart from conveying Marlow's early unpleasantness, Courtenay also makes the most of his tongue-tied embarrassment when confronted by a girl of his own class. At the prospect of being left alone with Miss Hardcastle, he makes a wild, desperate lunge towards Hastings to prevent him quitting the room; his voice emerges in a strained falsetto when he actually tries to speak; he endures all the agonies of the natural stammerer, who finds someone well-meaningly completing his sentences for him; and he signals frantically for help on "I see Miss Neville expecting us in the next room" like a shipwrecked mariner trying to attract the attention of a passing vessel. This is a perfectly calculated and timed demonstration of what Marlow himself accurately describes as the "Englishman's malady."

None of the other performances in Braham Murray's production quite comes up to this level. There is an admirable Hardcastle from James Cossins, rubicund and faintly tetchy; an agreeably warm-hearted, if insufficiently impish, Kate from Juliet

Michael Billington, "She Stoops to Conquer [Review]," *Plays and Players*, vol. 16, no. 10 (July 1969), pp. 51–53. Reprinted by permission of the author and *Plays and Players*, Hansom Books, publisher.

Mills; and a radiantly attractive Miss Neville from Ciaran Madden. For my taste, however, Trevor Peacock's Tony Lumpkin is strained and unfunny; the only actor I've ever seen to make the character believable was John Carlin in a Birmingham Rep revival some eight years ago and he did this simply by endowing him with a cherubic rural charm. Rosalind Knight's Mrs Hardcastle is also pushed too far towards the grotesque and misses some of the pathos of the ageing country-dweller pining for fashionable urban life. In short, there is a slightly uneasy division in this production between social comedy and downright farce.

The play itself, however, remains perennially engaging. The major reason for this is that Goldsmith combines excellent dramatic carpentry with a natural temperamental warmth. Another minor reason, however, is that the play bulges with off-stage characters who arouse one's fascination: there's Mrs. Oddfish, the curate's wife; little Cripplegate, the lame dancing-master; Mrs Grigsby, who goes to London for a month's polishing every winter, the two Miss Rickets of Crooked Lane, and, of course, the inimitable Bet Bouncer. Outside Shakespeare, it's hard to think of any English comedy that gives quite such a vivid impression of a little world existing beyond the frontiers of the play.

SHE STOOPS TO CONQUER [IN A 1975 PRODUCTION]
Jonathan Saville

It would be silly to say that Oliver Goldsmith's *She Stoops to Conquer* is a good comedy. It is a perfect comedy. It gives us full measure of those gratifications we expect from a comic play, and does so with ingenuity and grace. There is, first of all, the satisfaction we feel when young lovers surmount all obstacles and finally fall into each other's arms to the accompaniment of marriage chimes; it is that deeply remembered and deeply longed-for pattern of struggle and consummation, of desire frustrated and desire fulfilled; and the youth and handsomeness of the lovers makes their ultimate union all the more pleasurable—for them and for us. In *She Stoops to Conquer*, Goldsmith gives us two pairs of lovers, along with two varieties of frustration. George Hastings and Miss Constance Neville love each other heartily, but their love is opposed by Miss Neville's hideous aunt, Mrs. Hardcastle, who intends the young lady for her own son, the great booby Tony Lumpkin. What delight to watch the way Mrs. Hardcastle's plans are artfully confounded—that ever welcome defeat of repressive age by ardent youth, welcome because every member of the audience, no matter how old, automatically identifies with the lovers in their plots against the old lady's tyranny.

The other pair of lovers is considerably less conventional, and the gratifications provided by their adventures in love are of a different and more complex variety. Miss Kate Hardcastle is quite taken with the handsome Mr. Marlow, son of Sir Charles Marlow and heir to a large fortune; her parents welcome the match as enthusiastically as she does. The impediment to the romance is to be found not in any opposition by

Jonathan Saville, *"She Stoops to Conquer* [Review]," *Reader,* May 1, 1975.

the older generation but in a curious quirk in Mr. Marlow's own character. This young man has a certain problem in his dealings with women: working class wenches arouse all his youthful potency, but respectable women of the gentry paralyze him with shyness. Alas, he has succumbed to the age-old dilemma of men in regard to their womenfolk—the woman worthy of respect and love is treated as a lofty, non-sexual being, and the woman for whom one dares feel the stirrings of lust is defined as a low, fleshbound creature, created specifically for man's use. The poor female sex! Either saint or whore, but never in the middle range with the rest of humanity!

Kate Hardcastle, however, refuses to accept either of these roles, and she sets about to "cure" young Marlow of his double vision. Disguised as a servant girl, she seductively evokes his ardor (this is the way she "stoops to conquer"); then, revealing her name and social class, she forces him to re-unify his image of womankind, bringing the respectable and the sexual together until they blend in her own attractive person. All this is irresistible to an audience. The overcoming, in dramatic action, of a painful psychic split almost everyone, man and woman, suffers from (at least a little). The confutation, conversion and regeneration of a ridiculous eccentric (for that is what Marlow is, aside from being a romantic hero). The fun of seeing him made a fool of (for comedy engages many of our more ferocious instincts); the fun of participating vicariously in Kate's disguises and play-acting, with the wonderful sense of liberation from one's identity such things provide; and the fun of capping it all off with love, success, and getting the girl. What more could an audience ask for?

The final—and, for many, the chief—gratification of Goldsmith's play is Tony Lumpkin himself. Tony is the willful, spoiled infant we all once desired to be, before more mature aims lifted us out of that childish state. Gluttonous, slothful, disobedient, rude, concerned with nothing but his own vulgar comforts, yet full of a kind of amoral energy, irrepressibly cheerful, and—when it comes down to it—endowed with a heart that for one reason or another (perhaps laziness) knows no malice, Tony is one of those grand infantile creations—Falstaff and Cleopatra belong to the same anarchic class—that never cease to charm, simply because they represent the part of ourselves that has never submitted to being civilized.

The production of *She Stoops to Conquer* by John Houseman's City Center Acting Company did full justice to Goldsmith's marvelous play. Director Stephen Porter and his exceptionally able actors fleshed out the text, in itself already supremely comic, with masterly bits of stage business—Mr. Hardcastle furiously embracing the doorpost of his living room to emphasize to the arrogant Marlow that the house belongs not to the visitor but to the host; Tony devouring a huge bowl of cream; Mrs. Hardcastle imitating the postures of tragic drama as she tries to convince her son that Miss Neville's jewels have been stolen; the convulsive hee-heeing of a bumpkinish servant who has been instructed not to laugh at the jokes of his betters; and a hundred other touches of this sort, always in harmony with the playwright's intentions, always inventive, always funny. Goldsmith set out to write a comedy that would eschew tender sentiment and moral advice; true comedy, for him, meant a funny play, and the funnier the better. Mr. Porter's company took him at his word, and their staging of this ageless masterpiece succeeded in delivering a generous supply of those irreplaceable pleasures only true comedy can give.

Candide

The Classic Theatre's production of Candide *is an example of that widespread phenomenon, the theatrical adaptation. The play written for the stage—and performed as written—constitutes a simple and direct instance of the transformation from printed text to live performance. But we also have numerous examples, particularly in the modern theatre, of prose fiction adapted for the stage, of classical drama put into modern dress or otherwise modernized, of stage plays converted into musical comedies or operas—along with the ubiquitous procedure nowadays of turning theatre pieces into movies or television films. Every such adaptation demands fundamental changes in the original work to make it suitable to the new medium; each medium—fiction, drama, musical, film—has its own traditions, its own possibilities of expression, and its own limitations, and the same story in a book or on the stage (or on film) must be presented in radically different ways.* Candide *is a case in point: a television version, with actors, dialogue and scenic effects, of a story originally told in the form of prose fiction. Here, for the sake of comparison, are some chapters from the original—a few from the beginning of the tale, and a few from the end.*

CANDIDE
Voltaire

[Chapter One]: *How Candide Was Brought Up in a Handsome Country House and How He Was Chased from the Same.*

In Westphalia, in the country house of Monsieur the Baron of Thunder-ten-tronckh, there was a young man whom nature had given the gentlest of characters. His face revealed his soul. He had pretty good sense, with the simplest of intellects; it is for that reason, I believe, that he was called Candide. The old servants of the house suspected that he was the son of Monsieur the Baron's sister and of a good and honorable gentleman of the neighborhood, whom that lady would never marry because he could prove only seventy-one quarterings, and the rest of his genealogical tree had been lost by the ravages of time.

Monsieur the Baron was one of the most powerful lords of Westphalia, for his country house had a door and windows. His Great Hall was even decorated with a tapestry. All the dogs of his stable-yards formed a pack of hounds when necessary; his grooms were his huntsmen; the village vicar was his Grand Almoner. They all called him "Monseigneur" and they laughed when he told stories.

Madame the Baroness, who weighed around three hundred and fifty pounds, thereby won very great respect, and did the honors of the house with a dignity which made her even more respectable. Her daughter Cunégonde, seventeen years old, was rosy-cheeked, fresh, buxom, appetizing. The Baron's son appeared in everything worthy of his father. Pangloss, the tutor, was the oracle of the house, and little Candide listened to his lessons with all the trust of his age and character.

Pangloss taught metaphysico-theologo-cosmolo-nigology. He proved admirably that there is no effect without a cause, and that, in this best of all possible worlds, the country house of Monseigneur the Baron was the handsomest of country houses, and Madame the best of possible Baronesses.

From Voltaire, *Candide,* trans. and ed. by Peter Gay (New York: St. Martin's Press, 1963), Chapters 1, 3, 4, 29, 30. Copyright © 1963 by St. Martin's Press. Reprinted by permission of St. Martin's Press, Inc.

"It is demonstrated," he said, "that things cannot be otherwise; for, since everything was made for an end, all is necessarily for the best end. Note well that noses were made to wear spectacles; thus we have spectacles. Legs were obviously created to be breeched, and thus we have breeches. Stones were formed to be cut and made into country houses; thus Monseigneur has a very handsome country house; the greatest Baron of the province must be the best housed; and, since pigs were made to be eaten, we eat pork all year round. Consequently, those who have argued that all is well have talked nonsense; they should have said all is for the best."

Candide listened attentively, and believed innocently, for he thought Mademoiselle Cunégonde extremely beautiful, although he never found courage to tell her so. He concluded that next to having been born Baron of Thunder-ten-tronckh, the second degree of happiness was to be Mademoiselle Cunégonde; the third, to see her every day; and the fourth, to listen to Master Pangloss, the greatest philosopher of the province, and consequently of the whole world.

One day, Cunégonde, taking a walk near the country house, in the little forest they called Park, saw in the bushes Doctor Pangloss giving a lesson in experimental physics to her mother's chambermaid, a very pretty and very docile little brunette. Since Mademoiselle Cunégonde had a great inclination for the sciences, she observed breathlessly the repeated experiments she witnessed; she clearly saw the Doctor's sufficient reason, the effects and the causes, and returned home all excited, all pensive, all filled with the desire of being learned, thinking that she might well be the sufficient reason of young Candide, who might also be hers.

She met Candide in returning to the country house, and blushed; Candide blushed too; she said hello to him in a faltering voice, and Candide spoke to her without knowing what he was saying. The next day, after dinner, as people were leaving the table, Cunégonde and Candide found themselves behind a screen; Cunégonde dropped her handkerchief, Candide picked it up; she innocently took his hand; the young man innocently kissed the young lady's hand with a highly special vivacity, sensitivity, and grace; their lips met, their eyes sparkled, their knees trembled, their hands wandered. Monseigneur the Baron of Thunder-ten-tronckh passed near the screen, and, seeing this cause and that effect, drove Candide from the country house with great kicks in the behind; Cunégonde fainted; she was slapped by Madame the Baroness as soon as she revived; and all was in consternation in the handsomest and most agreeable of all possible country houses.

[Chapter Three]: *How Candide Escaped from among the Bulgarians and What Became of Him.*

Nothing could be so handsome, so smart, so brilliant, so well trained as the two armies. Trumpets, fifes, oboes, drums, cannon formed a harmony such as had never been in hell. First the cannon knocked down about six thousand men on each side; then the musketry took from the best of worlds around nine to ten thousand rascals who infested its surface. Also the bayonet was the sufficient reason for the death of several thousand men. The whole could well mount up to about thirty thousand souls.

Candide, who trembled like a philosopher, hid himself as well as he could during this heroic butchery.

Finally, while the two Kings had *Te Deums* sung, each in his camp, he decided to go reason elsewhere about effects and causes. He passed over piles of dead and dying, and first reached a neighboring village; it was in ashes; this was an Abarian village which the Bulgarians had burned according to the rules of international law. Here, old men, dazed by blows, watched their butchered wives dying, holding their children to their bleeding breasts; there, girls, disemboweled after they had satisfied the natural needs of a few heroes, breathed their last sighs; others, half burned, begged to be put to death. Brains were scattered over the ground beside severed arms and legs.

Candide fled as fast as possible into another village; it belonged to the Bulgarians, and the Abarian heroes had treated it in the same way. Candide, still stepping on quivering limbs, or across ruins, finally got away from the theater of war, carrying some small provisions in his knapsack, and never forgetting Mademoiselle Cunégonde. When he reached Holland his provisions were gone; but having heard that everybody was rich in that country, and that they were Christians there, he did not doubt that he would be treated as well as he had been in the country house of Monseigneur the Baron before he had been chased out because of Mademoiselle Cunégonde's pretty eyes.

He asked for alms from several grave personages, who all replied to him that if he continued to carry on this business, he would be shut up in a house of correction to teach him how to live.

Finally he addressed himself to a man who had just spoken about charity in a large assembly for a whole hour, all by himself. This orator, giving him a dark look, said to him: "What are you doing here? Are you here for the good cause?" — "There is no effect without cause," replied Candide modestly; "everything is necessarily linked, and arranged for the best. It was necessary for me to be chased away from Mademoiselle Cunégonde, to run the gauntlet, and it is necessary that I beg for my bread until I can earn it; all this could not have been otherwise." — "My friend," the orator told him, "do you believe that the Pope is Anti-Christ?" — "I have never even heard that before," replied Candide; "but, whether he is or not, I lack bread." — "You don't deserve to eat any," said the other; "get away, rascal; get away, wretch, don't ever come near me again." The orator's wife, having put her head out the window, and noticing a man who doubted that the Pope was Anti-Christ, poured over his head a full . . . O Heavens! To what excess religious zeal is carried in ladies!

A man who had not been baptized, a good Anabaptist called Jacques, saw the cruel and ignominious manner in which one of his brothers—a two-footed featherless being with a soul—was being treated; he took him home, cleaned him up, gave him some bread and beer, gave him a present of two florins, and even wanted to teach him to work in his factories of Persian stuff that is made in Holland. Candide, frantically falling at his feet before him, exclaimed: "Doctor Pangloss was right to tell me that all is for the best in this world, for I am infinitely more touched by your extreme generosity than by the harshness of that gentleman in the black coat, and of Madame, his wife."

The next day, taking a walk, he encountered a beggar all covered with sores, with lifeless eyes, the end of his nose rotted away, his mouth awry, his teeth black, and talking from his throat, tormented by a violent cough, and spitting out a tooth at each attack.

[Chapter Four]: *How Candide Met His Old Philosophy Teacher, Doctor Pangloss, and What Came of It.*

Candide, even more moved by compassion than horror, gave this frightful beggar the two florins which he had received from his honest Anabaptist, Jacques. The phantom looked at him fixedly, shed some tears, and threw his arms around his neck. Candide, terrified, recoils. "Alas!" says the wretch to the other wretch, "don't you recognize your dear Pangloss any more?" — "What do I hear? You, my dear teacher! You, in this horrible condition! What misfortune, then, has happened to you? Why are you no longer in the handsomest of country houses? What has become of Mademoiselle Cunégonde, the pearl of girls, the masterpiece of nature?" — "I am worn out," said Pangloss. Right away Candide took him into the Anabaptist's stable where he made him eat a little bread, and when Pangloss had recovered: "All right!" he said to him, "Cunégonde?" — "She is dead," replied the other. At this word Candide fainted; his friend restored him to his senses with a little bad vinegar which happened to be in the stable. Candide reopens his eyes. "Cunégonde is dead! Ah! best of worlds, where are you? But what disease did she die of? Isn't it from having seen me expelled from the handsome country house of Monsieur, her father, with big kicks?" — "No," said Pangloss. "She was disemboweled by Bulgarian soldiers, after having been violated as much as she could be; they smashed in the head of Monsieur the Baron, who wanted to defend her; Madame the Baroness was cut into pieces; my poor pupil treated exactly like his sister; and as for the country house, not one stone remains on another, not a barn, not a sheep, not a duck, not a tree; but we have been well avenged, for the Abarians did exactly the same thing in a neighboring barony which belonged to a Bulgarian Lord."

At this report, Candide fainted again; but, having come back to his senses and said all that was called for, he inquired about the cause and effect, and about the sufficient reason that had put Pangloss into such a piteous state. "Alas!" said the other, "it's love; love, the consoler of mankind, preserver of the universe, soul of all feeling beings, tender love." — "Alas!" said Candide, "I have known it, this love, this sovereign of hearts, that soul of our soul; it has never brought me anything but a kiss and twenty kicks in the behind. How could this beautiful cause produce such an abominable effect in you?" Pangloss replied in these words: "Oh my dear Candide! You know Paquette, that pretty attendant of our august Baroness; in her arms I tasted the delights of Paradise which produced these torments of Hell with which you see me devoured; she was infected with them, she may have died of them. Paquette got this present from a very learned Franciscan who had gone back to the source, for he had it from an old countess, who had got it from a captain of cavalry, who owed it to a marquise, who had it from a page, who had got it from a Jesuit, who, being a novice, had it in a direct line from one of the companions of Christopher Columbus. As for myself, I'll never give it to anyone, for I am dying."

"O Pangloss!" Candide exclaimed, "Here's a strange genealogy! Isn't the devil at the root of it?" — "Not at all," replied that great man; "it was an indispensable thing in the best of worlds, a necessary ingredient; for if Columbus had not caught, in an island of America, that disease which poisons the source of generation, which often even prevents generation, and which is obviously the opposite of the great aim of nature, we would have neither chocolate nor cochineal; it should also be noted that up to this date this disease is reserved to us in our continent, like controversy. The Turks, the Indians, the Persians, the Chinese, the Siamese, the Japanese do not yet know it; but there is a sufficient reason why they will know it in their turn in several centuries. Meanwhile it has made marvelous progress, and above all in those great armies made up of decent, well-educated mercenaries, which decide the destiny of states; we may be confident that when thirty thousand men fight in pitched battle against troops equal in number, there are about twenty thousand syphilitics on each side."

"Now that's admirable," said Candide; "but we must have you cured." — "And how can I be?" said Pangloss; "I don't have a sou, my friend, and in the whole extent of this globe, one can neither be bled nor take an enema without paying, or without having someone who pays for you."

This last speech made up Candide's mind; he went and threw himself at the feet of his charitable Anabaptist, Jacques, and painted such a touching picture of the condition to which his friend had been reduced that the good man did not hesitate to shelter Doctor Pangloss; he had him cured at his expense. In this cure, Pangloss lost only one eye and one ear. He wrote well and knew arithmetic perfectly. The Anabaptist Jacques made him his bookkeeper. At the end of two months, being obliged to go to Lisbon on matters of business, he brought his two philosophers along on his ship. Pangloss explained to him how everything was arranged for the best. Jacques was not of this opinion. "It must be," he said, "that men have corrupted nature a little, for they are not born as wolves, and they have become wolves. God has given them neither twenty-four-pounder cannons nor bayonets; and they have made themselves bayonets and cannons to destroy one another. I could take into account bankruptcies, and Justice which seizes the goods of the bankrupts to defraud creditors of them." — "All that was indispensable," replied the one-eyed doctor, "and private misfortunes make up the general good; so that the more private misfortunes there are, the more all is well." While he was arguing, the air darkened, the winds blew from the four corners of the earth, and the vessel was assailed by the most horrible tempest in the sight of the port of Lisbon.

[Chapter Twenty-Nine]: *How Candide Found Cunégonde and the Old Woman Again.*

While Candide, the Baron, Pangloss, Martin, and Cacambo were recounting their adventures, reasoning about the contingent and noncontingent events in this universe, arguing about causes and effects, about moral evil and physical evil, about free will and necessity, about the consolations one may find when one is in the galleys in Turkey, they landed on the shore of Propontis, at the house of the prince of Transylvania. The first objects that met their eyes were Cunégonde and the old woman, who were spreading out towels to dry on the lines.

The Baron paled at this sight. Candide, the tender lover, seeing his beautiful Cunégonde all brown, eyes bloodshot, flat-chested, cheeks wrinkled, arms red and chapped, recoiled three paces, seized with horror, and then advanced out of politeness. She embraced Candide and her brother; they embraced the old woman: Candide ransomed them both.

There was a little farm in the neighborhood; the old woman suggested to Candide that he acquire it until the whole group should enjoy better fortunes. Cunégonde did not know that she had grown ugly, nobody had told her so: she reminded Candide of his promises in so peremptory a tone that the good Candide did not dare refuse her. So he informed the Baron that he was going to marry his sister. "I'll never stand for such a sordid act on her part," said the Baron, "and such insolence on yours; I shall never be reproached with this infamy: my sister's children wouldn't be able to enter the Chapters of Germany. No, my sister shall never marry anyone but a Baron of the Empire." Cunégonde threw herself at his feet, and bathed them with tears; he was inflexible. "You supreme madman," Candide said to him, "I rescued you from the galleys, I paid your ransom, I paid your sister's; she was washing dishes here, she is ugly, I have the decency to make her my wife; and you still dare to oppose it! I'd kill you again if I listened to my anger." — "You may kill me again," said the Baron, "but you won't marry my sister while I'm alive."

[Chapter Thirty]: *Conclusion*

At the bottom of his heart Candide had no desire whatever to marry Cunégonde; but the Baron's extreme impertinence determined him to conclude the marriage, and Cunégonde urged him so strongly that he could not retract. He consulted Pangloss, Martin, and the faithful Cacambo. Pangloss wrote a fine memorandum in which he proved that the Baron had no rights over his sister, and that she could, according to all the laws of the Empire, make a left-handed marriage with Candide. Martin recommended that the Baron should be thrown into the sea; Cacambo decided that he should be returned to the Levantine captain and put back in the galleys, after which he would be sent to Rome to the Father General by the first ship. This was thought to be very good advice; the old woman approved it; they said nothing about it to his sister; the matter was carried out with a little money, and they had the pleasure of tricking a Jesuit and punishing the pride of a German Baron.

It was quite natural to suppose that after so many disasters Candide, married to his mistress and living with the philosopher Pangloss, the philosopher Martin, the prudent Cacambo, and the old woman, having in addition brought back so many diamonds from the country of the ancient Incas, would lead the most pleasant life in the world; but he was so cheated by the Jews that nothing remained to him beside his little farm; his wife, growing uglier every day, grew shrewish and insufferable; the old woman was ailing and was even more ill-tempered than Cunégonde. Cacambo, who worked in the garden and went to sell vegetables in Constantinople, was overworked and cursed his lot. Pangloss was in despair at not shining in some university in Germany. As for Martin, he was firmly convinced that people are equally miserable everywhere; he took things patiently. Candide, Martin, and Pangloss sometimes argued about metaphysics and morals. Often they saw ships passing under the windows of the farm, laden with effendis, pashas, cadis, who were being sent into exile at Lemnos, Mitylene, Erzerum; they saw other cadis arriving, other pashas, other effendis, who were taking the place of the exiles, and who were exiled in their turn. They saw heads properly empaled on their way to be presented to the Sublime Porte. These sights redoubled their discussions; and when they were not arguing, boredom was so excessive that the old woman dared to say to them one day: "I'd like to know which is worse: to be raped a hundred times by Negro pirates, to have a buttock cut off, to run the gauntlet among the Bulgarians, to be flogged and hanged in an auto-da-fé, to be dissected, to row in the galleys, in a word to undergo all the miseries we have suffered, or rather to stay here and do nothing?" — "That's a great question," said Candide.

This speech called forth new reflections, and Martin above all concluded that man was born to live in the convulsions of anxiety, or in the lethargy of boredom. Candide did not agree with that, but he asserted nothing. Pangloss admitted that he had always suffered horribly; but having once maintained that all was wonderful, he continued to maintain it and did not believe it.

One thing finally confirmed Martin in his detestable principles, made Candide hesitate more than ever, and embarrassed Pangloss. One day they saw Paquette and Friar Giroflée approach their farm; they were in the most extreme misery; they had very quickly gone through their three thousand piastres, had left each other, made up, quarreled, been put in prison; had escaped, and finally Friar Giroflée had turned Turk. Paquette continued her trade everywhere, and no longer earned anything with it. "I foresaw very well," Martin said to Candide, "that your presents would soon be dissipated and would only make them more miserable. You were once bloated with millions of piastres, you and Cacambo, and you are no happier than Friar Giroflée and Paquette." — "Ah! Ah!" Pangloss said to Paquette, "so heaven brings you back among us here, my poor child! Do you know that you cast me the end of my nose, an eye, and an ear? Now look at you! Eh! What a world this is!" This new adventure set them to philosophizing more than ever.

There was a very famous dervish in the neighborhood who was supposed to be the best philosopher in Turkey; they went to consult him; Pangloss was spokesman, and said to him: "Master, we come to ask you to tell us why so strange an animal as man was created." — "What are you meddling in?" the dervish said to him; "is that your business?" — "But, Reverend Father," said Candide, "there is a horrible lot of evil in the world." — "What does it matter," said the dervish, "whether there is evil or good? When His Highness sends a ship to Egypt, does he worry whether the mice in the ship are comfortable or not?" — "What, then, must we do?" said Pangloss. "Be silent," said the dervish. — "I flattered myself," said Pangloss, "that I might briefly discuss causes and effects with you, the best of possible worlds, the origin of evil, the nature of the soul, and pre-established harmony." At these words the dervish shut the door in their faces.

During the conversation the news had spread that in Constantinople they had just strangled two viziers of the Divan and the Mufti, and that they had impaled several of their friends. This catastrophe caused a great stir everywhere for a few hours. Pangloss, Candide, and Martin, returning to the little farm, met a good old man who was enjoying the fresh air under a bower of orange trees. Pangloss, who was as curious as he was argumentative, asked him the name of the Mufti who had just been strangled. "I have no idea," replied the good man; "and I've never known the name of any mufti or any vizier. I know absolutely nothing of the adventure you are telling me about; I assume that in general those who meddle with public affairs sometimes perish miserably, and that they deserve it; but I never try to find out what is going on in Constantinople; I content myself with sending there to sell the fruits of the garden I cultivate." Having said these words, he had the strangers come into his house; his two daughters and two sons presented them with several kinds of sherbet which they made themselves, kaimak flavored with candied citron peel, oranges, lemons, limes, pineapples, pistachios, Mocha coffee that had not been mixed with the bad coffee of Batavia and the Islands. After which the two daughters of this good Muslim perfumed the beards of Candide, Pangloss, and Martin.

"You must have," Candide said to the Turk, "a vast and magnificent property?" — "I have only twenty acres," replied the Turk; "I cultivate them with my children; work keeps away from us three great evils: boredom, vice, and need."

As Candide returned to his farm, he reflected deeply on the Turk's observations. He said to Pangloss and to Martin: "That good old man seems to me to have made for himself a lot far preferable to that of the six kings with whom we had the honor of dining." — "Greatness," said Pangloss, "is very dangerous, according to the account of all the philosophers: for after all, Eglon, King of the Moabites, was assassinated by Ehud; Absalom was hanged by his hair and pierced by three darts; King Nadab, son of Jeroboam, was killed by Baasha; King Elah by Zimri; Ahaziah by Jehu; Athaliah by Jehoiada; Kings Jehoiakim, Jeconiah, and Zedekiah were made into slaves. You know how Croesus perished, Astyages, Darius, Dionysius of Syracuse, Pyrrhus, Perseus, Hannibal, Jugurtha, Ariovistus, Caesar, Pompey, Nero, Otho, Vitellius, Domitian, Richard II of England, Edward II, Henry VI, Richard III, Mary Stuart, Charles I, the three Henrys of France, the Emperor Henry IV? You know . . ." — "I also know," said Candide, "that we must cultivate our garden." — "You are right," said Pangloss; "for when man was put into the Garden of Eden, he was put there *ut operaretur eum,* to work; which proves that man was not born for rest." — "Let us work without arguing," said Martin; "it's the only way to make life endurable."

The whole little society entered into this praiseworthy plan; each started to exercise his talents. The little property produced much. True, Cunégonde was very ugly, but she became an excellent pastry cook; Paquette embroidered; the old woman took care of the linen. Not even Friar Giroflée failed to perform some service; he was a very good carpenter, and even became respectable; and Pangloss sometimes said to Candide: "All events are linked in the best of possible worlds; for, after all, if you had not been expelled from a handsome country house with great kicks in the behind for love of Mademoiselle Cunégonde, if you had not been brought before the Inquisition, if you had not traversed America on foot, if you had not given the Baron a good sword thrust, if you had not lost all your sheep from the good land of El Dorado, you would not be here eating candied citrons and pistachios." — "That is well said," replied Candide, "but we must cultivate our garden."

In 1956, a musical version of Candide *opened at the Martin Beck Theatre in New York. The script was by the dramatist Lillian Hellman, the song lyrics were by the poet Richard Wilbur, and the music was by composer Leonard Bernstein; Tyrone Guthrie directed. The following excerpts give a good picture of some of the ways a prose narrative can be adapted for the musical stage; but in order to get a complete idea of what the adapters have done with the original, the reader should try to listen to the Bernstein-Wilbur songs (now available on recordings), since the music is one of the chief elements in the adaptation.*

CANDIDE: A COMIC OPERETTA BASED ON VOLTAIRE'S SATIRE
Lillian Hellman, Leonard Bernstein, and Richard Wilbur

[Act One, Scene One]

The Scene: Westphalia. Outside the castle of the BARON THUNDER TEN TRONCH. *At rise:* PANGLOSS *appears.*

PANGLOSS   I have been asked to tell you that this is Westphalia. It is a fine, sunny day. The sun shines on all wedding days, except, of course, when it doesn't, and then what does it matter? The women of Westphalia are very pure women.

(*The* WOMEN *of the* CHORUS *appear*)   I am told there are women in this world who are not pure, but the uneducated say a great many foolish things, don't they?

(*The* MEN *of the* CHORUS *appear*)   Our men are brave. The war is over, but we still have six divisions of artillery. It's been a long and bloody war, but if men didn't fight they would never know the benefits of peace, and if they didn't know the benefits of peace they would never know the benefits of war. You see, it all works out for the best.

(KING OF HESSE, *escorted by soldiers, appears*)   This is the King of Hesse, our hereditary enemy. We destroyed his army last week and took him prisoner. We treat him with great courtesy. He has a nice room in the basement. He comes out every day for exercise, and seems most content.

(HESSE *exits*)   Oh, forgive me. I am Pangloss, Doctor of Heidelberg, of Leipzig, and of Würzburg, in Philosophy and Metaphysics. I have long been resident tutor to the Baron's house. It's been a good life. Although, between you and me, I sometimes miss the cloisters of the university and small talk in Greek.

(GRETCHEN *comes toward him*)   Good morning, Gretchen.

GRETCHEN   You owe me money.

PANGLOSS   Ah, well. If she didn't think of money, she wouldn't think at all. Which certainly proves that all is for the best in this best of all possible worlds.

(*He sings*)   Look at this view! Mountains and towers!
Green meadows, too, bursting with flowers!
This is the heart of the best of all possible worlds.
Much the best part of the best of all possible worlds.

Lillian Hellman, *Candide: A Comic Operetta Based on Voltaire's Satire* (New York: Random House, 1957), pp. 3–22, 141–143. Copyright © 1957 by Lillian Hellman. Reprinted by permission of Random House, Inc.

The lyrics in *Candide: A Comic Operetta Based on Voltaire's Satire* by Richard Wilbur. Other lyrics by John Latouche and Dorothy Parker. Copyright © 1957 by Richard Wilbur. Copyright © 1957 by Richard Wilbur, John Latouche, and Dorothy Parker.

(CHORUS *sings*)   Yes, it's the heart of the best of all possible worlds.
    Much the best part of the best of all possible worlds.

(PANGLOSS *sings, gesturing toward the* CHORUS)
    Our men are lean, handsome and active.
    Where have you seen girls more attractive?
    None have more grace in this best of all possible worlds.
    No finer race in this best of all possible worlds.

CHORUS (*sings*)   No finer race in this best of all possible worlds.
    No better place in this best of all possible worlds.

(PANGLOSS *sings*)   And best of all, we now convene
    With keen anticipation,
    To watch a happy wedding scene
    And have a celebration.

(CHORUS *sings*)   A happy celebration.

(PANGLOSS *sings*)   All hail the groom
    And bride, of whom
    Our hearts could not be fonder.
    The love that reigns in Heaven above
    Is mirrored in the marriage of

(CANDIDE *and* CUNEGONDE *enter.* PANGLOSS *continues singing*)
    Candide and Cunegonde!

(CHORUS *sings*)   Candide and Cunegonde!

(PANGLOSS *sings*)   Wherefore and hence, therefore and ergo—

(CHORUS *sings*)   Wherefore and hence, therefore and ergo—

(PANGLOSS *sings*)   All's for the best in this best of all possible worlds.

(CHORUS *sings*)   All's for the best in this best of all possible worlds.

(PANGLOSS *sings*)   Any questions?
    Ask without fear. (*Touches his head*)
    I've all the answers here.

(CUNEGONDE *sings*) Dear master, I am sure you're right
    That married life is splendid.
    But why do married people fight?
    I cannot comprehend it.

(CHORUS *sings*)   She cannot comprehend it.

(PANGLOSS *sings*)   The private strife
    Of man and wife
    Is useful to the nation:
    It is a harmless outlet for
    Emotions which could lead to war
    Or social agitation.

(CHORUS *sings*)   A brilliant explanation!

(PANGLOSS *sings*)   Therefore, it's true.
    No one may doubt it:

(CHORUS *sings*)   Therefore, it's true.
    No doubt about it:

(PANGLOSS *sings*)   Marriage is blest in
                      This best of all possible worlds.

(CHORUS *sings*)   All's for the best in
                    This best of all possible worlds.

(PANGLOSS *sings*)   Next question?
                      Deep though it be,
                      There's none too deep for me!

(CANDIDE *sings*)   Since marriage is divine, of course,
                     We cannot understand, sir,
                     Why should there be so much divorce.
                     Do let us know the answer.

(CHORUS *sings*)   Do let us know the answer.

(PANGLOSS *sings*)   Why, marriage, boy,
                      Is such a joy,
                      So lovely a condition,
                      That many ask no better than
                      To wed as often as they can,
                      In happy repetition.

(CHORUS *sings*)   A brilliant exposition!

(PANGLOSS, CANDIDE, CUNEGONDE *sing*)
                   Wherefore and hence, therefore and ergo. . . .

(CHORUS *sings*)   Wherefore and hence, therefore and ergo. . . .

(PANGLOSS *sings*)   All's for the best in this best of all possible worlds.

(CHORUS *sings*)   All's for the best in this best of all possible worlds.

(PANGLOSS, CUNEGONDE, CANDIDE *sing*)
                   A brilliant exposition!
                   Q.E.D.
                   All's for the best.

(ALL *sing*)   A brilliant exposition in this best of all
                Possible, possible, possible, possible worlds!
                A brilliant exposition! Q.E.D.

(*The* BARON THUNDER TEN TRONCH *enters.*)

CUNEGONDE   (*Speaks*) Good morning, dear Father.

BARON   A good morning, dear children, on your wedding day. (MAXIMILLIAN *enters. He is hung with medals*) Good morning, son. Where did you get the medals?

MAXIMILLIAN   Oh, now, Father, I have one of my headaches.

BARON   Have you had a headache for three years? Why didn't you join the army when I sent for you? (*Points to* CANDIDE) My adopted son never left my side. He earned his medals.

MAXIMILLIAN   I sprained my ankle, Father. I have soft bones. I've explained it all before—

BARON   Candide didn't worry about his bones. He worried about mine.

MAXIMILLIAN   He has strong bones. Lower-class bones.

PANGLOSS   Baron, here are the marriage contracts in Latin, Greek and Westphalian dialect. A record for history.

MAXIMILLIAN   (*To* CUNEGONDE)   As your brother—and the future head of this house, God forbid Father ever dies—I must once again protest your marriage to a man of unknown birth. And if you hadn't paid so much for your wedding dress, I could have had a new uniform.

CUNEGONDE   (*Laughs*)   But it's a nice uniform. And certainly not touched by war.

BARON   (*To* CANDIDE)   Come sign the marriage contracts, my boy.

CANDIDE   (*Coming to table*)   Oh, sir, I can make no marriage settlement. You know I have nothing to give Cunegonde.

PANGLOSS   You have a pure heart. A woman wants nothing else.

CANDIDE   (*To* BARON)   You have been much too generous with Cunegonde's dowry. I cannot accept—

BARON   I haven't given her a damn thing.

CANDIDE   Thank you, sir. Thank you. And now I have a great favor to ask of you—

BARON   (*Very quickly*)   I can't afford anything. I must look out for my old age. What is it?

CANDIDE   This is the happiest day of my life and it pains me to think we have a prisoner in the house. Could we invite the King of Hesse to have wine and cake with us at the marriage feast?

(BARON *nods, signals to a soldier. The soldier exits to fetch the* KING OF HESSE.)

PANGLOSS   (*To* CANDIDE, *as they move away*)   Your old teacher is proud of you. Now make me happy. Throw yourself back through the years and repeat your lesson: tell me the golden rules of a high-minded Westphalian man.

CANDIDE   The heart of mankind is a generous heart; the honor of a man is all he needs on life's journey; the poor must be respected and so must the rich since they are always with us; the beauty of noble thought; the treasure that is sweet, sacred womanhood—

PANGLOSS   (*To a pretty girl who passes*)   Good morning, Paquette.

PAQUETTE   You owe me money.

PANGLOSS   (*To* CANDIDE)   Women are sometimes difficult. But if they weren't difficult perhaps nobody would pay any attention to them. Tell me, my boy, do you know much of women? Have you, I mean did you, perhaps, in a daring minute—

CANDIDE   What, sir? I don't know what you mean.

PANGLOSS   (*Delighted*)   Oh, I am so glad. So glad. (*To another pretty girl*) Hello, Irmentrude. You look charming—(*Quickly*) I paid you.   (*She disappears.*)

PANGLOSS   (*Hurries to* CUNEGONDE)   Cunegonde, my dear little girl, make your old teacher happy. Repeat the words of a high-minded Westphalian lady and swear that you will live by them.

CUNEGONDE   The honor of a woman is all she needs on life's journey. Dr. Pangloss, is that really all a woman needs?

PANGLOSS   Nothing else.

CUNEGONDE   Yes, sir. Do you like my dress?

PANGLOSS   Continue, dear girl: The treasure that is sweet, sacred womanhood—

CUNEGONDE   Treasure. Yes, sir. Do you think it will rain? If it rains, my hair won't curl—(*Pats* PANGLOSS *affectionately*) I'm a bad pupil. I always was. But don't be angry with me.

(PANGLOSS *smiles, kisses her, and moves to* MAXIMILLIAN.)

PANGLOSS   Maximillian, I have a new medal for you. Come along. (*They exit.*)

BARON   (*To* CUNEGONDE)   And how's my pretty daughter? Nervous as a bride should be?

CUNEGONDE   No, Father. I am not nervous.

BARON   (*As he exits*)   Oh, my God. Neither was your mother.

CANDIDE   We're alone. We shouldn't be.

CUNEGONDE   Why not? What silly old customs. We'll be married in a few minutes. Would you like to see my veil?   (*She moves toward him. He draws back.*)

CANDIDE   Cunegonde, you know that I am forbidden to see the wedding veil—

CUNEGONDE   For a daring hero, you're not very daring.

CANDIDE   I respect you and I—

CUNEGONDE   (*Too firmly*)   You should respect me. I'm very pure.

CANDIDE   You need hardly tell me such a thing.

CUNEGONDE   I've never even thought about another man. I've never kissed another man.

CANDIDE   (*Amazed*)   Of course not, Cunegonde.

CUNEGONDE   I think you should apologize, darling.

CANDIDE   I do. (*Bewildered*) Indeed I do.

CUNEGONDE   All right. I forgive. Now where are we going on our honeymoon?

CANDIDE   Well, we'll stay here and take a nice picnic basket—(*Sadly*) I can't take you anywhere, Cunegonde. You know I have nothing.

CUNEGONDE   I don't want anything, darling. And anyway, Father's rich.

CANDIDE   I won't take anything from your father. (*Desperately*) Cunegonde, I will work for you, I will give my life for you, but that isn't much to offer. I can't even give you a house of your own—

CUNEGONDE   Darling, darling. We've said all this before. I don't want houses or dresses or jewelry—they're all rather vulgar, aren't they? I'll live in this dress the rest of my life. These shoes will last me until death. I want nothing. Absolutely nothing but you.

(CANDIDE *sings*)	Soon, when we feel we can afford it, We'll build a modest little farm.
(CUNEGONDE *sings*)	We'll buy a yacht and live aboard it, Rolling in luxury and stylish charm.
(CANDIDE)	Cows and chickens.
(CUNEGONDE)	Social whirls.
(CANDIDE)	Peas and cabbage.
(CUNEGONDE)	Ropes of pearls.
(CANDIDE)	Soon there'll be little ones beside us; We'll have a sweet Westphalian home.
(CUNEGONDE)	Somehow we'll grow as rich as Midas; We'll live in Paris when we're not in Rome.

(CANDIDE)	Smiling babies.
(CUNEGONDE)	Marble halls.
(CANDIDE)	Sunday picnics.
(CUNEGONDE)	Costume balls.
(CUNEGONDE)	Oh, won't my robes of silk and satin
	Be chic! I'll have all that I desire.
(CANDIDE)	Pangloss will tutor us in Latin
	And Greek, while we sit before the fire.
(CUNEGONDE)	Glowing rubies.
(CANDIDE)	Glowing logs.
(CUNEGONDE)	Faithful servants.
(CANDIDE)	Faithful dogs.
(CUNEGONDE)	We'll round the world enjoying high life;
	All will be pink champagne and gold.
(CANDIDE)	We'll lead a rustic and a shy life,
	Feeding the pigs and sweetly growing old.
(CUNEGONDE)	Breast of peacock.
(CANDIDE)	Apple pie.
(CUNEGONDE)	I love marriage.
(CANDIDE)	So do I.
(CUNEGONDE)	Oh happy pair!
	Oh, happy we!
	It's very rare
	How we agree.
(BOTH)	Oh happy pair!
	Oh, happy we!
	It's very rare
	How we agree.
	Oh happy pair!
	Oh, happy we!
	It's very rare
	How we agree!

(*The people of the scene return to the stage.*)

CANDIDE (*Moves to the* KING OF HESSE) I would like to make you welcome at my wedding feast. Can you forget old battles on this happy day?

HESSE I am happy to forget old battles. I don't like battles. I hate war.

(*They shake hands and* CANDIDE *moves away. The* GENERAL *of the Hessian army appears, hiding behind a pillar, and taps* HESSE *on the shoulder.*)

HESSE'S GENERAL (*In a whisper*) Your Majesty.

HESSE Oh, my God, what are you doing here?

HESSE'S GENERAL Your Majesty, precisely at noon you will be rescued.

HESSE I don't want to be rescued. I don't want to go home. I like being a prisoner. Go away, please.

HESSE'S GENERAL We will not pay your ransom. We have been in conference all night and have decided it is cheaper to fight.

HESSE   Please leave me alone. I'm sick of war—

HESSE'S GENERAL   The honor of Hesse calls for the destruction of Westphalia. Have a little honor, Your Majesty.   (*He creeps off.*)

PANGLOSS   We shall now sing the first eighteen stanzas of the wedding chorale, omitting the eleventh, twelfth and thirteenth stanzas which have to do with fertility festivals. We shall use the St. Stanislaus version.

(CHORUS *sings*)   We subjects of this Barony
                     Are gathered here in pride and glee
                     To hail the lovely bride-to-be
                     And graft upon her noble tree
                     The flower of chivalry.

(*The* GENERAL *of the Hessian army appears, signaling to his men. They invade Westphalia. Through the noise of battle, we hear the cries of Westphalian ladies, the outraged shouts of Westphalian men. We see* CUNEGONDE *carried off by the* GENERAL *as* CANDIDE *rushes to her defense. Ladies rush across the stage in panic as Hessian soldiers pursue them. In the midst of the excitement,* PANGLOSS *climbs on the wedding table.*)

PANGLOSS   Gentlemen! Gentlemen! I have never before in my life used strong words, but I am forced to say this is unsporting. (*He is knocked off the table and disappears.*)

(*The last figures in the battle disappear. The stage is empty. After a second, the* BARON *and* MAXIMILLIAN *appear, struggle toward each other, and fall to the ground.* CUNEGONDE, *without her wedding dress, appears and falls to the ground trying to reach her father.* PANGLOSS *appears and struggles to reach the three figures.*)

PANGLOSS   Tut, tut, the good Baron. Tut, tut, the good Maximillian.   (*He moves toward* CUNEGONDE.)

PANGLOSS   Cunegonde. Cunegonde. Poor, pretty child.   (*He falls as* CANDIDE *comes stumbling on.*)

CANDIDE   (*Calling*)   Cunegonde, Cunegonde—

PANGLOSS   Candide—(CANDIDE *runs to him*) Cunegonde is dead. Westphalia is destroyed. Don't cry, don't stay to mourn us. The world is beautiful—go forth and see it.

CANDIDE   My Cunegonde—

PANGLOSS   Yes, I know. But think of it this way: If she hadn't died she'd never have been born. There is some sweetness in every woe. The world will be good to you, kind to you. Go now.

(*Music begins.* CANDIDE *moves slowly out of Westphalia.*)

[The end of the final scene]

CANDIDE   . . . Marry me, Cunegonde.

CUNEGONDE   (*Sadly, softly*)   It's too late. I'm not young, I'm not good, I'm not pure.

CANDIDE   And I am not young, and not worth much. What we wanted, we will not have. The way we did love, we will not love again. Come now, let us take what we have and love as we are.

PANGLOSS   I'd love to do a ceremony. I had three weeks of divinity school in the Würzburg Gymnasium. Now you must say after me, "Love between men and women is the highest order of love between men and women. Thus we promise to think noble and do noble. . . ."

CANDIDE   (*With force*)   No. We will not think noble because we are not noble. We will not live in beautiful harmony because there is no such thing in this world, nor should there be. We promise only to do our best and live out our lives. Dear God, that's all we can promise in truth. Marry me, Cunegonde.

(CANDIDE *sings*)   You've been a fool and so have I,
        But come and be my wife,
        And let us try before we die
        To make some sense of life.
        We're neither pure nor wise nor good;
        We'll do the best we know;
        We'll build our house, and chop our wood,
        And make our garden grow.
        And make our garden grow.

(CUNEGONDE *sings*)   I thought the world was sugar-cake,
        For so our master said;
        But now I'll teach my hands to bake
        Our loaf of daily bread.

(CANDIDE *and* CUNEGONDE *sing*)
        We're neither pure nor wise nor good;
        We'll do the best we know;
        We'll build our house, and chop our wood,
        And make our garden grow.
        And make our garden grow.

(*Cast begins slow entry. Sextette of* PANGLOSS, MAXIMILLIAN, OLD LADY, CUNEGONDE, CANDIDE *and* GOVERNOR *sing*)
        Let dreamers dream what worlds they please;
        Those Edens can't be found.
        The sweetest flowers, the fairest trees
        Are grown in solid ground.

(*Entire company sings*)
        We're neither pure nor wise nor good.
        We'll do the best we know.
        We'll build our house, and chop our wood,
        And make our garden grow.
        And make our garden grow.

Curtain

All the adaptations of Candide *attempt to convey, through their various media, the story and the meaning of Voltaire's original. H. N. Brailsford, in the following essay, analyzes* Candide's *philosophical ideas and its narrative techniques, and shows how effectively Voltaire has embodied his vision of life in this swiftly moving fantastic tale.*

CANDIDE
H. N. Brailsford

The earthquake that engulfed Lisbon in 1755 ranks among the decisive events of the eighteenth century. The destruction of the Cities of the Plain, four thousand years earlier, had set for the civilizations of the Eastern Mediterranean a similar problem. Orthodoxy in that age had found for it a simple and comforting solution: these cities had offended the police of the Universe by their abnormal wickedness. The eighteenth century was just struggling out of this naive anthropocentric view. To call it the Age of Enlightenment, as historians commonly do, is to flatter it grossly. It was an age of rabid and cruel superstition. It still burned witches; kings still "touched" for scrofula. An official astrologer, called to the royal bed-chamber, took the horoscope of Louis XIV as he came into this world; he quitted it wearing round his neck the bones of some departed saint that he might absorb their virtue, much as brown men will do to this day in the South Sea Islands. In Lisbon itself, the Holy Inquisition promptly appeased the wrath of Providence by burning a few Jews and heretics at the stake, whereupon a second shock shattered what was left of that city. None the less, on the fringes of all this official superstition, the Royal Societies and the Academies were busy, and with the Bronze Age view of life there co-existed a reluctant but fairly general belief that nature is governed by physical causation. On this first mechanistic glimpse of an orderly universe Leibnitz had built his celebrated system of optimism. Pope, with the help of Bolingbroke and Shaftesbury, popularized it in neat and pleasant verses, which soon appeared in an excellent French translation. It became the fashion in this complacent society to believe that all is for the best in the best of all possible worlds. Evil, to be sure, there is, but particular misfortunes viewed from a suitable distance are seen to compose the general good: many shadows are necessary in the scheme of any elaborate picture. The enlightened man of fashion may not have grasped the lofty metaphysical pedantry from which Leibnitz deduced this comfortable doctrine, but it served the normal purpose of all correct philosophy. It reconciled him with things as they are, among them the shadowy miseries of the many and the substantial privileges of the few.

Voltaire in his early manhood was dazzled by this doctrine, and for a time Madame du Châtelet swallowed the Leibnitzian system whole. He had his doubts, as Zadig's eloquent "But—" suggests. Some years passed, however, before he saw his way clearly through a rather elementary confusion. His final criticism, as witty and penetrating as need be, is to be found in his *Philosophic Dictionary* (Bien, tout est). Assuredly there is order everywhere. The agonies with which a stone in the bladder destroys a

From H. N. Brailsford, *Voltaire* (London: Oxford University Press, 1963), pp. 82–90. © 1963 Mrs. H. N. Brailsford. Reprinted by permission of Mrs. H. N. Brailsford.

valuable life are a perfect illustration of physical causation and system. "All is for the best" is true only in the sense that everything is subject to immutable laws. The doctrine is hardly consoling, and in addition it saps the Christian religion, since it deposes man from his seat as the centre of a creation designed for his good.

The event at Lisbon gave Voltaire the perfect text for a lay sermon on this theme. He set to work in creative excitement and produced in a few weeks his long poem on the earthquake. It is one of his best efforts in the style of this century, neatly phrased, closely reasoned, somewhat pedestrian in its orderly march, yet contriving to express sincerely and with a certain frank simplicity his distress, his perturbation at the unwelcome perception of a man's loneliness and impotence in a universe indifferent to his welfare. It ends with a confession of ignorance qualified by hope. The orthodox explanation is dismissed in a contemptuous line. Lisbon was no wickeder than other cities: "Lisbon is ruined and we dance in Paris." Leibnitz fares no better. Others, to be sure, may profit by my misfortunes, even by the death that ends my misery: "A fine consolation to be eaten by worms." There follow some passages that seem to be a conscious retraction of the most superficial of Voltaire's early works. With the letters on England he had published some *Preliminary Remarks on the Thoughts of M. Pascal* (1728). They reflect his temperamental dislike of Jansenism and his lifelong failure to understand a mystic. His own Deism permitted of the respect that a junior lieutenant in a smart uniform may feel towards an elderly and magnificent colonel. But the self-abasement of a finite creature before the infinite—this was as much beyond him as was Pascal's tormented sense of the dualism of human nature, its mingled pettiness and grandeur. Voltaire was always of a perfectly definite size, and that was not inconsiderable. In these *Remarks* he belaboured "the sublime misanthrope" for belittling our species and "addressing eloquent insults to the human race." He quoted one of Pascal's cries, the passage in which he looks around him, perceives that "the universe is dumb, man without light, abandoned to his own devices, lost in his corner of the earth, and unable to say who put him there or why, or what will come of him after death"; whereupon Pascal wonders that on "this desert island" man can escape despair. Voltaire's reply was that of a monumentally insensitive man of fashion: "For my part, when I look at Paris or London, I see no reason to indulge in this despair of which M. Pascal speaks. I see a city that in no way resembles a desert isle. It is populous, wealthy, civilized, and in it men are happy as human nature permits."

The poem on Lisbon actually contains some echoes of Pascal, which must have been conscious. "Nature is dumb, one questions her in vain." The conclusion, which one may translate thus, is worth quoting, for it reveals a new Voltaire:

> Atoms tormented on this ball of clay,
> The sport of death, of hazard's strokes the prey,
> Yet thinking atoms, atoms whose clear eyes
> Guided by thought have measured out the skies,
> Into the infinite we fling our gaze
> Yet cannot see ourselves, nor count our days . . .
>
> Humbly I sigh, submissive I await
> Without a challenge the decrees of fate.

More cheerfully, indeed, in bygone times
I sang of pleasure in seductive rhymes.
The times are changed and age has schooled my mind
To share the common frailties of mankind.
Groping in darkness for a guiding light
No murmur shall escape me in the night.
A dying Caliph, sick upon his bed
Turned to the God he loved, in prayer, and said,
'My King, I bring thee with my gratitude
All that thou lackest in thy plenitude.
Sin, ignorance and suff'ring and regret.'
But why did he the best gift, hope, forget?

This poem, which appeared with another on *Natural Law,* a rather bolder exposition of the tolerant, deist creed, was punctually burned by order of the Parlement of Paris (1759). A more closely reasoned refutation was furnished by Jean-Jacques Rousseau, of all men. In a not over-friendly letter he remonstrated with "this poor man, overwhelmed, so to speak, with prosperity and glory, who bitterly declaims against the wretchedness of this life." One smiles at this thrust, yet it was to the credit of this rich man that he did not confuse his own good fortune with the common lot. Out of this controversy sprang the one book of Voltaire's that is certainly immortal, his tale, *Candide* (1758).

Twice Voltaire seemed to have won immortality. His tragedies were, while he lived, the broad foundation of his fame. He had surpassed, it was thought, the Greeks, the rough English, the exuberant Spaniards, all his contemporaries, everyone, indeed, save Corneille and Racine. In his later years and for a generation or two after his death, what men read most eagerly were his histories and the pocket *Philosophic Dictionary.* These formed the mind of liberal Europe. The plays are dead. The graver prose works have ceased to be the indispensable possession of everyone who reads. But *Candide* lives on, and one may read it in any civilized tongue, in rich editions illustrated by great artists, or in paper covers sold for a few pence. The writer cherishes a cheap copy bought in a remote little town in Turkey, that has passed in his recollection through most of the vicissitudes known to Voltaire's hero; for it has seen a massacre, a conflagration, a siege, a bombardment, and three successive conquests. He read it as he camped among burned villages, and watched three epidemics in one winter decimate the population that had survived the artillery and the flames. In those surroundings there was much to be said for its argument, that this is not the best of all possible worlds. It is probable that it will never go wholly out of date.

What shall one call it? A tale, a satire, a philosophical romance that describes the life of Everyman? It is all these things, but also it is the most perfect model of written prose, in the language that is of all European tongues the best adapted for this art. You will not lay it down, if once you take it up, and as the years crowd upon you, you will find that you can read it over and over again. It is like a quartette of Mozart's: so light it seems, so graceful, so easy, that one supposes that none of its beauties can escape an attentive ear at the first playing, yet every repetition is discovery. Is it a tale? Then the story is at once the simplest and the most fantastic that ever came from the pen of man. The characters are thin outlines of humanity. The moral is obtrusive. What is it, then, that hurries the reader along enthralled? Partly it is the play of wit. Partly it is the fun of watching this preposterous thesis of optimism poked and tossed and chased and mauled with the most perfect grace and good manners, much as a mother cat may tease a clumsy kitten. Partly it is the never-failing invention. Lest we should tire of the crude horrors of the wars of the Bulgarians and the Abars, the earthquake at Lisbon, the prim brutalities of the Inquisition and the adventures of a Pope's bastard among Moorish pirates, there comes the relief of Candide's sojourn in Eldorado, and thereafter the highly sophisticated corruptions of Paris. With what perfect stage management are we introduced to the eerie supper party of the six dethroned kings, "who had come to pass the Carnival at Venice." With what art is that refrain repeated, and how tactfully we decline from the tragedy of the Sultan, the Tsar, Charles Edward Stuart and the two Kings of Poland, to the farce of Theodore of Corsica. The end of the whole story might seem idyllic, for in the tranquil garden by the Bosphorus, Candide, after all his harrowing adventures, has at last domesticated and even married the lady of his youthful passion, Mlle Cunégonde. This world, if not the best, wags passably well. But there are shadows. The lady has grown ugly and peevish, and as we talk in the miniature Eden, two viziers and the mufti have just been strangled and several of their friends impaled.

The tale, we said, is fantastic. It is so, however, only by accumulating an incredible number of extreme misfortunes on a single head. Candide is the Pilgrim of this Progress, the Everyman of this Mystery. He suffers nothing that is not the common lot. Voltaire is playing an absorbing game with us. The rules of it are strict enough. The king of his chessmen bears a charmed life—neither beatings, tempests, an earthquake, an *auto-da-fé,* a duel, nor even the attentions of French physicians can end it: Candide must stay on the board. But it is understood that no single incident in all the heaped-up horrors, all the multiplied coincidences, shall be in itself incredible, or even improbable. We watch Voltaire, but we never catch him out. Many of these incidents are actually historical—the earthquake, the subsequent doings of the Inquisition, the war against the Jesuit colony of Paraguay, the execution of Admiral Byng. The great actress who played Queens of England in Paris was really buried in a ditch. The six dethroned kings were all contemporaries. Do you doubt that a well-born young man could be kidnapped for a foreign army in Westphalia, and all but skinned alive when he tried to desert? Voltaire met this person, a French chevalier, lacking his nose and ears, as he trundled a wheelbarrow in the royal garden at Potsdam. King Frederick William's press-gang snatched him with many another, but he was the only one whom Voltaire could rescue by writing a set of verses. What else is improbable? Not the galleys rowed by slaves and convicts. Voltaire himself got some of them released. Do you doubt that a philosopher may catch the disease that Columbus brought to Europe? Maupertuis had that misfortune. As for Paquette, she endured only what all young women who drift into her profession must expect. Negro slavery was pretty much as Voltaire describes it at Surinam; indeed, he relates elsewhere this instance of it as a fact. Unwilling monks must often have suffered the distress that demoralized Brother Giroflée. Within the rules of the game, this is a veracious chronicle.

The reader need have no fear of wallowing in all these horrors. There is not a tear among them. Dr. Pangloss, who was hanged and thereafter dissected, is too well-mannered to exact this tribute. There are two ways of confronting cruelty and wrong. The more usual attitude, in countries of Anglo-Saxon speech, is to spend oneself in pity for the victim. This is productive of much disinterested distress and of guineas for Mansion House funds. The cruelty, none the less, persists. Pity, when all is said, is the last insult. It injures him who gives and him who takes. It was not Voltaire's way, though in real life it is recorded of him several times that he wept. His tears were not for paper. His answer to cruelty and wrong was militancy, reckless and merciless. Since, as he used to say, he had not "a hundred thousand mustachios at his command," his warfare was necessarily intellectual. He used that wit which is the Sword of the Spirit, piercing every joint of the Breastplate of Self-Righteousness. His thrusts, given a little time, were frequently mortal. A fair number of the wrongs and cruelties he assailed fell to his strokes. It is a common objection to this use of the intellect, that it is negative. This is singular logic. Every negation implies an affirmation. While Voltaire attacks, you may hear his credo chanted to the rhythm of his blows. When he renders cruelty hateful and injustice contemptible, he that has ears to hear will catch above the battle his hymn to brotherly love.

One asks how the thing is done. Wit so various and supple obeys no formula. But one secret of his power we can detect. He had the art of stripping human actions and relations of the trappings of abstract words in which they commonly go draped. He will not say that heretics were executed in an *auto-da-fé*. He tells us plainly that they were roasted over a slow fire. Listen to his account of the judicial murder of Admiral Byng, as Candide saw it. "Conversing in this way, they landed at Plymouth. A multitude of people covered the shore, and stared attentively at a rather burly man who was kneeling, his eyes bandaged, on the deck of one of the warships. Four soldiers, posted in front of this man fired, each of them, three bullets into his skull in the most peaceful way in the world, and the whole assemblage went home extremely satisfied." This is perfectly concrete. It compels us to see exactly what was done with a directness of vision of which few persons in that multitude can have been capable. The case is then analysed. Candide learns that Byng was shot "because he did not cause enough men to be killed: he gave battle to a French admiral, and the verdict was that he was not near enough to him." "But," said Candide, "the French admiral was just as far from the English admiral, as the Englishman was from the Frenchman." And then comes one of those swift, disconcerting thrusts to which there is no parry known. "In this country, it is well from time to time to kill an admiral to encourage the others." One might illustrate this method indefinitely: first see, with perfect definition, in the round, the cruelty in question: then thrust with the utmost economy of movement. One may choose at random another instance from *Candide*. That traveller saw at Surinam a negro, clad only in a pair of drawers, who lacked the left leg and the right hand, waiting for his master, M. Vanderdendur, the famous merchant. "Did he use you thus?" "Yes, sir," said the negro, "it is the custom. They give us a pair of drawers, as our only clothing, twice a year. When we work at the sugarmills, if the machinery catches a finger, they cut off a hand: when we try to escape, they cut off a leg: both things happened to me." Then comes the thrust. "That is the price at which you eat sugar in Europe."

But there is more in this tale than effective satire. Under all the bitter gaiety, there runs a parable of man's life on this earth, that is not without tenderness and kindly wisdom. This youth of excellent parts but great simplicity is the immortal idealist whose pilgrimage through life others also have traced. He is a juvenile Quixote; he is a less sedentary Faust. Though born in Westphalia, his mind had a positive quality that is wholly French. He fought no windmills; he had no truck with phantoms. He knew precisely what he wanted, to embrace Mlle Cunégonde, whom he once had kissed behind a screen. Yet for the ideal, in the pleasing corporeal form, did he not undertake a quest through battles and tempests across two continents and against the leagued powers of kings and priests, that might have done honour to any Knight of the Holy Grail? Him also "the eternal womanly" drew onwards. He travelled, indeed, with French eyes through an eighteenth-century world. Here were no Brocken spectres, no Helen, no homunculus, nothing at all of that thronged menagerie of symbols that peoples infinity for the Teutonic imagination. But was there not in his insatiable search, told to be sure in excellent French prose, something of that craving, for the ideal that ever eludes us, which men of other races and other centuries have described in language of a conscious exaltation? Candide was what Oswald Spengler calls a Faustian man: he craved, if not infinity, yet in no finite way, He met, as the idealist in this world-wide myth always meets, with disillusion. His Cunégonde, when he attained her, was ugly and old. The quest in the end was not worth achieving. And yet, not unlike the aged Faust, in creative work he found happiness. The parable of human life ends commonly in this way, though few have told its moral with the satisfying concreteness of this French romance. There is at its edifying close none of that choir of angels dropping roses that the German Goethe provided. But Voltaire assures us that Mlle Cunégonde became an excellent pastry-cook, and the whole society was passably happy, since they had learned to cultivate their garden.

The Rivals

In the following excerpt from her comprehensive biography of Richard Brinsley Sheridan, Madeleine Bingham discusses the issue of the sources of The Rivals *(in life and in literature), narrates the vicissitudes of its first performances, and describes in detail the nature of playgoing in the eighteenth century.*

[*THE RIVALS*]
Madeleine Bingham

Sheridan's nature was perfectly suited to the writing of comedies. He had a quick brain, and a ready wit. If he despised the theatre as being beneath the contempt of one who was born a gentleman, he did know the vicissitudes of the theatre and the way that plays were made. His mother had written comedies, his father had written a comedy, and from his early childhood he had heard talk of comedies and tragedies and stage effects. There are some things which people do not have to learn. They know them in their bones. For comedy and tragedy and all the effects produced in the theatre are instinctive things, and the appeal of the theatre comes from the stomach, which produces tears and laughter.

A comedy is a tragedy turned upside down. But it takes a man of good humour and wit to see how this can be done, so when Sheridan sat down to make some house-keeping money, the first thing which occurred to him was to turn his own life into comedy. He remembered the duels, the sighing of the lovers, himself and Eliza, and out of them he constructed *The Rivals.* In due course the experts have got to work on this comedy. They have proved to their own satisfaction that he took Mrs Malaprop from a comedy of his mother's, *A Trip to Bath;* that Sir Lucius O'Trigger was taken from a play of his father's; that Lydia Languish was not supposed to be Eliza, that Julia was; that this character and that were plagiarized from this literary source and that.

In his preface to *The Rivals* Sheridan wrote that he had not read many plays and went on:

> "Yet I own that, in one respect I did not regret my ignorance; for as my first wish in attempting a play was to avoid every appearance of plagiary, I thought I should stand a better chance of effecting this from being in a walk that I had not frequented, and where, consequently the progress of invention was less likely to be interrupted by starts of recollection; for on subjects on which the mind has been much informed, invention is slow of asserting itself. Faded ideas float in the fancy like half forgotten dreams; and the imagination in its fullest enjoyments becomes suspicious of its offspring, and doubts whether it has created or adopted."

This passage has been singled out as showing Sheridan's duplicity, as an attempt to spike the critics' guns before they were fired.

From Madeleine Bingham, *Sheridan: The Track of a Comet* (London: Allen & Unwin, 1972), pp. 113–124. © George Allen & Unwin Ltd. 1972. Reprinted by permission of George Allen & Unwin Ltd. and St. Martin's Press.

Whether he remembered the characters in his mother's *Trip to Bath* is irrelevant. The comedy of *The Rivals* was the love affair of Sheridan and Eliza. Lydia and Julia were both Eliza, as Jack Absolute and Faulkland are both Sheridan himself. By splitting the characters down the middle Sheridan with great skill, managed to put all the aspects of his love affair into four characters.

When Faulkland says, "Oh Jack! When delicate and feeling souls are separated, there is not a feature in the sky, not a movement of the elements, not an aspiration of the breeze, but hints some cause for a lover's apprehension," Sheridan is making fun of his own feelings. "What! *happy* and I away!"

His father was transformed into Sir Anthony Absolute, and all the comings and goings at Bath were made, with the witchery of wit, into brilliant and immortal comedy. He made things as he would have wished them to have been. Lydia was an heiress, Sir Anthony forgives his son, the sabre rattling is all in fun, the duel has no serious consequences and does not end in blood or threatened death as the real duel did. Once married to Eliza, Sheridan could afford to find the whole thing funny, for it had had a happy ending. All journeys should so end in lovers' meetings, that is one essential of a comedy.

Sheridan could almost have had later analysts and critics in mind when he made one of his characters say: "It *is* a grave comedy—it was ever my opinion that the stage should be a place of rational entertainment; instead of which, I am *very* sorry to say, most people go there for their diversion."

Comedy has been much more enduring than tragedy over the last two hundred years. Very few tragedies have survived. The suffering heroines and noble heroes have mostly been thrown into the theatrical prop basket, but Sheridan's comedies come up as fresh and bright as if they had been written yesterday.

In the winter of 1773, the young Sheridans left East Burnham and went up to London. For some time they lodged with Stephen Storace, a composer, and in the spring of 1774 they moved into their own house in Orchard Street, Portman Square. Mr Linley, who had by now been completely won over to the side of the young couple, furnished the house for them, and it was about this time that Sheridan wrote *The Rivals*.

On November 17, 1774, he wrote to his father-in-law:

> "If I were to attempt to make as many apologies as my long omission in writing to you requires, I should have no room for any other subject. One excuse only I shall bring forward, which is that I have been exceedingly employed and I believe very profitably. There will be a comedy of mine in rehearsal at Covent Garden within a few days. I did not set to work on it till within a few days of my setting out for Crome, so you may think I have not, for these last six weeks, been very idle. I have done it at Mr. Harris's (the manager's) own request; it is now complete in his hands, and preparing for the stage. He, and some of his friends also who have heard it, assure me in the most flattering terms that there is not a doubt of its success. It will be very well played, and Harris tells me that the least shilling I shall get (if it succeeds) will be six hundred pounds. I shall make no secret of it to-

wards the time of representation, that it may not lose any support my
friends can give it."

The notoriety which Sheridan had gained over his duels and despair were an asset.
Anyone who had been mentioned in the public prints was cash to a theatrical manager. But real life can always break through comedy, and in the same letter Sheridan
says, "I must ease my mind on a subject that much more nearly concerns me than any
point of business or profit. I must promise to you that Betsy (Eliza) is now very well,
before I tell you abruptly that she has encountered another disappointment and con-
sequent indisposition."

It was not surprising that Sheridan approached the subject of Eliza's miscarriages
with caution, for in a letter of June 26th, his father-in-law had warned him about her
delicate health and mentioned her "seminal weakness." Linley had reinforced his message by adding starkly: "You must absolutely keep from her, for every time you touch
her, you drive a Nail in her Coffin." This must have been a terrifying message for a
young man who was passionately in love with his wife. But it was a harsh age which
accepted infant mortality, the sudden death of the young, and the incessant pregnan-
cies of wives, as all part of life. A beautiful wife was a gift from the gods to Sheridan,
but it was a beauty which was essentially fragile.

In London the Sheridans were already being drawn into the life of fashion.
Crome, which Sheridan mentions in his letter, was the house of the Earl of Coventry.
And in Orchard Street the young Sheridans attracted many new friends and admirers.
Although Sheridan objected to his wife singing in public, he had no objections to her
singing for friends and soon his wit, and her enchanting voice, had made their house
a centre of gaiety. This modish circle of friends was likely to prove an asset to Sheridan's plays.

Apparently *The Rivals* was produced anonymously, although Sheridan had not been
averse to letting all his friends and acquaintances know that he was the author. Possibly it was one of those well-kept open secrets which can produce more publicity than
a play with the author's name on the programme.

The first night of *The Rivals* was on January 17, 1775, at Covent Garden, and the
following was the cast of the characters on the first night:

Sir Anthony Absolute	Mr Shuter
Captain Absolute	Mr Woodward
Faulkland	Mr Lewis
Acres	Mr Quick
Sir Lucius O'Trigger	Mr Lee
Fag	Mr Lee Lewis
David	Mr Dunstal
Coachman	Mr Fearon
Mrs Malaprop	Mrs Green
Lydia Languish	Miss Barsanti
Julia	Mrs Bulkeley
Lucy	Mrs Lessingham

"This comedy," says the prim Mr Moore, "as is well known failed on its first representation, chiefly from the bad acting of Mr Lee in Sir Lucius O'Trigger. Another actor, however, Mr Clinch, was substituted in his place, and the play being lightened of this and some other incumbrances, rose at once into that high region of public favour, where it has continued to float so buoyantly and gracefully ever since."

Behind those clear, simple sentences how many theatrical tantrums and how much green-room drama must lurk: the sacked actor, furious at being bereft of his part: the furious re-writing and cutting of dialogue by Sheridan, working by candlelight. For with the fluttering of fans and bright conversation of an impatient audience, a play could be damned and never seen again.

If eighteenth-century audiences were more restive it is not surprising. They sat on benches without backs, and as the house lights could not be dimmed there was a much more intimate rapport between the actors and the audience than there is in modern times, when a captive audience sits in the dark. Not only could the audience see the actors, but the actors were much more conscious of the audience. And the audience was not disinclined to give the actors a piece of their mind if they felt so inclined, as old Thomas Sheridan well knew, added to which the comings and goings in the side boxes did not help the actors to maintain the illusion.

The evening's entertainment started at six or earlier in winter. As there were no numbered seats, it was the custom in London, as in Dublin, for footmen to keep the seats for the nobility and gentry until they deigned to arrive. But if the seats were not filled by the time the curtain rose then anyone who was waiting for seats could take them. This led to open disputes, with others in the audience joining in the fray about who had priority. Some of the boxes had three tiers of benches which were hinged. Dresses could be torn and hands injured by a quick twist of the wrist, and the constant banging of the seats, and muttered imprecations, was no help to the more tender passages of a play.

Should a play prove popular and all seats be filled, the doors to the pit were screwed up, irrespective of fire dangers, to prove to the disappointed customers that there was positively no room either standing or otherwise. One uncomfortable denizen of the pit who had been trapped in this way yelled out to Mrs Jordan, playing Rosalind in *As You Like It:* "Ma'am, you lady, in boy's clothes, pray order the door to be opened or by God I shall be squeezed to death." As late as 1798 the *Gentleman's Magazine* said, "The spectator is obliged to ask his neighbour's leave to move his own arms and legs."

Another disadvantage to the actors was the fashionable audience in the boxes, for as their names were written in the "Box Book" at the entrance to the theatre, it could be referred to by any passer-by, and often the spectators were as great a draw as the actors. Notice would be taken of the dukes, duchesses, nobility and gentry who were to be present at the evening's performance. Should the play fail to hold the audience's attention, society ladies could be observed chatting and greeting their friends in their boxes. The ladies were gently illuminated by candles or lamps so that their toilettes and jewels could be seen by the *hoi-polloi,* and the actors on the stage in a shaky production thus had a good deal of competition from the feathers and furbelows in the stage boxes.

As many of the spectators could have been waiting for more than two hours, firstly in the street for the doors to be opened, and then jostling in the entrances to buy their un-numbered tickets, by the time they had finally fought their way to their seats they were in no mood for second rate entertainment.

A German traveller remarked:

> "Before the doors are opened, there is generally for an hour and longer such a crowd, and such a mobbing, that many a one, who perhaps is inclined to see a play performed, stays away, because he does not like to be jostled about for such a length of time, among a multitude where the least politeness is entirely out of the question and where pickpockets are extremely busy."

An additional hazard to success was that the theatres were unheated in the winter, and unventilated in the summer. It was not until 1796 that an elegant fireplace was introduced into the Royal Stage Box at Covent Garden Theatre "to the great surprise and no less comfort of their Majesties," said the *Morning Herald.*

Against this background it was not surprising if the success of Sheridan's first comedy trembled in the balance. After the first night, the critics were divided. One said that the "very imperfections of the play showed the man of genius, the gentleman and the scholar." But others voted it a bungle, and insufferably tedious. Some critics took exception to the natural dialogue, and Mrs Malaprop was voted "an exotic beyond the wilds of nature." One correspondent called it a "gulph of malevolence."

The actors did not come off much better. Lydia was informed she was a mere "mimic"; Lewis, who played Faulkland, was said to have "struggled with a very difficult character." Shuter (Sir Anthony) forgot his lines, and Woodward (Captain Absolute) was flattered by being told that he had "often appeared to greater advantage." The actors who played Lucy and Acres "exhibited their accustomed pert maid and country bumpkin." But the main fury of the critics was against Sir Lucius O'Trigger. This was "an affront to common sense, and so far from giving the manners of our brave and worthy neighbours (the Irish) that it scarcely equals the picture of a respectable Hotentot" [*sic*].

On the second night the part of O'Trigger was given to Clinch. But this had little effect at first, and Sheridan in despair wanted to withdraw his piece. But in one of those last minute conferences which are, and always will be, part of theatre life, Harris, the manager, persuaded Sheridan that with a little cutting and revision the play could get by, and the *Morning Chronicle* smugly recorded that the author, "willing to show his obedience to the will of the town, withdraws his comedy that he may prune, correct and alter it, till he thinks it worthy of the public favour."

Eliza was at Slough when the news of the disaster reached her. Her reaction was curious:

> "My dear Dick, I am delighted. I always knew that is was impossible that you could make anything by writing plays; so now there is nothing for it but my beginning to sing publickly again, and we shall have as much money as we like."

The usual offers for Eliza to sing were immediately forthcoming, but Sheridan was still adamant. "No," he said. "That shall never be. I see where the fault was; the play was too long and the parts were badly cast. I profited by his (Harris's) judgment and experience in the curtailing of it—till, I believe, his feeling for the vanity of a young author got the better of his desire for correctness, and he left many excrescences remaining because he had assisted in pruning so many more. Many other errors there were which might in part have arisen from my being by no means conversant with plays in general, either in reading or at the theatre."

The hurried changes were made, and the play reappeared on January 28, 1775. It was played on the same night as a "new musical entertainment called *The Two Misers.*" It should here be explained that an evening's entertainment at the theatre at this time commenced with what could be called a warm-up with a "good band of musick." They usually played two or three selections. If the audience did not like their choice of airs, they would call for something which was more to their taste. After the music came the prologue, then the main play which had two intervals of approximately ten minutes, and then a two-act afterpiece. The afterpiece could be a comedy, a farce, a burletta (an entertainment with music and dancing) or even at times shortened versions of Shakespeare's plays, either tragedies or comedies. Luckily for Sheridan his piece did not have to compete with a slice of *Measure for Measure* or *Romeo and Juliet.*

After the cuts in obedience to the will of the town, the critics changed their tune about *The Rivals.* Although they were still complaining about Lydia, and the attacks on lending libraries, they were even disposed to regret some of the cuts he had made, including Lydia's idea of real love: "How often have I stole forth, in the coldest night in January, and found him in the garden stuck like a dripping statue! And while the freezing blast numbed our joints, how warmly would he press me to pity his flame and glow with mutual ardour! Ah Julia, that was something *like* being in love."

The comedy ran for fourteen nights, which was a very long run. Sheridan's name and reputation were made, but as often with plays, it had been touch and go. Eliza's favourite sister, Mary Linley, wrote to her about the family's hopes and fears:

> "My dearest Eliza,
>
> We are all in the greatest anxiety about Sheridan's play—though I do not think there is the least doubt of its succeeding. I was told last night that it was his own story, and therefore called *The Rivals,* but I do not give any credit to this intelligence."

Possibly the family were bored with scandals about Eliza's suitors, and the human mind is always inclined to believe what it wants to believe. Mary added more practically, "I am told he will get at least £700 for his play." After the productions and the revisions she wrote again:

> Bath, January 1775.
> "It is impossible to tell you what pleasure we felt at the receipt of Sheridan's last letter, which confirmed what we had seen in the newspapers of the success of his play. The *knowing ones* were very much disappointed, as they had so very bad an opinion of its success."

An author can always rely on a circle of friends for discouragement.

"After the first night we were indeed all very fearful that the audience
would go very much against it. But now, there can be no doubt of its success, as it has certainly got through more difficulties than any comedy which
has not met its doom the first night."

Later, presumably after reading the play in Bath, she wrote again in a high state
of excitement.

Bath, February 18, 1775.

"What shall I say of *The Rivals!*—a compliment must naturally be expected;
but really it goes so far beyond anything I *can* say in its praise, that I am
afraid my modesty must keep me silent. When you and I meet I shall be
able better to explain myself, and tell you how much I am delighted with
it. We expect to have it here very soon; it is now in rehearsal. You pretty
well know the merits of our principal performers."

But she gives the cast with pertinent comments on some of the actors whose work, perhaps, her sister did not know:

"Faulkland . . . Mr. Diamond (a new actor of great merit, and a sweet figure).

"Miss Lydia . . . Miss Wheeler (Literally a very pretty romantic girl of
seventeen)."

This last was obviously a nice piece of contemporary type casting.

After the production, Mary reported delightedly:

"I waited the success of Sheridan's play in Bath; for, let me tell you, I look
upon our theatrical tribunal though not in *quantity,* in *quality* as good as
yours, and I do not believe there was a critic in the whole city that was not
there. But, in my life, I never saw anything go off with such uncommon applause. There was a very full house, nor did I hear, for the honour of your
Bath actors, one single prompt the whole night; but I suppose the poor
creatures never acted with shouts of applause in their lives, so that they
were incited by that to do their best. They lost many of Malaprop's good
sayings by the applause; in short, I never saw or heard anything like it;—before the actors spoke, they began their clapping. There was a new scene of
the North Parade, painted by a Mr Davis, and a most delightful one it is,
I assure you. Everybody says that yours in town is not so good. Most of the
dresses were entirely new, and very handsome. We only wanted a good Julia
to have made it quite complete. You must know that it was entirely out of
Mrs Didier's style of playing."

As Mr Didier was playing Captain Absolute, he had obviously wangled a part for
his wife to the detriment of the play. These are the hazards of comedies. Many a good
one has doubtless foundered because the manager put his mistress in a key part. . . .

Interpretation of the Julia/Faulkland scenes is of considerable importance in determining the kind of comedy Sheridan believed he was writing. One way of understanding the play is to see it as part of the attack on stage sentimentality initiated by Goldsmith two years previously, in his "Essay on the Theatre"; from this point of view, Faulkland and Julia must be considered objects of the playwright's ridicule, as the following paragraphs suggest.

[*THE RIVALS* AS AN ATTACK ON SENTIMENTAL COMEDY]
R. Crompton Rhodes

. . . John Bernard, in his *Retrospections of the Stage,* written forty years afterward, gave his own recollections of the first night, in which he describes *The Rivals* as an attack on the sentimental comedy of the period. Sheridan certainly declared it to be such in his Prologue for the Tenth Night, when he mocked at:—

> The Goddess of the woeful countenance,
> The sentimental Muse!

Bernard's account was:

> "It was so intolerably long, and so decidedly opposed in its composition to the taste of the day, as to draw down a degree of censure, which convinced me, on quitting the house, that it would never succeed. It must be remembered that this was the English 'age of sentiment,' and that Hugh Kelly and Cumberland had flooded the Stage with moral poems under the title of Comedies, which took their views of life from the drawing-room exclusively, and coloured their characters with a nauseous French affectation. *The Rivals,* in my opinion, was a decided attempt to overthrow this taste, and to follow up the blow which Goldsmith had given in *She Stoops to Conquer.* My recollection of the manner in which the former was received, bears me out in the supposition. The audience on this occasion were composed of two parties—those who supported the prevailing taste, and those who were indifferent to it and liked nature. On the first night of a new play, it was very natural that the former should predominate;—and what was the consequence? Why, that Faulkland and Julia (which Sheridan had obviously introduced to conciliate the sentimentalists, but which in the present day are considered heavy incumbrances,) were the characters which were most favourably received; whilst Sir Anthony Acres and Lydia, those faithful and diversified pictures of life, were barely tolerated."

Whether Bernard's recollections of Faulkland and Julia were correct or not is doubtful, but they may be left for the moment. "Sentimental comedy" had, besides its modern acceptation, a secondary meaning which it is well to emphasize. Robert Heron in an essay on Comedy in his *Letters of Literature* (1785) lays stress upon this characteristic:

From the Introduction to *The Rivals* in Richard Brinsley Sheridan, *The Plays and Poems of Richard Brinsley Sheridan,* Raymond C. Rhodes, Editor (Oxford: Blackwell, 1929; reprinted New York: Russell & Russell, 1962), Volume 1, pp. 8–10.

"Sentimental Comedy bore a very short sway in England. Indeed it was incompatible with the humour of an English audience, who go to a comedy to laugh, and not to cry. It was even more absurd, it may be added, in its faults than that of which Congreve is the model; for sentiments were spoken by every character in the piece, whereas one sentimental character was surely enough. If a man met with his mistress, or left her; if he was suddenly favoured by fortune, or suddenly the object of her hatred; if he was drunk, or married; he spoke a sentiment: if a lady was angry, or pleased; in love, or out of it; a prude, or a coquet; make room for a sentiment! If a servant girl was chid, or received a present from her mistress; if a valet received a purse, or a horsewhipping; good heavens, what a fine sentiment! . . .

"This fault I say was infinitely more absurd than that of Congreve; for a peasant may blunder on wit, to whose mind sentiment is totally heterogeneous. Besides, Congreve's wit is all his own; whereas most of the said sentiments may be found in the Proverbs of Solomon."

The Rivals was a three-fold attack on "the Sentimental Muse" first, in its return to pure comedy; second, in its exposure of the sentimentalist in real life, as exemplified by Faulkland; and third, in its playful ridicule of "the pernicious effect of the sentimental novel." The last, I think, was the initial dramatic motive. . . .

The failure of Sheridan's first version of The Rivals *and the success of his revision tell us something not only about English taste in 1775 but also about the characteristics of the play itself. C. J. L. Price touches upon these issues, and in particular attempts to assess the intention of the scenes involving Julia and Faulkland: are these scenes sentimental, or a satire on the sentimental, or an odd mixture of both?*

THE RIVALS
C. J. L. Price

The Covent Garden company had scored its greatest recent success in Goldsmith's *She Stoops to Conquer* (15 March 1773), and had gone on acting it, from time to time, ever since. Before Sheridan completed *The Rivals*, he could have seen the company in *She Stoops* on two occasions, 21 September and 8 November. We do not know that he did so, but it is interesting to speculate what the effect on him would have been, for *The Rivals*, like *She Stoops*, is a comedy based on farce and theatrical types. It is even more thought-provoking to observe that three of the actors and two of the actresses from this cast were also to take part in the first performance of *The Rivals*. Edward

From the Introduction to Richard Brinsley Sheridan, *The Rivals*, ed. C. J. L. Price (London: Oxford University Press, 1968), pp. 8–12. © Oxford University Press. Reprinted by permission of Oxford University Press, Oxford.

Shuter played droll old gentlemen, so he was Mr. Hardcastle and Sir Anthony. John Quick played young, countrified squires, and was a natural Tony Lumpkin as well as Bob Acres. Lee Lewes liked portraying the slightly arrogant, and took Young Marlow and Fag. Mrs. Green shone as the would-be gentlewoman full of airs and graces, so she created Mrs. Hardcastle and Mrs. Malaprop. Mrs. Bulkley excelled as the lively, open young woman, so was Kate Hardcastle and Julia.

Within a year Sheridan was to show how carefully he studied the capabilities of the likely performers in his plays when fitting out parts for them to act, and it seems likely that he took the same attitude now. Of course, there were several leading members of the cast of *The Rivals* who were not in *She Stoops,* but he could easily have noted their particular talents by a few nights' attendance at the playhouse. Henry Woodward, who played Jack Absolute, had recently acted Mercutio. W. T. Lewis (Faulkland) had been seen as Romeo, and John Lee (Sir Lucius), as Benedick.

The first performance of *The Rivals* took place on 17 January 1775, and was not a success. Sir Joshua Reynolds's nephew, writing a few weeks later, said it "but just escaped" damnation, "though some people admire it." This ambiguous result was caused partly by the play itself and partly by the incompetence of some of the actors. The prompter could be heard constantly when Shuter and Lee were on stage, and Lee was undoubtedly miscast as Sir Lucius. The comedy was criticized as being much too long and containing weak puns and coarse innuendoes.

The play might never have been performed again, but Thomas Harris was still enthusiastic and he insisted on Sheridan's revising it in the light of these criticisms. Fortunately the twenty-three-year-old dramatist was to show considerable talent as a "play doctor," and he saw just how the comedy could be improved. Later he said he looked upon the first-night audience as "a candid and judicious friend attending in behalf of the public, at his last rehearsal." That was more than an excuse for his own inexperience: it was an acknowledgement of what an audience could teach a young playwright about the nature of his craft and the taste of the day.

His own admiration for Congreve's *The Old Bachelor* (1693) and Vanbrugh's *The Relapse* (1696) had been evident, but he now had to learn that the wildness and freedom of speech of Restoration dramatists were no longer socially acceptable. He must capture their gusto without their grossness. He must remember that a mid-eighteenth century audience prided itself on its decorum, sensibility, and critical perception. So some of the coarseness associated with Sir Anthony's part and the more bizarre wordplay given to Acres and Mrs. Malaprop, were deleted. Sir Lucius was converted from a rather stupid fortune-hunter into a peremptory man of honour. Some scenes were removed, some speeches tightened, and the whole play was subtly given a more definite shape.

The revised version was presented on 28 January with the same cast, except for Lee. His place was taken by Laurence Clinch, a newcomer to the company but an old friend of the Sheridans. Loud applause greeted his Sir Lucius, and the play was generally admired. David Garrick, manager of the rival theatre, remarked early in the evening, "I see this play will creep." At the end he had to say, "I see this play will run."

It has been consistently successful ever since, and it is not difficult to understand why it has achieved such a place in the repertory. For one thing, it is full of the vitality, and the exaggerations, of youth. Acres and Mrs. Malaprop use language oddly but with great spirit. Sir Lucius and Lydia behave capriciously according to some high-flown code of their own. All four struggle to live in a world of their own making, and are fit subjects for laughter because their self-satisfaction is not justified. Yet while they may be foolish in some respects, they are by no means fools, and the process of stripping them of their self-regard is accompanied by felicities of language as well as verbal oddities.

The dialogue of the comic scenes is very well turned, and has a jauntiness and an ingenuity that comes over superbly.

The play has, too, a neat plot that develops amusingly and very clearly. The scenes move on briskly to make their points. Jack's downright refusal to marry the girl his father chooses for him, changes to eager acquiescence as soon as he finds that she is his adored Lydia, and to equal dismay when she objects to anything but a romantic elopement. Similarly, Sir Anthony demands that his son should give him implicit obedience, but is far from satisfied when Jack says that he is willing to marry niece or aunt:

> SIR ANTHONY: . . . The aunt, indeed! Odds life! when I ran away with your mother, I would not have touched anything old or ugly to gain an empire.
> ABSOLUTE: Not to please your father, sir?

This ability to turn the situation completely is one of Sheridan's great gifts, and in this example and a few others, the reversals spring from character.

In neither farce nor comedy of manners is it really necessary to develop character, for the interest of the one depends on situation and that of the other on ridiculing unusual behaviour. Consequently Malaprop, Languish, and O'Trigger, are merely what their names suggest. Only one relationship is developed beyond the requirements of the plot: that between father and son is touched in with a nice irony and a rich humour. In fact, their scenes have an imaginative force that makes them stand out in the theatre.

This is also the place to appreciate best the Julia/Faulkland scenes that appear so mawkish to modern readers. The eighteenth-century audience was moved by them, and the *Morning Post*, 24 January 1775, wrote that "the exquisite refinement in his [Faulkland's] disposition, opposed to the noble simplicity, tenderness, and candour of Julia's, give rise to some of the most affecting sentimental scenes." Julia still has all these virtues, but Faulkland seems fretful, and his language artificial, to the point of mania. Yet, watching him on the stage, we can make allowances: he is in love, and lovers are commonly jealous, prickly, and tiresome people. Although the prologue for the tenth night suggests that mockery of "the Sentimental Muse" was intended, no one can see the play without perceiving that while Sheridan laughed at Faulkland, he also luxuriated in his feverish sensibility. The reason is obvious: in Sheridan's own temperament there was an uneasy mixture of the satirical and the sentimental. In this comedy he was to reconcile these opposites to brilliant effect.

In a review of a recent revival of Sheridan's play, Stanley Price analyzes various ways of acting the roles and describes what he feels to have been only a moderately successful production.

THE RIVALS [IN A 1971 PRODUCTION]
Stanley Price

One of our daily theatre critics pointed out à propos this season's Chichester Festival programme that "the theatre is settling into a comfortable policy of middle-brow plays with star leads, and for better or worse this expectation is confirmed by its opening production."

I would not question his judgement, only his news sense. This policy has been evident at Chichester for several seasons now. The setting is still delightful, the efficient theatre-restaurant still serves its early-season, imported strawberries, the warning fanfares still reverberate regally round the well-groomed lawns.

This is typified, in the present production of *The Rivals*, by the fact that Carl Toms' attractive stage furniture is constantly changed by a dozen or so beautifully-liveried footmen who come on at evening's end carrying large, lighted candelabras. Chichester audiences still tend to dress for the occasion, and it is comforting for them to know the stage-management have done the same.

The current production illustrates another of the theatre's problems—the growing gulf between the old stars and the new, something which only firm and imaginative direction can solve. As in other recent productions, the stars come out and do their time-honoured thing, delighting if not exactly surprising their audiences, while the younger members of the cast seem strait-jacketed in productions that move about them with a certain military precision, and yet remain rather static and flat. Instead of the cast using that difficult but splendid stage, it now seems to be using them.

In terms of individual performance it is hard to fault any of the male leads in this production of *The Rivals*. As Sir Anthony Absolute, John Clements gives his definitive display of controlled anger running off the rails. His performance is a series of spluttering and exploding fireworks, but as a director Clements has failed to pull the whole together and strike enough sparks. In Peter Egan he has a Jack Absolute of striking presence with an attractive warmth and wryness, and from Edward Fox and Clive Swift there are two wonderfully comic performances. Yet the director seems to have preserved all three of these fine performances in aspic rather than integrating them into the fabric of the play.

Edward Fox plays Maitland as an eighteenth century forerunner of Count Sascher-Masoch, gaining an almost hysterical pleasure out of each of love's new torments. It is a wildly funny over-stated performance that could only be improved if the director had damped down a little of the initial over-statement. Clive Swift's ability to combine pathos with his clowning creates a Bob Acres comically aspiring to urban gentility while still trying to preserve his sensible rural skin intact. Only in the scenes Acres has with Sir Lucius O'Trigger is there a slight hiatus. Hubert Gregg, an actor whose

Stanley Price, "The Rivals [Review]," *Plays and Players*, vol. 18, no. 9 (June 1971), pp. 42 and 63. Reprinted by permission of the author.

forte is understated comedy, lacks the broad Irish panache for Sir Lucius, so that his goading of Acres becomes incongruously downbeat.

For the women, however, the situation is less happy. With the casting of Margaret Leighton as Mrs Malaprop one had hoped for something original and one is disappointed to have this promise only half-fulfilled. Her Mrs Malaprop is not the traditional vulgarian. She has a certain class, and is socially at home in the life of the Spa. Her endearing assaults on the language are never over-played. Unfortunately, Miss Leighton's costume, padding, wig and makeup remain in the pantomime tradition so that there is an uneasy gap between the possible initial intention and the final execution.

As for the young heroines, Lydia Languish and Julia Melville, this production comes no nearer solving the perennial problem of how to make Sheridan's heroines other than vapid debs, early prototypes of Cheltenham Ladies College who left before taking "0" levels. Possibly the answer to these traditionally unrewarding parts is a more careful consideration of the erotic character of the ladies in question, and of Sheridan's own satiric intention. Sheridan does state early in the play "And the cause of all this is love." It is said tongue-in-cheek, and Sheridan then sets out to satirise all the fashionable attitudes that forget the cause and object of that relationship in the excitement of intrigue and the mercenary social conventions of matchmaking.

The choice of the name Languish does suggest some early vision of Freudian vapours, and Lydia's fantasies about Beverley, part Valentino-crush, part teenage revolt, can lend themselves to both comedy and sensuality rather than the traditional straight-playing of a tiresome ninny conceived only as a butt for the author's satire. Angela Scoular, as a Lydia all wide-eyes and pouts, plumps for the latter approach, while Joanna David, as Julia, gives an equally simplistic interpretation, reacting with rather limp sincerity to all Maitland's masochistic writhings. The production has its straightforward pleasures, but overall one wishes that John Clements, as director of both the Festival and the initial production, had got the season off to a more flying start.

The Wild Duck

In her incisive essay on The Wild Duck, *the novelist and critic Mary McCarthy discusses the chief themes and techniques of the play and explains why she believes that only in this work (and in* Hedda Gabler*) did Ibsen shed his defects as a playwright and produce a "near-masterpiece."*

THE WILL AND TESTAMENT OF IBSEN
Mary McCarthy

GINA	Wasn't that a queer thing to say—that he'd like to be a dog?
HEDWIG	I tell you what, Mother. I think he meant something else by that.
GINA	What else could he mean?
HEDWIG	Well, I don't know; but it was as though he meant something else all the time—and not what he said.

*T*his short catechism—from the second act of *The Wild Duck*—is at first sight only a sort of road sign to the audience to look out for curves ahead. Hjalmar Ekdal's wife and daughter are discussing his friend, Gregers, the meddling fanatic who has inserted himself into the family speaking a dark language and pressing what he calls the claim of the ideal. In the scene just before he has expressed the wish to be a dog—an "extraordinarily clever dog. The kind that goes to the bottom after wild duck when they dive down and bite fast hold of the weeds and the tangle down in the mud." Translated out of this idiom into plain speech, this means that Gregers sees himself as the rescuer of the household which his father (the hunter) has wounded and sent down into the depths. These depths, ironically, are located in an attic, where Hjalmar, who plays the flute and has a windy, "artistic" personality, also plays at being a professional photographer and inventor while his wife does the hard work. In the neighboring garret room, behind a curtain, Hjalmar's disgraced, drunken old father, wearing a brown wig and his lieutenant's uniform, plays at being a hunter with an old double-barreled pistol, some barnyard fowls, pigeons, rabbits, and a real wild duck. Father and son "go hunting" in this make-believe forest, which is rather like photographers' scenery. Hedwig, the percipient little girl, who is not Hjalmar's real daughter but the illegitimate child of Gregers' father, is going blind. This blindness is a metaphor for the state of darkened self-deception in which the little family lives. Gregers believes that he has the duty to *open Hjalmar's eyes* to the true facts of his marriage. At the house of Gregers' father, who is also losing his sight, they are drinking Tokay wine and playing Blind Man's Buff.

In short, as Hedwig indicates to her uninstructed mother, the dramatist means something else all the time and not what he says. Everything, Hedwig precociously understands, is symbolic. The real wild duck is the child, Hedwig, who picks up Gregers' "loaded" suggestion and shoots herself. The tragic climax of *The Wild Duck* is brought about, thus, by an act of over-interpretation. Gregers, for once, was speaking literally when he said to the little girl: "But suppose, now, that you of your own free will, sacri-

Mary McCarthy, "The Will and Testament of Ibsen," in her *Theatre Chronicles 1937–1962* (New York: Farrar, Straus, 1963), pp. 168–178. Copyright © 1937, 1938, 1940, 1943, 1944, 1945, 1946, 1947, 1948, 1949, 1954, 1955, 1956, 1957, 1958, 1959, 1961, 1962, 1963 by Mary McCarthy. Reprinted by permission of Farrar, Straus & Giroux, Inc.

ficed the wild duck for *his* sake?" But Hedwig, confused and terrified the next morning by her supposed father's harshness (for Hjalmar's eyes have at last been opened), thinks that she has finally grasped Gregers' under-meaning and, presuming that she is the "sacrifice" alluded to, goes into the garret room and puts the pistol to her breast.

This ending, like so many of Ibsen's dramatic finales ("The mill race! The mill race!"), seems a little heavy and strained, like the last crashing chords of movie music. Yet it is utterly just. The child's suggestibility has a semantic grounding. She has been led by the Higher Critics around her to look for the real reality under the surface of language—that is, to schematize her life as she lives it. Gregers, with his "claim of the ideal," Hjalmar, with his talk of "a task in life," are both inveterate schematizers, one a truth-speaker, the other an aesthetician. As his wife says of Hjalmar, "Surely you realize, Mr. Werle, that my husband isn't one of those ordinary photographers." Everything has conspired to make Hedwig distrust the *ordinary* way of looking at things. In a peculiarly sinister scene in the third act, Gregers has been talking to Hedwig about the garret room where the wild duck lives. She tells him that sometimes the whole room and all the things in it seem to her like "the ocean's depths," and then she adds: "But that's so silly."

> GREGERS   No, you mustn't say that.
> HEDWIG   It is; because it's only an attic.
> GREGERS   *(looking hard at her)*. Are you so sure of that?
> HEDWIG   *(astonished)*. That it's an attic?
> GREGERS   Yes. Do you know that for certain? *(Hedwig is silent, looking at him with an open mouth.)*

Gregers preaches mysteries. Hjalmar's daily conversation is a flow of oratory. He always speaks of his brown-wigged bald father as "the white-haired old man." And his pretended "purpose in life" is a sort of parody of Gregers' "purpose to live for." Hjalmar too conceives of himself as a savior, the rescuer of his father. "Yes, I will rescue that ship-wrecked man. For he was ship-wrecked when the storm broke loose on him . . . That pistol there, my friend—the one we use to shoot rabbits with—it has played its part in the tragedy of the House of Ekdal." Again, a flight of metaphors, more disjointed and *ad libitum* in Hjalmar's case, a fact which points to the difference between the two rhetoricians. Hjalmar improvises idly on the instrument of language, but Gregers is in earnest, with his single unifying metaphor, of the duck and the bird dog and the hunter, which he pursues to the fearful end.

The men are poet-idealists; Hedwig is a budding poetess. Gina, the uneducated wife, belongs to the prosy multitude that was patronized earlier in the century by Wordsworth: "A primrose by the river's brim, A yellow primrose was to him. And it was nothing more." "That there blessed wild duck," she exclaims. "The fuss there is over it!" When Gregers, true to his metaphor, speaks of the "swamp vapor" that is morally poisoning the Ekdal household, Gina retorts: "Lord knows there's no smell of swamps here, Mr. Werle; I air the place out every blessed day."

The Wild Duck was written in the middle of Ibsen's career, after *Pillars of Society, A Doll's House, Ghosts, An Enemy of the People* and before the sequence of plays beginning with *Rosmersholm*. Ibsen regarded it as a departure from his earlier work, and it is often taken to be a satiric repudiation of "the Ibsenites" or even of Ibsen himself as a crusading social dramatist. In the figure of Gregers Werle, an ugly man in a countrified gray suit who appears on his mission of truth to rip the veil of illusion from a satisfied household, it is certainly possible to see a cruel self-portrait of the dramatic author who sought to "let in the air" on the stuffy Norwegian community, to expose its hypocrisy and commercial chicanery, its enslavement to a notion of duty and to a sentimentalized picture of family life. Gregers Werle's harping on the concept of "a true marriage," which shall not be based on lies and concealment, is certainly a mocking echo of the doctrines of *Ghosts* and *A Doll's House*. Moreover, Gregers Werle has been a radical before the opening of the play, and Ibsen, though he was a stock figure of respectability in private life, looked upon himself as a radical, even an anarchist, and throughout his plays, up to the very end, there is a doctrinal insistence on freedom and the necessity of self-realization that today has a somewhat period and moralistic flavor, as though the notion of duty, reappearing in the guise of Duty to Oneself, had become, if anything, more puritan, more rigid, more sternly forbidding, than the notion of duty to God or family or bourgeois custom. If Gregers Werle is Ibsen in his tendentious and polemical aspect, then indeed he is a demon that Ibsen is trying to cast out through the exorcism of this play—a grotesque and half-pathetic demon, in that he will never understand anything concrete, a demon, in fact, of abstraction who bursts into the play with his ugly face and ugly name like some parochial incorruptible Robespierre whose activities are circumscribed by a sad fate to the reform of a single bohemian family. But if Gregers Werle represents the demand for truth in its ultimate, implacable form, then the message of the play is, as some critics have said, cynical and nihilistic, since the converse of Gregers is a Dr. Relling, a lodger downstairs who believes that lies and illusions are necessary to human survival.

A softer reading of Ibsen's intention suggests that Gregers represents only the eternal interfering busybody, but this reduces the play to a platitude—an object-lesson in what happens when an outsider tries to tell married people how to run their lives. Shaw's opinion was that Gregers is simply a particularly dangerous case of idealism and duty on the rampage, and according to Shaw's thesis Ibsen spent his life doing doughty battle against the joint forces of duty and idealism—the vested interests of the day. But Ibsen was a more divided nature than Shaw allowed for, and the battle was within.

Ibsen is not an attractive personality, and his work has, intermittently, a curious confessional closet-smell, as though he were using his play-writing as a form of psychotherapy. This is especially noticeable in *The Master Builder,* where the hero is Ibsen in a symbolic disguise. The master builder (read sound dramatic craftsman) has first built churches (the early poetic plays), then houses for people to live in (the social dramas), and is finally erecting houses with steeples (the late, symbolic plays). This hero, Master Solness, is very darkly motivated; there has been a fire, years ago, through which, indirectly, he and his wife lost their children, but which, at the same time, permitted him to start on his successful career as a builder and real-estate developer. Now he is obsessed with jealousy of younger men in his profession, and he is suffering from a failure of nerve, which is connected with the fire, perhaps, or with his wife's compulsive sense of duty and her invalidism or with his abandonment of church architecture. The play is strangely thin, more like a scenario with several writers contributing suggestions in a story conference than like a finished play, and throughout its jerky development, there is a sense of something elusive, as though Ibsen, again, like Gregers Werle, meant something else all the time and not what he said. There is the same odd feeling in *Rosmersholm,* which is full of disjointed references, like the talk of an insane person—what are those white horses, really, and what is the mill race, and what is that quest for total innocence, on which the play seems to turn and yet not to turn?

The idea of guilt for some sin of the past, a sin, even, of the fathers, plays a great part in Ibsen. Like many of his characters, he has a secret in his early life—a poor girl whom he got in trouble and left to fend for herself. Hereditary disease, illegitimacy, the death of children haunt the Ibsen world; they are all in *The Wild Duck.* In the early plays, the guilt or the sin is localized; we know what the protagonist has done, in the past, which will spring the trap on him. But in the later plays, starting with *Rosmersholm,* the guilt has become diffuse, and it is no longer clear what is the matter. A kind of corny symbolism replaces the specific fact in the mechanism of the plot—white horses, steeples, trolls, a sailor, a mermaid, and the sea and a ring. And these symbols, which are only vague portents, correspond to a vague ache or yearning in the breasts of the principal characters, who talk about themselves distractedly, as though they were relating their symptoms in a session of group analysis. *Hedda Gabler* is an exception; next to *The Wild Duck,* it is Ibsen's most successful play. Hedda does not discuss herself; the General's daughter is too haughty for that. Instead, she behaves, and the subject of the play is visibly present, as it was in *The Doll's House,* as it still is in *The Wild Duck.* Her suicide at the end is less convincing than her burning of the manuscript, and her burning of the manuscript is less convincing than the transfixing moment in the first act when she pretends to think that the aunt's new hat, lying on the sofa, is the servant's old bonnet. But Ibsen is not very good at making big events happen; he is better at the small shocking event, the psychopathology of everyday life: Hedda and her husband's aunt's hat, Nora, when she nonchalantly pushes off the sewing on her poor widowed friend, Christine, Hjalmar, when he talks himself into letting Hedwig with her half-blind eyes do his retouching for him so that he can go off and play hunter with his father in the attic, Hjalmar cutting his father at the Werle soirée, Hjalmar eating butter obliviously while his hungry daughter watches him. These are the things one knows oneself to be capable of. If the larger gestures are less credible in Ibsen, this is possibly because of his very success in the realistic convention, which implies a norm of behavior on the part of its guilty citizens within their box-like living rooms. The realistic convention requires credibility, that is, a statistical norm; the audience must believe that the people on the stage are more or less like themselves, no worse and no better, in short, that they are ordinary, restrained by cowardice or public opinion from stooping too low or rising too high. The faculty for determining likelihood or credibility becomes more and more highly developed—a sensitized measuring instrument— as a society becomes more homogeneous and parochial and less stratified in terms of class.

But this very ordinariness, this exaction of truth to life, is a limitation on an artist, especially on one with "titanic" ambitions, like Ibsen. And this is where symbolism enters, as a device to deepen or heighten the realistic drama while keeping it within the frame of the three-wall stage. Symbolic thinking was already natural to him, as *Peer Gynt* and *Brand* indicate. Here, however, it was used in the old-fashioned way, to sustain a philosophical argument, that is, to make abstractions concrete and visible, with the text of the play serving as a kind of libretto to the music of the thought behind it. But starting with *Pillars of Society,* Ibsen began to reverse the process—to make the concrete abstract, in the "coffin-ships," whose rotting hulls are supposed to symbolize the whole of Norwegian society. But the temptation of this new, allusive method (the method described by Hedwig in the passage quoted) was that it led to grandiosity and cunning or more precisely, to the kind of schematic thinking exemplified by Gregers Werle, this schematic thinking being really a form of God-identification, in which the symbolist imposes on the concrete, created world his own private design and lays open to question the most primary facts of existence, i.e., whether an attic is "really" an attic or is not in fact a swamp or something else. The allusive, hinting language employed by Gregers is the language of all messianic individuals and interfering, paranoid prophets. And like Hjalmar's sentimental flow of metaphor, it is the language of bad art, art that is really religion or edification. This type of symbolism is often found in sermons and in addresses by college presidents, who liken the institution to a ship, themselves to the pilot at the helm, etc.

Ibsen sees all this in Gregers, and he sees, furthermore, that Gregers is incurable. In his last speech of the play, Gregers has merely shifted metaphors: "GREGERS *(looking in front of him)*. In that case, I am glad my destiny is what it is. RELLING. May I ask— what *is* your destiny? GREGERS *(on the point of going)*. To be thirteenth at table." This cryptic and portentous remark means something more than it says, evidently—either that the speaker is going to commit suicide or that he sees himself from henceforth as the odd, unassimilable man, the bird of ill omen, and that he finds a mysterious satisfaction in the picture.

Odious, baneful creature. And yet one cannot throw off the feeling that Gregers is something more than a repudiation of an earlier stage in the author's development. As in *The Master Builder,* where Solness is fond of likening himself fatly to a troll, there is a sense of confession here which lingers in that last remark and far from rounding off the play leaves it hanging, like an unanswered doubt. The fact is, in any case, that Ibsen, if he did unburden himself of a certain amount of self-dislike through the medium of Gregers, did not follow this up with any reforms. Quite the contrary. In the light of the later plays, this confession appears as a sort of indulgence bought for all future sins. The wild duck in the attic is revived as the carp in the pond of *The Lady from the Sea,* and here it is the *sympathetic* characters who hint that the carp is "really" a symbol of themselves in their brackish village. The pietistic talk of a "task" or a "purpose in life," which has already been heard in *A Doll's House,* is not silenced by the pistol shot in *The Wild Duck;* it breaks out again, irrepressibly, in *Rosmersholm,* in *The Lady from the Sea,* and even in *Hedda Gabler;* once more it is the sympathetic characters who voice the notions of Gregers and Hjalmar and who allegorize themselves as instruments of a hidden Will. The plays grow more grandiose as the symbolic content inflates them, and the scenery changes to cliffs and mountain tops that evoke the painted canvas settings of Hjalmar's photographic studio.

No doubt there is a good deal of bathetic "studio" art in all the great late nine-teenth-century writers, with the exception of Tolstoy. It is in Dickens and George Eliot and Dostoevsky, certainly; they paid for being titans and for the power to move a mass audience by a kind of auto-intoxication or self-hypnosis that allowed them to manipulate their emotions like a stage hand cranking out a snowstorm from a machine containing bits of paper. This effect of false snow falling on a dramatic scene is more noticeable in Ibsen than in any of his great coevals, and he left it as his legacy to the American school of playwrights, to O'Neill and now Tennessee Williams, Arthur Miller, and William Inge. (Shaw, who considered himself indebted to Ibsen, never learned anything from him, for he did not work in the realistic convention, though he may not always have been aware of the fact.) If Ibsen's followers are not better than they are, this may be partly because the master, compared to the great architect-novelists of his period, was only a master builder. The "Freudian" character of his symbols has often been remarked upon, and perhaps his most important contribution was clinical: he was the first to put a neurotic woman—Hedda, Ellida Wangel, Mrs. Solness, Nora—on the stage.

But his work, viewed as a whole, seems at once repetitive and inchoate. Twice, in *Hedda Gabler* and *The Wild Duck,* he created a near-masterpiece. The rest of his career appears as a series of false starts and reverses in an interior conversation that keeps lapsing into reverie. The goal of all Ibsen's heroes and heroines—self-realization—looms throughout his plays like one of his symbolic mountain peaks, which the toiling author himself could never reach.

Maurice Valency's book The Flower and the Castle *is a study of the conventional nineteenth-century drama from which Ibsen learned much of his dramatic technique and against which he struggled throughout his career. The following excerpt shows how, in* The Wild Duck, *Ibsen transformed what might have been a typical* pièce à thèse *(a play attempting to demonstrate a thesis about society, the family, or individual behavior) into a new kind of play which was to have great influence on the modern theatre.*

[*THE WILD DUCK* AND THE CONVENTIONAL THESIS PLAY]
Maurice Valency

. . . Ibsen spent rather more than a year thinking about this play; then he wrote it quickly. In June of 1883 he had written to Georg Brandes that he was contemplating a new play in four acts. A year later he wrote to Theodor Caspari: "I have just finished a play in five acts, that is to say, the rough draft; now comes the elaboration, the more energetic individualization of the persons and their mode of expression." At the beginning of September, 1884, he sent the manuscript to Hegel for publication,

From Maurice Valency, *The Flower and the Castle* (New York: Grosset and Dunlap, 1966), pp. 168–176. Originally published by Macmillan, 1963. Reprinted by permission of the author.

with a letter expressing his belief that he had done something new: "This new play in many ways occupies a place of its own among my dramas; the method is in various respects a departure from my earlier one. I do not want to say any more about this for the present. The critics will, I hope, find the points; in any case, they will find plenty to quarrel about, plenty to misinterpret . . ."

He was disappointed in his expectations. Although it was hissed a little at the opening performance in Copenhagen, the play was successful enough in the Scandinavian theatres; but the critics made little of it one way or the other. It was applauded in Berlin, howled down in Rome, received with indifference in Paris, and with frigidity in London. In a review of a series of Ibsen's plays, published in 1889, Edmund Gosse echoed, with characteristic acumen, what many had already said of *The Wild Duck:* "This is a very long play, by far the most extended of the series, and is, on the whole, the least interesting to read . . . There is really not a character in the book that inspires confidence or liking . . . There can be no doubt that it is by far the most difficult of Ibsen's for a reader to comprehend." But Bernard Shaw wrote in 1897, "Where shall I find an epithet magnificent enough for *The Wild Duck!*"

It was not immediately apparent in what way *The Wild Duck* seemed to Ibsen to mark a new departure in his method. Its style seems to be a development of the technique of *Ghosts,* and it resembles that play in more than one respect. Like *Ghosts* it involves a tragic action played, in part, by comic characters, and its effect is similarly strange. Structurally, it falls into the familiar mold of Second Empire drama. It is, in some respects, a *pièce à thèse* which demonstrates the advantages of domestic life, and the folly of destroying the home because of some supposed flaw in its moral foundation. As this thesis involves the idea that the paramount concern of the parents is the happiness of the children, it seems well out of line with the doctrine we associate with *A Doll's House.*

Up to a certain point, *The Wild Duck* was a rearrangement of materials that had already seen service. The chambermaid who was palmed off with a dowry upon the carpenter Engstrand in *Ghosts* becomes here the chambermaid Gina Hansen, who is bestowed in similar fashion upon Hjalmar Ekdal. Captain Alving's illegitimate daughter Regina has her equivalent in Hedvig, who inherits, like Osvald, the paternal infirmity, in this case a tendency to blindness. Haakon Werle appears to be a version of Consul Bernick in *Pillars of Society* and, like him, he has permitted his friend to expiate a crime he himself committed. Gregers Werle is in the nature of a vindictive Osvald come home to confront his father with the sins of his past.

The plot of *The Wild Duck* hangs upon a situation of the utmost banality. A husband discovers that his wife was pregnant by another man when he married her fifteen years before; in righteous anger, he casts her off and disowns his child, who thereupon kills herself. The death of the innocent child reunites the family in sorrow. The moral of the play is then announced by the family doctor: "It is best not to stir up old troubles." The English reviewer in *The Athenaeum* for May 12, 1894, commented: "The play must be a joke . . . it is a harmless, if not very humourous piece of self-banter, or it is nothing."

One might be excused for considering *The Wild Duck* a clumsy travesty. The play has a proper undercurrent of sentimentality, but the plot is all askew. The outraged husband is caricatured to the point of clownishness; the faithless wife is the mainstay of the family; they are all living on the proceeds of the sin on which their establishment is based; and the canonical scenes of accusation and reproach are all comic. Only the child suffers; and the introduction of a tragic note into a distinctly comic situation might well seem an unpardonable incongruity. At any rate, the melodramatic elements of the familiar play of transgression and retribution are obviously deformed in accordance with a new and radical concept. The figures and the design of the narrative are all recognizably traditional, but the manner of their representation goes somewhat beyond the demands of realism. One's first impression is of a familiar scene viewed in a distorting mirror. In fact, the technique is analytical in a manner that suggests the post-impressionists; and it is perhaps to an innovation of this sort that Ibsen referred in his covering letter to the publisher.

It is interesting to see how Ibsen arrived at the novel effect of *The Wild Duck*. He began with a theme on which he had already played several variations. Driven by an exaggerated sense of guilt, the idealistic Gregers comes as a savior to set the Ekdal family free through the truth. In precisely this manner, Julian came to liberate the world, and Brand to save it. The Ekdal family, however, has no use for the truth. It has managed in its misery to find a way of life which approximates happiness, and it would prefer to be left in peace. As old Ekdal demonstrates, the human soul has considerable ingenuity; it can construct a forest in an attic; it can build, if necessary, a world in a shoebox. The illusion serves quite as well as the reality so long as it is not disturbed. Consequently, nobody thanks Gregers for his idealistic efforts. On the contrary, his meddling results only in irreparable misfortune.

The doctrine that Dr. Relling, the *raisonneur* of the play, makes explicit in *The Wild Duck* is thus seen to be the same that was implicit in *Brand* and in *Emperor and Galilean,* and which was advanced cynically in *An Enemy of the People;* it is quite opposed to the idea we associate with the Ibsen of *Ghosts* and *Pillars of Society.* In these two plays it is Ibsen's position that felicity must be based on health, and that health, from the social standpoint, depends upon truth. The superstructure, however elaborate, that is raised on a false foundation must sooner or later topple: a house built on a lie cannot stand. If one is to have stability, the lie must be uprooted, the house must be rebuilt; and the event that brings about this outcome, no matter how disagreeable, is prophylactic and providential. *The Wild Duck,* however, depends on a less heroic concept. Dr. Relling in effect reiterates the words of Agnes when she exclaims at the folly of exacting All or Nothing from the human race in its poverty. In a world miserably patched together of lies and fancies, it is best to let things alone. Men have no use for truth: illusion alone makes life tolerable. "Rob a man of his life-lie," says Dr. Relling, "and you rob him of his happiness." Unlike Gregers, who pins his faith on the surgical efficacy of truth, Relling devises opiates for the incurable. Gregers demands All or Nothing; Relling speaks for the spirit of compromise which is the practical aspect of *deus caritatis.*

To illuminate these ideas in the situation of *The Wild Duck* it was necessary to destroy the theatrical conventions relating to the play of the deceived husband. Dumas would have done this through argument. Ibsen did it through laughter. Gregers reveals his secret to Hjalmar with theatrical impressiveness, and Hjalmar reacts as people do in plays, assumes the appropriate postures and speaks the time-honored lines. But it is clear that he is going through the necessary formalities of the outraged spouse without real conviction, and the resulting scenes are broadly comic. In the midst of a situation that rapidly becomes ridiculous, the action is brought up sharply by the sudden death of Hedvig, and the play acquires abruptly another dimension. The action has proceeded unobtrusively along several levels of reality simultaneously; all at once it is seen that what had no reality for some evidently had terrible reality for others. For Hjalmar, the deception that has shaped his life has not even as much validity as the forest primeval in the attic. His sufferings are largely histrionic. But for Hedvig, his sufferings are supremely real, and she must buy them with her life. The conclusion is plain: in this world it is necessary to look out above all for those who are capable of suffering. These are the sensitive children of life, the nobility of the race, and their lot is tragic. The rest are drugged to the point of insensibility. To expect of them a tragic response to life is to invite absurdity; and this truth is in its implications, perhaps, more poignant than the conventional tragedy of the theatre.

The development of *The Wild Duck,* like that of Turgeniev's *A Month in the Country,* or Chekhov's *Uncle Vanya,* is of the order of a chemical reaction. Into a situation which appears calm and limpid, a reagent is introduced. At once hidden tensions are released, the thing seethes, rages, and gives off fumes. There is a precipitation. Then equilibrium is re-established. Once again calm descends upon the scene, and it is as if nothing had happened; yet everything is changed. It is a simple and effective way of arranging a dramatic action, and quite different from the Scribean contest of intriguers.

The eruption of Gregers into the tranquil world of the Ekdals is very skillfully managed. There is the charming family scene reminiscent of a contemporary genre-painting—the father playing a Bohemian dance on the flute, the mother and daughter grouped happily about him. We are vaguely aware of discordant elements in this scene; nevertheless, it is a tableau suitable for framing. Now comes Gregers, a disagreeable man, advancing "the claims of the ideal," and he reveals their life for what it is—a patchwork of lies and pretenses, a tissue of illusion as pathetic as the imitation forest in the attic.

His motives are decidedly more questionable than Dr. Stockmann's in *An Enemy of the People;* but they are of the same order. Ostensibly he is interested only in truth and justice. In reality, he is a sadistic busybody, and he has personal reasons, besides, for wishing to embarrass his father. Whatever his inner motives may be, however, he has rationalized them in terms of his missionary zeal. He thinks of himself as a rescuer of fallen souls, "a really absurdly clever dog; the sort that goes in after wild ducks when they dive down and bite themselves into the weeds and tangle" at the bottom of the sea. It is in the furtherance of this mission, with its attendant requirements of All-or-Nothing, that he asks little Hedvig to sacrifice the thing she loves most in order to show Hjalmar how much she loves him:

> Ah, if only you had your eyes opened to what really makes life worthwhile! If you had the genuine, joyous, courageous spirit of self-sacrifice . . .

This is the final stage of the progressive vilification of Brand which marks Ibsen's middle period. In *Pillars of Society* the idealistic Hilmar is merely obnoxious with his *ugh* of disgust at the squalor of the world; in *An Enemy of the People,* Dr. Stockmann is funny

and lovable in his futility; but Gregers is hateful. It is interesting that he is cast in the
first instance as the *raisonneur* of the play.

In *The Wild Duck,* the *raisonneur* of the conventional *pièce à thèse* suffers an interesting transformation. The *raisonneur* of Second Empire drama was traditionally the author's representative, and was therefore intended to inspire respect and admiration.
Gregers, however, is unsympathetic. He has, moreover, a rival *raisonneur* in Dr. Relling,
who is very likable. Neither, of course, is trustworthy. Of the two manipulators of the
plot, the one is fanatic, neurotic, sadistic, and perhaps mad; the other is a drunkard
and a disgrace to his profession. These two angels battle for the soul of the hero, which
is worthless:

> GREGERS: Hedvig has not died in vain. Didn't you see how grief brought
> out what was noblest in him?
>
> RELLING: Most people feel some nobility when they stand in the presence
> of death. But how long do you suppose this glory will last in his
> case?
>
> GREGERS: Surely it will continue and flourish to the end of his life!
>
> RELLING: Give him nine months and little Hedvig will be nothing more
> than the theme of a pretty little party piece . . . We can discuss
> it again when the first grass grows on her grave. Then he'll bring
> it all up, all about the child so untimely torn from the loving
> father's heart! Then you'll see him wallowing deeper and deeper
> in sentimentality and self-pity.

Dr. Relling was destined, unhappily, to become a theatrical cliché, and in conceiv-
ing him as he did, Ibsen did what he could to dissociate himself from his doctrine. But
there can be no doubt that this estimable quack speaks for that side of Ibsen which
had by now supplanted Brand as the Ibsen "of his finest moments," an Ibsen who
viewed the world from a standpoint somewhere between contempt and compassion, but
always with a certain amusement. This is the Ibsen we see in his plays henceforth;
until we are confronted suddenly with the agony of *The Master Builder.*

The Wild Duck, like its relatives and descendants, *Il berretto a sonagli, The Playboy of the
Western World,* and *The Iceman Cometh,* indicates the use of illusion in a world of unbearable realities, but we cannot conclude from this that Ibsen advocated self-deception
as a panacea for the ills of humanity. The play is contemplative, not demonstrative.
It has the form, in general, of a *pièce à thèse,* but it is not a thesis play so much as
a play of antitheses. It proves nothing: it invites us to think. The mood is meditative,
lyrical, a mood of despair. In *The Wild Duck* the priest is drunk, the soldier is broken,
the idealist is mad, the doctor is ill. They have all sunk, metaphorically, into the ooze
at the bottom of the sea. Here, as in Gorki's *Na dne,* there is the comfort of hopeless-
ness: bad things happen and it makes no difference. There is no indication that out
of these experiences will come a better life; on the contrary, the expectation is that
after this brief period of turbulence, life will go on precisely as it did before, and in
this realization Ibsen finds an authentic source of emotion. Despair, for Kierkegaard,
is the terminal phase of each stage of the progress of the soul toward God. In *The Wild*

Duck nobody is capable of going beyond the initial stage; but even in the climate of despair it is possible to create a world in which one can live in something like joy.

Of this nature, it is intimated, is the sphere of art, the last refuge of aesthetic man, as pathetic a substitute for nature, perhaps, as a chicken coop in an attic, but very dear nonetheless, and well worth defending. In the absence of God, there is no plausible way of making life seem other than a pointless mummery. Maximus says at the end of *Emperor and Galilean,* borrowing, to express his discontent, a phrase out of Schopenhauer: "What is life worth? All is sport and make-believe. To will is to have to will!" It is evident that in the mood of these plays is prefigured the despair of the existentialist; but Ibsen had no faith in the redeeming power of engagement. In the power of fantasy, however, to find in chaos a home for the soul of man, Dr. Relling sees something godlike. At any rate, this is as close to God as he can come.

In *The Wild Duck* all the characters are formulated in terms of despair; but the source of emotion is the despair of the author, not the despair of the characters. The characters do not complain. It is the author who, by implication, bewails them. The pleasure of the play derives, accordingly, not from the identification of the audience with the protagonist, as in tragedy, but from a feeling of intimate communion with the author in the contemplation of the action, a feeling akin to the pleasure of poetry. As the spectator is never asked to surrender his autonomy, he is afforded an individual experience which is contrapuntal to, but quite distinct from, the emotions experienced on the stage. This technique differs materially from that of Dumas, for example. Dumas, through his *raisonneur,* is often on the stage as presenter and commentator, but the action is always intended to be a realistic demonstration, in academic terms, with a total illusion. Ibsen is never on the stage; but the entire action is portrayed impressionistically, so that we are constantly aware—as in impressionist painting—of the individuality of the author's perceptions. *The Wild Duck* thus marks a subtle, but important step away from the illusionism which especially characterizes realist drama, and it points the way toward a conception of theatre in which the author, rather than the characters, becomes the center of attention, a conception which Strindberg and, after him, Pirandello developed rapidly in the next decades.

The immediate effect of such plays as *Ghosts* and *The Wild Duck* was to stimulate in various quarters artistic currents such as the contemporary naturalistic dramatists had not succeeded in propagating. *The Wild Duck* had influence everywhere, save in France and England, and particularly on Russian drama. These plays, moreover, had interesting consequences of a non-dramatic nature. It was by breaking down the accepted stereotypes of the theatre that Ibsen revitalized the drama of his time, and very likely this is all he meant to do. But the social reflex was inevitable. The revaluation of the clichés of the theatre in time brought about a revaluation of the clichés of real life, which the stage ordinarily reflects and defines. Thus Ibsen, to his embarrassment, found himself once again a leader of public opinion, a position which flattered him, but caused him acute discomfort. As he felt the impulse to be extremely aggressive, yet desired to offend nobody, he was much concerned to resist definition, tacked constantly, changed direction from play to play, and while maintaining a certain general orientation, became exceedingly difficult to follow. . . .

One of Ibsen's most striking techniques in The Wild Duck *is his use of symbols as a means of characterization and as a way to communicate themes. Hermann J. Weigand devotes several highly perceptive pages to the function of symbolism in* The Wild Duck, *as part of his thorough analysis of the play.*

[SYMBOLISM IN *THE WILD DUCK*]
Hermann J. Weigand

. . . Gregers' idealism is the attempt of a superfluous man—one who feels it his destiny to be the thirteenth at table—to dignify his existence by persuading himself that he is of some use in the world. He is an empty vessel, hungering to be filled with the fermenting overflow of a personality; a man of the kind Strindberg would have ranged in his gallery of vampires. He has no personality of his own. Brand's inexorable idealism had been but a corollary of the immanent law of his life: "Be thyself." Apply this maxim as a touchstone to Gregers, and the chasm between the apostle of the ideal and its salesman is seen to yawn.

Gregers could have been rendered pathetic; instead Ibsen chose to turn the shafts of his ridicule upon him. His blind worship of Hjalmar through the successive acts of the melodrama gives rise to mocking laughter. Even Gina, handicapped by the servant's native respect for her betters, is this gentleman's superior in knowledge of human nature. And in his own way, Gregers is as literal as Gina. The principle that life is to be founded on truth, he has learned by rote without grasping its meaning. His hobby at present is the true marriage. He expects to see it consummated by acting the part of officious informer. Quack that he is, he tries to apply truth externally, incapable of realizing that the truth Ibsen postulated must be a leaven pervading a man's whole existence. Of course, his experiment fails; but to make its failure the more grotesquely humiliating, Hjalmar has to make the mortifying observation that the marriage which Gregers' detested father is about to enter corresponds to his formula of the true marriage, literally applied.

The interpretation of Gregers' character is most closely bound up with the symbolism of the play. The symbolism of "The Wild Duck" has taxed the ingenuity of interpreters to the utmost. The wild duck has given the play its title; it is the topic on which a large portion of the dialogue turns; and it is an indispensable factor in the plot, as the motivation of Hedwig's suicide hinges on its presence.

Werle is the first to employ this symbolism in alluding to the fate of Old Ekdal. "There are people in the world," he tells Gregers, "who dive to the bottom the moment they get a couple of slugs in their body, and never come to the surface again." In his mouth the figure is perfectly natural, the experience of his duck-hunt in the marshes still being fresh in his mind; and it fits the Old Man, just as it would have fitted John Gabriel Borkman thirteen years later.

But when Gregers, on his first visit to the Ekdal studio, sees the wounded duck exhibited and hears its strange history, all the details of its story crystallize in his mind

From Hermann J. Weigand, *The Modern Ibsen* (New York: Holt, 1925; reprinted by Dutton, 1960), pp. 160–165. Copyright 1925 by Holt, Rinehart and Winston, Inc. Copyright 1953 by Hermann J. Weigand. Reprinted by permission of Holt, Rinehart and Winston, Publishers.

into a pattern symbolizing the fate of Hjalmar Ekdal, in accordance with his fixed idea of Hjalmar's character: Hjalmar of the fiery temperament is Werle's wounded victim, he has dived deep down and bitten himself fast in the marsh of the garret, where he is certain to die unless a clever dog dives after him and forcibly drags him up to the light of truth. Gregers feels it his mission to be this dog; and without our being expressly told so, we are aware how keenly Gregers enjoys the irony of fate that has singled out him, the despoiler's son, for the mission of opening the eyes of his father's victim. The symbolism which he has detected gives to his mission an added dignity; and henceforth his language reflects his esoteric insight, causing the child to remark after his departure: "It seemed to me that he meant something different from what he said—all the time."

A coincidence the next morning bestows on Gregers' mission, as it were, its consecration. He had left the house the night before, his mind agitated by the parallelism between the garret and the sea-bottom to which the wild duck, i.e., Hjalmar, had dived, and he has been unable to think of another thing ever since. Now, in the course of his talk with Hedwig, he hears to his astonishment that she also associated "the whole room and everything in it" with the depths of the sea. She displays a child's natural embarrassment in confessing her secret, as if it were something stupid; but there is nothing strange in her linking the treasured relics of a vanished "flying dutchman"—the big cupboards full of books, the old bureau with drawers and flaps, and the marvelous clock—with the depths of the sea, which her fairy tales must have told her also abound with strange wonders. But upon Gregers her confession must have had the effect of a sign from above. "Out of the mouths of babes and sucklings—" he must have thought, as the sudden gravity of his rejoinder indicates.

HEDWIG	But that is so stupid.
GREGERS	You mustn't say that.
HEDWIG	Oh, yes, for you know it's only a garret.
GREGERS	*(Looks fixedly at her.)* Are you so sure of that?
HEDWIG	*(Astonished.)* That it's a garret?
GREGERS	Are you quite certain of it?

Up to this time Gregers had resolved the symbolism of the wild duck in his own mind. But in the course of the scene following, when Hjalmar's emotions are agitated by his account of the pistol and of his invention, and he is presumably in a receptive mood, Gregers attempts to use the symbol of the wild duck as a vehicle for conveying to him the truth about his condition. Hjalmar's quick move in self-defense, the moment he senses the danger to his comfort, frustrates the first attempt; but Gregers succeeds in cornering his victim during their walk together, when Hjalmar's caution had unwisely yielded to his curiosity. Henceforth the symbolism, no longer confined to Gregers' solo part, reappears as a duet, chanted by the two luckless men in unison. In Act IV Hjalmar proclaims himself in Relling's presence "Mr. Werle's wing-broken victim."

What is the purpose of all this symbolism? There can be no doubt that its prime function is to characterize Gregers; for all this symbolism, applied to Hjalmar, is grotesquely inept. There is nothing of the wild duck in his make-up. The more Gregers harps on their fancied likeness, the more vividly does the incongruity between

Hjalmar's domestic rabbit-soul and that creature of the wilds impinge upon our consciousness. What this symbolism does is to reveal the mentality of Gregers. We perceive his penchant for wallowing in symbols—his *Geheimniskrämerei* as the Germans would say—to be one of the most conspicuous traits of his character. Symbol-mongering is his favorite way of evading the drab color of matter-of-fact reality. It is his way of achieving the illusion, the stimulating principle of life. It is to him what the garret is to Old Ekdal, his invention to Hjalmar and his demonic nature to Molvik. And we see Ibsen's eyes fixed upon the symbol-monger in grim amusement.

Yet to assert that the wild-duck symbolism was interwoven with the play solely for the purpose of satirizing Gregers would seem to me somewhat rash. It must be remembered that we catch Ibsen's satirical intent in exhibiting the symbol-monger rather late; the choicest bits of satire—among them, what I have called the consecration of Gregers' mission—are so subtle as almost to escape detection. Ibsen obviously delights in laying traps for the reader, in mystifying him as to his intentions, in making him sift the most innocent allusion as to a symbolical meaning lurking underneath. It must have amused him to find critics racking their brains to interpret the symbolism of Ekdal's fowling-piece that would no longer shoot. He was prepared for that sort of thing; he predicted it when he posted his manuscript: "My critics will, at any rate, find several things to squabble about and several things to interpret." He knew his own, not undeserved, reputation for juggling symbols. So we will hardly go wrong in numbering the wild-duck symbolism as among those bits of "tomfoolery" which made the work of writing this play so entertaining to Ibsen. Having once caught Ibsen's sly wink, we relish this symbolism like a subtly compounded sauce imparting to the whole dish an exotic flavor of particular delight for the aesthetic gourmand.

What has been said here about the symbolism of the wild duck does not apply to the transparent symbolism immanent to the situation proper of the play. Relling's comment—too explicit to be natural—makes its interpretation sufficiently obvious. Those dwellers of the garret, each cherishing his distinct illusion, reflect the need of the average man for a life-lie, an ideal, with which to paint over the grim face of reality. Rob them of their illusions, and their happiness is gone, either for good, or until their ingenuity develops some new make-believe to stay their despair. Gregers' bungling anticipates the conclusion which Rosmer arrives at: "Men cannot be ennobled from without."

The cynic has the last word. Gregers sums up his point of view in the words: "If you are right and I am wrong, then life is not worth living." To which Relling makes answer: "Oh, life would be quite tolerable, after all, if only we could be rid of the confounded duns that keep on pestering us in our poverty, with the claim of the ideal."

The cynic has the last word. Little perspicacity is needed, however, to see that he serves Ibsen only as a convenient foil for giving the quack his deserts. In his sodden debauchery Relling has ups and downs which raise the mean average of his existence very little—if any—above the plane of the other frequenters of the studio. He is one of the menagerie swept by the poet's range from his high perspective.

In his broad-ranging study of dramatic technique, The Elements of Drama, *J. D. Styan investigates the way Ibsen manipulates* tempo *in* The Wild Duck *in order to enhance the dramatic effect and to convey meaning.*

[TEMPO IN *THE WILD DUCK*]
J. D. Styan

. . . A meaningful tempo, while promoting the realization of an impression, must also affect its *depth.* By this is meant that one impression is empowered to carry a greater value in relation to another. The obvious example of this is the climax in tragedy, which is often strikingly effective because it is quieter, more still and slower than the sequence which preceded it, despite the fact that it is the crux of the play. So it is in *Romeo and Juliet,* in *King Lear,* in *Macbeth.* We are given a point of rest to free our minds to make their own vital contribution. Part of the unconscious task forced upon us in the theatre experience is to be constantly evaluating what we are receiving, and tempo is a cogent means of controlling our response.

It tends to be true that simpler patterns of tempo are only fully acceptable in non-realistic drama. Tempo in real life is more delicate, certainly less deliberate, more irresponsible, and where a dramatist introduces a formal rhythmic pattern, one senses theatricality in the play. On the other hand, no realistic play rejects the advantages of rhythmic control. The control may be only better disguised for purposes of realism. The exciting climax of *The Wild Duck* shows how Ibsen at his best did not neglect this aid.

The suicide of Hedvig must carry with it the cumulative meaning of the play, and from the moment earlier in Act V when the shot from the attic is heard, we are taken up with the problem of who or what has been shot, but more with the bigger but related question why the shot was fired. It was ingenious of Ibsen to insist that our answer to the first is impossible without our answer to the second. At the same time as we scrutinize the evidence after the shot, Ibsen compels us to estimate its intention and to judge the guilty. The tempo up to the discovery of Hedvig dead in the attic is deliberately contrived to drive us to the conclusions he wants.

So strong with ironic statements is the dialogue of Gregers and Hjalmar preceding the shot that the audience has the pleasure of being at least less in doubt about the cause and nature of the shot than the characters are. Hjalmar had said immediately before it was heard,

> If I asked her then, "Hedvig, are you willing to give up life for my sake?"
> *Laughing sarcastically.* Oh yes, I dare say! You'd soon hear what answer I got!
> *A pistol shot is heard in the attic.*

The scene that follows strains to retain its irony until the discovery of the body, while sustaining the suspense that had been growing since Hedvig entered the attic. Here is the passage that includes the last of the series of thrusts and parries towards the solu-

From J. L. Styan, *The Elements of Drama* (Cambridge: Cambridge University Press, 1960), pp. 148–152.
© Cambridge University Press 1960. Reprinted by permission of Cambridge University Press.

tion of the mystery and the resolution of the tension. These thrusts and parries control the tempo of movement and speech to the climax, and this same tempo controls the drift of the imaginative argument in our minds.

HJALMAR   *going across and throwing the kitchen door open.* Hedvig, come along! Come in here to me! *Looking round.* No she's not here.

GINA   Then she's in her own little room.

HJALMAR   *from outside.* No, she isn't here either. *Coming in.* She must have gone out.

GINA   Well, you didn't want her anywhere about the house.

HJALMAR   Ah, if only she'd come home soon—so that I can really tell her . . . Now all will be well, Gregers; for now I really believe we can begin life over again.

GREGERS   *quietly.* I knew it; it will all come right through the child. *Old Ekdal comes to the door of his room; he is in full uniform and is busy fastening on his sabre.*

HJALMAR   *amazed.* Father! Are you there?

GINA   Were you shooting in your room, Father?

EKDAL   *indignantly, coming forward.* So you go shooting alone, do you, Hjalmar?

HJALMAR   *anxious, bewildered.* So it wasn't you who fired the shot in the attic?

EKDAL   I? Fire a shot? Hm.

GREGERS   *calling to Hjalmar.* She has shot the wild duck herself, don't you see?

HJALMAR   What is all this? *Rushes across to the door of the attic, pulls it aside, looks in and gives a scream.* Hedvig!

As Hjalmar eliminates alternatives by looking into the kitchen, then by looking into Hedvig's own room, the characters on the stage seem to endorse the view that Old Ekdal fired the shot on behalf of Hedvig. The quickening of the action during this search is relaxed while all three are busy with their own sentiments, Gina struggling with her maternal tears, Hjalmar with his remorse and Gregers happy to put a conclusive idealistic interpretation on the issue. In the pause we have time to ventilate our own thoughts about the statements. Hjalmar's lame and inopportune optimism, "now I really believe we can begin life over again," by this time must jar against our sense of propriety. We have respite enough to tell ourselves that neither Hedvig can begin life over again, nor Hjalmar, whose self-indulgence, even self-love, is ingrained, a view that is substantiated at the last by Dr Relling. On the other hand, Gregers's suggestion that "it will all come right through the child," we suspect to be true in a way quite other than he thinks. Ironically, his statement points directly to the substance of the play's meaning, in which is implied a sin and an atonement. In the immensity of this crisis, now that the event is seen naked, Gregers's error suggests, not merely that he has not grasped the solution of the mystery, but that his values are hopelessly inept and sterile. This is understood, with that strangely mixed urge upon our intellect and upon our emotions this author often conjures, by our cold refusal to accept Gregers's reasoning and by our warm sympathy with an unwitting victim. A precise flexing of the tempo of this episode will permit our maximum imaginative activity. Now Ibsen can flourish his trump-card.

The entry of Old Ekdal is the final thrust, and immediately anticipates the discovery. But even with this, Ibsen keeps his finger on the pulse of the climax to its end. Hjalmar and Gina for a fraction stand in amazement: with no word from Ekdal, they are granted the pause in which to search for understanding. We, meanwhile, are many moves ahead of them, and sit in suspense. Even then Ekdal's reply is no reply to their question, and once more progress limps. He enters, a ridiculous figure, ignorant of his part in the killing of his granddaughter: "So you go shooting alone, do you, Hjalmar?" Again we wait as Hjalmar painfully makes his next deduction. And again we wait while Gregers, who has had a more intricate problem to work out, offers the last possible alternative explanation: "She has shot the wild duck herself, don't you see?"—one last restraint by which Ibsen delays Hjalmar's impulse to look in the attic, a tormented moment measuring an age of feeling, before passion is released. With a sudden access of speed in speech and movement, Hjalmar runs to the door of the attic followed by the others, and the climax is attained.

The calculated tempo of this scene is not theatrical panache: it aids meaning. Because by this time we are certain of the outcome, we are absorbed by the grossness of the mistake that Hjalmar and Gregers are making, and the size of the monstrosity engendered is measured the more precisely as we grow more certain. Each false deduction by a character makes more acute our insight into the motive for the error: each hesitation condemns. It would be true to add to this that the attic, till now a whimsical curiosity, at the most a symptom of the family's malady difficult to assimilate because so concrete, rises here to a proper dramatic status in becoming fully part of the play: it becomes at the last a symbol for tragic self-deception.

Tempo is an artificial imposition upon language. Ibsen's precision of effect suggests he has balanced the demands of psychological realism with elements that regulate tempo, reconciling as always life with dramatic necessity. Even if a particular rhythm is inseparable from a particular character, even if "every passion has its proper pulse," effects of excitement and relief, of squeeze and relax, must be shrewdly regulated to enlarge or reduce the size of the image. Ibsen's achievement is a compromise: through a character's mood, the prominence of an idea, or the duration of a speech, the actor can identify rhythm and at the same time behave realistically. . . .

In reviews of two modern productions of The Wild Duck, *Harold Clurman and Robert Cushman discuss the nature of Ibsen's art and the problems of staging his plays.*

[*THE WILD DUCK* IN A 1967 PRODUCTION]
Harold Clurman

"No conflict, no drama" is a classic axiom. It seems to be borne out even today when the conflicting forces are not readily identifiable. Protagonist and antagonist appear to merge. *Avant-garde* plays reflect (I can hardly say "dramatize") conditions rather than situations. A man in a state of collapse is in a "condition"; if he does something to recover, or if someone comes to help him, we have a situation. The lack of purposive action makes many contemporary plays on the whole less interesting to wide audiences than the older drama. It is in the nature of humankind to act, and once you begin to do so you are likely to encounter hardship, hence conflict. That is why drama interests us: we participate in its "stories." Quiescent drama is rarely rousing. Yet even in such drama there is some implicit conflict: the conflict may resolve itself to the difficulty of staying inactive.

I have been thinking on these matters because many of the plays I have recently been reading by would-be playwrights are little more than yammers of prostration in which four-letter imprecations are hurled against nothing in particular—not even destiny or God—and I have come to the conclusion that the artists who most firmly hold my attention are those in whom the conflicts they depict arise in the first place within themselves. When such conflicts are settled once and for all, when the warring elements within them are completely subdued, they have for me very little of interest to say. Peace of mind in the artist is gratifying only when we realize the desperate struggle that he has gone through to achieve it. And even then we must not be certain that the battle has come to a full stop.

The impression we gather from most of Ibsen's critics is of a grim and resolute moralist. He was a dogged and implacable warrior who knew what he wanted. When so presented on the stage, he becomes gray and slightly dull, worst of all, "old-fashioned."

There can be no question about it: Ibsen was a severely logical artist. He came of age in the heyday of scientific rationalism. This was the weapon with which to annihilate the hierarchy of bugaboos. He would give no quarter to the constriction of social-ethical notions that no longer corresponded to the facts of the industrial era. He was going to batter falsity down with moral and intellectual rigor. He wasn't joking about it.

Such characters now strike us as unsympathetic, insufficiently human. We prefer greater flexibility. Humor, we believe, is the saving grace. Chekhov maintained that Russian actors couldn't play Ibsen because Russians (those in Chekhov's time at any rate) were more vulnerable, softer, less consistent—delightfully or frantically bewildered. Compared to characters in Turgenev, Chekhov or even Gorky, Ibsen's people are unyielding.

Harold Clurman, [Review of *The Wild Duck*], *The Nation*, vol. 204, no. 5 (January 30, 1967), 156–157.

But just as we are eager in our theatre today to discover the comedic aspects of Chekhov's plays so that we may not suffer their intrinsic sadness, so we are beginning to look for Ibsen's lighter side. In both cases we fall into error. For Chekhov's laughter arises from tenderness and compassion; it is not escape from pain. It is an embrace of our total human experience in which the tragic and the comic are complementary, the two being more semantically than substantively differentiated.

Comedy in Ibsen is a symptom of a laceration in Ibsen's spirit. Chekhov smiles because he forgives and accepts. Ibsen is tougher; he is too "logical" for such an attitude. He is fighting all the time, and—this is his pathos—he is generally fighting himself. He says "either, or." Since neither the one nor the other quite satisfies him because he contains both, his laughter is harsh, a godlike judgment, proud and inexorable. Ibsen is relentless, constantly punitive. Neither Chekhov nor Ibsen is "funny."

In a little-known play, *Emperor and Galilean,* Julian the apostate says: "The old beauty is no longer beautiful, and the new truth is no longer true." Throughout his life Ibsen was haunted by a vision of grandeur which was being destroyed and had to be destroyed, while he felt trapped in a world which diminished manhood. He was torn by the conflict between justice and love. He sought the ideal and demanded the practical. He was divided by contrary impulses, and each of his plays is the justification of one or the other of his urges: Christianity and paganism, aristocracy and democracy, individualism and socialism.

Brand insists on self-abnegation and wrecks everyone as well as himself. Peer Gynt wants to be triumphantly independent and constantly compromises with all that stands in his way, finally becoming attenuated into a dry and empty shell, waste matter for the Buttonmolder. Hedda Gabler, a general's daughter, desires a life of glorious splendor and finds herself reduced to a middle-class housewife. Solness dreams of building towering mansions but succeeds only in constructing ordinary dwelling places. In devotion to his art, Rubek in *When We Dead Awaken* renounces passionate fulfillment through the love of a woman and finds that in doing so he has failed both as artist and man. Gregers Werle in *The Wild Duck* pursues truth unremittingly in the belief that it will save, only to find that it may ruin.

All this may explain something about the APA production of *The Wild Duck* at the Lyceum. It is decent and intelligent enough. It is not so trim a production as that of *Right You Are* because the latter is, for all its twists and turns, a simpler, more linear play. *The Wild Duck* demands far more from its actors.

The weakling Hjalmar Ekdal, your "average man," and his sensible peasant-like wife, both brilliantly drawn and on the whole comedic figures comparatively easy to project, never fail to register. But Gregers Werle, presumably the butt of Ibsen's criticism (directed, it may be, against himself), carries the real challenge of the play, and it is rarely met in performance. The reason is that directors try to make a pathetic caricature of him. His idealism is naive to the point of folly; his motivation neurotic. But though there is a certain mockery in Ibsen's portrait of Werle, he must not be made petty. (Dr Stockman, the "enemy of the people," may also be given a humorous touch as a fumbling innocent, but in the end he must retain something of the heroic.) The bourgeois realist Ibsen was ultimately interested in nothing less than the grandiose: his "cottages" are really cathedrals. The weakness of the APA production—and one should not be scornful of it on this account—is that its Werle is a slight, almost an inconsequential, personage.

Werle may be cramped, even a little absurd, but he is still Ibsen and, despite all, a mighty being. For what does Werle say about himself as the curtain falls: that he is forever destined to remain *"The thirteenth man at the table."* Yes, says Werle-Ibsen, I may be a troublemaker, a spoil sport, even "crazy," but my function is incessantly to go on clamoring for the truth and the ideal, even if I never attain them or am never able to ascertain their exact nature.

I have seen *The Wild Duck* in many different productions. It is still worth seeing at the APA-Lyceum.

THE WILD DUCK [IN A 1971 PRODUCTION]
Robert Cushman

Most playwrights invented the anti-hero, but it was Ibsen who patented the invention. He seems to have done so almost by accident. Setting out, anachronistically, to write a verse tragedy he found his protagonist had escaped from him across the gulf—always a narrow one—which separates noble intransigence from insufferable selfrighteousness. By the end of *Brand* we hardly know where we stand; this man has aroused his villagers from their moral torpor (it is perhaps hardly his fault that they sink back into it at the first opportunity) and he knows a vested interest when he sees one. On the other hand, he destroys his wife and mother. The violence of the avalanche which destroys him is as much as anything the author's desperate method of resolving his own ambiguities. An ampler response was the whole substance of his next play. *Peer Gynt* is the worm's eye view of *Brand,* the hero seen frankly as *poseur.* He, too, causes his fair share of suffering but escapes censure in precisely the areas where Brand invites it. He ensures that his mother dies happy (by literally talking her into it) and he even, albeit in peculiar circumstances, winds up with the girl.

I think of these two figures as a double-headed eagle raised aloft the Ibsen canon. They define the territory in which nearly all his major figures exist. The only departure is in the middle period social plays: *Ghosts,* for example, though it may not be just a

Robert Cushman, "The Wild Duck [Review]," *Plays and Players,* vol. 18, no. 4 (January 1971), pp. 34 and 59. Reprinted by permission of the author.

play about syphilis is still concerned with disorders which are, in the very long run (and we're not there yet) curable; the same could be said of *Pillars of Society. An Enemy of the People* disqualifies on rather different grounds. Its hero is certainly stamped with the Brand image; the trouble is that he shows no traces of the sensibility that created Peer Gynt. (Ibsen asserted in later life that he did indeed see the absurd side of Dr Stockman, though in the play itself there are few intimations that we are not meant to take him at his own valuation.) But the mature plays return us to Ibsen's central preoccupation.

The preoccupation is at once social and aesthetic. Ibsen was the first post-tragic dramatist. He could almost create tragic heroes (or figures, like Solness and Hedda Gabler who feel they owe it to themselves to behave like heroes), but he was too acute to put them in a tragic context for no such thing now existed. If you write *Brand,* you have to balance·it with *Peer Gynt,* and if, as an Ibsen hero, you attempt to behave like Brand the element of Peer in you will find you out. If you are lucky *(cf. The Lady from the Sea)* it may find you out before you throw your life away. This, of course, rarely happens. When Solness emulates Brand by going climbing he just keels over. Small consolation that young Hilde hears harps in the air the while; never trust a girl who believes in symbols.

But even a parody hero provides a juicy opportunity for a star, and this is how Ibsen usually reaches us. He makes West Enders of us all. The RSC seem to have undertaken *Ghosts* principally (and dimly) as a vehicle for Peggy Ashcroft; they have not repeated the venture. The National gave us two beknighted master builders playing, from opposite ends of the spectrum: Redgrave (nobly Branded) took Solness to the top of his steeple; Olivier (mischievously Peering) pushed him off. Maggie Smith has taken deadly accurate aim at Hedda Gabler. And now we have the Play Company of London whose professed policy is to lure international stars to appear in their productions. For the nonce they have Hayley Mills, though in general the starriness on display is of the homely variety, an impression strengthened by the inclusion in the programme of the kind of garish colour portraits that used to adorn your local Gaumont.

The acting, being of the same Rank, is a little below the requirements of the play. *The Wild Duck* is the great pivotal work in which Ibsen provided the fullest exposition of his theme. As has often been pointed out, the play is in part self-parody. But this means more than a retraction of certain opinions expressed in *Ghosts* and *A Doll's House* about the paramount importance of unblinkered truth in human relationships. If this were all there would be little to cavil at in the production at the Criterion. But (if I may give my hobby-horse a final canter) there is much more. When Gregers Werle adopts Hjalmar Ekdal as his hero, he is casting Peer Gynt as Brand and, of course, Peer leaps at the chance; this is how he sees himself anyway. But even Peer makes a fairly good showing for three acts out of five: he is a failure on a swaggering scale.

Hjalmar may well be one of the great unplayable roles; a glance at the English stage history of the play, appended to Michael Meyer's published translation, shows that actors of the part have been castigated alternately for being too comic or not comic enough. Mr Meyer himself warns against "the temptation to play Hjalmar as ridiculous and farcical," and then contradicts himself by insisting that "his ridiculousness must be given full play; it is a baroque role for a baroque actor."

So what is the actor to do? Michael Denison lends the role his usual mellifluous boom; he is not quite a baroque actor, but he is difficult to take with total seriousness. So we see through Hjalmar from the start. The wonder is that Gregers fails to. This, admittedly, is a cardinal weakness of the play. It depends on the conjunction, not merely of two very silly men, but of two whose stupidities interconnect like hand and glove. Ibsen overcompensated, if anything, by stuffing the last scenes with psychological explanations of them both. Mr Denison overcompensates too; once he reaches his own hearth he tones down Hjalmar's threnodies as if afraid of them. He might perhaps be helped by direction, which encouraged him to stride about a bit. Nobody in this production ever moves very far. That the opening party scene is both undermanned and under-active can perhaps be blamed on economics and a cramped stage, but this is no excuse for the stasis of the main action which is charmingly and quite spaciously set in what I take to be (isn't it good?) Norwegian wood.

The general tone is so muted that Paul Hardwick's typically robust Dr Relling has no difficulty in taking over the play. Here, obviously, as we are always told, is the author's mouthpiece, shrewd and unsentimental. But if this is really the case, *The Wild Duck* is not much of a play; it stacks its cards quite monstrously. Surely, when Relling and Gregers are left alone together at the end, we are meant to glean that the truth lies somewhere between them, that the doctor's cynicism is really as limiting as Gregers' gullibility. He, too, is a disappointed unloved man; Mr Hardwick gives full value to the brief moment with Mrs Sorby which makes this clear, but the point is nowhere followed up. If the play has a moral centre it belongs with Gina, who distrusts both men's influence over her husband. Maybe Dulcie Gray conveyed this—but I was so irritated by her refusal to act the slightest bit common that most of her performance passed me by.

Nine years ago Glen Byam Shaw received deserved acclaim for a most delicate treatment of *The Lady from the Sea.* But the same approach will not work here. For one thing, he had real stars then—Leightons and Redgraves and such—to fill the evening out. Here his carefulness betrays him, and Ibsen's mannerisms are left unbecomingly exposed. The wild duck itself, for example, comes uncomfortably close to being a real symbol instead of a snare for people who insist on looking at life that way. When Gregers solemnly informs Hjalmar that "There's a lot of the wild duck in you," we could almost be meant to believe him. It would take very robust playing to obviate this danger (and how any director can get around Old Ekdal's leadenly meaningless remarks about the forest claiming its own, I have really no idea).

And there remains the awful problem of Hedvig, who, at Gregers' suggestion, swallows the symbolism so entirely that she dies of it (a Solness-Hilde situation in reverse). This is the grimmest joke of all, but it is always liable to be swallowed in pathos—the pathos that a fourteen year old girl *who is going blind* can hardly help evoking long before she lays a finger on the fatal shotgun. At Edinburgh last year Anna Calder-Marshall avoided this danger by sailing headlong into it; she was so moving that other considerations just disappeared. Hayley Mills attempts nothing so hazardous and achieves a modest success. It is difficult to see why she should want to play another little girl at this stage of her career; but that's her problem. At least she isn't fey.

Hedda Gabler

In all the productions included in The Classic Theatre, *a crucial question for the viewer is this: to what extent does the play embody feelings, conflicts, character types and social settings peculiar to the age and culture in which it was written, and to what extent does it respond to the particular needs and problems of a modern audience? In other words: what kind of a play was it in the past and what kind of a play is it in the present? A case in point is Ibsen's* Hedda Gabler, *which was written in 1890 for a particular European audience, yet—some eighty-five years later—is still being performed, and in media (such as television) the author could not have dreamed of. Herbert Blau, in the essay below, addresses the problem of* Hedda's *relevance to a mid-twentieth-century audience, showing the significant differences between Ibsen's world (and the theatre that reflects it) and our own.*

HEDDA GABLER: THE IRONY OF DECADENCE
Herbert Blau

I

To many devotees of the theatre, especially those of the realistic tradition, some of the plays of Henrik Ibsen have become uncomfortably anachronistic. The basis for this discomfort is not elusive; and, for me, it was crystallized as the result of a recent involvement in a production of *Hedda Gabler*. First inclination was to modernize it. Is it not, after all, universal? And Hedda the prototype of the "modern woman"? These questions arose quite naturally in early discussions of the play, but soon attached themselves to a more generic one: did Ibsen actually manage in the constricted bourgeois parlor of the play to gather meanings pertinent to the future, or have the physical limitations of its scene by now exhausted the spiritual wealth of the drama itself?

In an age where our library of produceable plays is down to the classics and the trash, the answer to this question is relevant to the fate of the theatre. It is easy, we know, to attack the opinions of tradition and cynically deride many works which have become reputable through time; but it is equally easy for those addicted to a standard repertoire to confuse the tendency to revive a play with the actual merit of that play. Most students of the drama are aware that managers more often look for good parts than for good meanings. And if one looks for good meanings in most of our contemporary drama, he will either despair of the theatre or be labeled a reactionary. For, we are told, there are no "good" meanings. Meanings are relative, and what is good for you is not good for me.

Now a few minutes of sober thought will reveal the difficulty here. With such an ethic it would be impossible, for example, to convince a recalcitrant student that *Hamlet* is superior to *The Moon Is Blue*. Nevertheless, cultural relativity is the popular attitude today, and it is almost as dangerous to be a critic as to be a Communist.

II

But to return to *Hedda Gabler*: what is the argument of the play? And what breadth of meaning does it have for the present age? How steadily does it gaze at life

Herbert Blau, *"Hedda Gabler:* The Irony of Decadence," *Educational Theatre Journal*, vol. 5, no. 2 (May 1953), 112–116. Reprinted by permission of the American Educational Theatre Association.

and how much is it willing to see? To begin with, we might consider the common assumption that Hedda is the first "modern woman," the predecessor of all those inhibited and neurotic souls who have haunted our stages since the death of chivalry unsexed. Obviously Hedda suffers from the same pointless intensity and latent irritation that has become prevalent in a society which, once liberated and expansive, has at last grown in on itself. But for Hedda there is no reality: she experiences a boredom that hasn't even the virtue of being exquisite; she has neither the outlet of hedonism nor the recourse of a business suit. Her breeding prevents her from making her own way; her husband is incapable of making it for her. She has only the consolation of heirlooms—her pistols, symbols of the paternal heritage—and of an occasional illicit conversation with the suave, informed, cautiously lecherous, and ultimately insensitive Judge Brack. In that she wants something beyond what she has (something vague, something imaginative and Bacchic, something which the romantic indiscretions of Lövborg seem to embody for her, but something which is never really defined), she is indeed representative of an entire class of women. But there is a difference; and the difference is that between the generalized modern woman and what is indeed, in some respects, an anachronism.

For if we compare Hedda with a more contemporary heroine who resembles her, Nina of O'Neill's Freudian experiment, *Strange Interlude,* we notice that whereas Nina, motivated by the emotional trauma of aborted first love, recklessly compensates in sexual indulgence and flight *from* her past, Hedda attempts with meticulous desperation to retreat *to* her past, or rather, to impose it upon the present, a present too imperceptive to appreciate it, no less accept it. Nina, it is true, eventually reassumes her familial character, but her tragedy consists of her unsuccessful efforts to escape it, and the process involves fundamental change. But Hedda never changes; she remains General Gabler's daughter until the end. But because General Gabler is dead, Hedda is impotent, cut off from her natal source; and one of her most affective characteristics is a disturbing sterility that approaches the masculine.

Blanche DuBois, of Tennessee Williams' *Streetcar Named Desire,* affords another contrast. Bred in a vanished past, Blanche does not strive to restore it or maintain it (this struggle is antecedent to the drama), but rather to make herself over in the image of the present. Hedda detests Tesman; Blanche clings to Mitch, and she is quite willing, to the point of hysteria, to marry into his world.

Hedda's essential sterility is revealed in her antithetical, but not dialectical, pairing with Mrs. Elvsted, who enjoys a primitive fecundity without understanding either the source of her power or the value of her fruits. Certain symbolism is obvious: Hedda's hair is sparse, Mrs. Elvsted's is abundant; Hedda wants no child, Mrs. Elvsted must have one, if only a brain child. Mrs. Elvsted, in short, must participate in a creative act, if only vicariously; Hedda contributes only to the act of destruction. She has none of the Christian qualities of sacrifice, charity, or love, which Mrs. Elvsted, the devoted Aunt Juliana, and even Tesman unconsciously exhibit.

All this is well known. Hedda is repulsive and fascinating at once (an ambivalence which has attracted so many actresses to the part); and her demoniac resistance to entrapment reveals a quick and cynical mind, but also, surprisingly, a definite naïveté (how easily she is handled by the competent old roué Judge Brack!). She is the vessel of all the forms and instincts of a tradition which is lost and which, as these forms and instincts persist in her, sinks to oblivion in her death. What alone redeems her is a sense of dignity and honor that no one else in the play, including Judge Brack, shares. For Brack has all the accoutrements of Hedda's class—the wit, the charm, the manners, and the dress; but one suspects he is a latecomer to it, and that his prerogatives are not those of birth. Hedda's only legitimacy is her breeding, and it is this, however perverted, which, under the circumstances, guarantees her suicide.

In the social scene represented in Tesman's home, the standards of Hedda's class have disappeared. She herself is inaccurately aware of them, her impulses dissociated from the values which once gave them substance. Within the structure of the play there is no instrument for evaluating the dislocation of sensibility which is imitated in the action. Therefore, when Hedda commits suicide, both responses to her act are woefully inadequate to it. Poor pedantic innocuous Tesman can only shriek: "Shot herself! Shot herself in the temple! Fancy that!"—an ejaculation which he might have made upon uncovering an old manuscript. And Brack, who would have known better were he really of Hedda's class, half faints in an armchair, muttering: "Good God!—people don't do such things."

III

The effect is that of irony; but the irony is that of decadence, the same irony that appears more bewilderedly and plaintively in Henry Adams' *Education,* and more sophisticatedly and self-derisively in T. S. Eliot's *Prufrock*—in all three the irony of a civilization which no longer trusts itself. The argument governing the irony is that the imaginative and cultivated sensibility of a vanished age cannot exist in the tedious, purblind, materialistic present, and in fact hardens in resistance and torments itself to death. The attitude of the play, however, emerges by negation.

To see this in the action, one might approach the part of Hedda as an actor trained in the Stanislavski system would do. If we were to place Hedda's objective in the form of an infinitive, we would find first of all that its statement is very difficult. Indeed, the determination of a precise objective is the surest indication of a misinterpretation of the role. We must satisfy ourselves, therefore, with a sublimated objective: Hedda, not able to realize herself on her own terms and by her own means, decides that she must possess another human being. This Mrs. Elvsted has almost done, unwittingly to be sure, but efficiently enough to stir Hedda's jealousy. Hedda's objective infinitive, then, is: "to have the power to mold a human destiny." Now in the drama of other periods, say in *Oedipus* or *Hamlet,* when we set down the objective infinitive of the protagonist, we find that though the protagonist may himself be destroyed in the process, the objective is eventually consummated. Thus, Oedipus sets out "to hunt the murderer of Laius" or "to determine his own reality"; in either case he does precisely what he has set out to do. The tragic effect resides in the disaster logically implicit in the triumph. Oedipus gets what he wants, but he gets more than he bargained for. So too with Hamlet, who starts out "to destroy the ulcer in the body politic" but unfortunately destroys a good deal more, including himself.

Hedda, like Oedipus and Hamlet, dies. But her death is not a triumph and her objective infinitive is never fulfilled. It is in fact virtually reversed. To split her major objective into components: she marries Tesman "to obtain security," and finds his position threatened by Lövborg and her plan of entering society obstructed; she attempts "to intimidate" Aunt Juliana, and she is herself intimidated when the old lady, refusing to be insulted, musters a belated dignity; she tries "to control" the timid Mrs. Elvsted, and she realizes that Mrs. Elvsted has dared what she herself has never done and is actually the stronger. In these relationships we see even the weak characters have the better of Hedda. But her failure is most crushing in respect to Judge Brack and Lövborg. Her intimacy with Brack leads to her enslavement: she tries "to make Brack serve" her and ends by almost serving him. As a last resort she attempts "to persuade Lövborg to perform one last act of beauty" and, of course, he perishes along with her dream in an event, not an act, of ugliness. Intending to possess, she is instead possessed, and her only escape is that of suicide.

Such frustration is certainly not unusual in modern society. But Hedda lacks an essential quality of literary modernity: a sense of alienation. For at no time during the action does she feel that she doesn't belong. It is, for her, the others who are intruders, though she is living in a strange house, enjoying another woman's servant, wheedling thrills from another's experience, and making the worst of a life that is not hers. She has the intellectual assurance of heredity, but the incertitude of the emotionally timid. In a later age and another environment she might, were there not something natively frigid about her, release her repressions, like Nina and Blanche, in aimless promiscuity. But as it is she wants something from the new bourgeois culture which it is incapable of giving, and yet she is not critical enough to understand why. The members of the Lost Generation of the 1920's were at odds too with specialization and materialism, but they understood it, not as a clash with their past, but as inimical to their future. And it is a future which Hedda simply does not have.

IV

The cultural problem which Hedda magnifies, then, is considerably diminished, although the emotion concomitant with it endures. Like Baudelaire, Ibsen deals with the horrible state of Ennui—but the significance of this state in the play is reduced for lack of standards by which to judge it. Mr. Yvor Winters discusses Ennui as a poetic subject in his essay on T. S. Eliot: "Now Ennui, as it appears in much romantic literature is very much the same sin as the Christian sin of acedia, or spiritual torpor, and it might well be regarded as the most deadly of sins because it leads to all the others and interferes with one's struggling against them: it would be above all other sins the one most likely to appear, if we accept Christian postulates, in a man or society deprived of grace." But the world of *Hedda Gabler* is not deprived of grace because it has been too long deprived of its Christian postulates. And Hedda cannot be said to be suffering from any sin, for Ibsen has himself immolated the notion of sin along with other traditional values on the pyre of social criticism. We cannot call his study of Hedda, as we can the poems of Baudelaire or Shakespeare's *Macbeth,* a study of evil, for there is in this world of Ibsen's no way to evaluate evil; hence the effect of negative irony. Hedda is and Hedda expires: the judgment, if any, is outside the play.

Hedda Gabler provides, thus, a fragment of reality. Its protagonist is directionless, and though sharing certain attributes of our age, is not fully typical of it, nor sufficiently positive to make us warm to her as we do even to Blanche DuBois, who at least has qualities of tenderness and charity that, in a revised environment, might possibly fructify. Williams disappoints because he intimates that the environment he portrays is the partial projection of a whole which is brutal and calloused. Ibsen disappoints because he gives us a Will impoverished by lack of self-understanding and which, because it is active only in destruction, deserves itself to be destroyed. In both plays the failure is a failure of perception—the image is limited.

Our age, erratic enough, and anxious to redeem the time by restoring purpose, has had its fill of perversion and eccentricity; it has seen far too much of destruction. Neither the myth of automatic perfectibility nor the shock of nihilism can account for our dilemmas or set us right, nor can any pseudo-orthodox consolations. Our age wants neither the guarantee of predetermined sanctity nor the best of a bad job, alternatives which T. S. Eliot offers in *The Cocktail Party*. It wants to work for its living. And it wants simply to know from its artists, old and new, what the normal aspiring person, he who is willing to struggle and sacrifice and suffer so long as there is a chance that it is not in vain, must do to achieve some satisfactory salvation. Our age wants this, even if it is not always aware of it, for the very tension which marks it is a result of its ageless desire to know.

Ibsen has dealt elsewhere with the problem of self-realization. Nora in *A Doll's House* represents more than the emancipated woman, she represents potential actuating itself. But Nora's conflict, though it is philosophically and dramatically perennial, loses potency when the circumstances in which it arises are no longer felt as real. It has more value than Hedda's, but it is subject to greater loss. It is necessary, therefore, in producing both of these plays to avoid "modernizing" them. For if you modernize them, you ruin them. What worth persists in *Hedda Gabler* will only be realized in so far as its cultural situation is theatrically and mimetically restored.

Only in the tight omnipresent suffocating realistic parlor can we suggest what is important in Ibsen. Shakespeare is more easily modernized because place in Shakespeare is an act of the imagination; in Ibsen it is a specification. The Castle of Elsinore is an atmosphere, an essence, not a scene; Tesman's home is the real stuff, brocade and majolica ornaments included. It is the very solidity of this home that repels Hedda, for she antedates it. Mrs. Elvsted could live in it; Nora could leave it; Hedda could only die.

The character of Hedda, which of course is central to the meaning of the play, is sufficiently complex and ambiguous to have invited a wide variety of interpretations, both by those who go to (or read) plays and by those who stage them. In the following excerpts, three students of the theatre, looking at the same Ibsen play, discover three radically different Heddas. For Harold Clurman, she is an ordinary woman whose problems are typical of the nineteenth-century middle class. For Joseph Wood Krutch, she is a sterile and cowardly neurotic, perverted by the dullness of a complacent society. For G. Wilson Knight, Hedda is heroic, a person of great spiritual stature, an embodiment of the amoral, life-seeking energies of the Greek god of wine and ecstasy, Dionysus. These interpretations may seem contradictory. But nothing could better demonstrate the richness of interpretive possibility in a great dramatic work than the fact that each of these interpretations is solidly based on what is to be found in Ibsen's text.

[*HEDDA GABLER* AS THE TRAGEDY OF THE NINETEENTH-CENTURY BOURGEOISIE]
Harold Clurman

If I had to explain to a foreign visitor one of the most grievous defects of the American theatre I should say: "You see, Monsieur, our 'big' public—the one that pays the high prices to see our appallingly costly productions (and even productions which look modest are costly)—this public does not as a rule care for old plays. I refer not only to Shakespeare, Congreve, Sheridan or Goldsmith, but to Shaw, Chekhov, Wilde and O'Neill. This public does not care for such plays simply because they are old: there is no 'story' in them, no news value. In order to see plays by the authors we loosely label 'classics,' one has to go to a special—usually a tiny—theatre where, because of the extremely limited means at the producer's disposal, young actors do their very best to cope with the difficult material. For the better the play, the knottier the problems it poses for the director and his company.

"When I was a young man an admirable producer, Arthur Hopkins, offered a whole cycle of Ibsen plays on Broadway with Nazimova, Lionel Atwill, Roland Young (settings by Robert Edmond Jones). Some years later an enterprising organization produced *Hedda Gabler* with Emily Stevens, Dudley Digges, Louis Calhern—every one of them of star stature. But in those days the cost of production was not high, the price of tickets was moderate. In the late twenties Eva Le Gallienne at her Civic Repertory Theatre on 14th Street presented Chekhov and Ibsen to large audiences for $1.50 the orchestra seat. (But that was a privately subsidized theatre.) Today Chekhov and Ibsen are usually played in a theatre of 199 seats, earnestly directed and sincerely acted, but without the full equipment of background, maturity and scope of talent to do justice to these masters. But since they are masters, and since the public which has retained an appetite for plays of substance still exists, these productions, for all their artistic inadequacies, are sometimes hailed as high points of theatrical art—and no decent person is disposed to deny it. For if we rejected such honorable efforts in the off-Broadway

Excerpted from Harold Clurman, [Review of *Hedda Gabler*], *The Nation*, vol. 191, no. 20 (December 10, 1960), 462–463.

areas we should have to go without any reminder at all of what the best dramatists of the past had to say."

So Ibsen's *Hedda Gabler* (4th Street Theatre) is rediscovered. Many people who have spoken or written about this production give the impression that they have neither seen nor read the play before; or if they had, regarded it as one of those classics which it was better to talk about than to know.

I have seen four previous productions of *Hedda*—the three just referred to—and one in France. Two seasons ago I had occasion to use *Hedda Gabler* as a kind of text for a lecture I gave on Chekhov and Ibsen. Rereading it, I realized once again that though, subjectively speaking, I prefer Chekhov, *Hedda* is indeed a masterpiece and still a play to be treasured not merely as a "model" but as a living work of art.

I need not emphasize the perfection of its construction, which breaks down at only one point: in the last act where Ibsen's need to preserve the unity of time makes him pack too many psychological metamorphoses into too brief a section of the play. Nor are we aided to appreciate the play by viewing Hedda herself as an evil woman, a horrendous *femme fatale,* a freak like the "vampires" of stage and screen in the era of Theda Bara.

Nazimova played Hedda that way—and I remember that John Corbin, who was then critic of *The New York Times,* condemned her for it. He was right. Hedda is, at bottom, an "ordinary" woman. She is afraid to combat the conventions of her class and her environment. She will not break any rules. The descendant of what must have been a sort of military aristocracy now deprived of its privileges, money and status, she cannot abide the mediocrity of middle-class life in a tight community. Yet she will not marry an outcast intellectual to whom she is strongly attracted and perhaps even loves. She is jealous of an old schoolmate, an innocent nincompoop (according to Hedda), but a woman who through love is able to escape the bonds of her social position.

Hedda does the only thing left for her to do: she marries into a respectable milieu to which she considers herself superior by virtue of her heritage and "temperament." Like so many middle-class women, she hopes that her husband's stock will rise—either by his becoming more affluent or by achieving a "name"—and thus render her life more tolerable. She wants to be a successfully normal woman, comfortably safe with attributes of glamour and dash. On no account will she be "had" (lose her "independence") either by becoming a mother or some man's mistress. As a result, she is warped. Whatever is superior in her—that is, humanly lively (for in no other way does Ibsen portray her as superior)—becomes destructive through her self-enforced conformism. But the point that one must forever bear in mind is that Hedda is not by nature demonic. She is, as I have said, ordinary, almost representative.

The play then is the tragedy of the nineteenth-century bourgeoise. Her equivalent is still with us. Even if we cannot see the correspondence between Hedda and many women we know today—despite their "emancipation"—the play embodies the truth that healthy impulses, thwarted either by lack of social encouragement or by lack of personal resoluteness, will ultimately grow either flabby or nihilistic.

Flaubert said, "I am Madame Bovary." He meant that though he was a romantic at heart, he felt historically obliged to tame his yearning for grandeur, color and eloquence so that he might serve the ends of the strictly realistic, antiheroic novel. Somewhat similarly, Ibsen was a Hedda Gabler, compressing his passion to the manner and themes of the middle-class theatre. His last play—*When We Dead Awaken*—tells us that the man who sacrifices his affective life for "art" or a like ambition—it is "business" in *John Gabriel Borkman*—becomes a monster whose works will inevitably reveal the deformed nature of their origin. But the force of Ibsen's passion and its compression in the narrow mold of the realistic stage gives his plays at their best an elevation, an intensity, a symbolic sweep and extension that break through the grayness of their caution and logic.

[HEDDA AS A NEUROTIC]
Joseph Wood Crutch

The most exciting event of a busy week in the theater was not any of the new plays revealed but the production of "Hedda Gabler" by the Civic Repertory Company now operating at the Broadhurst. Miss Le Gallienne's performance of her part has always been admirable, but the production as a whole is vastly more finished than the one formerly seen on Fourteenth Street, and it comes as a fresh reminder that at least one of Ibsen's plays is almost as exciting as it ever was. Even in "Ghosts" the burden of a now granted thesis seems to grow heavier and heavier; even in the best of the later "symbolic" plays much of the iridescent mist which used to surround them looks more and more like mere fog; but Hedda remains a character as enduringly real and as perversely fascinating as ever. Among all the inventions of her creator she is, perhaps, the most complexly human, the least explicable as merely the projection of an idea. And for that reason there is about her something of the "infinite variety" of an even greater character whom age cannot wither nor custom stale.

Hedda is a neurotic. Even the blindest of Ibsen's contemporary critics saw that and denounced it. But what they did not understand, or rather what they understood just sufficiently to revolt against it in horror, was the fact that her creator saw deep enough into her soul to understand her perversity and to make her, not a monster, but a woman. Ibsen was no decadent show-off prating of "splendid sins" and magnificent cruelties. Hedda's mean acts, conceived and executed in the rage of impotence which can feel power only by destroying, remain plainly mean. But Ibsen saw in her perversities something which only a few men of his time—Dostoevski, for example—would have been capable of seeing: namely, that her reactions are not merely evil or merely the evidences of a malady to be disposed of when it has been called disease. She is rebelling perversely and unsuccessfully against something which should be rebelled against. The things which exasperate her—the complacent spiritual poverty of her group and the dull "goodness" of her vegetating husband—are exasperating things. She is therefore not merely a villain, an evil woman. She has made an unsuccessful adjustment to a situation which any vital person would have found intolerable; and the play built

Joseph Wood Krutch, [Review of *Hedda Gabler*], *The Nation*, vol. 139, no. 3624 (December 19, 1934), 720–721.

about her was "immoral" in the shocked eyes of such respectables as William Winter because it laid the blame no more upon Hedda, whom dullness had perverted, than upon the others, whom it had merely stultified. Those famous "vine leaves" which she hoped to see in Lövborg's hair are only a symbol of the neurotic's perverted version of that "joy" whose absence from the lives of his fellow-citizens Ibsen was so continually lamenting. . . .

Interpretations of Hedda are as various, almost, as interpretations of Hamlet, and for much the same reason. Like Hamlet she is wonderfully convincing as a person even when one is least sure what rational account to give of her motives. But in the light of her creator's own working notes there can hardly be doubt any longer concerning the main outlines of his intention. She is a heroine *manquée* and not only *a* heroine but *the* Ibsen heroine. She longs for all the things which Ibsen desired and thought most admirable. She wants to be "free," to seek the joy and the meaning of life without regard for convention or safety. To her, as to the author of so many plays about very limited people, the meaning of life is to be found in ecstasy. But though she perceives the fact, she is incapable of rising to the heights which she despises others for not being even aware of. She is a coward and she is sterile. But, so Ibsen seems to say, it is something to be capable of even a sickness like hers. . . .

[HEDDA AS THE DIONYSIAN WOMAN]

G. Wilson Knight

. . . The neglected powers appear to be most active, or at least most easily focused, in women: in Furia, Hiördis, Gerd, Nora and Rebecca. *Hedda Gabler* (1890) makes the Dionysian woman its central concern.

As in *Rosmersholm,* the note is aristocratic, though here our new Rebecca descends, as it were, from the heroic element in the Rosmers. Hedda's father, now dead, was General Gabler, whose portrait overwatches the action. A great heroic tradition is behind her, harking back to Hiördis, fire-arms replacing arrows. Hedda's interests are aristocratic; she used to ride with her father, and she still possesses, and amuses herself with, his pistols. In strong contrast she has recently married a middle-class academic nonentity, Tesman, who is researching (I. 18) on the "Domestic Industries of Brabant during the Middle Ages." Hedda despises his work and loathes domesticity. The prospect of a child is to her an agony. She is in a state of boredom swirling with unharnessed energies, "raising her arms and clenching her hands as if in desperation" (I. 25). She is deliberately cruel to her husband's sweet-natured if slightly ridiculous aunt, such "impulses" coming over her "all of a sudden" (II. 76). Her dislike of living always with "the same person" (II. 67) in marriage, and her infuriation at people's well-meant interest in her approaching maternity—the absurdity, she says, is "killing" her (IV 161)—

From G. Wilson Knight, *Henrik Ibsen* (New York: Grove Press, 1962), pp. 62–67. Copyright © 1962 by Grove Press, Inc. Reprinted by permission of Grove Press, Inc., New York, and Curtis Brown Ltd., London, on behalf of G. Wilson Knight.

are in line with Ibsen's denigration of the sexual-biological in *Love's Comedy,* and indeed throughout his dramatic quest. Of this quest Hedda is an exact, if extreme, personification. Sexually she seems half-male. The word "love" sickens her, and she hates amatory advances (II. 68, 71), though she enjoys listening to sex-secrets from the male angle (II. 99–100; 113). Though her imagination can to this, male, extent be sexually heated, she is terrified, as was Ibsen himself—the play is strongly autobiographical—of scandal, and admits to cowardice (II. 101–2). Her descent blends iron heroism with conventional respectability, and this dual conditioning, together with her abnormal sexuality, forces her into a state of inhibited violence. If she shuts out the sun (I. 19–20) that is because she dare not face her own fire. Despite her external cautions, she has a "craving for life" (II. 102), and despite her cruelty, a horror of ugliness (III. 130). The clamped pressure of these opposites is unendurable; she lets off her father's pistols for relief, she is, like the fire-veined Furia in *Catiline,* whom we first meet in a precisely similar state of volcanic boredom, fire personified.

Hedda appears to lack the more positive qualities of both normality and abnormality, being without the social ease of the one or the daring of the other; and yet she is certainly impressive. Much, perhaps too much, is left to the performer, whose business it will be to convince us of Hedda's stature. We have to recognise that she is "unlike the generality of women" (II. 81), facing difficulties correspondent to her uniqueness.

Contrasted with Tesman's dry-as-dust researches is the more creative talent of Eilert Lövborg, with whom Hedda had once, before her marriage, had a close association, which she broke off for fear of scandal (II. 97–102). He has since sunk to vice through drink and been rehabilitated by Mrs Elvsted, an old school-companion whom Hedda used to bully, threatening to burn her hair (I. 39). Hedda discovers that the seemingly "fragile" and "soft" Mrs Elvsted has had the courage to leave her husband and look after Lövborg, has been the inspiratory force behind his successful book on "the march of civilisation" (I. 29, 33), and has since collaborated with him in a still more important and as yet unpublished work of prophetic significance. We recognise a typical Ibsen set-up: a breaking-free from conventional restrictions, advanced thought, and a woman-inspirer acting on a man of ability if not genius. And yet, as we discovered, in *Ghosts, The Wild Duck,* and *Rosmersholm,* intellectual enlightenment alone, however praiseworthy, may not be adequate. The greater powers are not so easily placated; and Hedda is their implement.

She deliberately tempts Lövborg back to drink, and in a terrifying scene burns his new manuscript. Why? Partly, of course, from thwarted jealousy. Mrs Elvsted has done what Hedda would like to do, moulding "a human destiny" (II. 114), and if she may not do it positively she will do it destructively, like Bishop Nicholas when he burns the crucial letter in *The Pretenders.* Hedda's jealousy is, however, the obverse of a positive, if darkly-apprehended, belief that could she find it she has something better to offer. Intoxication is a power in *Peer Gynt* and *Ghosts,* and mystically honoured in *Emperor and Galilean*; and in recalling Lövborg from literary brilliance to drink Hedda may be seen as drawing him from a limited intellectual achievement to all the fiery vitalities defined by Shakespeare in Falstaff's speech on sherris-sack (2 *Henry IV,* IV. iii. 93–136). Ibsen himself on occasion drank heavily. In normal terms such experiences may be bought too dear, but Hedda is not thinking in normal terms. She is not thinking at all; she is finding an action correspondent to her state of being; and it has an imaginative, if not a logical, ratification. That is why she takes such keen pleasure in envisaging Lövborg "with vine-leaves in his hair" (II. 114–15; III. 125, 136, 150–1). In submitting himself to temptation she believes that he will regain his whole, Dionysian, self and be henceforth "a free man for all his days"; and she claims that her trust is greater than Mrs Elvsted's, whose surface reformation has left him no better than a half-man and unfree (II. 114). When Hedda hears of the miserable result, all she can say, quietly, "gazing straight before her," is, "Then he had no vine-leaves in his hair" (III. 136). Lövborg's failure repeats Julian's: searching for Dionysus, he finds himself in a police-station.

Ostensibly Hedda burns his manuscript in a paroxysm of jealousy because it has been the "child" (III. 152) of the supposedly reformed Lövborg and the trivial, mouse-like, Mrs Elvsted. But if we remember Ibsen's cauterising satire on writing—Falk's burning of his books in *Love's Comedy*, Julian's comic pamphlets, and the philosopher on the battle-field anxious for his own safety in order to complete his great work "On Equanimity in Affliction" (*The Emperor Julian*, V. iii. 460)—we may again see Hedda's action as motivated from the very depths of her being. She had wanted to make Lövborg great; action to further that greatness has failed; action can yet define what that greatness was not. Whatever it might have been, and neither she nor Ibsen clearly knows, it certainly was not a matter of pen and ink. Therefore the manuscript must be burned.

As in *Rosmersholm*, realisation in life has been proved impossible. Hedda, functioning as a Sibylline authority, formulates what *Rosmersholm* left dark. Lövborg has hinted at suicide (III. 150):

HEDDA   Eilert Lövborg—listen to me.—Will you not try to—to do it beautifully?

LÖVBORG   Beautifully? [*Smiling*] With vine-leaves in my hair, as you used to dream in the old days—?

HEDDA   No, no. I have lost my faith in the vine-leaves. But beautifully nevertheless! For once in a way!

She gives him one of General Gabler's pistols. Here, faced by the ultimate negation, the positive drive within Hedda's actions is rendered explicit. And when she hears of Lövborg's death, shot in the "breast," she is sorry that it was not "in the temple," but content (IV. 168–9). At last she has found "a deed worth doing," "the one right thing"; and it gives her a sense of "freedom" to know that such "deliberate courage" and "spontaneous beauty" is still "possible." He has dared to live his life after his own fashion and pay the price (IV. 169–74).

When Hedda discovers that his dying was in fact neither voluntary nor beautiful and that he was shot in the bowels, it seems to her that whatever she touches turns "ludicrous and mean" (IV. 176). Judge Brack, whose attentions had formerly served as an acceptable diversion, now increases his hold over her; he warns her that she may be implicated in Lövborg's death and arouses her deep-seated fears of scandal. As a composite and ambivalent personification of both sexual intrigue and social judgment he stands for all that Hedda most hates and fears in the society around her. She is trapped. While Tesman and Mrs Elvsted are piecing together the notes of Lövborg's manuscript, Hedda plays wild, exultantly Dionysian, Tarantella, dance-music; a shot sounds from General Gabler's other pistol; and she lies dead. The prophetic work has, it is true, in part survived, but in death Hedda succeeds where Lövborg failed (IV. 185):

> TESMAN   Shot herself! Shot herself in the temple! Fancy that!
> BRACK   Good God!—people don't do such things.

Or if they do, they do not do it so exquisitely, showing such pride, scorn, and indomitable spirit. "In the temple." The mind is both man's highest possession and worst foe, and consequently the spirit's right antagonist and target.

With a fine austerity of purpose Ibsen refuses his heroine any softening that might prevent her spiritual stature from asserting itself in independence of moral value. Probably in no other drama in existence is the positive essence within the apparent negations of a criminal temperament so exactly exposed, accepted, and driven to an honoured conclusion, as in this story of a general's daughter. In *Hedda Gabler*, in its sun-fire wine, its pistols, and its burning, the fiery veins of Ibsen's fearful quest are nakedly apparent. . . .

In focusing on the complexities of Hedda herself, critics (and directors) have sometimes tended to overlook the subtle traits of personality Ibsen gave to the other characters in the play. In his study of Hedda Gabler, *Hermann J. Weigand has persuasively drawn our attention to some of these neglected subtleties—for example, in his detailed reinterpretation of the character of Tesman.*

[TESMAN]
Hermann J. Weigand

. . . The portrait of Brack is executed with a vividness that makes it one of the unforgettable pieces in Ibsen's gallery of characters. An even more distinctive position, however, is reserved for Tesman. In Tesman Ibsen has handled a thoroughly commonplace character with a degree of finesse which he rarely, if ever, equaled. I know of no single situation that illustrates Ibsen's peculiar genius more strikingly than Tesman's relation to Lövborg. An uncanny penetration into the secret springs of conduct combines here with an objectivity of rendering calculated to conceal rather than reveal the author's esoteric knowledge of Tesman's character. To my knowledge, the equivocal nature of Tesman's complete line of conduct, after his finding of the manuscript, has failed to arouse the suspicions of a single critic. In the nature of things, Tesman's brainless scholarship and his ludicrous naïveté have drawn the caustic sarcasm of all commentators; but many—and not the meanest of them—have stressed his large-hearted

From Hermann J. Weigand, *The Modern Ibsen* (New York: Holt, 1925; reprinted by Dutton, 1960), pp. 267–273. Copyright 1925 by Holt, Rinehart and Winston, Inc. Copyright 1953 by Hermann J. Weigand. Reprinted by permission of Holt, Rinehart and Winston, Publishers.

kindness and simple honesty as endowing him with some genuine human value in contrast to Hedda's corrosive perversity. The findings of our analysis will be seen to differ sharply from those commonly accepted.

Tesman is keenly aware of the fact that he is intellectually Lövborg's inferior. When Brack advances the theory that his appointment to the professorship may be made contingent upon the outcome of a competition with Lövborg, he is thoroughly alarmed. Indignant gesticulation at the very idea is his first reaction to the news. For Lövborg to challenge his right to the position would be showing the most incredible lack of consideration toward him, a married man, who had run deeply into debt on the strength of mere prospects. On finding himself alone with Hedda he betrays his discouragement. "It was adventurous to go and marry and set up house upon mere expectations," he tells her. Eager as he is to snatch the merest straw of comfort, he finds balm in the reassuring words of Aunt Julie. And when the tension finally breaks, when Lövborg tells him in language which does not disguise his contempt, that he has no intentions of standing in the way of Tesman's appointment, Tesman is so little master of his feelings that he draws Brack's and Hedda's ironical comment.

However, even a fool like Tesman cannot be insensitive to the humiliation which a victory of Lövborg's in the open forum would entail for him. It is natural that his consciousness of being the weaker should make him secretly hope for some eventuality to arise to thwart his rival's success.

His stocks rise in consequence of the developments at Brack's party.

For one thing, he finds consolation in the reflection that if Lövborg outdistances him in brilliancy of intellect, he more than neutralizes this deficiency by the shining example he sets Lövborg in the matter of decent behavior. The satisfaction he experiences in contrasting his own socially accredited virtue with Lövborg's lack of self-control is so great that he can weep crocodile tears of regret over Lövborg's incorrigible weakness. More than that, he feels his own moral superiority so securely established that he can afford even to confess to a stirring of jealousy, as he listened to his rival's brilliant essay.

Of even greater psychological importance is the fact of his find. From the outset his feelings with regard to the precious manuscript in his possession are quite complicated. At the root of his act of concealing it is the instinctive, unavowed wish to deprive his rival of the material evidence of his superiority. However, Tesman's conscience will not permit that wish to come to the surface of his consciousness. He obscures it instantly with superficial motives which serve to explain his action on high moral grounds. In the state Lövborg was in, he persuades himself, he didn't dare return it to him at once. For Eilert's sake, in order to spare him a keen humiliation, he concealed his find from his companions, and he enjoins Hedda not to tell a soul about it.

Time is gained, at any rate, by procrastination; and generous motives easily suggest themselves to Tesman for justifying further delay. He wants to give "Eilert, poor fellow, time to have his sleep out," before he surrenders the book. All this time, as his words to Hedda betray, his mind is dwelling upon the fact that there is no second copy of the manuscript in existence.

The day passes, and evening arrives without Tesman having divulged his secret. In the afternoon he had looked in at Lövborg's rooms but failed to find him. Perhaps he counted on his being out, as might well be the case, considering his presumptive state of mind on discovery of his loss. Certainly the fact that Tesman departed without leaving a note is an item of the gravest significance. Then he met Thea rushing about distractedly, but he clung to his secret. From Thea he gathered that Lövborg had called at the house that morning and talked incoherently about having torn the manuscript to pieces. Thea's own ignorance made it sufficiently plain that Hedda had followed to the letter his injunction to keep silence. When he nevertheless asks Hedda, "But of course you told him that we had it?" he is certain, in advance, of a negative answer.

"You ought to have told him," he tells Hedda. "Fancy, if, in desperation he should go and do himself some injury!" His reply is strictly in accord with the demands of his conscience. Yet the apparent concern of his phrasing only disguises the secret hope that such a contingency might already have occurred, and it absolves him in advance of any blame for what may have happened.

Now Tesman declares his resolve to take the manuscript to Lövborg at once. Precisely what he had in mind to do must remain mere conjecture. Perhaps he hoped that Hedda would dissuade him from acting in haste. Or there was always the possibility of Lövborg's not being at home. And again, he was possibly prepared to find Lövborg in such a state of distraction to justify his deciding that it would be dangerous to tell him of his find at once even now. Be that as it may, his conscience at any rate required some sort of gesture for its temporary pacification. All that we can be certain about is that his conscience, while permitting him to drift passively into crime, was too active to allow his forming any deliberate, consciously avowed plan to suppress Lövborg's work.

Conjecture as to what might have happened is checked by Hedda's announcement that she had burned the manuscript. The first shock is almost too much for Tesman. In mingled joy and terror he screams: "Burnt! Burnt Eilert's manuscript!" Then, as he collects himself, he formulates the significance of her act in language suggestive of Torvald Helmer: "Do you know what you have done, Hedda? It's unlawful appropriation of lost property."

Swayed by a mixture of fear of consequences and sarcastic deviltry, Hedda explains that she committed the deed for love of him, and to make sure of his dancing altogether to the tune of her pipe she gives him to understand that he is to become a father. The effect of this second revelation is marvelous. Tesman claps his hands together. He shouts. He laughs in irrepressible glee. In his excitement he even gets off an excellent pun:

> No, by-the-bye—that affair of the manuscript—of course nobody must know about that. But that you burn for me, Hedda, Aunt Julie must really share my joy in that.

Our insight into Tesman's complex state of mind makes us realize what a masterly flash of intuition on Ibsen's part prompted the timing of Hedda's announcement of her pregnancy at this juncture. The news that he is to be a father releases of a sudden all of Tesman's pent-up emotions. When Hedda announced the destruction of Lövborg's work he longed to cry out with glee at the materialization of his secret wishes, but his conscience restrained him, except for his first equivocal shout; he had to persuade himself that he deplored the deed on Lövborg's account. Now it is different. The second piece of news opens the floodgates of his feelings, and in the tumult of his paternal joy the waters from the first source mingle undetected with the current that has just found its legitimate release. Now he can rejoice to his fill, and no voice of conscience dares to inhibit the spontaneity of his exultation!

Fate has been kind to Tesman. Without his having had to commit an act or utter a word that he need to ascribe to any save the most honorable and exalted motives, his rival's work has been destroyed. And Fate has a still greater kindness in store for him. As Brack brings the news of Lövborg's suicide, there is indeed a flutter of suspense; Tesman's conscience, aroused again, gives him a few uneasy moments; but the situation is saved and Tesman's peace of mind definitely assured, when Thea produces her bundle of notes—the jottings from which Lövborg dictated his book. There is a task for Tesman! With his talent for arranging other people's work, he is the very man to restore the lost manuscript. How will his conscience dare to stir in the face of his resolve to dedicate his life to this task, to make his own researches wait upon the completion of this monument to Lövborg's memory? Could friendship be more generous, could devotion be more self-sacrificing? Considering it from whatever angle one will—the appeasement of his conscience, the establishing of his scholar's reputation, the appraisement of his character as a man,—it is certain that this piece of editing will be the keystone in the making of Tesman's career.

Rarely, if ever, has Ibsen handled a commonplace character with such a degree of subtlety. The extraordinary finesse displayed in the treatment accorded to Tesman lies precisely in the equivocal nature of every single phase of his conduct. For the reader to lump Tesman with Brack, as another cold-blooded, unscrupulous rascal, were to miss the point of our analysis. Far from being a clever villain, Tesman is every bit as honorable as the average run of commonplace people. He has a conscience as efficacious as that of the average run of people: It keeps aggressive wickedness from stalking in freedom; and for the rest it keeps the mind busy building up fictitious lines of motivation to serve as covers for the manifestation of impulses that are not recognized as respectable. Ironical side-lights fall, to be sure, on the texture of this average morality, revealing its fabric to consist so largely of fraud and make-believe as to throw its wearer almost wholly upon the mercy of fortuitous circumstance. When Fate is kind enough, however, to prevent the frail tissue from being rent by any overt act, the Tesman type of conscience obligingly relapses into its normal state of quiescence. It shows no disposition to develop into the malignant tumor, the destroyer of vital tissue, as which we behold another type of conscience in the tragedy of Master-Builder Solness.

The problem of interpreting the characters in a dramatic work becomes immediate and acute when it is a matter not merely of reading and reacting to the text, as in the previous essays, but of putting the play on the stage. The director, the actors, and the set and costume designers must transform the printed script, with all of its various possibilities of interpretation, into a living performance that decisively conveys a coherent set of meanings. Eva Le Gallienne has throughout her career been deeply involved with Hedda Gabler, *as actress, director and translator, and she has therefore given much thought to all the practical details of production. Her reading of the play—the series of choices she has made in interpreting all its elements—is fully outlined in a lengthy preface she wrote for an edition of her own translation of* Hedda. *In the excerpts that follow, Miss Le Gallienne discusses the early scenes of the play, recording her ideas about the set, the costumes, and the characterization of Hedda and Tesman, and closely analyzing the scene in which Hedda questions Thea about her relationship with Lövborg.*

FROM *PREFACE TO IBSEN'S "HEDDA GABLER"*
Eva Le Gallienne

[The set for the opening scene]

. . . The room should be cheerful; bright morning sun through the french windows (there is a sun in Scandinavia!). It should be in good taste, though Hedda has not furnished it herself, and will "want to change a few things here and there"; it should be a room that might please her, though she will always grumble and ridicule: "What might be called the Aunt Julia atmosphere," "a touch of decay about it," etc. There should be one or two pieces of really good furniture, which she will notice and appreciate, for she has taste. The only things that she brings with her from her old life are her piano, a large portrait of General Gabler which hangs over the sofa in the inner room, and her pistols. Important symbols, all three, of her personal, private life. . . .

[Characterization of Tesman]

. . . Tesman is a man of few facets, and nearly all of them are touched on in this first scene of his with Aunt Julia. His healthy, active, almost bustling vitality—"I've been up since day-break," his pleasure in the small everyday things of life, show a buoyant, cheerful nature. Everything delights him; he is like a child, but not a silly child. He is delighted, astonished, bewildered, eager, troubled, dismayed, interested, enthusiastic, hurt, tender, excited, as a child might be—whole-heartedly. He gives himself up to the feeling of the moment, whatever it may be, with all of himself. There are no dark corners in him, no shadowy veiled places. He is what he appears to be at that particular moment. He is a man with a certain charm; the charm of honest, wholesome, good-nature. Men like him. People respect him. He is dependable, lovable, a thorough, conscientious worker and student, a painstaking, careful scholar. What a bril-

Excerpted from Eva Le Gallienne, *Preface to Ibsen's "Hedda Gabler"* (London: Faber and Faber, 1953), pp. 8–9, 10–12, 18–21. Reprinted by permission of Eva Le Gallienne and Faber and Faber, Ltd.

liant man would perceive in a flash of intuition, he arrives at through months of patient plodding study. But what he knows, he knows thoroughly and for ever. Men far
more brilliant than he are glad to discuss their work with him, to ask his opinion and
advice, to test their more daring and erratic flights of thought, in the slow but sure
dependability of his solid knowledge. He is himself slightly bewildered at finding himself the husband of Hedda Gabler, but I don't think it really makes him uncomfortable. He is extremely male, and his masculine superiority protects him.

Her incessant gibes (mostly subtle and oblique, but nevertheless constant) for the
most part drop off him as water off a duck; but if one is too blatant to ignore, he
imagines there must be something wrong with this feminine person and asks "Is anything the matter with you, Hedda, eh?" He looks on women as queer creatures; incomprehensible and therefore inferior to men, but charming and to be treated with
care. He is very proud of Hedda; proud of having a wife in his home so distinguished
and well-bred and beautiful and helpless. "I had looked forward to seeing you a brilliant hostess surrounded by distinguished guests"—"I daresay several of my friends are
a bit jealous of me, eh?" It is most important that Tesman himself should never feel
ridiculous or "funny." He is highly self-important, in a pleasant way. His tricks of
speech—"just think" or "think of that—eh?"—(the "fancy that" of the Archer version is
pure archerism; in the Norwegian he says "Taenk det"—but Archer has a way of fan-
cying things up!)—should never be unduly stressed; we all have habits of speech of that
sort—we are not even aware of them, they slip out quite casually, and can be extremely
annoying to people once they get on their nerves, and almost everything about Tesman
gets on Hedda's nerves. If an actor can say quite simply at the end of the play "Shot
herself in the temple—think of that" and not get a laugh, he has played the part well,
for of course there are frequent occasions throughout the play when he should get a
laugh through this habit of speech.

[Characterization and costume of Hedda]

Into this quiet, comfortable, *gemütlich* atmosphere comes Hedda. Her appearance is
enormously important. She should not be obviously "exotic" in any way. Ibsen is extremely definite in his description of her. " . . . Her face and figure show refinement
and distinction—her steel-grey eyes express a cold, unruffled repose," etc. For several of
his notes on Hedda he uses the expression "Cold"—"ice cold."

Some actresses have played the part completely disregarding Ibsen's wishes; have
dressed Hedda in an exaggerated *femme fatale* style; have made her appearance so extremely neurotic and peculiar that Tesman would never have dreamed of marrying
her, even had he wished to, which would be doubtful, for his tastes would surely lean
towards the conventional, and outwardly it is important that Hedda should seem conventional and in every way impress one as a highly-bred woman of distinction and
poise.

Ibsen describes her clothes as "tasteful." They should be becoming and should
have a certain individuality, no matter what period is chosen for the play; they should
never look like exaggerated fashion-plates, for a European woman of taste is not nearly
as regimented in her dress as her American equivalent. Hedda would choose her clothes

carefully and with a subtle art. They would be quite definitely "her own," for she is in everything an individualist while never going beyond the bounds of good taste and refinement. She is enormously aware of the impression she creates, very self-conscious always, and exquisite. She thinks of herself, one can be sure, as someone rare and romantic, a kind of *princesse lointaine.* It is probable that one of the most irritating things she found on the "wedding journey" was Tesman's good-natured willingness to conform to all the petty rules and regulations, his exactness about trains and time-tables, his careful economy and budgeting, all so "vulgar" and bourgeois; never the slightest inclination towards the unscheduled or the unexpected. And then for nearly six months to be cooped up in small hotel rooms or tiny railroad carriages; under such conditions to find oneself "everlastingly with one and the same person"—yes, indeed—poor Hedda must have been "bored to distraction."

So, on this morning, when we first meet her, she is probably in a good mood. When she woke up, Tesman had already disappeared and she was able to get up in a leisurely fashion, to prepare herself gradually to face the day, without the irritation of Tesman's noisy, bustling vitality.

On the whole, the house made a fairly agreeable impression on her the night before, and now she will take stock of it all, and decide on the changes and improvements she must obviously plan for. She comes in carrying her pistols—"General Gabler's pistols"—intending to put them on her old piano where she likes to see them as she sits for hours playing Chopin and sentimental waltzes, and not playing very well, but with a good deal of "expression." When she realizes that Aunt Julia is there with George it is too late to escape (though she has the impulse) and she tries to make the best of it. Her manner could be taken for gracious, though perhaps there is too much stress on the "early visitor," "how kind of you," and she can't resist, in her annoyance, the almost imperceptible dig at Tesman, "Yes—fortunately. . . ."

[The conversation between Hedda and Thea]

. . . When Thea is first announced, Hedda has no idea of the reason of her visit. She only knows that Lövborg has, for the past few years, been living near the Elvsteds and she is avid for news of him. Her feeling for Lövborg is not love—is Hedda capable of that? What is it then? Certainly there was between them a strong physical attraction. Hedda had a great, a consuming desire for Lövborg. But she is not like Thea. Passion with her could never be simple, pure, and inevitable. It must always be perverse and complicated. . . .

Hedda is now acutely aware that Thea is in love with Lövborg and is determined to find out the whole truth of the matter.

All during Thea's scene with Tesman she watches her, taking note of every expression, every nuance of tone and emphasis. She realizes that she must get Thea alone if she is to win her confidence.

During this scene she hears for the first time about Lövborg's rehabilitation, about the success of his published book, and the fact that Thea was closely associated with it. With a woman's eye for detail she observes her plain, almost shabby dress, the poorness of her accessories; her gloves, her bag; all meticulously neat, but indicative of the strictest economy. Thea later says: "It doesn't cost much to keep me—I'm not expensive." This has been obvious to Hedda from the beginning.

She now sends Tesman into his study to write a "long friendly letter" to Lövborg, asking him to call. In this way she manages to get Thea to herself. Also, knowing Lövborg as she does, she is probably right in thinking that "he may not care to come of his own accord" and she is consumed with curiosity to see him again, and judge for herself the extent of his "reformation." Tesman bustles happily off to write the letter and the two women are alone. The scene that follows must be played by Hedda with the utmost finesse.

In order to achieve a successful performance in an Ibsen play, it is necessary that the actor be capable of such concentrated thinking, that his thoughts actually take shape; the audience must see the thought, must be made a part of it. And this must be achieved without any external commotion whatever; not even a flick of the eyelash should be needed. The actor must, through the truth and power of his thinking, transfer his thought to the audience, compel them into awareness of the hidden inner life of the character portrayed. This is not a simple business. All great actors make use of this power to some extent, no matter what the play. But Ibsen makes the use of it imperative.

In the scene under discussion we have a perfect example.

Thea must be genuinely convinced of Hedda's good will, of her friendly sympathy and understanding. In everything she does and says Hedda must inspire confidence, must charm Thea and disarm her; the external pattern of the actress's performance must take care of that. Yet the audience must be acutely aware of the true thread of Hedda's thinking; to them her motives must be unmistakable. And this must be achieved by power of thought; there must be no dark looks behind Thea's back, no baleful glances towards the auditorium. It must all be very quiet, very relaxed, very sure. If the actress playing Hedda handles the scene clumsily, Thea will seem a fool. And that would be wrong.

It is true that when she finds herself alone with Hedda, Thea's first impulse is to escape. She mistrusts her; her clear, uncluttered instinct warns her against this woman. Hedda is quite aware of this. She is insistent that Thea "can't be in such a hurry," that they must have "a nice friendly chat"; she conjures up a purely fictitious childhood friendship—makes much of "after all, we were at school together"—refuses to notice Thea's weak denials of former intimacy, and finally overwhelms her into staying. Thea is shy and unwilling to give offence, she gives in.

And then her loneliness, confronted by this charming woman, who seems all warmth and strength and understanding, betrays her into revealing her secret.

Hedda starts by asking her questions about her "life at home." She is now in full control of the situation and plays with Thea as a cat plays with a mouse. There is always in her attitude a slightly superior tone—the snob in her comes out in almost imperceptible ways as in her question, "You were engaged as housekeeper, weren't you?"—the colour of the word "housekeeper" is unmistakable, though veiled with the good manners of the high-born talking to an inferior. Thea just senses it, for she comes back quite strongly with "I was supposed to go as governess," etc., and then in a few minutes Hedda brings out the frustration of her married life. She prompts her skilfully:

"But isn't he a bit old for you, dear? There must be about twenty years between you." All this with the greatest concern and sympathy.

Gradually Thea forgets her shyness, and all the pent-up grievances and misery of the past few years come tumbling out. She has been so alone, and it is a relief to talk about herself.

When it transpires that Thea has left her home for good, has run away, in fact, to be where Lövborg is, Hedda is definitely taken by surprise. To begin with, she hadn't suspected the importance of the Thea-Lövborg relationship; she now realizes that she is face to face with a woman who loves so deeply and so purely that she will dare anything for the sake of that love. Here is no little "ninny," no weak little female without character or courage; on the contrary, Hedda understands only too well the power and integrity of Thea's love. She is filled with envy as well as amazement. She would be entirely incapable of such an act. To face the condemnation of society, to dare to stand alone against all criticism, to be that true to oneself and to God—these are things that Hedda in the innermost recesses of her being would long to do—but would always refuse. She understands that Thea is far stronger than she.

I think there is a grudging admiration in her feeling; but her envy and resentment, yes, her jealousy, overcome it and her every thought, from now on, will be to poison and destroy Thea's love.

She herself dared not take Lövborg, but she can't endure the fact of anyone else having him.

Though Thea is unaware of it, Hedda has now become her bitter enemy. And the more she gives herself away, the truer this becomes. She feeds, through her guileless trust in Hedda, the resentment and jealousy that smoulder there.

When she speaks of sharing Lövborg's work, and particularly when she admits Lövborg's use of the term "comrade," she has unwittingly delivered herself and her love into Hedda's ruthless and destructive power. Lövborg had called Hedda, too, in the "old days," his "comrade" (men have an unfortunate way of repeating their patterns where women are concerned), and it is unbearable for Hedda to realize that he found "ample consolation" (as she puts it) elsewhere.

Her egotistical nature would have had him forever crushed and lost, since he could not have her. In fact, it is she who has been frustrated and lost through not having dared accept his love, through not having had the courage to really live.

But, at the very end of the scene, Thea lets fall a remark that provides Hedda with a very dangerous weapon. She reveals the fact that she feels "there is a shadow between Lövborg and me; a woman's shadow"; Hedda instinctively guesses who this woman is, and when Thea admits that "when they parted she threatened to shoot him" there is no room for doubt. This knowledge makes it clear to Hedda that she still has the "power" to disturb Lövborg, that the poison of their unresolved passion still works in him as it does in her. It is now only a question of how she can make circumstances serve her purpose. She is resolved.

This is a masterly scene. It is so clearly and brilliantly conceived from a psychological point of view, so closely knit, so economical in writing, so unerringly accurate, that the actresses concerned need do nothing but be honest. But they must be that. There is considerable comedy in the scene, for it is handled with a light touch, and the double values, of which the audience is aware, provide a number of reasons for ironic laughter.

In general, it is true that Ibsen's mordant humour is too often neglected. Actors are prone to handle his plays too heavily. They are afraid of "getting laughs." This is a mistake. Ibsen's sense of humour may not be gay or pleasant, but it is very potent all the same, and to discount it is to rob his plays of one of their most powerful assets. . . .

Hedda Gabler is one of the great female roles of the modern theatre. It is a tremendously demanding part, and a testing ground for the abilities of any actress. Furthermore, as the preceding excerpts have shown, Hedda's character can be understood—and hence acted—in many different ways. Here are some reviews of several eminent actresses of the past and present in the role of Hedda, including some quite antithetical opinions about Eva Le Gallienne and about the great Italian tragedian Eleonora Duse. These reviews give a vivid sense of the various interpretations of Hedda that have been seen on the stage, of the risks an actress takes in attempting the part, and of the dissension that is so often to be found among even the most intelligent and experienced critics when they try to assess the quality of a performance.

[DUSE AS HEDDA]
J. T. Grein

GREAT individual manifestations of genius are apt to unsettle our critical judgment. When one comes away in raptures from such a performance as Eleonora Duse's Hedda, the spell of her magnetism would induce the exclamation: "She is the greatest of them all—the only one." In our ecstasy the heroine of the hour effaces all other memories; we forget that other great artists have elicited the same cry, the same enthusiasm, the same adoration. But the very fact of this momentary exaggeration proves that the player who thus ensnares her hearers must possess unique power of transmitting her emotions to the multitude. In achieving this Duse employs no theatrical means. She does not put pressure on her vocal powers. She does not indulge in excessive facial changes or carefully studied gesticulations. She does not even practise the art of diction in perfect articulation. Compared to the methods of other artists, hers is a performance in a minor key, almost of nonchalance. Seemingly there is no stage for her, and there are no footlights; as for the public, they are, as it were, hidden by an imaginary fourth wall. Duse acts *in camera*. Her first dogma seems to be: "I will behave and speak as ordinary mortals do under ordinary circumstances." Whether she cows little Teja Elvsted into mortification, gently, cunningly, almost imperceptibly; whether

From J. T. Grein, "Duse in *Hedda Gabler* [Review, October 7, 1903]," in his *Dramatic Criticism 1903–1904* (New York: Benjamin Blom, 1969), pp. 293–294. First published 1904; reissued 1969 by Benjamin Blom, Inc.

she tempts Lövborg to drink in defiance of Teja, with the subtle ways of the Paradisiacal snake; whether she cajoles Tesman, her noodle of a husband, or toys with Brack, the lecherous provincial beau, she does it all without emphasis or effort. As we behold and listen to her, the sensation overwhelms us that she is wholly human—that she is one of us in peculiarly painful circumstances of life.

The immediate effect of this simple procedure is that those who have hitherto failed to understand the play, and sought in vain for subtle meanings unexplained, now grasp the whole situation. The case is now no longer even one of pathology. We see clearly why this lofty character, placed in juxtaposition to puny personalities in narrow circumstances, yearns and battles and clamours for deliverance. This Hedda cannot thrive, nor breathe, nor live in the stifling atmosphere vitiated by memories of the past, deadly by reason of the smallness of any thought that is uttered. And thus this Hedda, a Magdalene in countenance, a weary soul in a languid, worn-out body, stands before us, a doleful picture of woe, a sympathetic victim of circumstances. In this respect Duse's conception differs from that of all her sisters in art: in the others we are mostly attracted by the great outline of the character and repelled by its sharp edges and neurotic outbursts. In Duse's Hedda we merely feel moved to pity for the agony of a woman. The final rôle is one of immense sadness.

[DUSE AS HEDDA]
Max Beerbohm

. . . It may be that what I am going to say about Signora Duse as Hedda Gabler is vitiated by incapacity to understand exactly her rendering of the part as a whole. She may be more plausibly like Hedda Gabler than she seems to me. Mark, I do not say that she may have conceived the part more intelligently, more rightly, with greater insight into Ibsen's meaning. And perhaps I should express myself more accurately if I said that Hedda Gabler may be more like Signora Duse than she seems to me. For this actress never stoops to impersonation. I have seen her in many parts, but I have never (you must take my evidence for what it is worth) detected any difference in her. To have seen her once is to have seen her always. She is artistically right or wrong according as whether the part enacted by her can or cannot be merged and fused into her own personality. Can Hedda Gabler be so merged and fused? She is self-centred. Her eyes are turned inward to her own soul. She does not try to fit herself into the general scheme of things. She broods disdainfully aloof. So far so good; for Signora Duse, as we know her, is just such another. (This can be said without offence. The personality of an artist, as shown through his or her art, is not necessarily a reflection, and is often a flat contradiction—a complement—to his or her personality in life.) But Hedda is also a minx, and a ridiculous minx, and not a nice minx. Her revolt from

From Max Beerbohm, "An Hypocrisy in Playgoing [Review of Duse's *Hedda Gabler,* October 10, 1903]," in his *Around Theatres* (New York: Simon & Schuster, 1954), pp. 279–281.

the circumstances of her life is untinged with nobility. She imagines herself to be striving for finer things, but her taste is in fact not good enough for what she gets. One can see that Ibsen hates her, and means us to laugh at her. For that reason she "wears" much better than those sister-rebels whom Ibsen glorified. She remains as a lively satire on a phase that for serious purposes is out of date. She ought to be played with a sense of humour, with a comedic understanding between the player and the audience. Signora Duse is not the woman to create such an understanding. She cannot, moreover, convey a hint of minxishness: that quality is outside her rubric. Hedda is anything but listless. She is sick of a life which does not tickle her with little ready-made excitements. But she is ever alert to contrive these little excitements for herself. She is the very soul of restless mischief. Signora Duse suggested the weary calm of one who has climbed to a summit high above the gross world. She was as one who sighs, but can afford to smile, being at rest with herself. She was spiritual, statuesque, somnambulistic, what you will, always in direct opposition to eager, snappy, fascinating, nasty little Hedda Gabler. Resignedly she shot the pistol from the window. Resignedly she bent over the book of photographs with the lover who had returned. Resignedly she lured him to drunkenness. Resignedly she committed his MS. to the flames. Resignation, as always, was the keynote of her performance. And here, as often elsewhere, it rang false.

However, it was not the only performance of Hedda Gabler. There was another, and, in some ways, a better. While Signora Duse walked through her part, the prompter threw himself into it with a will. A more raucous whisper I never heard than that which preceded the Signora's every sentence. It was like the continuous tearing of a very thick silk. I think it worried every one in the theatre, except the Signora herself, who listened placidly to the prompter's every reading, and, as soon as he had finished, reproduced it in her own way. This process made the matinée a rather long one. By a very simple expedient the extra time might have been turned to good account. How much pleasure would have been gained, and how much hypocrisy saved, if there had been an interpreter on the O.P. side, to shout in English what the prompter was whispering in Italian! . . .

[INGRID BERGMAN AS HEDDA]
Janet Flanner

Henrik Ibsen's *Hedda Gabler,* practically unknown here, was last played as a full-dress Paris performance nineteen years ago, during the war, and so was seen by few. It has just been revived on the same stage—that of the Théâtre Montparnasse—for Ingrid Bergman. She is the only international star who can play at ease internationally, in French, English, Italian, German, and Swedish. Undeflected by this cosmopolitanism, the native Scandinavian essence of Bergman's interpretation, done here in French, gives to Ibsen's evasive, destructive, and frigid Nordic woman the melting weight of tragedy, at last. Hedda was the first modern married female egotist, as flighty and undomestic as a sea gull, and the erratic prototype of too many twentieth-century Western women to come. With cold invention, Ibsen brought her to life too soon—in 1890—so for two decades or more, while human nature caught up with her, she seemed a matronly freak, and for years was played as such, even by the best actresses, to whom her frantic hyperesthesia must have seemed a special intellectual puzzle. Bergman plays her as if Hedda were completely visible as a character only in her worst moments—as if the Northern Lights of the play's climate suddenly fell full upon her in focussed illumination only during her cruel minutes, such as when she makes fun of Aunt Julia's new bonnet, when she lies so easily to her loving, stupid husband, when she threatens to set fire to Mme. Elvsted's pale hair, when she murderously thrusts Eilert Lövborg's great manuscript into the stove. The rest of the time, unlighted by anything stronger than the parlor lamp, her Hedda has shadows enough to make her seem only a normally unhappy married woman, lonely and even pitiable. It is a logical, integrated conception, brilliantly performed. Bergman's strong, idle hands, her long-stepped, gliding walk, her Northern voice, and the liberty-loving tilt of her head seem her special physical assets for her incarnation of Hedda. The stage is perhaps better dressed than the star. The Tesman parlor is properly cluttered with stylish bourgeois draperies and furnishings. Miss Bergman looks undeniably handsome in a vivid green velvet evening jacket, though an overfull striped skirt destroys her fine slenderness. She attains her full beauty only in the last act, dressed tightly and tragically in beautiful black, as she glides out of the room with her pistol in her hand.

It is a memorable production by a completely intelligent, superior cast, well suited to acting in what is, after all, the most penetrating psychological study and the best-constructed modern play now showing in Paris—no question about it. Claude Dauphin does not hesitate to make poor, erudite Tesman silly enough for the audience to laugh at out loud—a rare sound at an Ibsen masterpiece.

Genêt [Janet Flanner], "Letter from Paris [Review of Ingrid Bergman's *Hedda Gabler*]," *The New Yorker,* December 15, 1962, pp. 175–176. Reproduced by permission; © 1962 The New Yorker Magazine, Inc.

[NAZIMOVA AS HEDDA]
Joseph Wood Krutch

Alla Nazimova's performance in *Hedda Gabler* (Longacre Theater) is something of a triumph for both actress and playwright. It is nearly thirty years since she first essayed the role, and it is no small thing that both the character itself and her interpretation of it should remain as vital as they do. . . .

As for Madame Nazimova, I saw her first some fifteen years ago in *The Wild Duck*. Even then she was, as she shook the black hair from about her eyes, less a little Norwegian girl than some almost unearthly creature who would have seemed exotic in any environment. All that might have been urged against her then might be urged with at least equal force today. If one stops to think, it is obviously impossible to assume that she could have been accepted by the people among whom she moved as a passably ordinary person, not an extraordinary phenomenon. I might even go so far as to add that, in the abstract, I prefer the conception of those who play the character with more emphasis upon a certain contrast between an outward conventionality of manner and the inner diabolism of her character. But Madame Nazimova makes one forget all this. She is both technically superb and capable of projecting a personality too strong to permit a question. I have seen Heddas who seemed more credible in retrospect; I have never seen one who imposed herself so inescapably. . . .

Excerpted from Joseph Wood Krutch, [Review of Nazimova's *Hedda Gabler*], *The Nation*, vol. 143, no. 22 (November 28, 1936), 641–642.

[ANNE MEACHAM AS HEDDA]
Robert Brustein

Off Broadway this season has been just as depressing as Broadway, but two recent productions merit a few remarks.

The first is *Hedda Gabler,* now being presented by David Ross as the initial offering in his projected Ibsen cycle. Since this cycle will at least expose audiences to the full amplitude of Ibsen's formidable powers, it is heartily welcome. Welcome also is the present production, though less heartily, for I am not happy about the performance. Anne Meacham, opening in the title role with only a few days preparation, is to be applauded for her heroism, but I wish she had transferred some of this quality to the part of Hedda. On her first entrance, I was staggered to see her made up like some ghastly cadaverous apparition (bloodless face, blood-red lips, green-shadowed eyes), and even more disheartened when she proceeded to interpret Hedda as a pathological case just two shrieks away from insanity. Hedda's strained romanticism proves a disaster to everyone, but the play is dialectical: she also possesses a vital heroic streak which is meant to contrast favorably with the mean-spirited world in which she lives. All this has now been reduced to Method psychopathology: gritted teeth, nervous gestures, staring eyes. Ibsen, who is closer to Shakespeare than to Tennessee Williams, needs actors with grandeur and style. And he needs a more tough-minded translator than Michael Meyer who has weakened the text even more than his Victorian predecessor, William Archer.

[EVA LE GALLIENNE AS HEDDA]
George Jean Nathan

As again in the case of the ice skating shows, one review of Miss Le Gallienne is perforce much like another. The monotony of the former is matched by the monotony of the lady's long, ambitious and manly but unsuccessful efforts to establish herself as an acceptable actress. That she is a completely sincere, hard-working, and extra-theatrically intelligent person is obvious. That she further has conducted her career on no low level but has sought to do the higher things in drama is similarly obvious. And that she has, unmistakably, been motivated by a commendable desire to assist the theatre in every way within her small means is not less so. But, and I believe that most

Robert Brustein, [Review of Anne Meacham's *Hedda Gabler*], *The New Republic,* vol. 143, no. 23 (November 28, 1960), p. 39. Reprinted by permission of *The New Republic,* © 1960, The New Republic, Inc.

Excerpted from George Jean Nathan [Review of Eva Le Gallienne's Hedda Gabler], in his *Theatre Book of the Year, 1947–1948* (New York: Knopf, 1948; reprinted Cranbury, N.J.: Thomas Yoseloff, 1975), pp. 300–303. Reprinted by permission of Mrs. G. J. Nathan and Thomas Yoseloff.

of my colleagues at last agree, her limitations as an actress are so serious and her intelligence is so generally at theatrical fault that her labors unfortunately seem bound to come to little.

When I speak of Miss Le Gallienne as an actress, I use the term only with the greatest liberality. What she is, as I have often remarked before, is rather merely an expert reciter of the roles in which she casts herself, with acting in any strict definition no part of her performances. She reads her lines well, but she does not dramatize them in her person and seems unable to achieve character more than half an inch below her vocal organs. She impresses us, in short, as one who is letter-perfect at the first rehearsal of a play which is thereupon abandoned. She is, in the second place, also possessed of so arctic a personality, despite her attractiveness of face and figure, that her performances take on the air of an *Icetime of 1948,* minus only such a show's proficiency and audience appeal. She is so cold that a spectator is sometimes surprised that a frosty mist does not issue from her mouth when she opens it to speak her lines. And, thirdly, that chill is accompanied always by one of the most damaging qualities in an actress, which is the suggestion that her mind is constantly operating over rather than under her lines and is putting her emotions in their place, with a whip. She should learn her Rachel. "Think out your role thoroughly before the curtain goes up," said that famous actress, "and then forget everything and let go." Even in roles themselves intrinsically cold, like this Hedda, Miss Le Gallienne carries ice to Newfoundland.

She additionally exploits herself too greatly in other directions wherein her competences are doubtful. She sets herself to adapt various classics to her personal advantage as an actress and in the process rips much of their life from them. She sets herself to direct plays, and her direction imparts to her fellow players either a share of her own refrigeration or here and there such a violently contrasting heat that the stage seems to be occupied by a number of firemen feverishly trying to put out a Frigidaire. And, when serving in the capacity of her own producer, she allows her conviction that she is gifted with histrionic versatility to resolve itself into repertory programs which only accentuate her shortcomings.

"I begin to have hopes of a great metropolitan vogue for that lady now," Shaw once wrote ironically of Janet Achurch after viewing her performance as Shakespeare's Cleopatra, "since she has at last done something that is thoroughly wrong from beginning to end." Were he to have seen Miss Le Gallienne's Mrs. Alving and Hedda, he would, I fear, have omitted fifty percent of the sentence.

There are several different justifiable ways to play Hedda, but Miss Le Gallienne's is not, I feel, among them. Connoisseurs of the absurd may, for example, recall with delight her previous venture into the role some years ago when she equipped it with a modern sports costume and a carton of Lucky Strike cigarettes, and further played it as if Hedda had just stepped into it for a few minutes from a Michael Arlen comedy and was on her impatient way into one by Maugham. In this later interpretation she does not permit her idiosyncrasies to go quite that far, but she nevertheless gives every evidence of still accepting too literally Grant Allen's nineteenth century view of Hedda: "I take her into dinner twice a week," and of believing that the character is out of the pages of *Town And Country,* that the Stork Club is situated just around the corner from Tesman's house, and that Lövborg in some ways resembles Don Ameche. In other words, her attempt to invest the character with an approximate modernity invests it only with caricature.

I appreciate that almost everyone has his prejudice as to the one manner in which Hedda is best to be played and that, for all the fact that I personally do not hold anything of the kind and believe, as I have said, that there are several ways in which the role may honestly be acted, I nevertheless will be charged by the reader with the single conception. Very well, I accept. My idea of the way it should be played is to play it for the greater part in exactly the opposite way to the way Miss Le Gallienne plays it. Which is to say to act its cold calculation into some projectional warmth; to compose its artful deliberation not merely and solely in features set into an expression which hints at a paralysis of the facial muscles; to realize that under its icy surface, as under all icy surfaces, there is fluidity, and that that fluidity is not without some depth; and practically to dramatize the periodic absence of what is conventionally called emotion not into a vacuum but into something at least histrionically implicative.

One of Miss Le Gallienne's severest personal and professional handicaps seems to be a lack of humor. It is, for example, her periodic observation to interviewers, as it is Miss Margaret Webster's, her associate in various productions, that she has little use for criticism of her endeavors and that, accordingly, she does not elect to read what the critics say of them. As one of the critics whom she does not choose to read, I certainly have no criticism of her on that score. But, though she says that she does not read criticism, she seems in some occult way nevertheless to wax very angry at what the critics whom she does not read have written of her and her enterprises, as does also Miss Webster, which, it may be allowed, is slightly puzzling even to the more accomplished rebus addicts. . . .

[EVA LE GALLIENNE AS HEDDA]
Joseph Wood Krutch

. . . Paul Leyssac plays Tesman with a true appreciation of the humor in the part, and indeed the whole of the present production reveals a fine sense of those elements of cruel comedy involved. As for Miss Le Gallienne's "Hedda," it is, I think, one of her best roles and remarkable for its delicacy as well as its strength. Too often the character is played luridly, as though Hedda were a vampire in the Kipling tradition. Miss Le Gallienne remembers that Ibsen himself described her as "distinctly a lady, by her position and by her character." She is, in other words, as dangerous as she is for the very reason that her disease is not evident on the surface. . . .

Excerpt from Joseph Wood Krutch, [Review of Eva Le Gallienne's *Hedda Gabler*], *The Nation,* vol. 139, no. 3624 (December 19, 1934), p. 721.

The following review of a stage production of Hedda Gabler *by the Swedish film director,
Ingmar Bergman, contributes a number of acute observations and ideas to the various subjects discussed in all the preceding excerpts. Here, in the words of Martin Esslin, is still another view of
Hedda: she is at once a true tragic heroine and a victim of society, her creativity and love turned
to destructiveness and hate by the frustrations of convention and class. Here too is an interpretation
of Tesman, embodied in the reviewer's approval of the way the part was acted in Bergman's production. In addition, Mr. Esslin describes and evaluates the other players, including the Hedda of Maggie Smith. Finally, he gives us some sharp insights into the way a director—through cuts, sets, staging, pacing, casting, and coaching of the actors—can create a whole new dramatic experience out of
a familiar, classic script.*

[INGMAR BERGMAN'S *HEDDA GABLER*]
Martin Esslin

One of the most difficult aspects of drama criticism is the work of the director:
where does the actors' contribution end, where does the director's contribution start?
Was an actor's brilliant performance due to his own creative imagination or was it suggested by the director? If only one could see the same director's work on the same play
with a totally different set of actors! Then one could really separate the actors' and the
director's share of the total success or failure of the production.

To those who have had a chance of seeing Ingmar Bergman's production of *Hedda
Gabler* at the Royal Dramatic Theatre in Stockholm (and briefly at the World Theatre
Season at the Aldwych), a visit to the same production with the actors of the British
National Theatre at the Cambridge Theatre therefore offers a unique opportunity for
studying Bergman's personal contribution by comparing the two performances.

First of all: there is the overall conception. A non-naturalistic setting—the scene is
all blood red, a few pieces of furniture, only the essentials: a piano, a settee, a chair or
two, a bookcase. A small movable screen indicates that the set can represent not one
but two—communicating—rooms in Tesman's house. And this underlies the basic conception of Bergman's approach: it enables him to counterpoint Ibsen's scenes by showing characters who are not on stage in Ibsen's text alone in the next room. This allows
the director to use one of the theatre's greatest assets as against the cinema: the simul-
taneity of two sequences of events happening side by side. For example: the play
opens—in Ibsen's text—with the dialogue between Aunt Julia and the maid: happy gos-
sip about the returned honeymoon couple. But Bergman opens the play in the other
room, with Hedda looking at herself in the mirror and expressing her utter disgust and
nausea at knowing herself pregnant. And while the aunt and the maid indulge in their
sentimental chit-chat we see Hedda in the other room staring in front of herself in despair and utter boredom.

The possibility of this split stage is used with the utmost intelligence and subtlety
throughout, culminating in Hedda's suicide in full view of the audience, while the
other characters sit in the next room in smug ignorance of what is about to happen.

Secondly there is the handling and adaptation of the text: Bergman has cut and

Martin Esslin, *"Hedda Gabler* [Review]," *Plays and Players,* vol. 17, no. 11 (August 1970), pp. 38 and 41. Reprinted by permission of the author.

modernised the play and freed it from such period romanticism as the famous phrase about vineleaves in Lövborg's hair. As a result the play, while still essentially concerned with the problem of the frustrations of women in a Victorian bourgeois society becomes wholly accessible to a mid-twentieth century audience.

Moreover, Bergman has speeded the action up, playing the text in a continuous sequence—with one interval, but without elaborate pauses to indicate the lapse of time. This gives the action a filmic quality which is completely acceptable in an age as inured to television as ours.

The result is astonishing: theme and motivation of this allegedly enigmatic masterpiece emerge with blinding clarity. And we realise the depth of Ibsen's insight into the moral and human dilemma of gifted women in his time. The conventional view of Hedda as a wicked vixen disappears: this Hedda is a victim of society, of convention, of her upper class status. Ibsen shows us a gifted woman denied a creative outlet— because society does not allow a lady to work; and a passionate woman kept from the man she loves because society threatens the direct sanctions to those who break its sex taboos. Lövborg, a gifted man but an alcoholic, is not in a position to marry. Hedda loved him but when he wanted her to become his mistress, she threatened to shoot him; as a general's daughter she was afraid of scandal. Having got tired of dancing at provincial balls she finally *has* to marry and marries the dull but devoted scholar Tesman. When she returns from her honeymoon she learns to her horror that another woman, Thea Elvsted, *has* had the courage to run away from her husband and her home to live with Lövborg. And that her defiance of convention has enabled Lövborg to write a great book.

Hedda cannot endure seeing another woman achieve what she lacked the courage to do. Hence her hatred of Thea, her destruction of the manuscript which was the fruit of Lövborg's relationship with Thea, her destruction of Lövborg and finally her suicide. Hedda Gabler's destructiveness is frustrated creativity, her hatred frustrated love. That is why, in spite of her incredibly wicked actions she moves us as a true tragic heroine.

Maggie Smith's Hedda in many ways resembles her Swedish counterpart Gertrud Fridh in looks and gesture. But she is more regal, more majestic, cooler. And she has, in all her tragic frustration, the sense of humour and the timing of a born comedienne. This is a truly memorable performance. The three men in Hedda's life are less stately, less serious, and younger than the Swedish actors who played these parts. Jeremy Brett's Tesman is a wholly credible character. Not the usual bungling fool, but a very presentable, handsome young man who just happens to be somewhat too dull, too scholarly and socially inferior to his wife.

Robert Stephens as Lövborg is much less of the impressive scholar than Georg Arlin presented in the Swedish production. But he is very credibly a man of immense charm whose passionate nature has led him into dissipation—precisely because women of intelligence and breeding were unattainable, he has been driven into the brothels. John Moffatt (Brack) worthily completes the trio: he is a far younger man than conventionally cast. And quite rightly so, for in Norway one entered the career of a judge on leaving university. There is therefore no need for him to be an old codger. A younger Brack is far more convincing as a cynical seducer of married women. John Moffatt suggests the right mixture of dignity, cunning and coarseness.

This, then, is a rewarding evening: impeccable acting under a great director.

Trelawny of the "Wells"

Pinero's Trelawny of the "Wells" *is a play about theatre folk, but at the same time it is a play about playwriting, written by an author very much conscious of the theatrical tradition of which he was the heir. This is the tradition of the "well-made play," which descends in the nineteenth century from popular French playwrights such as Eugène Scribe, Victorien Sardou and Eugène Labiche, through Tom Robertson (portrayed as Tom Wrench in* Trelawny*), to Pinero himself. John Russell Taylor's* The Rise and Fall of the Well-Made Play *traces this tradition of playwriting up to Pinero and beyond, making clear what its aims and techniques were and showing how they developed in the work of various writers. The excerpts that follow discuss Pinero's chief predecessors, define his kind of drama, and analyze the excellences of* Trelawny, *which is perhaps the author's most successful "well-made" play.*

FROM *THE RISE AND FALL OF THE WELL-MADE PLAY*
John Russell Taylor

[Scribe, inventor of the well-made play]

Nothing comes from nothing, and certainly all sorts of precursors can be found for Scribe and his form of play. But for our purpose it is sufficient to say that what had been done occasionally, patchily and empirically by others Scribe did regularly, consistently and in full consciousness of what he was doing. He was born in 1791, and his first play appeared in 1815. By this time he had already been in the theatre for some years, and had learnt more about the sheer *technique* of catching and holding an audience than many much greater dramatists learn in their whole working lives. His prime originality lay in his realization that the most reliable formula for holding an audience's attention was a well-told story. Note the well-*told;* Scribe was living in the first heyday of Romanticism, and his theory of drama was not, could not be, a classical one of balance and proportion in the construction of an intrigue. To appreciate fully what Scribe meant by a *pièce bien faite* one must always bear this in mind; that what he set out to do was not to tame and discipline Romantic extravagance, but to devise a mould into which any sort of material, however extravagant and seemingly uncontrollable, could be poured.

He saw that all drama, in performance, is an experience in time, and that therefore the first essential is to keep one's audience attentive from one minute to the next. Romantic drama tended to neglect this requirement, or at least do little deliberately to satisfy it. Which was all very well if, say, the central character was so absorbing that an audience was willing to go along with anything that he or she did, or if the big scenes of spectacle and sensation were so spectacular and so sensational that the audience would just sit there and wait for the next to cap the last. But these were unduly chancy considerations, depending upon the author's qualities of imagination or at least of sheer invention. For a poet or novelist who might dabble in the theatre when he felt in the mood—or "inspired"—to do so, they could well be enough. But a full-time professional playwright needed something more certain to go by.

Excerpted from John Russell Taylor, *The Rise and Fall of the Well-Made Play* (London: Methuen, 1967), pp. 19–21, 52, 53–54, 56–57, 78–80. Reprinted by permission of A. D. Peters & Co. Ltd.

This something was what Scribe provided. His plays inculcated, not the overall construction of a drama such as Racine would have understood it, but at least the spacing and preparation of effects so that an audience should be kept expectant from beginning to end. That, and that only, is what Scribe meant by a well-made play, and it is, if not perhaps the most one might hope for from a playwright, at least a very proper and by no means despicable minimum. . . .

We are here, then, still a far cry from what Pinero, say, would have regarded as the well-made play. For essential to the well-made play of the 1890s, the sort of play Archer analyses in his book *Play-Making,* are two elements Scribe was not really interested in at all: clear, neat, balanced overall construction, and the appearance at least of verisimilitude. If Scribe was a crucial influence in putting serious British dramatic writing back into the theatre after too long spent in Elizabethan closets, the particular way that this new theatricalism found expression was specifically English. It was guided above all by the bourgeois realism of Tom Robertson, who took Scribe's unashamedly non-literary approach to dramatic story-telling and applied it to commonplace elements of contemporary middle-class life in a fashion which prompted Archer to call him, not unfairly, "a Pre-Raphaelite of the theatre. . . ."

[Tom Robertson]

. . . The British well-made play, as it turned out, developed in a very different direction from the French *pièce bien faite*—something much nearer, if one must have a French comparison, to Dumas fils and his famous emotional drama *La Dame aux Camélias,* for long unproduceable in England. But even that is ultimately remote in its effect from the drama of Robertson, of Henry Arthur Jones, and of Arthur Wing Pinero. The French model remained in front of them, but their Englishness transformed what they learned from it into something very different. And the first dramatist to do this was T. W. Robertson. . . .

What Robertson was (and is) famed for above all is having introduced on to the mid-Victorian stage a realistic picture of everyday middle-class life. Well, of course the term is relative. To us, now, Robertson's plots seem often hardly less improbable and melodramatic than those of the unashamed melodramas he was reacting against, while his plays abound in such conventions as soliloquy, aside and simultaneous conversations on stage by characters who are supposed not to be aware of each other's presence. Nor was Robertson the first dramatist of his age to deal with current social problems in what was meant to be a realistic way—even Lord Lytton, author of the most phenomenally successful romantic melodrama of the period, *The Lady of Lyons* (1838), also dabbled, according to his lights, with everyday realism in plays like *Money* (1840), the very title of which has a Robertson-like ring.

But undoubtedly Robertson went further in this direction, wrote better while doing so, and hit exactly the right moment for doing so—hence his historical importance, even if as a dramatist he remains very much in the minor league. He was born in 1829, his family background including a number of actors, writers, painters and professional artists of various sorts. He himself went on the stage in early childhood, and continued to act with modest success for some years. He also had the itch to write, however, and seemed all set for early success when a play of his, *A Night's Adventure,* was accepted for production by a major London company in 1851.

But though this piece of period flummery about Jacobites, Hanoverians and a romantic highwayman in disguise was in no way challenging and was by all accounts in general rather better than the run of such plays at the time, it had no success at all, and its unfortunate author was reduced to churning out innumerable adaptations, mainly "from the French." Among those he wrote in the mid-1850s were, significantly perhaps, *The Ladies' Battle* from *La bataille des dames,* by Scribe and Legouvé, and *A Glass of Water,* from Scribe's *Un Verre d'eau.* Thus the great innovator-to-be was thoroughly familiar with Scribe's work and methods some years before his own major original successes were written, and no doubt learnt from them quite a lot about Scribe's concept of the *pièce bien faite,* which was as we have seen above all the art of telling a story to maximum effect in specifically theatrical terms.

Robertson's first success with a play of his own did not come until 1864, by which time he had completely given up acting for writing and spent some time as a drama critic, of the *Illustrated Times.* And even the first play to make any sort of a name for him, *David Garrick,* was in fact an adaptation, admittedly free, from a French play, de Melesville's *Sullivan,* which in its turn was only one of many variations on the old notion of a stage star deliberately disenchanting an infatuated young admirer by cutting a very unflattering figure off-stage. The main thing which distinguishes the play from any number of others cast in a similar mould is the love-scene in the last act, which though inevitably sentimental has a lightness and charm which convinced audiences at the time that it was very true to life—or at any rate a good deal truer than most of what they were currently offered on the stage.

Girded with this success Robertson went on almost at once to offer an original play of his own: *Society,* written in 1864 and produced in November 1865. This had a resounding success, and marked Robertson's definitive arrival as the dramatist of the day, especially when confirmed by the success of *Ours* in 1866 and *Caste,* his most famous play, in 1867. These slight, graceful, rather silly plays do not look much like the start of revolution, and it does not seem to have been a vital part of Robertson's purpose to call anyone in the theatre to arms. Indeed here even Pinero's funny, nostalgic and not essentially inaccurate picture of Robertson in *Trelawny of the "Wells"* errs somewhat; Robertson wrote what his nature made him write, not in response to any doctrinaire programme. . . .

[Pinero]

With the career of Sir Arthur Wing Pinero (1855–1934) we come to the high point of the well-made play's career in Britain. Not a very high point, it has been usual to say for the last fifty years or so. And yet, whatever else may be said of him, Pinero is a dramatist whose best plays—half a dozen or so, and not just one or two—remain constantly revivable and find new audiences in each generation. Moreover, he was the only British dramatist who consistently managed to make the well-made play work, not only on its first audiences but on succeeding generations, and not only in farce, where well-madeness is necessary, and comedy, where it is desirable, but in serious drama—

precisely the type of play generally supposed most capable of standing on its own legs without the adventitious aids of mere technique, and most liable to be vitiated by the failure in sincerity which is, to our incorrigibly romantic English minds, always felt to be somehow implied by a clear knowledge of what one is doing before and while one is doing it. . . .

So Pinero's effective career as a dramatist lasted about a quarter of a century, and during that time he wrote some score of plays, among which three farces and three dramas or dramatic comedies have been regularly revived, and two or three more would probably bear reviving if anyone thought to do so. He had—we may as well concede it at the outset—no "philosophy of life," no message that he was burning to deliver to the public, no deep-rooted personal obsessions which had willy nilly to find expression. He was a professional writer who took his profession seriously, and his plays, where they triumph, are above all a triumph of craftsmanship. Not just craftsmanship, of course: that could hardly keep his plays alive for more than fifty years. He had ideas too: not so much ideas about life, but ideas for subjects which would make interesting plays. He was, for what it is worth—and that is not a little—a writer who could tell interesting stories to maximum effect on the stage. Many, setting out to do much more, have succeeded in doing much less.

I would not like to be misunderstood. All this is true, and yet it should not be taken to imply that Pinero was a very self-conscious craftsman, let alone artist. Though he knew fairly well what had been and was going on in the popular French theatre—he spent quite a bit of his dramatic apprenticeship adapting "from the French" or acting in such adaptations by other people—he seems to have spent little energy on considering exactly what he was up to as a dramatist and how his aims might best be expressed in general terms. He was a practical dramatist, he wrote plays. He relied on his instinct to show him what would and would not be effective on the stage, and if his instinct led him astray once he knew better next time.

When Archer asked him about his routine of composition he said "Before beginning to write a play, I always make sure, by means of a definite scheme, that there is *a* way of doing it; but whether I ultimately follow that way is a totally different matter." And later he characterized the slavish following of a drawn-up scheme as "carpenter's work, belonging to a lower form of composition." He firmly believed, moreover, that the only regulators of his plays' construction were the characters in them—"The beginning of a play to me is a little world of people. I live with them, get familiar with them, and *they* tell me the story." Which, if he was not being disingenuous—and there is no reason to suppose he was—simply shows how well he had assimilated the principles of the well-made play without even being conscious that he had done so. Certainly it is noticeable, and notable, that after that bad but interesting transitional work *The Profligate,* whenever there is an evident weakness of construction it always coincides with a weakness, a failure of confidence or courage, in the depiction of one of the characters involved. . . .

With Pinero, as with all those who subscribe somehow to the theory of the well-made play, the issue is simply stated: how to convey the appearance, the impression of real life unmanipulated, while at the same time manipulating it as much as one needs to fit into a play which keeps the audience held unquestioning as long, at least, as the play lasts? "Willing suspension of disbelief" is a phrase much bandied about in this context, but it is a misnomer. No one ever willingly suspended disbelief, or could if he would. Audiences have to be made to suspend disbelief, and on the degree to which Pinero succeeds in making his audiences follow him and his stories without question depends his lasting effectiveness as a dramatist.

As to the difficulty of doing so, we can judge only by results. In comedy, it would seem, it must be relatively easy to keep one's audience believing even while writing in an unmistakeably artificial form. Obviously it is not true that so long as you mean to be funny anything goes, as many aspiring humorists have found to their cost. But it does seem that even if obvious devices like extravagant inconsistencies of character, incredibly neat coincidences and the like are as little acceptable in the central matter of comedy as they are in the central matter of drama, we are willing to take a more charitable view of such evident contrivance on the margins of comedy, and even find positive pleasure in the preternatural neatness with which the pieces of comedy are finally made to fit together. Not so in drama, and to this extent at least Pinero's successful experience on the lighter side of the well-made play need not be a help and might prove a positive hindrance when it came to applying his talents to straight drama. . . .

[*Trelawny of the "Wells"*]

. . . If *The Benefit of the Doubt* is the play in which Pinero's technique is most dazzlingly, shamelessly on show, *Trelawny of the "Wells"* is the play in which he comes nearest, not only to banishing it from his audience's consciousness, but banishing it from his own as well. Ready for once, unpredictably, to give Pinero credit where credit was due, Shaw saw in it "a certain delicacy which makes me loth to lay my fingers on it." Of course he attributed this to the fact that in it Pinero was for once writing not about the present, which in Shaw's view he knew nothing about and had little sympathy with, but about the past, about the theatre as it was when he was five, in 1860, and about a world in which he was really, under it all, much more at home than in his own. There is no doubt some truth in this, at least insofar as it concerns Pinero's sympathy with and nostalgia for the period he was depicting. In it, one may suspect, Pinero comes as near as he does anywhere to wearing his heart on his sleeve, and a very gentle, old-world, sentimental heart it turns out to be.

The story is simple—for once really simple, and not just seemingly so. Rose Trelawny, popular star of Bagnigge Wells, is about to marry a young gentleman and abandon the stage for good. Her old companions in the theatre give her a farewell party, and she goes off to spend a sort of probationary period with her prospective husband's family. But she soon finds this boring, disgraces herself and leaves to return to the stage. The deep distress of all this has humanized her soul, however, and she is unable any more to play with conviction the silly old melodramas and sentimental tales in which she once shone. On the other hand, she is now woman enough to do justice to the simple, true dramas written by her friend Tom Wrench (a thinly disguised portrait of T. W. Robertson). And in the last act all is settled when not only is her erstwhile fiancé's grandfather prevailed upon to finance a production (spurred by sentimental recollections of her mother), but her fiancé, who has meanwhile renounced his family and taken to the stage, turns up as her leading man and the happy couple are reunited with the old man's blessing.

A slight story, though holding enough to keep the audience interested and constructed with all Pinero's ease and fluency. And strong enough to carry the superstructure which really interested him: the contrast between the old, worn-out drama which was the stock-in-trade of Bagnigge Wells and the, in its time, so new and realistic drama of Robertson, and the contrast between stage people and the stuffy rest of the world. Both contrasts are in some sense illusory. Robertson's drama, as we have seen, was not so different in essence from the sort of play it replaced; it merely changed the social and physical setting in which it took place, and as Allardyce Nicoll has aptly pointed out, if the line from *The Second Mrs. Tanqueray* goes back directly to *Caste,* the line from *Caste* goes back just as directly and recognizably to *The Castle Spectre* and the wildest extremes of gothic melodrama. And the contrast between the warm, human stage folk and the cold, unnatural rest, if one of the hoariest clichés of theatre in life as in fiction, does not stand up to serious examination.

But the important thing is that Pinero believed them to be real; at least they were significant myths for him. So much so that he is able for once to accept all his characters in their own terms, to see the old actors like the Telfers, who were too old and too set in their ways to change, with sympathy of the same sort that he gives to the more obviously congenial Tom Wrench. He is even able to be kind to crusty old Sir William Gower, or anyway to appreciate from the inside what it must be like to see the world through Sir William's eyes.

We have said that this, ultimately, was what he failed to do with Paula Tanqueray or Agnes Ebbsmith; if he understood what it was like to be either, he recoiled from his understanding, and in recoiling wrecked the perfect mechanism of the well-made plays in which he had placed them. But in *Trelawny of the "Wells"* form and content are one, indivisible from beginning to end—it is the greatest triumph of Pinero's technique because the most lightly, unselfconsciously worn. It is no small thing to write a play as controlled and perfectly shaped as *His House in Order,* or as challengingly adroit as *The Benefit of the Doubt.* But it is a sign of greater art to write with such ease, real as well as apparent (*Dandy Dick* was written in under a month) farces which can hold the stage for eighty years and genuinely amuse after almost indefinite re-seeing. And perhaps it is best of all to write a play like *Trelawny of the "Wells",* which is natural-seeming because it is natural, and well-made because its author could hardly any more do otherwise than make a play well, having forgotten more about sheer stagecraft than most of his more fashionable rivals would ever know.

Trelawny was received appreciatively when it was first performed in 1898. In the following contemporary review, J. T. Grein comments on the production, the play and the author.

TRELAWNY OF THE "WELLS"
[IN ITS ORIGINAL PRODUCTION, 1898]
J. T. Grein

Mr. Pinero, with a modesty bordering on humility, calls this delightful play a comedietta. He wants us, therefore, to take it lightly, and not to consider it as a finished picture of some theatrical and non-theatrical folk of the crinoline and horse-hair sofa days. But however light his touch, however sketchy his characters, however thin the thread of plot that strings the four acts together, there is far more depth in this little work than in many volumes of bulky proportions.

The question is, will the large world of playgoers see and understand the play as it ought to be seen and understood? Mr. Pinero has oftentimes done things which enchanted the few and bewildered the many; *The Times* is an example; the memorable *Cabinet Minister* is another; yet another is *The Amazons;* and all of these, for which he has been sparsely praised, are of his later and glorious days. Earlier, when he had not yet "arrived," and wrote in that same half satirical, half pathetic style which is all his own, he was roundly abused. No man has encountered more treacherous nails and splinters upon the ladder of fame than our Pinero. And even now, while we hail him as the premier playwright of the English-speaking world, it would seem that the public is slow to appreciate Pinero at his best; it would have little of the fascinating "Princess and the Butterfly," and it is by no means certain whether it will enjoy to the full the exquisite charm of "Trelawny." For our author leads us into a sphere which is foreign to most, even though their memory reaches back to the period when the eccentric theatre—*i.e.,* the theatre on the fringe of West London—was in the lowest water.

Yet what a field of humour and of true comedy, what a treasure-trove for an observant man! And Pinero, whose eyes dwell as keenly on the past as they do on modern society, has drawn a wonderfully vivid picture of the simple-minded, kind-hearted, rough-and-ready "cabotins" who flourished at the "Wells," and of the fossilized gentlefolk who lived in cold monotony in fashionable squares. This Rose, who, like "bon chien chasse de race," is not happy when she is taken from the stage to the noble mansion of her fiancé's grandfather, to see how she would acclimatise; this Tom Wrench, sick of stiltedness and convention, and yearning to give something of his simple, natural self in a play of unconventional form; this Avonia, common little creature, wont to please the lowly crowd with her freaks and funny little ways, yet warm-blooded and kind of heart as the best of women; these mummers all, whose H's rise and fall like the tide, are no mere puppets of the author's conceit. No; they are sketched from life, and, perhaps, a little rouged and made up for the purpose of the stage; but, if we try to understand them, we can feel for them, and live with them. The author is not quite so happy in his portraiture of the non-theatrical folk; here the satirist is uppermost,

J. T. Grein, "Trelawny of the 'Wells' [Review, January 1898]," in his *Dramatic Criticism* (London: John Long, 1899), pp. 32–34.

and, if young Gower, who wooed Rose, is a normal type of a young gentleman of the sixties, the Vice-Chancellor, Sir William Gower, his sister, and his friends, are more or less caricatures, obviously overdrawn for the purpose of contrast, but, for this reason, the weaker part of the play.

However, it matters little that the collateral characters are more fanciful than real; I would even venture to say that the very exaggeration enhances the charm of the play. It is from beginning to end highly diverting; it is episodically deeply interesting, and, to those who are intimate with the world behind the footlights, it is a conceit of amazing cleverness.

As usual, Mr. Pinero has the good fortune to be well interpreted. I have but to take exception to two impersonations. Mr. Dion Boucicault is undoubtedly clever, but he seems to forget that our London palate is more sensitive to the condiment of "over-doing" than colonial taste. His performance as the old Vice-Chancellor constantly reminded us that a comparatively young man endeavoured to embody old age; it reminded us also of how great a loss the Court Theatre sustained in Arthur Cecil. And in the abundantly paragraphed Mr. James Erskine, however painstaking he was, I discovered none of those qualifications which justified his being preferred to one of the many tried and hard-working actors who appear to be "resting" just now. Acting in "thinking parts" and a thorough training in elocution and deportment, would, I submit, be of greater service to Mr. Erskine than his present occupation. Miss Irene Vanbrugh was a charming Rose; the part is long, difficult, and somewhat unsuited to her delicate style, but she conquered the obstacles with flying colours. Miss Hilda Spong had to do what would have been a fitting task for Marie Wilton; that she did not altogether fail is to her credit. Mr. Athol Forde as the old actor, Mr. Robson as the funny little Colroys, and Mr. Paul Arthur as Wrench, the yearning author, were an admirable triumvirate. But smaller parts were equally well done by Miss Bateman, Miss Le Thiere, Miss Eva Williams, Mr. Du Maurier—in fact, I should like to transcribe the whole cast with a menu of fitting adjectives, for Mr. Pinero always chooses the right people. On purpose I have not yet named Miss Pattie Browne, who was the joy of the evening as Avonia. True, the part plays itself, as it were; but Miss Pattie Browne endowed it with so much vivacity, so much *savoir faire,* engendered by vast experience, that the character, which is only secondary, stood out in brilliant prominence.

All things considered, *Trelawny of the "Wells"* will hold its own in the record of Mr. Pinero, and if London is to be taken by charm, it will assuredly capitulate.

Trelawny *still seems to be a viable theatre piece, as the following review of a modern production attests. The critic's comments also serve to locate Pinero's contribution to the modern theatre in relation to two other playwrights in the present series: Ibsen and Shaw.*

[*TRELAWNY OF THE "WELLS"* IN A 1965 PRODUCTION]
Ronald Bryden

. . . The best thing about the National Theatre is not *Othello* but the evidence it has given of working slowly and systematically up the foothills of drama, training its players to cooperate in acquiring skills forgotten and unnecessary on the plains of the West End. . . . On this sort of ground, I'm prepared to cast a kindlier eye on Desmond O'Donovan's production of *Trelawny of the "Wells"* than I did at Chichester in July.

Clearly there's an element in the choice of Pinero's old "comedietta" of blandishing a pre-Christmas public with a bit of superior Victorian music hall. Marks of this straggle like gift-wrapping over the first half of the evening: the licensed hamming of the old stagers whom Pinero satirised is dressed up with a good deal of unjustified period camp in the production—the last things Pinero, champion of naturalism, would have approved are painted backcloths and doorless flies for his theatrical digs in Brydon Crescent, the clatter of an old thunder-sheet for his second-act storm. But as the story of Tom Robertson's capture of the rowdy old stage of the 1860s for polite comedy and three-walled rooms with real doors and door-knobs went on, the Old Tyme knockabout subsided and the play got more interesting. For all its sentimentality, it's a rare document of an important shift in theatrical styles, educative in a way Pinero cannot have foreseen.

Shaw made an exception for *Trelawny* in his general slating of Pinero and all his works. As he pointed out with malicious accuracy, it's the one play in which Pinero was true to the real nature of his talent, which belonged to the period he satirised rather than the Nineties he ruled. When he tried to out-Ibsen Ibsen in *The Second Mrs Tanqueray* and *The Notorious Mrs Ebbsmith,* he only succeeded in writing old-fashioned melodramas disguised in a Sardou tailoring of telegrams, letters and mohair sofas. Chronicling in *Trelawny* the triumph of naturalism, he only succeeded in betraying his affinity with the pre-Robertson days of untrammelled romance and rhetoric, the stage of such "splendid gipsies" as Kean.

Shaw had his reasons to defend this hankering after the bad old days. As a leading "Ibsenite," he was offically committed to the theatre of naturalism, to Duse rather than Bernhardt. But around him he could see it becoming merely another weapon of the Edwardian revolt against Victorian moral passion, of the new, brutal "realism" which was tearing down the old pruderies in order to lounge in leather chairs being smuttily jocose about black men and ballet. He knew well that Ibsenism was more than naturalism; he was also a Victorian and Wagnerian. In an essay written not long before his review of *Trelawny,* he dissociated himself from William Archer and his Ibsenite canons of theatrical verisimilitude:

Excerpted from Ronald Bryden, [Review of *Trelawny of the "Wells"*], *New Statesman,* vol. 70, no. 1811 (November 26, 1965), 851–852. From *New Statesman,* London, reprinted by permission.

To him acting, like scene-painting, is merely a means to an end, that end being to enable him to make believe. To me the play is only the means, the end being the expression of feeling by the arts of the actor, the poet, the musician. Anything that makes this expression more vivid, whether it be versification, or an orchestra, or a deliberately artificial delivery of the lines, is so much the good for me, even though it may destroy all the verisimilitude of the scene.

We are still fighting our way out of naturalism's three-walled room with real door-knobs into the greater theatre, ancient and modern, which Shaw opened up for us. The value of *Trelawny*, as Shaw saw, is that through the door which Pinero presented as the gate of the future we can catch a glimpse of the pre-Pinero past, with its heroic, unrealistic vividness. It is one of the very few plays which offer modern actors a bridge from naturalism to the lost kingdoms of rhetoric which lie between Shakespeare and ourselves. It is also, within its limits, a funny and charming old piece. To anyone who takes an interest in the growth of the company, it also justifies itself by the further opportunities for expansion it offers Robert Stephens (a quiet but superbly thought-out performance as the Robertson-character) and Derek Jacobi (wildly funny in the tiny part of a mahogany-headed officer with Dundreary whiskers like huge fan-tailed goldfish).

If Voltaire's Candide *can be made into a musical and a television play, then perhaps even Pinero's* Trelawny of the "Wells" *could undergo one of these theatrical transformations and come out renewed and revivified. According to the following review, however, a recent attempt at a musical version of* Trelawny *sacrificed more than it gained. It is interesting to speculate whether the adaptation was simply an inept one, or whether there are certain things inherent in a play like* Trelawny—*its themes, its characters, its dramatic techniques, its concept of the theatre—which resist any change of medium.*

[*TRELAWNY OF THE "WELLS"* AS A MUSICAL]
Kenneth Hurren

. . . The business at hand is the gala reopening production of the Theatre Royal— in which, coincidentally, there has been another attempt at refurbishment and the fusion of old and new which hasn't come off at all. The show is called *Trelawny of the "Wells."* The new part of it is a set of songs by Julian Slade, to accommodate which Mr. Slade and his collaborators, Aubrey Woods and George Rowell, have foolhardily thrown out most of the things that were endearing in Pinero's exuberant portrait of

From Kenneth Hurren, [Review of the Bristol Old Vic's musical version of *Trelawny of the "Wells"*], *The Spectator,* vol. 228, no. 7491 (January 22, 1972), p. 125. Reprinted by permission of *The Spectator.*

mid-Victorian mummers (the play was set in the 1860s) as the new-fangled "cup-and-saucer" drama of T. W. Robertson was about to engulf them. The celebrated scenes in the lodging-house frequented by these "dissolute gipsies" are especially regrettable omissions; the scenes illustrating their involvement in a pantomime are especially regrettable, indeed almost unendurable, interpolations.

It is easy to see what made the thing seem so appealing for the present occasion; apart from the notion of blending something old with something new, with which the management is infatuated, the climax of the work is the reopening of an old playhouse looking hopefully into a new theatrical era; and musicals have been based on far more unlikely material (the works of Chaucer and St Matthew, for handy examples). It might even have been thought that some of the "well-made play" mechanics of Pinero needed the frivolous assistance of songs to mitigate their absurdities for contemporary audiences, and this, I suspect, is where the enterprise is misconceived.

The manoeuvres and coincidences whereby the actress-heroine, Rose Trelawny, is reunited with her young "swell" (whose rigidly exacting family has proved too constricting for her independent spirit to bear), while at the same time her loyal friend, the aspirant dramatist Tom Wrench, gets his play financed and produced, are quite preposterous, but they were acceptable enough because Pinero took them far less seriously than he did the equally absurd contrivances of earnest melodramas like *The Second Mrs. Tanqueray* and *His House in Order*. Set protractedly to music, I'm afraid they really do look pretty foolish, and at the same time the main themes—the innovatory struggles of Tom Wrench (a character based directly on Robertson) and the sense of the theatre in transition—are lost.

Julian Slade's laboured lyrics are far less interesting than the dialogue they have replaced, and his score is routine, tum-ti-tum stuff. The songs, indeed, are little help to the players; nor they, as it happens to them. Pictorially, Hayley Mills is a Rose to set Harry Wheatcroft's whiskers a-quiver (and her gameness ensures that one or two of Pinero's "moments" retain their sentimental kick), but her voice when raised in song only occasionally coincides with the notes. Ian Richardson, as Tom Wrench, is at a similar vocal disadvantage, and besides finds fewer pickings on the stripped bones of his part than would seem to justify his fervent attack on them. Most of the bearable singing comes from Elizabeth Power as Avonia and John Watts as Rose's suitor; and Timothy West, settling for talking his songs, does a dignified job of constructive character acting as the lad's irascible parent.

The Three Sisters

Chekhov's dramatic techniques—his treatment of plot, mode of characterization, use of language, ways of conveying meaning—differ radically from those of the other dramatists represented in The Classic Theatre. *Maurice Valency, in his study of* The Three Sisters, *describes these techniques; differentiates them from the techniques used in earlier drama, particularly the "well-made play"; shows how they contribute to the unique tone and effect of* The Three Sisters; *and indicates a basic theme of the play that is virtually inherent in the techniques themselves.*

[DRAMATIC TECHNIQUE IN *THE THREE SISTERS*]
Maurice Valency

[Plot]

The principal structural innovation is in the arrangement of the interlaced stories. The traditional design of Western comedy from the sixteenth century on involved the simultaneous management of two or more plots of climactic nature, subordinated according to the rank, age, or social condition of the participants, connected by common incidents which affect each plot line differently, the whole complicated by misunderstandings, deceits, mistaken identities, or disguises, and resolved by means of recognitions, discoveries, and peripeties. In *The Three Sisters* Chekhov made use of a novelistic technique in which several lines are unfolded simultaneously without any evident thematic dependence, no subordination, no surprises, and very little convergence of plot. The result is a story that seems relatively plotless.

Beyond the several actions which the play develops, there is, however, the enclosing symbol which defines the whole and gives it unity and point—Moscow, the unattainable city toward which all the action tends, the dream which all the events of the play combine to thwart. The principal motif of the play is thus not so much an action as a tension, and what is emphasized is not what happens, but what does not happen. As the play is conceived, each of the principal characters has a story of his own. These stories are not of equal importance and they hardly bear on each other, but, developed in canon, they make an effect that is curiously polyphonic. The opening scenes, as is usual with Chekhov, are directly and efficiently informative. By the end of the first act, there are set on foot the stories of Vershinin and Masha; of Natasha and Andrey; of Irina, Tusenbach, Solyony, and Chebutykin; and lastly, the very uneventful story of Olga. These narrative strands, while dramatically independent, are interwoven so as to give the effect of texture. In consequence, the play, though it is crowded with incident, has very little forward impulse and gives the impression of stasis, a composition rather than a narrative. . . .

[Characterization]

. . . It is this imprecision, this unstudied reluctance to assign precise motives for the actions of his characters, that characterizes Chekhov's style as a dramatist. As an im-

Excerpted from Maurice Valency, *The Breaking String: The Plays of Anton Chekhov* (London, Oxford: Oxford University Press, 1966), pp. 211–212, 219, 230–231, 237–238, 240–241, 243–244, 245–246, 248–250. Copyright © 1966 by Maurice Valency. Reprinted by permission of Oxford University Press, Inc.

pressionist he was chiefly concerned with the surface, and he made no obvious inference as to what, if anything, lay beneath it. His plays represent behavior in meticulous detail, the thing done, and the thing said; the rest is left to the spectator. The dramatist's easy assumption that he knows his characters to the bottom of their souls is a type of literary pretentiousness to which not even professional Freudians can lend themselves with dignity. It was a result of Chekhov's impressionistic attitude that he forbore the usual analysis of motive; it was also a mark of his extraordinary probity as a writer.

The result of this resolute objectivity is an immense gain in the vitality of the characterization. Modern drama, with its rigorously analytic method, often gives the impression of an autopsy, an examination of the walking dead. But Chekhov's characters spring to life readily, in all their dimension, intact and self-contained the moment they are contemplated. They are neither analyzed nor dissected; their inner life is their own. They remain mysterious, and their mystery interests us particularly because the author does not suggest that he understands it; and if he understands it, he makes no move to betray it. Thus, while in general the characters of drama make the impression on the stage of characters in a play, Chekhov's characters give the impression of living people.

The advantages of this method are too clear to require emphasis. Its chief disadvantage is that the play exercises very little control over the actors; and this Chekhov discovered to his cost in his various disagreements with the Moscow Art Theatre. It is possible to rationalize Chebutykin's behavior, but at best he is and remains a puzzle. Nevertheless, he must be played; and the actor who plays him will not play the part properly unless he has some idea of what he is doing. Upon his analysis and his conclusions, obviously, the success of the characterization will depend. It is understandable that all this puts an unusually heavy burden upon the actor, and one can only sympathize with Stanislavsky in his effort to secure a maximum identification of actor and character through a projection of the actor's inner experience upon the data furnished by the author. When the character is presented by the author as an enigma, the answer can be sought only in the inner life of the actor, and that only when he is completely alive in the part. Since something creative along these lines can be looked for only in actors of extraordinary intuition, it is to be expected that characters of this sort will commonly be presented in accordance with the usual stereotypes of the theatre, and, indeed, this is what generally happens. . . .

[Dialogue]

. . . This passage illustrates quite well the manner in which Chekhov motivated his dialogue. The speeches are seemingly inconsequential; but their sequence reveals the underlying train of thought in each of the characters, and it is seldom that the associative links are completely lacking. It is entirely probable that the seemingly disjunctive nature of Chekhov's dialogue reflects his own habit of mind. His friends have commented on his way of interpolating a complete irrelevancy into a conversation in such a way as to indicate that he had been carrying on a train of thought quite apart from the subject under discussion. Of this idiosyncrasy, Chekhov made ample use in characterization, and the resulting technique, traces of which may be found in *Uncle Vanya* and in *The Sea Gull,* was brought to its perfection in *The Three Sisters* and, later, in *The Cherry Orchard.* It resulted in a dialectic texture of extraordinary richness, the beauty of which is immediately apparent, although its intricacy can be judged only if one takes the trouble to follow the course of the individual strands of thought as they weave below the surface, and then are brought up to mesh in the design. The brilliance of Chekhov's scenes, all the more remarkable since they are normally not at all eventful, is due in great measure to the fact that Chekhov very skillfully managed in this way to keep all his characters alive all the time they are before our eyes. Their silence is quite as expressive as their words, and the subtle play of associations keeps us continually aware of the hidden currents of thought and feeling which work below the surface of the visible action, and give it another dimension, the nature of which is intimated but the full extent of which can only be surmised. . . .

[Chekhov's drama as lyrical and naturalistic]

. . . The lyrical quality of a play conceived along these lines is achieved, necessarily, at the expense of more usual dramatic values. A fine play in the Scribean manner is a marvel of ingenuity, in which every line serves either to advance the action, or to characterize the speaker, or both. In such plays, no words are wasted; whatever does not serve to propel the plot is judged to be extraneous and dispensable; and the characters work their way forward with all their might, each intent on his desire. This kind of drama conveys, accordingly, a sense of urgency which in real life we feel only in our more hysterical moments, and also an enhanced awareness of the play of motives, the interchange of pressures, and the clash of wills. The design is primarily mechanical in principle, and the result is a piece of dramatic engineering, a machine.

Chekhov's plays are of another stamp. In general, his characters feel no urgency and transmit none; they create no suspense. In comparison with the characters of well-made plays, they seem languid and bored. Aside from the comic characters of such vaudevilles as *The Bear* and *The Proposal,* the personages who convey a sense of energy in Chekhov's plays are exceptional, and seem to belong to another world than the rest of the cast. The usual Chekhovian character is a half-hearted participant in an action that barely excites his interest. His desires, when they are manifested, seem to run against the grain of the action. The bustle which characterizes Scribean drama is nowhere evident in Chekhov's theatre. There is a certain tension; but nobody is in a hurry, and even when, like Elena in *The Wood Demon,* a character desperately wishes to escape, there is nowhere to go. This very lack of direction is a source of uneasiness. . . .

After *Ivanov,* Chekhov's mistrust of melodrama, and his fear of overstatement, were such that he rarely permitted his climaxes to rise much above the level of the preparatory action. In *Uncle Vanya* the climax is deflated by Vanya's ineptitude; in *The Sea Gull,* it is sabotaged by Nina's determination to play a tragic scene; in *The Three Sisters,* the climaxes are so unobtrusive that one is hardly aware of them. Evidently Chekhov did not see life in terms of climaxes and *scènes à faire,* that is to say, in terms of theatre. None of his later plays is theatrical; and the indefinable sense of paradox that his works evoke is very likely the result of the application of a dramatic system designed to arouse passion to a subject-matter which stubbornly resists any such treatment.

This curious incongruity was the consequence of Chekhov's naturalistic bias. In his opinion, a dramatist who desires to depict life honestly must put on the stage the experiences of ordinary people, and deal with the laughter and tears inherent in ordinary happenings. In real life what is visible is generally trivial and commonplace. But for centuries playwrights had been in the habit of associating drama with moments of high excitement, great gestures, and impressive utterances, precisely those things which are lacking in our ordinary experience. The result was the impassable gulf which has always divided reality from the fantasies of the theatre.

It was Chekhov's ambition to bridge this gulf. As he said:

> After all, in real life, people don't spend every moment in shooting one another, hanging themselves, or making declarations of love. They do not spend all their time saying clever things. They are more occupied with eating, drinking, flirting, and saying stupidities, and these are the things which ought to be shown on the stage . . . People eat their dinner, just eat their dinner, and all the time their happiness is taking form, or their lives are being destroyed.

There was nothing especially new in this idea. But while both Zola and Maeterlinck had quite recently described the drama of everyday life, nobody had so far attempted actually to write such a play. It was very difficult in the theatre to relinquish the extraordinary. The novelty of Chekhov's technique lay not in his theory, but in his practice. He was the first dramatist to write realistically for the stage.

Because he was primarily a realist, one looks in vain to Chekhov for that quality of neatness which was so highly prized by the dramatists of the Second Empire. Chekhov's plots are not neat. "Plays should be written badly, insolently," he told his brother Alexander. In his later plays, when the action ends, the narrative is not concluded; it is merely suspended. *The Three Sisters* ends with a tableau. The audience is invited to contemplate for a moment those who have departed, and those who remain. For a moment the play is at rest. But in fact, nothing is at rest—the tableau holds together only for that moment. Like the final tableau in *The Revizor*, the scene is charged with energy and ready to fly apart the moment the author relinquishes his control.

Here, as elsewhere, Chekhov succeeds in giving his characters an extension of vitality that goes beyond their dramatic utility. They have a dimension that is peculiarly theirs, in which they are free to live. As characters, they are enlisted to serve the plot; but they have an autonomy of their own. Certain characters—Chebutykin, for example—appear at a certain point to secede from the ensemble, as if they refused to take any further part in the action. In general, Chekhov's personages preserve the imprecise outlines and the enigmatic quality of people. They exhibit a normal reluctance to engage themselves, and the author makes no effort to penetrate their reserve. The consequence is not only the strange relation of character to narrative that is peculiar to Chekhov's plays, but also a derogation of plot which presages a different order of drama from anything that properly belongs to the nineteenth century.

[Chekhov's impressionism and the view of life it conveys]

. . . *The Three Sisters* is Chekhov's masterpiece, the flower of impressionism in the drama. No play has ever conveyed more subtly the sense of transitory nature of human life, the sadness and beauty of the passing moment. The action seems to be haphazard and amorphous, not because the play has no definite shape—it has a very definite shape—but because this shape seems to be constantly changing, like a cloud in the summer sky. . . .

The life which we glimpse in *The Three Sisters* is a continuum in which a few events are seen to make a vortex, a shape which is swallowed up in the flux as quickly as it was formed. In the story of *The Three Sisters* nothing is presented as other than ephemeral, and no event bears any special emphasis. The play simply marks a moment in eternity. In the impressionist view of things, of course, eternity is essentially a matter of moments. But Chekhov is by no means simply an impressionist. To understand him, it is important to add to the sense of episode, the sense of process, and, after that, the all-enveloping doubt.

The Three Sisters concentrates attention momentarily on what may be considered a trivial aspect of the evolutionary pattern, namely, the plight of the individual in the cosmic scheme. Evolution makes nothing of individuals. But within its outlines, insofar as they are intelligible, the drama of the individual may be magnified, if one has a mind to it, to something like universal proportions. In respect to the universal, the human drama is necessarily a microscopic art, and it is important for the dramatist to preserve his sense of scale. But once it is conceded that a particular destiny can have in itself no more than minimal importance, one is free to generalize its significance in terms as vast as the heavens; there is no limit to the artist's fancy. A drop of water can reflect a world. . . .

[Contrasted characters and philosophies in *The Three Sisters* as a reflection of Chekhov's own spiritual conflict]

. . . In *The Three Sisters*, Vershinin evidently speaks for Chekhov, and his views are clear. But Chebutykin also speaks for Chekhov, and his views are equally clear. The old skeptic believes in nothing, and expects nothing. He is cynical, spent, a little wicked, yet in his way quite as sympathetic as Vershinin, and for him it is all nonsense, the past, the future, and the present—it all adds up to nothing, and the play virtually closes with his words: *Vse ravno! Vse ravno!*—"It's all one! It's all one!"

The indeterminate area between faith and skepticism measures the extent of Chekhov's spiritual discomfort. Vershinin speaks for his faith; Chebutykin, for his doubt. Chekhov's soul was capacious. There was room in it for the one and for the other, and he saw no way to reconcile the two. We cannot doubt that this continual inner altercation was of major importance in his life as a dramatist. Possibly it represented in conscious terms the dynamic principle of his art, the polarity which gave it movement. His mind was calm, but his soul was not placid and, more clearly than any other of his plays, *The Three Sisters* reflects his spiritual tension. . . .

Chekhov's technique of creating character and conveying theme by means of casual, apparently irrelevant bits of dialogue and action is illustrated in the following detailed analyses by David Magarshack. The first excerpt discusses the character of Chebutykin; the second analyzes the theme of the sisters' yearning for Moscow.

[THE IMPORTANCE OF "CASUAL" DETAIL IN *THE THREE SISTERS*]
David Magarshack

[Chebutykin]

. . . Chebutykin is the constant butt of Solyony. He is the fourth and last doctor in Chekhov's plays, but he derives from the improvident Triletsky in *Platonov* rather than from the wise and humane Dorn or the idealist Astrov. It is characteristic of Chebutykin and Solyony that, though they always argue, they are so preoccupied with themselves, that they never seem to listen to each other. For instance, in their furious quarrel in Act II about the meaning of "cheremsha," a wild onion, and "chekhartma," mutton roasted in the Caucasian manner, Chekhov has chosen two unusual words that would sound alike to people who are not so much concerned with convincing each other as with proving that their opponent is wrong. And in contrast to the great issues discussed by Vershinin and Tusenbach, the subject of their disputes is always trifling. All this is brought out immediately on their first appearance in Act I. Solyony is preoccupied with his hands. He is trying to convince Chebutykin that with two hands he can lift a weight three times as heavy as with one hand (an absurdly futile argument considering that he wants only one hand to kill a man). But Chebutykin is not listening to him. He is reading his newspaper, which is treated by Chekhov as the symbol of Chebutykin's crass ignorance. He never reads serious books, or indeed any books. He has forgotten all he has ever known about medicine. His mind has been frittered away. His soul, too, is empty. The popular newspaper (in the earlier versions of the play Chekhov actually mentioned the two popular newspapers Chebutykin is reading) is the only source from which he can fill his vacant mind, since a vacant mind has to be filled with something. (It is very likely that the idea of using the newspaper as one of the visual symbols of Chebutykin's character was indirectly suggested to Chekhov by Nemirovich-Danchenko, who in one of his letters urging Chekhov to get on with the writing of *The Three Sisters* warned him against reading newspapers as they tended to distract the mind from serious work.) But Chebutykin not only reads his newspaper, he also puts down everything that strikes him as important into his note-book, a pathetic reminder of his university days when he used to take down his lectures in the same way:

> CHEBUTYKIN (*walks in reading a paper*). For falling hair—130 grains of naphthaline in half a bottle of spirit—dissolve and apply daily. (*Writes it down in his notebook.*) Let me make a note of it.

Excerpted from David Magarshack, *Chekhov the Dramatist* (New York: Hill & Wang, 1960), pp. 239–245, 253–255. Copyright © 1960 by David Magarshack. Reprinted by permission of Farrar, Straus & Giroux, Inc.

His very first words, then, give the audience a clear idea of this old doctor whose medical knowledge has been reduced to taking down some absurd prescription from a popular newspaper. But while in the stage directions the newspaper appears many times, it is only on three occasions that Chekhov actually makes Chebutykin read out an item of news from it. The second time it supplies Chebutykin with one of his most famous lines: "Balzac was married in Berdichev." This line comes after the argument between Vershinin and Tusenbach about happiness. Vershinin argues that happiness does not exist, or, at any rate, that it cannot and must not exist for them. "We must only work and work, but happiness—that's for our remote descendants. *(Pause.)* If not for me, then at least let it be for the descendants of my descendants." Tusenbach does not agree, for he, poor man, is happy! And he goes on to argue that life will always be the same, for it follows certain laws which man will never know. And when Mary asks him whether he really thinks that life has no meaning at all, he replies: "A meaning? Look, it's snowing. What meaning is there in that?" Mary, however, refuses to accept such a complete dissociation of man from his fate, and she insists that man must have faith, or must seek some kind of faith, for otherwise his life is empty. Man, she demands, must know what he is living for, or else (and here she would have been justified in pointing to Chebutykin who was immersed in reading his paper) nothing in life matters any more. Vershinin, looking at Mary, with whom he could have been happy, bursts out: "All the same it is a pity that I'm no longer young." Mary, catching the hidden meaning of his words, quotes the last line from Gogol's famous story of the quarrel between Ivan Ivanovich and Ivan Nikiforovich (another literary echo!): "It's a boring world, my friends!"

> TUSENBACH. But I say it's difficult to argue with you, my friends. Oh, let's drop the subject—
>
> CHEBUTYKIN (reading his paper). Balzac was married in Berdichev. *(Irene hums softly)*
>
> CHEBUTYKIN. I think I'll make a note of that. *(Writes it down in his notebook.)* Balzac was married in Berdichev. *(Reads his paper.)*
>
> IRENE *(laying out patience, reflectively)*. Balzac was married in Berdichev.

What is the meaning of this thrice repeated phrase? Berdichev, the Wigan of Russia, is the last place one would expect one of the greatest of French writers to be married in, or, to go back to the rather inconclusive ending of the argument about happiness, to find happiness in. And it is Irene who has been counting the days (there were seemingly only a few of them left) before her return to Moscow, where alone she believed she could find happiness, who repeats the line reflectively: happiness (and this is emphasised again and again by Chekhov whenever the Moscow theme is brought up) is not only to be found in Moscow, where people are also searching in vain for happiness, but even in such a proverbially dull town as Berdichev, and not only ordinary people can find happiness there, but even a great genius like Balzac. It is in this way that Chekhov uses the chorus element both to provide an answer to an inconclusive argument and a comment on one of the main themes of the play. (The association of marriage with happiness is here purely subjective: Irene's dreams of Moscow revolve round her illusion that it is only there that she would meet the man with whom she would fall in love; Tusenbach is happy because, having sent in his resignation from his regiment, he is now more than ever convinced that Irene will accept his proposal of marriage; and Vershinin's as well as Mary's thoughts of happiness also revolve round their own intimate feelings for one another.)

The other two symbols associated with Chebutykin are the silver samovar and the porcelain clock. To present a young girl of twenty with a tea-urn for her birthday could have occurred only to a man who had lost all touch with life. He wanted to get a really expensive present for Irene, the daughter of the only woman he ever loved, and a silver samovar (usually given as a silver-wedding present in middle-class families) was the only thing he could think of! He is therefore quite incapable of understanding the gasp of horror his present has produced.

> OLGA *(covers her eyes)*. A samovar! That's awful! *(Goes out.)*
>
> IRENE. Oh, you poor darling, what are you doing?
>
> TUSENBACH *(laughs)*. I told you.
>
> MARY. Really, doctor, you ought to be ashamed of yourself!
>
> CHEBUTYKIN. My dear, sweet darlings, you are all I have. You're all I hold most dear in the world. I shall soon be sixty. I'm an old man, a lonely, insignificant old man. There's nothing good about me except my love for you, and but for you, I should have been dead long ago. *(To Irene.)* My darling, I've known you ever since you were born—I used to carry you about in my arms—I loved your mother—
>
> IRENE. But why such expensive presents?
>
> CHEBUTYKIN *(through tears, angrily)*. Expensive presents! Don't talk such nonsense! *(To his orderly.)* Take the samovar to the other room. *(In a mocking voice.)* Expensive presents! *(The orderly carries off the samovar to the dining room.)*

This complete divorce from life and living people is of course characteristic of the old doctor. His callousness towards his patients is only another side of it. Life, in fact, no longer exists for him. It is all a delusion. "Perhaps," he mumbles drunkenly in his soliloquy in Act III, "I am not a human being at all, but merely imagine that I have hands and feet and a head; perhaps I don't exist at all, but just imagine that I walk, eat and sleep. *(Weeps.)* Oh, if only I did not exist!"

Chebutykin is "not a human being at all" and in this phrase Chekhov has stripped him of all the finer attributes of man, but, unlike Natasha, whom her husband also describes as "not a human being," he had been a human being once when he was capable of devoted and selfless love for a woman, and his final degradation, his final dehumanisation, is symbolically represented in his smashing of the porcelain clock which had been one of the treasured possessions of the woman he loved. It happens shortly after his soliloquy in Act III. Vershinin announces that the brigade to which he is attached is to leave the town soon for some distant destination. Irene declares emphatically that they, too, will leave the town.

IRENE. And we are going too.

CHEBUTYKIN (*drops the clock which breaks*). Smashed to bits! (*Pause: everyone is upset and embarrassed.*)

KULYGIN (*picking up the pieces*). To smash an expensive thing like that! Oh, doctor, doctor, zero minus for conduct!

IRENE. That was mother's clock.

CHEBUTYKIN. Possibly. So it was your mother's clock. Perhaps I didn't smash it, but it just seems as though I did. Perhaps we only imagine that we exist, but we don't really exist at all. I don't know anything. Nobody knows anything.

But somewhere deep inside him the smashing of the clock has aroused bitter memories of his own wasted life, for as he is about to leave the room, he suddenly stops and shouts at them furiously: "What are you looking at? Natasha is having a disgusting affair with Protopopov and you don't see it. You're just sitting about here while Natasha is having her disgusting affair with Protopopov and you don't see it. (*Sings.*) Won't you accept this little present from me? (*Goes out.*)"

Chebutykin's degradation is completed in Act III. In Act IV he is no longer a human being. Nothing makes any impression on him any more. The officers forget to take leave of him, but he just dismisses it with a shrug. Throughout the whole of the act he is, according to the stage direction, in a goodhumoured mood sitting in a chair in the garden and waiting to be called to the duel between Solyony and Tusenbach. He could have stopped the duel by telling Irene about it, but as he says to Mary: "One baron more or less in the world—what difference does it make?" It does not occur to him that Tusenbach's death will also affect Irene. When Irene tries to find out from him about the quarrel between Solyony and Tusenbach the day before, he refuses to tell her anything. "What's happened?" he says. "Nothing. Rubbish. (*Reads his newspaper.*) It makes no difference." Kulygin has also heard rumours of the impending duel, but Chebutykin refuses to enlighten him. "I don't know," he says. "It's all nonsense." It is then that Kulygin tells his funny story about the divinity student whose essay his professor marked with the word "nonsense," which the student, thinking it was written in Roman and not in Russian characters, read as "renyxa." (The Russian word for nonsense—*chepukha*—when written out can be mistaken for a "Latin" word since all its letters are identical with the letters of the Roman alphabet.) The nonsense word "renyxa," which strikes Chebutykin as the very quintessence of nonsense and which he repeats with such relish, epitomises his own attitude towards life. And when he returns from the duel, he just announces the news of Tusenbach's death and sits down, still in his goodhumoured mood, reading his paper and humming "Tararaboomdeay." He has been reduced to the state of an idiot to whom nothing matters and who keeps his good humour irrespective of what calamities may be happening around him. . . .

[The theme of Moscow]

. . . The idea that the yearning of the sisters for Moscow is the main theme of the play and expresses, as a modern Russian critic put it, "a kind of poetic symbol which introduces a certain unreality in the delineation of everyday facts," is far from true. The producers of *The Three Sisters* make too much of this all too obvious theme in conformity with the popular notion that the chief characters of the play are "Chekhovian" ineffectual characters, whereas the truth is that they are far from ineffectual. The important fact that the play does not end on a note of resignation but on a note of triumph is somehow completely ignored by them. It must be remembered that the Moscow theme is to a large extent autobiographical, expressing, as it does, Chekhov's own yearning to return to Moscow from the Crimea where his illness kept him confined for the last five years of his life. In his play Chekhov uses it to point a moral rather than to wallow in one of those moods which critics are so fond of ascribing to him, but which in fact he detested. It is significant that every time Moscow is mentioned in the play, Chekhov immediately underlines the absurdity of such a purely romantic craving for the unattainable. He does so at the very opening of the play in the chorus scene of the three sisters. Then, in the middle of Act I, Vershinin, in reply to the ecstatic cries of Olga and Irene when they find out that he, too, had been in Moscow, tells them of the "gloomy bridge" which made him feel so depressed every time he had to cross it, and—immediately after Irene's remark that her mother was buried in the cemetery attached to the Novo-Devichy Monastery, one of the oldest monasteries in Moscow (Chekhov was buried there), Vershinin says that with time "what seems so very important to us now, will be forgotten and will seem trivial." In Act II, in the scene between Andrey and Ferapont, Andrey's wish to sit in a large restaurant in Moscow where he would not feel as lonely as he does at home, is countered with Ferapont's story of the merchant who choked himself to death with a pancake in a Moscow restaurant, the whole point of the story being that Moscow can be as coarse and as uncivilised as the least cultured provincial town. A little later in the same act the whole unreality of Irene's dream about Moscow is emphasised twice. First, in her unconscious failure to realise that Andrey's losses at cards would prevent her from going to Moscow.

> IRENE. A fortnight ago he lost, and in December he lost. I wish he'd hurry up and lose everything he's got—perhaps we'd leave for Moscow then. Oh dear, I dream of Moscow every night. I'm going quite off my head. *(Laughs.)* We move there in June, and before June there is still—February, March, April, May—nearly half a year!

And later in the same act when Irene is laying out the cards in a game of patience—

> IRENE. It's coming out—I can see. We shall go to Moscow.

> FEDOTIK. No, it won't come out. See? The eight of spades is on top of the two. *(Laughs.)* That means that you won't go to Moscow.

> CHEBUTYKIN *(reads the paper)*. Tsitsihar. A smallpox epidemic is raging here.

Here again, as in the case of Berdichev, Chekhov introduces an apparently irrelevant statement, but what he really does is to use the chorus element as a detached comment on the dialogue, in this instance Irene's remark about Moscow. Tsitsihar—what an exotic place, even more desirable and unattainable than Moscow, and yet in reality it is nothing but a pest hole. (An English spectator would see the point of Chebutykin's line more clearly if Chekhov had used Samarkand instead of Tsitsihar.) And a little later after Mary's remark that if she had been in Moscow she would not notice the bad weather, Vershinin tells them the parable of the imprisoned French Cabinet Minister who for the first time in his life found real delight in watching the birds from his prison window, but who did not notice them any more after his release from prison. "So," Vershinin goes on, "you won't notice Moscow when you live there."

Chekhov ends Act II and Act III with the Moscow theme, but in both these curtains it is used merely to emphasise the delusive nature of Irene's dream. In Act II it follows close upon Natasha's departure for her sleigh ride with Protopopov, the two persons who will rob the sisters of their fortune and will make it impossible for them to go to Moscow; and in Act III it follows Irene's decision to marry Tusenbach, who has got himself a job far away from Moscow. Indeed, a little earlier in the same act Irene herself realises at last that she would never go to Moscow.

In Act IV comes Irene's final reconciliation with the idea that she would never see Moscow again. She says: "What I have decided is that if I am not going to live in Moscow, then it just can't be helped. I suppose it's fate, and there's nothing to be done about it." And the same note of reconciliation rather than resignation is sounded by Olga at the end of Act IV: "There won't be a single soldier left in town tomorrow, everything will become just a memory, and for us of course a new life will begin. Nothing has turned out as we expected. I did not want to be a headmistress, but I've become one. Which means that I shall never go to Moscow. . . ."

The whole thing, in fact, is nothing but a delusion, and the time has now come for the sisters to face reality, and they do it with courage and hope, as the final chorus of the three sisters shows—and it is this and not Moscow that is the leitmotif of the play. . . .

The Three Sisters was first performed on February 13, 1901 by the Moscow Art Theatre, under the direction of Konstantin Stanislavsky and Vladimir Nemirovich Danchenko. The crucial importance of this production for the modern reader or playgoer rests on two facts: Chekhov wrote The Three Sisters explicitly for the Moscow Art Theatre, with its particular traditions of acting and direction; and this first production was consequently so authoritative that it has influenced all subsequent stagings of the play. Here is Stanislavsky's own brief account of how he and his actors rehearsed Chekhov's play, followed by a detailed description of the production.

[THE FIRST PRODUCTION OF *THE THREE SISTERS*]
Konstantin Stanislavsky

Now, after the success of both Chekhov's plays, our Theatre could not get along without a new play from his pen. We began to attack Anton Pavlovich to have him fulfil the promise he gave us in the Crimea to write us a new play. We were forced

From Konstantin Stanislavsky, *My Life in Art*, trans. J. J. Robbins (New York: Theatre Arts Books, 1952), pp. 370–375. Copyright, 1924, by Little, Brown and Company. Copyright, 1948, Elizabeth Reynolds Hapgood. Copyright renewed 1952. Published since 1948 by Theatre Arts Books. Reprinted with the permission of the Publisher, Theatre Arts Books, New York.

to tire him with our continual questions and hints. It was hard for him to have us continually beating at the gates of his soul, it was hard for us to force ourselves to violate
his will. But there was nothing else for us to do. The fate of the Theatre from that
time on was in his hands; if he gave us a play we would have another season, if he
didn't the Theatre would lose all of its prestige. Unhappily the health of Chekhov
seemed to be on the wane. The freshest news from his quarters came from Olga Knipper
from the Crimea.—Strange!—We began to suspect her.—She knew altogether too much
about everything that was going on in Yalta—of the state of health of Chekhov, of the
weather in the Crimea, of the progress of work on the play, of the coming or not coming of Chekhov to Moscow.

"Aha," said we, Petr Ivanovich and I.

At last, to the pleasure of all, Anton Pavlovich sent the first act of the new play,
still unnamed. Then there arrived the second act and the third. Only the last act was
missing. Finally Chekhov came himself with the fourth act, and a reading of the play
was arranged, with the author present. As was our custom, a large table was placed
in the foyer of the theatre and covered with cloth, and we all sat down around it, the
author and the stage directors in the center. The atmosphere was triumphant and
uplifted. All the members of the company, the ushers, some of the stage hands and
even a tailor or two were present. The author was apparently excited and felt out of
place in the chairman's seat. Now and then he would leap from his chair and walk
about, especially at those moments when the conversation, in his opinion, took a false
or unpleasant direction. After the reading of the play, some of us, in talking of our impressions of the play, called it a drama, and others, even a tragedy, without noticing
that these definitions amazed Chekhov. One of the speakers, who had a self-evident
Eastern accent and tried to display his eloquence, began to speak of his impressions
with pathos and the common vocabulary of a tried orator:

"Although I do not agree with the author in principle, still—"

Anton Pavlovich could not survive this "in principle." Confused, hurt, and even
insulted, he left the meeting, trying to go out without being noticed. He succeeded, for
we had not understood what had happened, and least of all could explain the cause
that had made him leave us. Afraid that it was his state of health that had forced him
to leave the Theatre, I went at once to his home and found him not only out of spirits
and insulted, but angry. I do not remember ever seeing him so angry again.

"It is impossible. Listen—'in principle' !"

At first I thought that the flatness and the out-of-place use of the commonplace
phrase and the vulgarity of pronunciation had made Anton Pavlovich lose his patience. But the real reason was that he had written a happy comedy and all of us had
considered the play a tragedy and even wept over it. Evidently Chekhov thought that
the play had been misunderstood and that it was already a failure.

The work of stage direction began. As was the custom I wrote a detailed *mise en
scène,* who must cross to where and why, what he must feel, what he must do, how he
must look,—things that are considered strange, superfluous and harmful at the present
time, but which were unavoidable and necessary at that time because of the imma-
turity of the actors and the swiftness of production.

We worked with spirit. We rehearsed the play, everything was clear, comprehensive, true, but the play did not live; it was hollow, it seemed tiresome and long. There was something missing. How torturing it is to seek this something without knowing what it is. All was ready, it was necessary to advertise the production, but if it were to be allowed on the stage in the form in which it had congealed, we were faced with certain failure. And then what would happen to Anton Pavlovich? And what would happen to the Theatre? Yet, nevertheless, we felt that there were elements that augured great success, that everything with the exception of that little something was present. But we could not guess what that something was. We met daily, we rehearsed to a point of despair, we parted company, and next day we would meet again and reach despair once more.

"Friends, this all happens because we are trying to be smart," some one suddenly pronounced judgment. "We are dragging the thing out, we are playing bores on the stage. We must lift the tone and play in quick tempo, as in vaudeville, without any foolishness."

We began to play quickly, that is, we tried to speak and move swiftly, and this forced us to crumple up the action, to lose the text of our speeches and to pronounce our sentences meaninglessly. The result was that the play became worse, more tiresome, from the general disorder, hurry and flying about of actors on the stage. It was hard to understand what was taking place on the stage and of what the actors were talking. The prevalent mistake of beginning stage directors and actors is that they think that the heightening of tone is the quickening of tempo; that playing in full tone is loud and quick talking and strained action. But the expressions the "heightening of tone," "full tone," "quickening of tempo" have nothing to do with the actor and all with the spectator. To heighten tone means to heighten the mood of the audience, to strengthen the interest of the spectator in the performance; to quicken tempo means to live more strongly and intensively and to live over all that one says and does on the stage. And in talking and acting so that the spectator does not understand either the words or the problems of the actors, all that the actor really accomplishes is the letting down and lowering of the interest of the spectator in the performance and the general tone of his spiritual state of being.

At one of our torturing rehearsals the actors stopped in the middle of the play, ceased to act, seeing no sense in their work and feeling that we were standing in one place and not moving forward. At such times the distrust of the actors in the stage director and in each other reaches its greatest height and threatens to cause demoralization and the disappearance of energy. This took place late at night. Two or three electric lights burned dimly. We sat in the corners, hardly able to restrain our tears, silent, in the semigloom. Our hearts beat with anxiety and the helplessness of our position. Some one was nervously scratching the bench on which he sat with his finger nails. The sound was like that of a mouse. Now again there happened to me something incomprehensible, something that had remained a secret to me ever since an analogous happening during the rehearsals of "The Snow Maiden." Apparently the sound of a scratching mouse, which must have had some meaning for me at an early period of my life, in conjunction with the darkness and the condition and the mood of the entire night, together with the helplessness and depression, reminded me of something important, deep and bright that I had experienced somewhere and at some time. A spiritual spring was touched and I at last understood the nature of the something that was missing. I had known it before also, but I had known it with my mind and not my emotions.

The men of Chekhov do not bathe, as we did at that time, in their own sorrow. Just the opposite; they, like Chekhov himself, seek life, joy, laughter, courage. The men and women of Chekhov want to live and not to die. They are active and surge to overcome the hard and unbearable impasses into which life has plunged them. It is not their fault that Russian life kills initiative and the best of beginnings and interferes with the free action and life of men and women.

I came to life and knew what it was I had to show the actors. I had to show them what was to be done on the stage and how. And they also came to life. We began to work; it was clear to everybody that the dress rehearsal was not far away at last. Olga Knipper still had some trouble with her part, but Nemirovich-Danchenko worked privately with her. At one of the rehearsals something seemed to open in her soul and her role began to progress excellently.

Poor Anton Pavlovich did not wait, not only for the first night, but even for the dress rehearsal. He left Russia, giving his failing health as an excuse for going. I think there was another reason also—his anxiety over the play. This suspicion of mine was borne out by the fact that Chekhov did not leave an address where we could telegraph him of the reception of the play. Even Olga Knipper did not know where he had gone. And it seemed—

But Chekhov had left a viceroy in the person of a lovable colonel who was to see that there should be no mistakes made in the customs of military life, in the manner and method of the officers' bearing in the play, in the details of their uniforms, and so on. Anton Pavlovich paid a great deal of attention to this detail of his play because there had been rumors that he had written a play against the army, and these had aroused confusion, expectation, and bad feelings on the part of military men. In truth, Anton Pavlovich always had the best of opinion about military men, especially those in active service, for they, in his own words, were to a certain extent the bearers of a cultural mission, since, coming into the farthest corners of the provinces, they brought with them new demands on life, knowledge, art, happiness, and joy. Chekhov least of all desired to hurt the self-esteem of the military men.

During the dress rehearsals we received a letter from Chekhov abroad, but again there was no mention of his address. His letter stated, "Cross out the whole speech of Andrey and use instead of it the words 'A wife is a wife' ." This was typical, for it gives a good picture of the laconism of Chekhov. In the original manuscript Andrey delivered a fine speech which defined wonderfully and censured strongly the prosiness and smallness of many Russian women. Till marriage they kept alive in themselves a bit of poetry and femininity. But once married, they wore dressing gowns and slippers at home, and rich but tasteless clothes outside. The same dressing gown and the same tasteless clothes were apparent in their spiritual life and relationships. Is not this whole thought of Chekhov expressed without the use of unnecessary words in the secret meaning and the undercurrent of his short sentence, so full of helplessness and sadness: "A wife is a wife"?

THE THREE SISTERS IN THE PRODUCTION OF THE MOSCOW ART THEATRE
M. N. Stroeva

"Following the success of *The Seagull* and *Uncle Vanya*, the Moscow Art Theatre could no longer get along without a new Chekhov play," wrote K. S. Stanislavsky. "Thus, our fate from that time on was in the hands of Anton Pavlovich: if a play arrived, there would be a season; if not, the theatre would lose its flavor."

The Three Sisters was the first play written by Chekhov specifically for the Moscow Art Theatre, "commissioned" by it, as it were.

Work on the production began under the direction of Stanislavsky. After a preliminary talk, Nemirovich-Danchenko went abroad and Stanislavsky himself now carried on the rehearsals. . . . The first striking thing in Stanislavsky's new direction is his view of the play as an integral whole, as a symphonic work unfolding harmoniously. In *The Seagull* there were still individual bits which functioned only as external "transitions" for the actors, while in *Uncle Vanya* certain characteristics of the *dramatis personae* did not always tie in with the general mood of the play. This time all these elements were drawn systematically into the general fabric of the production and given logical coherence through the integral thinking of the director which disclosed the idea of the whole performance.

One might define this idea as representation of the inner struggle of man with the "power of banality." Stanislavsky had dealt before this with man's confrontation of his environment but neither in *The Seagull* nor in *Uncle Vanya* did it come so plainly into the foreground. The main thing, though, is that this confrontation now acquired an entirely new character.

Formerly, in *Uncle Vanya* and especially in *The Seagull*, the prosaic background tended to have a passive, descriptive function; it only explained the reasons for one kind of mood or behavior in people as opposed to another kind. In *The Three Sisters*, however, in full accordance with the author's thought, banal everyday life becomes an active, aggressive, far more dangerous force. It almost eats into people's lives, gradually enveloping everything, even the most intimate aspects of their lives, dogs all their actions, at every step smothers their dreams, with indifferent mockery reduces to nought their bursts of energy, their strivings. But no richly gifted Chekhovian man of sensibility can remain static. His inner life has the same dramatic intensity as the inner life of the heroes of *Uncle Vanya;* but now this inner activity all the more demands resolution in the external world, is imbued with an even greater sense of purpose. The purpose or goal here is to find the true path to happiness, to a free and bright life of labor.

The clash of two hostile forces constitutes the dramatic pivot in the director's prompt book. This clash begins in the second act. The first act, as is always the case with Chekhov, makes up a bright, joyous prelude—the "nameday, spring, high spirits;

M. N. Stroeva, *"The Three Sisters* in the Production of the Moscow Art Theatre," in *K. S. Stanislavskij: materialy, pis'ma, issledovanija, Teatral'noe nasledstvo,* I (Moscow, 1955), pp. 653–670, abridged and translated by Robert Louis Jackson. Reprinted from Robert Louis Jackson, Ed., *Chekhov: A Collection of Critical Essays* (Englewood Cliffs, N.J.: Prentice-Hall, 1967), pp. 121–135. © 1967. Reprinted by permission of Prentice-Hall, Inc., Englewood Cliffs, New Jersey.

the birds are singing; the sun is shining brightly." "Branches with buds barely turned green" peer into the windows "which have just been opened after winter." Irina is preparing feed for the birds; one can hear their "chirping outside beyond the bay window." "Andrei, full of spring feeling, is playing some melodious sonata off in the wings." . . . There are lots of flowers on the stage and from time to time one hears music, loud laughter, joyous exclamations. The mood of contemplation is quickly broken off; tears are erased by a smile. Stanislavsky even introduces entire scenes of laughter, of good-natured quarreling and unexpected bursts of gaiety, in his effort to heighten the mood of buoyancy and good cheer. Dreams about Moscow easily muffle the sadness arising from recollections of the past. The struggle between these two motifs and the quick triumph of vernal hopes for the future lies at the basis of the director's development of the beginning of the performance.

This resolution of the first act shows how correctly the director understands the unique way in which a Chekhov play is put together. In *The Three Sisters* (just as in *The Seagull* and in *Uncle Vanya*), the first act, full of hopes and confidence, is followed by a second in which reality—the banal everyday life enveloping the heroes—replaces the dream. Later on, in the third act, there is a clash between these two planes of the play and an explosion which leads to the complete defeat of all the hopes of the heroes to realize their dreams in actuality; only the self-sacrificing faith in a better future for mankind remains intact.

In full accord with this development, the second act—in contrast to Stanislavsky's first act (in the director's prompt book)—begins almost somberly; at the very outset the director, in the handling of lights and sound alone, conveys the feeling of anxiety that has crept into the house which till now had been warmed by joyous hopes.

> The beginning: It is dark in the living room; the fire in the stove is going out, only a streak of light falls from the open door leading to Andrei's room. From time to time Andrei's shadow flickers in this streak of light; he is walking up and down in his room, recalling his lectures. One can hear Andrei's footsteps as well as the sound of conversation, the monotonous undertone, occasional coughing, sighs, blowing of the nose, the shifting of a chair. Everything falls silent; he stops at his table and leafs through a notebook (the rustle of pages). Perhaps a sound hinting at tears, and once again a blowing of the nose, steps, a lower murmuring, and his shadow on the stage. The lamp is about to go out in the dining room; it flares up, then again begins to die out. The windows are frozen over. Snow on the roof. Outside it is snowing. A storm. The piano has been moved, and it obstructs the bay window.

And, as if to explain the reason for the changes that have taken place in the house, the director points out: "The appointment of the room is in Natasha's taste." It immediately becomes clear that she has filled the place with herself; her Bobik is everywhere: "A child's blanket, baby sheets, cushions, swaddling bands, and the like are strewn over the sofa. On the table next to the sofa are toys: a little barrel-organ (with a squeaky sound), a harlequin clapping cymbals together. On the floor next to the piano—a large rug; on it are pillows from the sofa, toys—a child's harmonica, a top, a little wagon. On the piano are pieces of material, scissors, a towel." One gets the impression that not a single space is left in the room which has not been taken over by Natasha's philistine existence. Light and air have been banished. The only sounds in the darkness are "monotonous strokes of the pendulums of two clocks"; "the wind howls in the chimney of the stove," while the snowstorm "beats at the windowpanes." And as though to make this atmosphere of hopeless anguish heavier still, the "sound of a harmonica drifts in now and then"; "a troika rushes down the street to the sound of drunken shouts" and you hear "far off the drunken singing of a stray reveler."

It becomes clear now why Andrei's shadow shifts about the room so restlessly, why Anfisa, "her slippers scraping," drags herself along so despondently "as she carries a pitcher with kvass into Andrei's room." "Anfisa has changed," the director emphasizes. "She has become shrunken, pale; she gathers up the toys, gets down on her knees, expresses exhaustion, weariness." When Natasha appears, Anfisa in a state of fright sets about putting away the toys, while "a fat custodian zealously gives her a dressing down." Natasha, according to the notation of Stanislavsky, only enters in order to extinguish all the lamps. It gets quite dark. Andrei is obliged to light a candle and by its uncertain flickering light he carries on a conversation with Ferapont, or more correctly, a conversation with himself: "How terribly life changes, deceives one!" . . .

One should note that in Stanislavsky's direction of *The Three Sisters,* he adheres rigorously and consistently to the principle of introducing only ideologically important, necessary details from everyday life. The sounds of the harmonica and the drunken voices which invade the room are justified not only on the plane of everyday life (it is Shrovetide), but also on the ideological plane (they emphasize, in the director's thinking, the hopeless banality and crudity of the surroundings).

The scene of Masha and Vershinin, for example, is constructed as follows. On their appearance in the room "it grows lighter." But the elated, dreamy conversation-confession of the two lovers has at the basis of its construction the fact that the conversation is interrupted; during the pauses, for instance, "the scraping of a mouse" is occasionally heard, and they chase it away, knocking on the sofa, while from Andrei's room there is heard at first "a frightfully plaintive melody on the violin," then the "sound of a saw. . . ." "Overcome by depression in his room, he is obviously casting about now this way, now that, but nothing holds him," explains the director. In this context Vershinin's bitter and unanswerable question inevitably comes to mind and becomes relevant: "A lofty way of thought is characteristic of the Russian man in the highest degree, but tell me why it is that in life he strikes so low? Why?"

The idea of the disjunction between dream and reality seems to be graphically confirmed at every step. Thus Irina declares despairingly: "Work without poetry, without ideas—" And in the pause—the dreary "scratching of the mouse." Irina once again begins to dream of Moscow, but at this moment Vershinin "picks up a toy lying on the table—Petrushka with the cymbals—and makes a noise with it—then he holds this toy in his hands and every now and then makes a noise with it," thus producing as it were an ironic accompaniment to his words. Irina doggedly continues. "We are moving there [to Moscow] in June"—once again one hears the mocking "noise of Petrushka." Here Stanislavsky employs quite the same device as Chekhov does in Act I of the play when Olga's words, "One longs so passionately to go home," are accompanied—seemingly accidentally, but actually with clear mocking intent—by a rejoinder of Chebutykin: "The devil take it!"

The same device of contrasting details is introduced even more clearly by the director in the "philosophizing" scene which follows: "Let's at least philosophize a bit," suggests Vershinin. Tusenbach has found a little music box, plays it. "About what?" "Let's dream—for example, about what life will be like when we are gone, in two or three hundred years." Pause. Tusenbach turns the music box two or three times, it emits some vague sounds. "And in a thousand years man will be sighing the same: 'Ah, how hard it is to live!'" Tusenbach holds the music box in his hands and now and again gives it a turn; it emits plaintive sounds. But Vershinin energetically retorts: "In two or three hundred years, or even in a thousand years—it's not a matter of a particular time—a new, happy life will come into being. We will not participate in this life, of course, but we live for it now, we are working, well, suffering, we are creating it—and in this alone is the purpose of our being and, if you will, our happiness." And Stanislavsky notes: *"It is very important to stir up the audience, [speak with] spirit, raise the voice."* But just here, opposite those same words of Vershinin, he writes: *"In the distance the harmonica and the drunken voices seem deliberately to bring to mind the thought that everything about which Vershinin speaks is a long way off"* (italics are Stanislavsky's).

It is striking to see how profoundly Stanislavsky penetrates into the author's conception, into the intense drama of the scene. Chekhov convinced people that "a new, happy life will come into being" not at all in order to calm and lull in them the feeling of protest against the system of life of those times; on the contrary, he aroused it. And it is remarkable that Stanislavsky, who considered it "very important" to convey to the spectator an inspiriting faith in the future, simultaneously instills in him a sense of distress by creating the oppressive atmosphere of the everyday world surrounding Chekhov's heroes.

Obviously in such conditions joy cannot be complete. It would seem that Masha is happy in this scene; she is cheerful, laughing. But the director notes: "Masha's laughter is nervous, she could as well burst into tears; therefore she quickly puts out both candles." The scene that follows is without light: "Darkness. Snow. The moon. Only the glow of the cigarettes is visible." And how expressive it is: the lonely glow of cigarettes in the gloom as people dispute "passionately" about happiness, work, the future. But the dispute gradually dies down and ends with the "quiet singing—some song about wasted youth." Then even the "singing somehow gets out of tune and stops. All fall silent." And when Masha does not want to give up and tries again to talk with Vershinin about happiness, about Moscow, she is interrupted by an "ominous ring from the anteroom." The letter to Vershinin ("the wife has taken poison again") tears him from Masha.

The whole second act is worked out in this way by the director. There is constant emphasis upon the contrast between the people's inner state, their strivings, impulses, and that life which in every detail seems to say to them: "No." But for Stanislavsky it was important to show that people do not give up, that their thirst for life does not die out, but, on the contrary, revives, as appears in the structure of the encounter between Natasha and the guests who have gathered at the house of the Prozorovs. The director introduces a whole "laughing scene" after Natasha's French phrases: "Some hiss; others rock with laughter." After she goes, Tusenbach feels somehow liberated and starts to sing, dances a little waltz on the proscenium, . . . laughs, leaps about gaily, and goes to the piano: 'I'm sitting down to play!' Masha hears the waltz, jumps up, and begins to dance—singing to herself, she dances alone and in despair. Roday takes hold of her and they go on dancing together." Then when Natasha unceremoniously sends the guests packing, the director stresses that this is a "comic, cheerful departure."

The "appearance of the maskers" was transformed by Stanislavsky into a whole scene; in just the same way, he meant it to introduce a fresh breath of life into the desolate semidark atmosphere of the house. "You see them; you hear gay voices—the sound of bells." But (on Natasha's orders) the maskers are not allowed in: "Silence. All the gaiety is shattered; somebody whistles. A pall descends upon the gay spirits of the crowd. They are even sort of embarrassed."

The entire finale of the act is dominated now by Natasha and Protopopov. The bells of Protopopov's troika ring out and stifle the sound of voices: "In the course of the Kulygin-Irina-Olga-Vershinin scene one can hear the troika standing at the front gate; the horses are shaking their manes; their bells are jingling." Thus the anguished despair of Irina in the finale is prepared and justified: "Irina stands motionless—sadly she makes her way to the piano. Natasha walks past. The departure of the troika. Pause. The lamp in the dining room starts to go out, flickers; a mouse scratches. Irina groans as though in pain: 'To Moscow, to Moscow.' She leans against the piano. The pendulum."

The clash of hostile forces increases in the third act. The whole atmosphere of the action becomes extraordinarily tense. Stanislavsky makes a special point about it: "Wherever possible one must accent the sense of nervousness and the tempo. Do not abuse the pauses. Everybody's transitions and movements are nervous and rapid." Gone now are the scraping mouse, the squeaking sounds, the music box and revelers' singing—these do not create the "mood." The "ever intensifying heavy-sounding bell of the fire alarm" clangs through the entire act, "the firemen thunder past the house, across the yard," "a red light falls in patches on the floor."

Taking advantage of everybody's anxiety and distraught condition, banality takes the offensive. Natasha takes over as sovereign mistress of the house. In the second act she could still deal with Andrei or Irina "very tenderly," "almost caressingly." But now, in the scene with Anfisa, she "speaks without shouting, but very commandingly and boldly drives her out with a gesture." And later with Olga she begins to speak "without shouting, but firmly; at Olga's slightest movement she gets more and more irritated. She ends up with a squealing hysterical scream. She squeals with tears in her voice." And, after establishing herself in this manner as mistress of the house, Natasha walks by from time to time without looking at anybody, crosses the room, candle in hand, angrily slamming doors. It should be noted that the last *mise-en-scène* was close to what the author wanted when he wrote Stanislavsky: "Better if she [Natasha] crosses the stage, in a straight line, without looking at anybody or anything, *à la* Lady Macbeth, with a candle—this would be simpler and more terrible." Originally it was proposed—as Stanislavsky wrote Chekhov—that "Natasha, while making the rounds of the house, at night, should extinguish all the lights and look for burglars under the furniture."

In these circumstances the dissatisfaction with life that Chekhov's heroines feel reaches a point of unbearable suffering. Irina "groans with misery, clutches her head, agonizes—throws herself on the bed, sobs behind the screen." "I can't, I can't bear any more! I can't, I can't!" She hasn't the strength to tear herself away and, pleading with the others to help her, "with a groan she almost shouts: 'Throw me out, throw me out, I can't stand it any longer!' " After this, "veritable hysteria breaks out behind the screen, growing more and more intense (only, for God's sake, not in real!!!!!!!!!!)" writes Stanislavsky.

Act III for the sisters is marked by a search for a way out, a search for action. Masha, stronger and bolder, seems to have found this way out; she has decided to break with the cheerless, tedious banality of her life. Here is how the director set up her confession to her sisters: "Masha quickly gets up, agitated, in a state of decision; she is nervously excited, nervously stretches out her arms, gets on her knees, just as does Olga, at the head of Irina's bed, embraces Irina with one arm and Olga with the other. She speaks quietly ("I love that man, in a word, I love Vershinin"), drawing the heads of Olga and Irina closer to her own. The three heads of the sisters are close to one another. Masha looks upwards with an ecstatic look, recalls her whole romance." After the words of Olga: "Please stop this. I'm just not going to listen," Masha, "with vexation brushing off her dress, gets up, briskly goes up to Olga; the tone is desperate; she's turning her back on everything; she's come to a decision."

Stanislavsky stresses that Olga, in essence, understands Masha, sympathizes with her (something which Chekhov does not reveal in this scene). "Olga tenderly caresses her, the sinner, as she does the innocent Irina. Olga tenderly kisses Masha, strokes her." The director felt it was important to show that common strivings unite the sisters; it is interesting in this respect to note his instruction: "Masha is solicitous over Irina, although this is not in her character." Again the sisters' community of strivings in their struggle to find a way out is revealed with special clarity in the scene of Masha's departure: "The departure of Masha—hurriedly, impetuously, very nervous and upset, she embraces Olga firmly and talks as she moves toward the door. At the door Olga kisses Masha tenderly, in a motherly way. In reality she understands her; in the depths of her heart she acknowledges that she would act the same way. Now she does not censure her, but pities her. Therefore she kisses her tenderly, as a mother would." And as though to emphasize the importance of this moment, so crucial to Masha's fate, the sounds of the conflagration are carried in again from the street: "The firemen thunder past the house and across the yard: the clatter of hooves, bells, empty barrels, the shouts of two voices; against the background of this tumult—the kiss of Olga and Masha."

Act IV brings a shattering of all hopes; the dream about a possible happiness must be relinquished. "There is no happiness; there should not be and will not be for us. We should only work and work, and as for happiness—that is the lot of our distant descendants"—this is the leitmotif of the last act. In contrast to the first act with its springlike atmosphere, Stanislavsky notes here: "The mood. Autumn. It is cool, everyone is wearing coats (the light summer kind). Here and there yellow leaves are falling from trees during the whole act."

The curtain rises at a moment when one hears a treble peal of bells (after Mass-prayers on the occasion of the departure of the troops). The director creates the troubled and confused atmosphere surrounding departure by introducing the activity of many people: porter, orderly, cook, maid, all seeing the officers off. They are hauling all sorts of things. The garden gate is being slammed all the time.

Each of the heroes bears his suffering, the sorrow of departure. Tusenbach continually has a troubled look; he looks at his watch frequently and coughs nervously. Irina is aware of his state and looks at him anxiously. He knows that the duel is inevitable and senses its tragic end; but when he says goodbye to Irina, he tries to stifle his sorrow and vainly strives to appear gay. This is the way the director structured the farewell scene:

> The music comes closer. Violin and harp. Tusenbach caresses Irina, smooths her hair, wraps her more warmly in her shawl, kisses all the fingers of her hand. Irina is tense, does not take her eyes off Tusenbach. He pats her on the head. She presses more closely to him. Tusenbach: "I'm happy"—he becomes much more cheerful, inspirited, livelier. "It's time for me to go now"—quickly kisses her hand, leaves, takes hold of the gate handle, opens the gate. Irina runs after him with an anxious glance, grabs him by the hand and holds him back. Tusenbach makes an effort to smile. Irina embraces him and nestles close to him. Tusenbach pensively looks off toward the garden.

We find Masha also in the same state of waiting for unhappiness. "The cranes fly by; Masha gets up with a start. She is distraught; tears well up. Harp and violin in the distance. Masha rubs her forehead, sighs deeply, shakes her head. She looks at her watch, is very nervous, pensive."

While the troubled, unhappy atmosphere of departure gradually deepens outside in the garden, the house lives its own, special life, quite alien to these suffering people. Natasha and Protopopov now reign undisputed there. From time to time, echoes of this life carry their loud, indifferent dissonance into the garden. In order to shut herself off more completely from what is now taking place out there, Natasha "draws a curtain over the balcony" and from time to time one hears loud laughter; moreover, "a deep bass, obviously that of Protopopov, can be distinguished amidst the laughter."

On the stage—the delicate, restrained lyricism of sorrow; but it is lacerated by indifferent, happy "voices, the sound of a top, the sound of a large ball bouncing on the floor, the noise of a wooden sphere rolling on the floor. Frequent laughter—a bass may be distinguished." Stanislavsky considers it necessary to show how this balcony world penetrates into the garden: "At one point a ball bounces from the balcony; the nurse picks it up in the garden and returns to the balcony." The director even went so far as to consider bringing Protopopov himself out onto the stage. "Make a try at having Protopopov himself pick it [the ball] up; in this way he would appear before the public for a moment. It might turn out magnificently or dreadfully. It should be tried at one of the dress rehearsals," writes Stanislavsky, sketching the image of Protopopov in several strokes. "This would be a marvelous role. Just imagine: suddenly a fat man with a cigar between his teeth would unexpectedly leap from the balcony; he would run after the ball, bending over several times since he could not catch it at once. Then he disappears forever with the ball."

But when the most trying period of the departure arrives and human sorrow fills the scene, the director banishes banality from the stage. "Up to this moment [i.e., the moment when Masha bids farewell to Vershinin—M.S.] one can still hear conversation and the noise of the ball and games on the terrace, though it does not interfere with the action; after this moment, a calm sets in, things gradually come to a halt, and the balcony empties."

"Masha, all distraught, comes rapidly along the garden path. Vershinin: 'I came to bid farewell.' Masha: 'Farewell'—sobs in Vershinin's arms; he himself barely restrains his tears; he is deeply moved. Olga wants to comfort Masha. Irina advises her not to interfere and to let her weep."

The surmounting of suffering is, for the director, the most important thing in the finale. He sees "an inspiriting thought of the author" in the fact that Chekhovian heroes even in a moment of profound sorrow find the strength to raise themselves to dreaming of people's future happiness. The director accompanies the concluding monologue of Olga with an emphatic note: *"As much as possible, speak more spiritedly."*

In the first version of Chekhov's play, which Stanislavsky worked with, Olga's words "If we only knew" are followed by this stage direction of the author: "The music gradually dies down; in the background of the stage there is a bustle; one can see a crowd watching the baron, killed at the duel, as he is being carried away; Kulygin happy, smiling, carries a hat and cape; Andrei is pushing another pram in which Bobik is sitting."

Stanislavsky, as he finished his work on the director's plan, came to the conclusion that the body of Tusenbach must not be carried across the stage. The director gave detailed reasons why it seemed important to him to change the author's stage direction:

> Call Anton Pavlovich's attention to the fact that in his version it would be necessary to insert a scene involving the populace, the chatter of the crowd which is accompanying Tusenbach; otherwise we would have a ballet. During the procession across the narrow stage all the scenery would rock. The crowd would make a racket with their feet, bump into things—all this would produce an anticlimactic pause. And as for the sisters—is it possible to leave them indifferent to seeing Tusenbach carried away? One would have to think up something for them. I am afraid that, after chasing so many hares, we shall lose what is most important: the final inspiriting thought of the author which atones for many of the somber parts of the play. The removal of the body will either turn out to be boring, anticlimactic, unnatural, or (if we succeed in overcoming all these obstacles) terribly oppressive, and would only reinforce a feeling of oppression.

The reason for Stanislavsky's reluctance to intensify the "feeling of oppression" of the play was, first of all, that he wanted to emphasize its affirmative aspect. This fully accorded with the desires of the author himself who, as we know, even at the first reading of the play in the theater objected to the view of *The Three Sisters* as "an oppressive drama of Russian life," and affirmed that he had written a "comedy." For this reason Chekhov gladly agreed to strike out the episode with the carrying of Tusenbach's body; he had had doubts about it even earlier but had left it in on the insistence of Stanislavsky ("Even at that time," he wrote Olga Knipper, "I had said that it would be inconvenient to bear away the corpse of Tusenbach across your stage, but Alekseev [Stanislavsky] insisted that there was no getting along without the corpse."). . . .

Stanislavsky understood the idea of Chekhov's play as being the clash between two hostile forces in the milieu of the Russian intelligentsia of that period. The social significance of this clash consisted in the fact that, in spite of the external triumph of "banality," that is, the philistine, bourgeois element, moral victory rested on the side of the antiphilistine, antibourgeois elements, that is, on the side of the three sisters who had inwardly liberated themselves from the "power of everyday environment." Thus, the performance was supposed to be a rebellion against the "external slavery" of the Chekhovian heroes, and was intended to arouse a feeling of social protest. At the same time the affirmative aspect of the play is clearly emphasized in Stanislavsky's prompt book—the dream of Chekhov's heroes which is opposed to the horror of reality. . . .

In a way, as he worked on the director's plan for *The Three Sisters,* Stanislavsky in a practical sense came close to realizing his concept of "a through-line of action." This made it possible for him to show in a Chekhovian manner the natural "current of life," not simply as a chain of accidental episodes, details from everyday life strung together, but in movement, when each seemingly accidental word that is dropped, everything that strikes the eye, emphasizes and brings out the author's thought.

Stanislavsky sought to concentrate heavily around Chekhov's heroes such a crushing and stifling atmosphere—expressing itself everywhere, even in the tiniest details—that the thought would of itself arise: how unbearable this existence is—and a conflict with reality would inevitably take shape. But this conflict could only really become the *active* pivot of the performance if the people drawn into it stepped forward as an active force of opposition. And herein lay the chief difficulty of rehearsal with the actors. Because really: how is one to disclose this active element in people who do not come out in open struggle with the banality surrounding them, who, so it seems, only suffer and yearn, and in this way are doomed to inaction?

Stanislavsky found the correct answer—as he writes—"unexpectedly" at one of the rehearsals, and only then did "Chekhovian people come to life." "It turned out that they are by no means moping about in anguish but, on the contrary, are seeking gaiety, laughter, animation; they want to live and not just vegetate. I sensed that this was the true approach to Chekhov's heroes, it inspired me, and I intuitively understood what had to be done." It should be emphasized that all of Stanislavsky's preparatory work on the director's prompt book led him to this resolution of the question.

It might appear that this assertion contradicts Stanislavsky's statement cited above, that it was only at rehearsals that the main idea was found. But, first of all, the path from conception to realization is always complex and contradictory. Now, for example, if Stanislavsky immediately, at the first rehearsal, had set before the actors the task of "seeking gaiety, laughter, animation," then one can say for certain that Chekhov's idea would not have been disclosed. Through such an approach it would have been impossible to perceive and transmit the genuinely Chekhovian inner action, the activity of the heroes. It was first necessary for the actors at rehearsals to live deeply into this unbearable state of a life without exit, in order then to feel a hatred for it, to feel the necessity for inner liberation. . . .

It is characteristic that the performance began to live a full life when its "supertask" was defined—Stanislavsky's formulation that "Chekhovian people . . . are seeking gaiety, laughter, animation; they want to live and not just vegetate." Only such an active, operative "supertask" could help the actors to "live" on the stage, and not to "act," because truth of life in the theatre is born through correctly discovered stage action. One of the important achievements in the rehearsal work on *The Three Sisters* lay in the fact that—basing themselves on the work on *Uncle Vanya*—the actors and directors of the Moscow Art Theatre now came close to mastering on a practical plane the central principle of the "art of experience"—not to act, but to live, i.e., to feel and live.

In his book *From the Past,* Nemirovich-Danchenko writes that in its work on Chekhovian performances the Moscow Art Theatre came close to the goal advanced by Chekhov himself when he said at a rehearsal for *The Seagull* in St. Petersburg: "There is too much acting, everything must be as it is in real life." "Nothing must be acted"—this is how Nemirovich-Danchenko defined that classic demand which he and Stanislavsky made to the actors at that time. "Absolutely nothing. Neither feelings, nor moods, nor situations, nor words, nor style, nor images."

This is a decisive refutation of the false notion that a certain "mood" was a goal in itself for the directors of Chekhov performances in the Moscow Art Theatre. In fact, what Stanislavsky and Nemirovich-Danchenko understood by the notion "mood" was the realistic atmosphere of the performance; it served only as a means for re-creating on the stage the truth of life as refracted through the prism of Chekhov's world view.

"The difference between the stage and life is only in the world view of the author," wrote Nemirovich-Danchenko in reporting to Chekhov on the progress of rehearsals of *The Three Sisters.* "All *this* life, the life shown in this performance, has passed through the world view, sensibility, temperament of the author. It received a special coloration which is called poetry."

Nemirovich-Danchenko began to take part in rehearsals only in the middle of January 1901 (the first performance was given January 31), i.e., at a time when Stanislavsky had carried the work on the performance to the point of rough dress rehearsals.

[In a letter to Chekhov of January 22, 1901] Nemirovich-Danchenko disclosed his understanding of the essence of the future performance. . . . "The fable: the house of the Prozorovs. The life of the three sisters after the death of the father, the appearance of Natasha, her gradual taking possession of the whole house, and, finally, her complete triumph and the isolation of the sisters. The fate of each of them—take the fate of Irina—runs like a red thread: 1) I want to work, [she is] happy, gay, healthy; 2) a headache from work, it doesn't satisfy; 3) life is smashed, youth passes, she agrees to marry a man who doesn't appeal to her; 4) fate trips things up, and the bridegroom is killed."

This interpretation of the play differs considerably from the one which is revealed to us on the pages of Stanislavsky's prompt book. Of course, the basic design is the same. But what is obviously missing in Nemirovich-Danchenko's interpretation is the element of struggle, an emphasis upon the active side of Chekhov's heroes who try to resist the onslaught of banality. Quite the contrary, he emphasizes their passive submission to their fate: "These people are like chessmen in the hands of unseen players." (It should be noted that in his production of *The Three Sisters* in 1940, Nemirovich-Danchenko reexamines the old traditions precisely in this manner.)

Thus, Nemirovich-Danchenko comprehends the Chekhovian "current of life" more in the way of epic narration which broadly and fully embraces all life, not merely its "heaving heights and falling depths." "The events in the play seem to creep along, like life itself in that epoch—sluggishly, without any apparent logical connection. People act more under the influence of chance happenings, they are not themselves the builders of their life," wrote Nemirovich-Danchenko later on; he was setting forth his view of the unique character of the play, a uniqueness—so it seemed to him—created by the peculiar features of the epoch. While rehearsing the play, he stressed the following in a letter to Chekhov: "The fable develops, as in an *epic* work—without those stimuli which were supposed to be used by the old-style dramatists—in the midst of a simple, faithfully perceived current of life. The nameday, Shrovetide, the fire, the departure, the stove, the lamp, the pianoforte, pies, drunkenness, twilight, night, the living room, the dining room, the girls' bedroom, winter, autumn, spring, etc., etc., etc."

But if we recall that the performance occurred on the boundary-line of the new century (December 1900–January 1901), on the threshold of the first Russian revolution, then it becomes clear that the characterization of the epoch given by Nemirovich-Danchenko, far from being accurate, is one-sided. We must acknowledge that Stanislavsky's position in this case was more progressive, since the intense dramatic character of the clash of two hostile forces in modern society better reflected the progressive moods of the epoch than the passive-epic narrative about how "some splendid people could fall into the clutches of a most common vulgar woman."

As a whole, Stanislavsky's direction of the performance strove to represent through *The Three Sisters* the tragedy of the Russian intelligentsia of that day, to awaken in the audience a protest against unbearable conditions of life and at the same time to see to it that faith in man himself did not perish—in that man who was straining toward a renewal of life, who was expending himself in dreams of the bright future of his country.

The Moscow Art Theatre continues to perform The Three Sisters *according to the guidelines established for the first production, three quarters of a century ago. According to reviewer Kenneth Tynan, this production remains as effective as ever, particularly because of the total identification of the actors with their roles.*

[THE MOSCOW ART THEATRE'S *THREE SISTERS* IN 1958]
Kenneth Tynan

. . . Peter Ustinov contends that team-work and Chekhov are, in acting terms, incompatible. The characters, he maintains, are all soloists who occasionally interrupt each other's monologues but never listen to what anyone else is saying. They are deaf

Kenneth Tynan, [Review of the Moscow Art Theatre's production of *The Three Sisters*], in his *Curtains* (New York: Atheneum, 1961), pp. 435–436. Copyright © 1958, 1961 by Kenneth Tynan. Appeared originally in The New Yorker Magazine. Reprinted by permission of Atheneum Publishers.

and blind to the world outside them—which is why they are funny and also why they are appalling. Fair comment, and in *Three Sisters,* a much more complex work than *The Cherry Orchard,* this technique is carried as far as it can go without blowing the play centrifugally apart. The very theme is estrangement: a brief brushing of lips is as close as anyone ever gets to another's soul. Of the three girls yearning for Moscow, Olga will never marry, Masha has married badly, and Irina is cheated of marriage by a tragic duel. Their brother, Andrey, is yoked to a prolific and faithless shrew. Two nihilists look on: one active—the savage Solyony, who scents his hands because, like Lear's, they smell of mortality—and the other passive: Chebutykin, the doctor, jilted by the girls' mother and now drunk past caring. And so all sit, mourning and mumbling, making out of their inconsequence a choral lament on human isolation.

The Moscow production, based on the original staging by Nemirovich-Danchenko, gets all of this and infuses it with that strange dynamic apathy that is Chekhov's greatest demand on his actors. The sisters themselves are new to the roles and as yet unsettled in them: Mlle. Yurieva's Masha comes nearest to the wry fatalism we are looking for. Her Vershinin, M. Massalsky, is unduly restrained, tarred with the pomade of the *matinée* idol; but the elder parts are filled to overflowing with beard and rasp and detail. M. Gribov's Chebutykin, in particular, is all I had heard of it; encrusted with corruption, a ponderous fish-eyed shrug of a man, he is yet capable, while remembering his dead love, of a sudden and transfixing pathos. The last act is, I suppose, the high-water mark of twentieth-century drama, yet this superb company meets its challenge as if opening the door to an old friend. The sound-effects and lighting are brilliant throughout: we weep, apart from anything else, for a lost world so lovingly revived. How these actors eat; and listen; and fail to listen; and grunt and exist, roundly and egocentrically exist! They have become, with long rehearsal, the people they are playing: they do not need, as our actors do, to depend on the lines alone for their characterisation. We act with our voices, they with their lives. Where we leave off, they begin. Don't be deterred by the language barrier. This is not verbal acting, like ours, but total acting: Stanislavsky often made his players rehearse without words, to be sure that their faces and bodies were performing as well. Read the play before going, and you will be safe. Safe, and enriched. . . .

However authoritative the Moscow Art Theatre production may still be, it remains only one way of staging Chekhov's play. Each new production must interpret the script anew, and questions of how to play characters such as Masha or Chebutykin or how to stage a scene such as the final one of the play have by no means been settled for all time. Indeed, these questions never can find a definitive answer, so long as The Three Sisters *remains alive in the theatre. In the following review, Frank Cox describes a recent (and apparently quite successful) Czech production, which seems to have differed significantly from the tradition established by Stanislavsky and Nemirovich-Danchenko.*

Review on the following page: Frank Cox, [Review of *The Three Sisters*], *Plays and Players*, vol. 16, no. 10 (July 1969), pp. 54–55. Reprinted by permission of the author.

[*THE THREE SISTERS* IN A 1969 CZECH PRODUCTION]
Frank Cox

Regular readers of these pages will be aware from David Hare's guide to the World Theatre Season in the April issue, and in detail from Peter Roberts' reports last November on the Belgrade and Venice Festivals, that The Theatre Behind The Gate is a splinter-group from the Czech National Theatre, sharing the Laterna Magica Theatre in Prague under the direction of Otomar Krejca and with Josef Svoboda as resident designer. What they will now no doubt wonder, having sampled the work of this company in London, is what on earth the Czech National Theatre is doing, bereft of at least six of its most outstanding actors, its master-director and its renowned designer! For Krejca and his team visiting the Aldwych last month gave their *Three Sisters* at least one world-class performance which made our own National Theatre production seem by comparison uneasy and underpowered, and which swept firmly away what memories remain of that much-abused though, to my mind, badly underrated Actors' Studio one of four seasons ago.

Svoboda's settings are the least satisfactory feature, being not so much simple as poverty-stricken and lacking even the gaunt splendour of his NT version, but here he does have the excuse that the company's productions must of necessity be easily transported, since The Theatre Behind The Gate tours extensively as part of its lengthy rehearsal schedule. Nevertheless the visual success of this *Three Sisters* lies not in its dull grey flattage and spare furnishings but in the appearance and groupings of the actors and in the sensitive area-lighting by Vlastimil Tretera which isolates and so pinpoints the solitude of the characters most feelingly.

Krejca's view of the play is totally unsentimental. His Masha is a bit of a bitch, supercilious in company, caring for no-one until Vershinin comes along, offering besides his maturely dashing presence the chance, however second-hand, of a link with Moscow; Andrei has already sunk with pudgy complacency into provincial life years before we meet him, and in the last scene he seems not the slightest bit incongruous pushing the pram; Solyoni is a nasty little neurotic with smarmed hair and the thoughtless stare of an unpractised voyeur, just the type to commit licensed murder for no better reason than envy, and Chebutykin (Krejca himself, bulky, balding and self-effacing in the best actor-manager tradition—you can't tear your eyes away from him!) is no cuddly old uncle figure but an ungainly, inadequate onlooker, his helpless detachment summed up in one powerful stage-image in the last act when slumped in the garden swing which, with one spindly tree, comprises the scenery, he lolls grotesquely like some uniformed baby in its harness.

The comedy of the play is neither exaggerated nor diminished, but there is a boisterous quality in the playing which seems much closer to Chekhov's intention than our own traditionally awed approach. So Krejca's ending to the play cuts across the rhetoric which threatens to sink so many productions; when the news of the Baron's death is brought to Irina, the three sisters scurry headlong about the stage, clutching at each other and spinning in a near-hysterical dance which counterpoints the blaring military music of the departing soldiers. The effect is dazing when compared with, say Olivier's statuesque grouping at the National, but essentially it is a more convincing solution of the play's most dangerously portentous moments. . . .

The Playboy
of the Western World

In most audiences' experience of The Playboy of the Western World, *there are two major centers of interest, and the impressions produced by the two are equally memorable. First, there is Christy, with his horrifying and at the same time comical attempts to kill his father; and then, as a dramatic counterweight, there are the people of Mayo, with their extravagant language, behavior and morals. In a brief and incisive essay, Norman Podhoretz sees the relationship between these two dramatic elements as the fundamental theme of the play, which he defines as "the radical incompatibility of Hero and society."*

SYNGE'S *PLAYBOY:* MORALITY AND THE HERO
Norman Podhoretz

Synge's *The Playboy of the Western World* is a dramatic masterpiece. On this, it seems, there has been critical unanimity. Yeats, for example, called it "the strangest, the most beautiful expression in drama of that Irish fantasy which . . . is the unbroken character of Irish genius." But the critics have not been very helpful in explaining what makes the play a masterpiece. "It brought to the contemporary stage the most rich and copious store of character since Shakespeare," writes P. P. Howe, but he goes no further by way of interpretation than a summary of the plot. Yet that there is something to interpret should be obvious from even a casual glance at the plot, which clearly has the myth of rebellion against the father at its basis.

Christy, we are told, "kills" his father for two reasons: he is tired of being goaded on the score of his physical and sexual timidity, and, more immediately, he refuses to marry the old woman who had nursed him as a baby. The primitive people of Mayo (with whom Christy has taken refuge) not only refuse to give him up to the police, but make a hero of him instead. Encouraged by their admiration, Christy begins growing into manhood with full command of his physical and sexual powers. With the suggestion of the myth in mind, we can appreciate the significance of Christy's reception by the Mayoites. First of all, it must be noted that there is another "murderer" in the play who, like Christy, has escaped punishment but who is nevertheless despised in Mayo—the Widow Quin. Hers "was a sneaky kind of murder did win small glory with the boys itself." A more important pointer is that the second time Christy "kills" his father, the Mayoites turn on him. Michael James, who had told Christy that "a daring fellow is the jewel of the world, and a man did split his father's middle with a single clout should have the bravery of ten, so may God and Mary and St. Patrick bless you and increase you from this mortal day," now invokes the curse of God against him: "If we took pity on you the Lord God, would, maybe bring us ruin from the law today." Obviously Synge knew what he was doing and meant us to understand that the Mayoites saw a great difference between the three murders. An examination of their reasons carries us to the heart of Synge's meaning.

The Mayoites are primitive people who live almost entirely in an imaginative world of their own creation. They are all poets *manqués;* their life is all language, and

Norman Podhoretz, "Synge's *Playboy:* Morality and the Hero," *Essays in Criticism,* vol. 3 (July 1953), pp. 337–344. Reprinted by permission of the author.

it is only what they can make poetry out of that is important to them. Pegeen's complaint that there is no material in "this place" for her imagination to work on is revealing:

> It's a wonder, Shaneen, the Holy Father'd be taking notice of the likes of you; for if I was him, I wouldn't bother with *this* place where you'll meet none but Red Linahan, has a squint in his eye, and Patcheen is lame in his heel, or the mad Mulrannies were driven from California and they lost in their wits.

It is no accident, then, that Christy who is, as will be seen, the undeveloped poet coming to consciousness of himself as man and as artist, should be accepted with such fervour. This was no ordinary, everyday murder he had committed, but an act of great "daring" such as the Mayoites have never had before their very eyes until this day. Moreover, they recognize that there was something heroic, something *necessary* about the deed, which makes the question of crime irrelevant. "Up to the day I killed my father," says Christy, "there wasn't a person in Ireland knew the kind I was, and I there drinking, waking, eating, sleeping, a quiet, simple poor fellow with no man giving me heed." And Pegeen answers: "It's near time a fine lad like you should have your good share of the earth." Consciousness, maturity, self-realization were bound up with revolt against the father, and Pegeen, with her sure earthy instinct, senses this.

Gradually Synge tells us more and more about the earlier Christy and his sexual timidity, which is characterized throughout in animal images:

> PEG. It was the girls were giving you heed, maybe . . .
> CHR. Not the girls itself, and I won't tell you a lie. There wasn't anyone heeding me in that place saving only the dumb beasts of the field.

Mahon, Christy's father, later confirms this, using almost identical imagery:

> If he had seen a red petticoat coming swinging over the hill, he'd be off to hide in the sticks, and you'd see him shooting out his sheep's eyes between the little twigs and the leaves, and his two ears rising like a hare looking out through a gap. Girls, indeed!

The results of Christy's revolt are what we should expect them to be: sexual assertion and a new awareness of self:

> PEG. Wasn't I telling you, and you a fine, handsome young fellow with a noble brow?
> CHR. *(with a flush of delighted surprise)* Is it me?
> PEG: Aye. Did you never hear that from the young girls where you come from in the west or south?
> CHR. *(with venom)* I did not, then. Oh, they're bloody liars in the naked parish where I grew a man.

And Christy's soliloquy at the end of Act I, when the forces have all been set in motion, is exact evidence of Synge's comic genius:

Well, it's a clean bed and soft with it, and it's great luck and company I've won me in the end of time—two fine women fighting for the likes of me—till I'm thinking this night wasn't I a foolish fellow not to kill my father in the years gone by.

If we stop to analyse the humour of this passage, we see that it derives from an absurd moral position, and indeed, what Synge has grasped here is nothing less than the paradox on which civilization (according to the myth, at any rate) seems to rest—individual achievement and communal progress depend on murder. The moral consciousness has found a way out of the dilemma for civilized man: he commits a *symbolic* act of murder in place of physical violence by rejecting the father and his values, but in the primitive world of Act I there is as yet no sign of morality. Synge will begin to draw it into his play slowly in Act II, and it becomes so important to the dénouement that I will have to return to a discussion of the whole problem later. We cannot understand the climax of the play without appreciating Synge's profound sense of the relation between symbolism and morality.

The second reason for Christy's success in Mayo is, of course, his greatness as a poet. Indications of this are so numerous in the text that it would be difficult to quote them all, but several passages in which the theme is stressed are worth looking at. "I've heard all times," Pegeen says rhapsodically, "it's the poets are your like—fine, fiery fellows with great rages when their temper's roused." Again, when Christy has been boasting to the girls who come to pay homage to his heroism, and has been expanding his deed into epic proportions, Susan's only comment is, "That's a grand story," and Honor agrees, adding that "he tells it lovely." And finally, the Widow Quin (she senses more than she knows) snorts at one point, "There's poetry talk for a girl you'd see itching and scratching, and she with a stale stink of poteen on her from selling in the shop." Synge's dialogue, we may note in passing, is never irrelevantly lyrical: the quality of the language itself is organic to the play's meaning. Language is the very being of these people, and so they naturally pay tribute to the great master of language who has come among them. Moreover, it is the poetic, the symbolic deed which has set their imaginations afire: the murder has for them the reality of fitness and beauty but never the reality of fact. Christy, who is taken in by the poetic glory of what he has done no less than Pegeen, neglects to remember the harsh details:

> I just riz the loy and let fall the edge of it on the ridge of his skull, and he went down at my feet like an empty sack, and never let a groan or grunt from him at all.

The last phrase is enormously revealing: Christy has no notion of what he has done to his father: he cannot see the suffering his act has caused and he is not aware of its brutality, which is only a way of saying that he has no moral consciousness. And so with Pegeen; she will not allow Shawn to call Christy a "bloody handed murderer." That there should have been blood cannot occur to her, because the murder is "a gallous story," a symbolic event, an expression of what is fine in the human spirit. Christy had a right to kill his father; and more, it was necessary and good that he should do so.

They all regard the murder essentially in terms of symbolic and imaginative overtones, and indeed, symbolic is precisely what the first murder turns out to be. The "old man of the tribe" has not been killed, and the fact that his appearance terrifies Christy tells us that the first murder was not so emancipating as it seemed. Still another act of violence is necessary if Christy is to triumph over his father, over, that is, those forces which have prevented the full emergence of his identity. And here the moral paradox of which I spoke above asserts itself most strongly. The original act represented the instinctive stirrings of manhood in Christy, while for the people of Mayo it was "a gallous story" rather than "a dirty deed." Christy, however, murders again not instinctively but deliberately, out of a desire to protect his newly-found independence:

> Shut your yelling (he says), for if you're after making a mighty man of me this day by the power of a lie, you're setting me now to think if it's a poor thing to be lonesome, it's worse, maybe, go mixing with the fools of earth.

This, of course, is a moral act, the result of a choice, and partly for that reason, the Mayoites now turn on Christy. The sight of blood makes them aware of the realities of suffering and murder, and Pegeen, at least, realizes how great a gap there is "between a gallous story and a dirty deed." From the point of view of society, the second murder is certainly a dirty deed; Pegeen's downfall is assured when she shows herself unable to consider it from any other point of view:

> Take him on from this, *for I think bad the world should see me* raging for a Munster liar, and the fool of men. (My italics)

But another valid point of view is presented—Christy's; he can see no real alternative to the second murder:

> And I must go back into my torment is it, or run off like a vagabond straying through the unions with the dust of August making mudstains in the gullet of my throat; or the winds of March blowing on me till I'd take an oath I felt them making whistles of my ribs within?

Christy, then, makes a choice, but it remains to be noticed that he does so without knowledge of the consequences: Synge is careful to show that Christy had not believed his admirers would turn on him; his immediate motive for killing his father again is that they have taunted him with a lie. His absurd and magnificent willingness, however, to kill his father yet a third time ("Are you coming to be killed a third time, or what ails you now?") is the product of a full moral consciousness. He knows that they will hang him if he raises the loy once more, but the necessity of ultimate triumph is more important, is absolute. This finally establishes Christy as the Hero who has the courage to face up to that paradox on which civilization rests, who will commit the act of violence which all feel to be necessary and which society cannot afford to condone. And it is beautifully proper that Christy's triumph does not entail self-destruction. For Synge is telling us, I think, that the Hero, the poet who does in fact challenge morality with its own contradictions will not be destroyed, that he will be saved by a kind of Grace. There is, unfortunately, no other word (unless it be "luck") for the power which saves Christy and which resolves the dilemma lying at the heart of the play. And we should not be surprised at the invocation of the idea of Grace in a work so saturated with religious awareness. Synge's religion is not Father Reilly's, but it is a religion nonetheless. He believes (to borrow a phrase from Henry James) in the salubrity of genius: Christy is the poet, the playboy, triumphant in games, who will spend his life "romancing" and "telling stories" now that he has been made "a likely gaffer in the end of all." Society has not been able to countenance him and all he represents, and in the name of order and peace they have driven him out into "the lonesome west":

> MIC. By the will of God, we'll have peace now for our drinks. . . .
> SHA. It's a miracle Father Reilly can wed us in the end of all, and we'll have none to trouble us when his vicious bite is healed.

But nothing can heal Christy's "vicious bite" as far as Pegeen is concerned. She realizes when Christy leaves declaring that he is "master of all fights now" what she has lost, what the meaning of his strange salvation is, and she knows that she is consigned to a life in society with the likes of Shawn Keogh: "Oh, my grief, I've lost him surely. I've lost the only Playboy of the Western World."

A few remarks are necessary, finally, to clarify Synge's attitude towards society and the Hero. The charm with which he invests the people of Mayo, and the fact that he is constantly critical of Christy, are enough to dissociate Synge from the currently fashionable school of "alienationists"—he is not defending the frail artistic sensibility from the onslaughts of a morality that stunts the artist's growth. The Hero and society are incompatible in the sense that they pursue different objectives, but the relation between them must be understood as one of reciprocal benefit no less than of antagonism. Christy develops into a Hero only when the superior instinct of society approves what he had done in ignorance and bewilderment, and the Mayoites, on the other hand, move from a primitive state of consciousness to a sense of civilization and its values through their contact with him. The West is a lonesome place, Synge tells us early in the play, but Christy has made his choice: "If it's a poor thing to be lonesome, it's worse, maybe, go mixing with the fools of earth." What he has to do, Christy must do alone. Synge, then, is alive both to the possibilities of the Shawns and the Michael Jameses, and to the worth of the Christies, and his sympathy is patently divided between those two extremes. His pity, however, Synge reserves for Pegeen, who—to paraphrase Eliot—has been visited by the vision of greatness for a few days and will for ever after be a haunted woman. The tragic implications of *The Playboy of the Western World* are that the type represented by Pegeen—those who can perceive greatness but cannot rise to it, who are weighed down by the "society" within them—can neither live in the lonesome west playing out their days, nor be happy in the little world of daily preoccupations. The Christies are somehow taken care of, and so are the Shawns; it is the Pegeens who suffer most from the radical incompatibility of Hero and society.

Focusing on the complex ironies in Synge's play, J. L. Styan analyzes the subtle means by which the playwright (in conjunction with his actors) conveys meaning to the audience and controls our response.

MAKING MEANINGS IN THE THEATRE [*THE PLAYBOY OF THE WESTERN WORLD*]
J. L. Styan

. . . Dialogue between characters proceeds by assents and dissents, by one speaker echoing another or differing from him, with all the degrees of harmony or discord between these extremes. Since we receive our dramatic impression when we apprehend a discord in a certain context, it follows that judgment upon the quality of a performance rests upon our ability to see how it clarifies the variety of the text. Not that the playgoer needs to read the text to prepare the ironies before he sees the play. The intensity required of his attention will indicate the delicacy of texture in the play and its performance. Conversely, the spectator's degree of attention, as well as whatever the scene has to say to him, will be dependent upon the gradation and shading of the speech and action. Each actor will indicate in the appositeness of his reactions both his dependence upon another actor and his independence from him, that is, the integrity of his character. For such is the way the good dramatist sees the play as he constructs it.

The Playboy of the Western World is good drama for this reason, that the plot is simplicity itself, but nevertheless the response of the audience is subtle and delicate and of considerable complexity. In urging this it has the economy of great playwriting. It is an amalgam of ironies, and the complexity of the audience's response is due to the way in which the author manages with the visual and aural detail of his dialogue to flex and vary and refine our impressions. The meaning of the scene is intenser, its outline sharper, its importance greater, although by comparison the narrative action on the stage is bald. Thus the triple twist to the tail of the play is not a perversity, but a natural outcome of a play which is a mosaic of twists.

The first act carefully sets the tone and drift of the ironies. From Christy Mahon's first entrance, the stage presents a pattern of fluctuations in the tempo and movement of the characters as they veer between doubt of and respect for Christy. At first those in the shebeen patronize him:

> PEGEEN. There's a queer lad. Were you never slapped in school, young fellow, that you don't know the name of your deed?

Their interest in the crime increases rapidly upon Christy's "I'm not calling to mind any person, gentle, simple, judge or jury, did the like of me," to the crisis, "Don't strike me. I killed my poor father, Tuesday was a week, for doing the like of that." On this admission they retreat from him in some respect. But it remains a doubtful respect until they hear the manner of the crime: "I just riz the loy and let fall the edge of it on the ridge of his skull." From here Christy's confidence begins to grow with their esteem.

From J. L. Styan, *The Elements of Drama* (Cambridge: Cambridge University Press, 1960), pp. 57–63.
© Cambridge University Press 1960. Reprinted by permission of Cambridge University Press.

This is a severe summary of the line of the action, but it shows how the audience's regard for Christy will contrast with Pegeen's and Michael's, Philly's and Jimmy's. The life of the whole play is in that contrast. Our attitude to him was in part determined by his bathetic entrance:

> For a perceptible moment they watch the door with curiosity. Some one coughs outside. Then Christy Mahon, a slight young man, comes in very tired and frightened and dirty.
> CHRISTY in a small voice. God save all here!

The first impression of his slightness is the foundation of the spectator's estimation of him. Interest in Christy will grow as the characters' interest grows, but the nature of our response will differ in inverse proportion. When they glorify Christy

> PHILLY. There's a daring fellow.
> JIMMY. Oh, glory be to God!

our instinct is to vilify him. We do not do this because, of course, we do not readily jump to conclusions when a scene is still in progress. We are more bothered by the difference between our reaction to Christy and that of the characters. Christy is the focus of attention for the characters on the stage, but the spectator's attention embraces the whole stage picture.

Having thus prepared his audience, Synge goes on to sharpen the impression with this:

> PEGEEN. That'd be a lad with the sense of Solomon to have for a pot-boy, Michael James, if it's the truth you're seeking one at all.
>
> PHILLY. The peelers is fearing him, and if you'd that lad in the house there isn't one of them would come smelling around if the dogs itself were lapping poteen from the dung-pit of the yard.
>
> JIMMY. Bravery's a treasure in a lonesome place, and a lad would kill his father, I'm thinking, would face a foxy divil with a pitchpike on the flags of hell.
>
> PEGEEN. It's the truth they're saying, and if I'd that lad in the house, I wouldn't be fearing the loosed khaki cut-throats, or the walking dead.
> CHRISTY, swelling with surprise and triumph. Well, glory be to God!
>
> MICHAEL, with deference. Would you think well to stop here and be pot-boy, mister honey, if we gave you good wages, and didn't destroy you with the weight of work?
> SHAWN, coming forward uneasily. That'd be a queer kind to bring into a decent, quiet household with the like of Pegeen Mike.
> PEGEEN, very sharply. Will you whisht? Who's speaking to you?
>
> SHAWN, retreating. A bloody-handed murderer the like of. . . .
>
> PEGEEN, snapping at him. Whisht, I am saying; we'll take no fooling from your like at all. To Christy with a honeyed voice. And you, young fellow, you'd have a right to stop, I'm thinking, for we'd do our all and utmost to content your needs.

The question arising in the discussion is, Will a murderer make a good pot-boy?—one grotesquerie among the many that compose the fabric of the play. All the characters except Shawn are trying to persuade Michael to employ the stranger; superficially, therefore, we get an accumulation of arguments for it. Christy is reluctant to say where he killed his father, so Pegeen attributes to him "the sense of Solomon." The peelers have not followed him, so Philly twice suggests they "is fearing him, and if you'd that lad in the house there isn't one of them would come smelling around." And finally, to complete this trio of advisers, Jimmy points out that killing one's father takes bravery, so it is argued that Christy is brave, and "Bravery's a treasure in a lonesome place." We are not intended to feel incongruity between the three speeches, since they are in accord. Irony does not arise therefore by any comparison between what they say. But each echoes the illogicality of the other, the folly of the reasoning in each case making the total argument more and more ridiculous, especially as each contributor raises his voice a tone higher and speaks with increasingly assertive Irishisms. We are being asked to believe by implication that a killer would be just the one to have in a lonesome place with you, that black is white, that two and two make five. There is irony in the wit here of course, and we laugh at the incongruity of it, but such irony and such laughter are of the surface only.

The real incongruity, the real irony and the real control over the spectator springs from their *agreement.* We would have expected Philly to contradict Pegeen, Jimmy to contradict Philly, and finally we would have expected Pegeen to stop the progress of an argument moving so quickly towards the ludicrous. Instead she pursues it with a note of flirtatiousness in her voice and manner. Pegeen the single girl, Pegeen who will have to work with him, live in the house with him, caps them both with, "if I'd that lad in the house, I wouldn't be fearing the loosed khaki cut-throats, or the walking dead." She would prefer Christy to a Tommy and to a spectre; if she had with her a killer with a loy, she would not fear a killer with a knife; if she had with her a man whose conscience was burdened by the ghost of a dead father, she would not fear a ghost itself. Impression A does not confound impression B: it underlines it, and underlines impressions C and D as well. Our imagination is daringly distorted. The spectator asks himself what statement Synge is making, what to believe. Because there is a strict antithesis between our logic and theirs, and because they are thinking in unison, we can only deduce by our standard of behaviour that they are mad, the more so for appearing so serious in what passes for their reasoning. We bridge the theatrical gap between our minds and theirs with a mental gesture of half-dismissal: we laugh. But now Synge can weave his bizarre magic on us.

Christy is surprised too: "Well, glory be to God!" So they are not all in a conspiracy of madness, and their response was not wholly to be expected after all. Perhaps our first impression of Christy as rather a contemptible young man was a right one: Christy's remark evidently confirms us in this. But the attention of Pegeen, Philly and Jimmy has been directed on Michael, and now our attention is led there too. Michael will surely resolve the contradiction. We wait in the slight pause, savouring the situation and trying the weight of Michael's decision. We anticipate something like "The saints forbid that ever I should do the like of that!" but instead we hear a gentle, deferential voice: "Would you think well to stop here and be pot-boy, mister honey. . . . ?"

And Michael goes on to offer good wages and light work. The gap is strained again. We are not certain what to think. Is impression A in relation to impression B unmeaning? Is our recognition of a criminal, supported as it is by a code of right and wrong, to have no support from the characters on the stage and to bear no relation to any code of values within the play? We are left wondering again at the characters' irrational behaviour. Perhaps we are to dismiss it as we dismiss it in farce? But the stage action as it has been described is not complete.

Our critical response is not allowed to be so simple, because Shawn is on stage too, cowering in the corner, and, observe, reacting to Christy in a manner quite different from the others. Synge has been at pains through the first ten minutes of the act to fill out the character of Shawn. He is not there simply to contrast with Christy. He is there in chief to establish and show the conventional response to a murderer and a patricide. It is then intended that he should be our chorus, and as *raisonneur* represent our feelings towards Christy? No, for how could this be? His is an excessive physical cowardice and a fanatical and hyper-religious attitude. We must be reluctant to let this sort of example be our guide: "God help me, he's following me now, and if he's heard what I said, he'll be having my life, and I going home lonesome in the darkness of the night."

Yet it is Shawn who now speaks our *own* comment: "That'd be a queer kind to bring into a decent, quiet household." Was it accident that we phrased the comment we anticipated from Michael as Shawn would have spoken it? So Synge judges us, and uses Pegeen, who was earlier taking her death with the fear, to reprove Shawn and us: "we'll take no fooling from your like at all." We observe she says "we," and draws together the majority against Shawn. By the movement of her body and the change in her tone, she isolates him, the outsider, one not in the compact. And she reduces his eminent reasonableness to "fooling." But who is fooling?

We are left undecided, our attitude unsettled, with no certain finger left us to wag, our received impression askew. But we are forced to reconcile and make shapely this grotesquerie if we are to sit comfortably through the play. If we choose to accept Synge's coloured view of his Irish peasant characters, and can stomach this extraordinary method of revealing it to us, the play will supply a nice insight into human nature. We may even care to echo what Mr Edmund Wilson said in 1931, that this was the most authentic poetic drama the century had seen. If not, we may boo with the first audiences who saw it at the Abbey Theatre in 1907. There are not many plays in which the author is so playful with his audience, or juggles with its feelings and adjusts the focus of its imagination so sportively to achieve his ends. *The Playboy* is a bold use of the theatre, and a good example of how extravagant a dramatist can be. . . .

In the following excerpt from an article about Synge and the Welsh poet Dylan Thomas, Terence Hawkes emphasizes the "Irishness" of The Playboy of the Western World. *According to this view, both situation and language in Synge's play reflect the unique nature of Irish culture.*

PLAYBOYS OF THE WESTERN WORLD
Terence Hawkes

The language spoken by a human community contains that community's "culture" embedded in it: or, to put it another way, any language is "designed" by its speakers to enable them to talk about, and so to reflect, their particular way of life. This places many modern writers, whom we often casually group together as part of "English literature," in rather an odd position. Many of them are not English, and have no wish to write about England. However, as an accident of fate, politics, economics or whatever, they find that they have only the English language at their disposal. As a result, they are forced into the position of having to write about one way of life in the language of another. Not surprisingly, in such circumstances, the English language often undergoes distinctive modifications at their hands, as an attempt must inevitably be made to make it "fit" a non-English culture.

Neither J. M. Synge nor Dylan Thomas would care to be described as English, yet each wrote in that language because no other really suited the purpose. Synge knew Irish, had studied it in fact, but could not use it for his plays. Thomas knew only a few words and phrases in Welsh; he made no attempt to acquire a mastery of that language, and wrote entirely in English. Each experienced a kind of love-hate relationship with his respective native culture, and left it as a young man, only, as is often the case, to return there for protracted visits later in life. Each, as his work developed, similarly returned to the culture in the literary sense. Thomas frequently set his later poems about childhood in Wales; Synge's account of his journey to the Aran Islands speaks for itself. The work of each reaches a sort of climax with a play in which the values and way of life of the culture are celebrated in a microcosmic form as "different" from or "better" than those of the larger and alien world outside. Synge in *The Playboy of the Western World* and Thomas in *Under Milk Wood* both exhibit the natural desire of the non-English writer to write about, to express through language, his own culture. Each chooses a small community representative of that culture, and examines it in dramatic and symbolic terms far removed from those of realism. Accuracy in the factual or documentary sense is not in question. Synge's Aran lies as far from reality as Thomas's self-explanatory (if reversed) "Llareggub."

These works are vastly different in many ways: one a stage play written for the Abbey Theatre, Dublin, one a "play for voices" commissioned for radio by the BBC. What gives them a community of interest is that the voices which animate them are not English voices. They are the voices of two distinct cultures to the west of England over which the English language has long held dominion. They are, so to speak, the voices of those "western worlds" where English is spoken *faute de mieux;* and the use made of English by Synge and Thomas in these plays, the language of these "play-

From Terence Hawkes, "Playboys of the Western World," *The Listener,* vol. 74, no., 1915 (December 9, 1965), pp. 991–992. Reprinted by permission of the author.

boys," constitutes a large part of their dramatic effect. Each tackles the problem of expressing one culture in the language of another in a different way, and in so doing shows an aspect of himself as a writer which is revealing; for Thomas's failure in the matter is as interesting as Synge's success.

The Playboy of the Western World focuses its interest almost at once on Christy Mahon and the reception the villagers give him when he announces that he has murdered his father. They welcome him as a hero because of what he has done. When it transpires that his father is in fact still alive, they turn against him (although Christy has by then achieved another kind of triumph over his father). The full weight of the play rests on this idea of "reversal of values"; by means of it Synge surprises his audience by denying their expectations, and by inviting them to approve of values which are the opposite of their own. The comic effect of the play lies in this, as does its effect on a deeper level. Christy's "killing" of his father enacts an archetypal desire, perhaps, of which a hidden part of us approves; we all have fathers to "kill" and we find ourselves possibly unwillingly and irrationally agreeing with the villagers' verdict on Christy. In terms of Irish culture, such a suspension of rational, "normal" values must have seemed rather more disturbing. Irish father-figures such as the Roman Catholic Church (whose priests are "fathers"), or the English government, may or may not be implied by the figure of Christy's father. But the repressive nature of such institutions to some of the Irish, and the (perhaps subconscious though often articulate) compulsion to "kill" them finds an adequate and accurate representation in Christy's situation.

In the sense that the situation is a funny one, that the theme of the reversal of values here is not too seriously treated, the play is a comedy. But on a deeper level it identifies itself very closely with the "core" of Irish culture. Set in the west of Ireland, it shows us a world, a "western world," which is self-contained, enclosed, closely confined. The "murder" itself takes place outside its boundaries, and Christy describes that alien area as "Oh, a distant place . . . a windy corner of high distant hills." By contrast, the play explores a small world; literally a microcosm. Not only does the setting imply that this world symbolizes Ireland and Irish culture, but Synge's preface to the play hints at a similar design. In it he expressly makes the point that the language used mirrors the ancient culture of Ireland. He has written, he claims, an accurate version of the English these people speak, and he has used only "one or two words" which he has not heard among "the country people." The "form" of the language, he claims, reflects the "reality" of the Aran Islands; such a "rich and living" language, he seems to say, has fully informed the play and its ideas. Earlier he had painted the famous picture of himself listening to the people of Aran through "a chink in the floor of the old Wicklow home where I was staying." The language, this seems to argue, contains the culture, and transmits it through the ear, by means of speech: the "chink in the floor" is the gateway to the culture.

The precise nature of this language, then, should be of central importance in the play. I want to suggest that its main characteristic resembles that of the play itself, and, as a result, that *The Playboy of the Western World* constitutes an almost perfect example of the way in which the language reflects the culture which the play depicts.

This passage, from the scene in which Christy is accepted and made much of because he is a murderer, is typical:

Pegeen: Let you stop a short while anyhow. Aren't you destroyed walking with your feet in bleeding blisters, and your whole skin needing washing like a Wicklow sheep.

Christy: It's a nice room, and if it's not humbugging me you are, I'm thinking that I'll surely stay.

Jimmy: (Jumps up) Now, by the grace of God, herself will be safe this night, with a man killed his father holding danger from the door, and let you come on, Michael James, or they'll have the best stuff drunk at the wake.

The situation is comic and grotesque; the murderer is given the status of a perfect night-watchman: "a man killed his father holding danger from the door." The "grace of God" is ironically called for in circumstances which can hardly warrant it, and the play's theme of reversed values receives a clear and ironic statement. Nevertheless the language obviously carries a great deal of this irony embedded within itself, and not only because the words used blandly ignore the "normal" view of the facts which confront the characters. The most important way in which this language differs from "standard" English is clearly not a matter of vocabulary at all, but one of syntax. The word-order of phrases like "let you stop," "if it's not humbugging me you are," "let you come on," and "they'll have the best stuff drunk at the wake" have an odd ring to English ears, as do similar syntactical patterns which abound in the play. They upset "standard" word order, and seem to want to turn it on its head.

Such structures may well be closer to those of Gaelic than English, but to describe the play's language as simply "Anglo-Irish," formed of English words with Gaelic word-order, minimizes its total effect in terms of the dramatic structure of the play's ideas. Rather, the important fact about the play's language, what makes it potent in the play and gives it the status almost of "taking part in" the play as a "character" itself is surely that it involves an actual re-shaping of English to make it "fit" a non-English culture. The language thus becomes congruent with the culture, and reflects it with some precision. After all, the culture which the play examines and presents is one where the values of the "big world" have been tragi-comically reversed, so that a "murderer" can be accepted and treated as a hero. The syntactic structure of the language reflects this perfectly, because it reverses the "standard" word order of English, just as the culture of Aran turns the "standards," the moral "order" of the "big world," on its head.

The play thus exhibits in its totality, and practises in its language, what "standard" English speakers mockingly call the "Irishism"; a way of speaking the language which, by means of syntax, makes the speaker imply almost the opposite of what he means to say. By the extensive use of this kind of syntactic device in the play, the language becomes, on the stage, what the play depicts; "reversal" describes both the culture as we see it in action, and in a sense the language itself. As Synge hints in his preface, its "form" gives the "reality" of the culture; a truly Irish culture which neatly turns the mockery of the English "big world" into a means of self-expression, thus mocking its mockers. The "sound" of the play echoes its "sense" on the structural level of both language and ideas, and the "western world" of the title is realized perfectly by this means. . . .

A 1946 production of The Playboy of the Western World *in New York, generally panned by the critics, gave rise to the following review article by John Gassner. In his analysis of the play and its production, Mr. Gassner suggests that unless actors and director understand the central dramatic vision (what he calls the "spine") of a play, they will tend to make serious mistakes in all aspects of staging: tempo, emphasis, acting style, rendering of lines, even sets and lighting. His own definition of this play's "spine" involves society, the conscious self of the individual, and unconscious fantasies—all in a complicated and contradictory interrelationship.*

[THE "SPINE" OF *THE PLAYBOY OF THE WESTERN WORLD*]
John Gassner

Theatre Incorporated wanted to perform a service in reviving John Millington Synge's masterpiece, *The Playboy of the Western World*, and there were some revealing moments in Burgess Meredith's performance. But it is curious how well-intentioned and talented theatre folk managed almost to commit mayhem on a superb artist's work. The production was kept uniformly slow, apparently in order to enable audiences to understand and relish Synge's flavorsome peasant dialect. If the tempo was speeded up toward the end, it was done precisely when the director might have taken time to underscore the villagers' *volteface* once the "playboy" Chris knocks his father down in their presence. The theme of the play is "What Price Hero-Worship?" since Chris is a hero so long as he killed his father in a distant county and not in the villagers' own backyard. In a sense, the play is also a rueful account of the development of a boy who must realize at the end that strength lies in oneself and not in the ill-founded admiration of others.

The meaning of the play was largely lost in a literal evocation of folk comedy, which in turn failed to work because of a mixture of acting styles ranging from the genuine Dublin article (in Edith Dunne's and J. M. Kerrigan's performances) to Shubert musical comedy in the costuming and playing of the village maidens. Burgess Meredith was excellent in the first act when he conveyed the weariness and loneliness of the runaway Chris, but he lost much intensity in his role as the youth who basks in admiration and gathers strength at the end. Meredith relied too much on a studied lyricism and was slowed up by the necessity of speaking a dialect which mastered him instead of being mastered by him. The revival was languid instead of exuberant as folk comedy; some of it actually seemed slow-motion humor. Yet for all the muted quality of the performances, the production failed to convey the disenchantment at the core of Synge's comic writing.

Disenchantment! That is, indeed, a true key to *The Playboy of the Western World*, whose very title is ironic. But the quality of irony was hardly in evidence in the production. And once we raise the question of irony, as I suspect the producers, directors, and leading actor did not do, we can understand the production problem they failed to solve. They were misled by the superficial criticism and publicity from which the

---

Taken from John Gassner, "*The Playboy of the Western World*, 1946 [Review article]," in his *The Theatre in Our Times* (New York: Crown, 1954), pp. 537–543. © 1954 by John Gassner. Used by permission of Crown Publishers, Inc.

play has suffered virtually from the beginning. That criticism and publicity, supported by Synge's celebrated preface, have invariably thrust into the foreground the *folk-comedy premise,* according to which Synge patriotically and innocently compounded a rich brew of humor out of the naïve, colorful, "primitive" life of the Irish countryside.

Although the countryside was primitive, Synge decidedly was not. He was fundamentally a sophisticated artist—even a *décadent* one—whose view of life remained sceptical and saturnine; almost Baudelairian, even after he left France at Yeats's suggestion. Yes, he returned to Ireland and steeped himself in the folkways and idiom of Western Ireland and the Aran Islands. But what the artist observes and records as "local color" is never what he *creates.* The reason why most folk-plays rarely have merit and even more rarely possess greatness is because they are the work of writers who *see* the local color and *hear* the local dialect rather than of writers who use what they have seen and heard creatively. Great writers build a more or less autonomous world of art that conforms to a personal, rather than a mere *folk,* view of reality.

Irish patriots who rioted at the Dublin premiere of *The Playboy* on the grounds that the author misrepresented the Irish people came closer to the truth about Synge's work than those who, led by Yeats (who has always impressed me as a great baby as well as a great poet), defended the play. Of course, Synge misrepresented Ireland. Only his motives were different from those attributed to him by the rioters. He was not critical of the Irish, he was critical of the human race. And in being that, he *represented* himself in his work.

Synge's view of reality was saturnine, as anyone could have seen in his very first play *In the Shadow of the Glen,* and as he was to prove later in *The Tinker's Wedding* and *The Well of Saints.* Even his sense of tragedy included a large sense of desperation about the human lot, a negative attitude toward the possibility of happiness. Nothing at all could be done about the tragic situation in *Riders to the Sea.* Man did not cause it and man could not avert it. Nor was a single person in the play itself actively engaged in the tragic action of fate.

For a tragedy of fate, *Riders to the Sea* is at the opposite pole from that greatest of tragedies of fate *Oedipus the King,* throughout which Oedipus is vibrantly engaged in discovering the fatality of circumstance in which he is enmeshed. Oedipus, to put the case colloquially, is "in there," fighting all the time, whereas the characters in *Riders to the Sea* are not fighting at all. The play is truly, profoundly "static drama," the theory for which was laid down by another "symbolist" successor of Baudelaire, Verlaine, Rimbaud, and other *décadents,* Maurice Maeterlinck.

In Synge's last play, *Deirdre of the Sorrows,* it is true, there is much activity, and its main characters are decidedly active to the end. But even here, in a work that may be designated as heroic drama, the decisive factor is Deirdre's fatalistic belief that love like hers with her lover cannot last. She courts death for him and for herself by prevailing upon him to return to the king who is insanely jealous of him and will kill him in order to possess Deirdre. This is Synge's special interpretation of the great Irish legend which formed the substance of several plays by other writers. It is Synge alone who insists on the motivation of disbelief in the power of love to hold the lovers together for a long time—and this in the case of two of the most romantic characters in all literature!

What has this to do with the Theatre Incorporated production of *The Playboy of the Western World?* Everything! The work is one of thoroughgoing irony—not only about the general fallacy of hero worship to which I have already alluded, but to all the particulars in the play. When Chris thinks he is telling the truth in reporting that he has killed his father, he is not only deceived, but self-deceiving; he builds himself up on the strength of the wishfully entertained deed. He is viewing himself as a marvel when he reports his "murder" in the village to which he has fled. The weakling has become a hero—because he has murdered. The villagers are entranced with him, and two women, one young and another middle-aged, fight over him—because he has murdered; not merely because he proves himself so successful an athlete in the village sports. And what is it that gave him the confidence that resulted in victory? The fact that he murdered his father, as well as that much has been made of him as a marvel because he did so!

Following his athletic feats, the lad's father turns up suddenly with a bandaged head and robs his son of his claim to uniqueness and glory. Not only Chris, but others feel let down. Just think of it, the boy *didn't* murder his father! And Chris is so desperate at discovering that his father is perversely alive that he strikes him down again! And so active is the wishful thinking, the murder fantasy, of Chris and those who glorified a parricide—a fact that should not be glossed over by explanations of the simplemindedness or "naïveté" of the villagers—that everybody instantly assumes that the father is dead. By comparison with so mordant a development of the theme, the rest of the development of the action is actually mild, although it would be sharp enough for many plays. Because the second "murder" occurred in their own village, Chris ceases to be a hero and becomes a criminal whom they are ready to deliver up to justice. And even here the irony cuts deeper than the mere idea that heroism is relative to time and place, or that one is a hero for doing something elsewhere and a criminal for doing it in our presence. (How many mute inglorious Napoleons must be sentenced to death in the villages of France by judges for whom the Emperor at Paris, Austerlitz, or Jena is a glorious figure!) The deeper irony is that the villagers do not realize that they are guiltier than Chris, for it is they who gave him social sanction for his second assault on his father by glorifying him for his first. No wonder Chris is bewildered rather than repentant when they bind him with ropes. Here, if we wish to labor the moral, is the whole history of mankind in a nutshell—punishment for crimes hallowed as heroism under different circumstances, society putting a premium on murder since the beginning of the primal clan and then punishing those who have been taught and encouraged to kill. Finally, there is the gentler irony that the boy becomes a hero in the eyes of his own father, when the latter revives, because Chris has shown *spunk* in *assaulting* him. Change the word "spunk" to "character" and the irony becomes sharper. Change the word "assaulting" to "trying to kill" and the bitterness of the play becomes fully apparent.

The fact is that *The Playboy* cuts deep. It does not owe its greatness to its mere rusticity. Synge worked on several levels in writing it—on the levels of genre painting and universal observation, folk-comedy and universal satire, conscious behavior and "fantasia of the unconscious." As a result, the work is a system of intense and subtle tensions, whereas the Theatre Incorporated production was a work of little and rather superficial tension. I do not claim that those involved in the production should have followed my analysis to the letter or even agreed with it in every detail, especially since I have made no reference to other nuances. And I have not mentioned the obvious point that Synge dissolved the mordant qualities of his play in a glow of good-natured comedy, providing a healing laughter as well as a cutting one, for he was a poet as well as a satirist. But the production would have been more emphatic and provocative if the producers had sensed the implications that exist on the various levels of the play.

And, for "practical" purposes of succeeding in the theatre with *The Playboy,* one consideration is even more important. If irony had been more sharply defined in the production—if, for example, the action had been more stylized or given a more keen-edged extravagance—the result would have been very much more comic. The saturnine Synge was a comic genius. The casual, languid Theatre Incorporated production was only mildly comic. My reactions to it, shared by others, were confused—that is, divided into feelings of lukewarm emotion, on one hand, and a sense of comedy, on the other, that came only in brief spurts instead of welling forth with any steadiness or force. As for any glow in the production, it could be found here and there in Burgess Meredith's performance, especially in the first half of the play, but the staging, as well as setting and lighting, had virtually none.

The ultimate lesson to be derived from the production of . . . *The Playboy of the Western World* is simply this: In order to produce a play, especially a distinguished work, we must not be content until we have found its *spine.* By this I mean not a mere notion on which to hang a production but a spine to which every turn of action, every suggestion, and every implication is attached. And having found that spine, we must not rest until all the emphases and the nuances of the performance relate to it so distinctly that we really do have a spine instead of a thin thread from which all things dangle and flap like so many clothes from a clothesline in windy weather. . . .

The spine of *The Playboy* cannot be so epigrammatically summarized. It has taken me a number of paragraphs to explicate it, and I am aware that I have been only partly successful in that enterprise. To have succeeded entirely, I should have had to argue out a variety of points and analyzed actions and entire scenes in considerable detail. But this much seems to me clear: *The spine is an ironic statement on the contradictions of human behavior and "society," including the contradictions between consciousness and the fantasia of the unconscious*—in which fantasy of murder as a form of gratification or "glory" is present. In serving that spine only fitfully and vaguely, the Theater Incorporated production gave us only a low-voltage and confused comic experience.

Let us note finally how the texture of distinguished writing communicates the spine of the play. The lines call for various inflections, intonations, stances, movements—and what not—from the performer. Let us listen, for example, to the publican Michael, whose daughter Pegeen has taken a fancy to the "playboy" Chris Mahon. Michael approves of marriage between them. Irony impacted in contradiction can hardly go further as Synge makes Michael say to them:

> . . . I seeing a score of grandsons growing up like gallant swearers by the
> name of God . . . *(He joins their hands.)* A daring fellow is the jewel of the
> world, and a man did split his father's middle with a single clout should

have the bravery of ten, so may God and Mary and St. Patrick bless you,
and increase you from this mortal day.

Christy, called a liar when his father Old Mahon suddenly turns up in the Mayo village to which Christy fled, remarks:

It's himself was a liar, lying stretched out with an open head on him, letting on he was dead.

Pegeen, who turns on Christy after he has struck down his father, declares, "there's a great gap between a gallous story and a dirty deed." Earlier, Pegeen had scorned a respectable suitor Shawn as "a middling kind of a scarecrow, with no *savagery* or fine words to him at all." Widow Quin, in trying to get Christy to marry herself rather than Pegeen, says to him:

Don't be letting on to be shy, a fine, gamey, *treacherous* lad the like of you.

When in Act I, Pegeen wants to know whether Chris, who struck his father with a "loy" or spade, shot his father dead, Chris replies indignantly:

I never used weapons. I've no license, and I'm a law-fearing man.

And when she asks whether he buried his father, Chris explains patiently:

Aye. I buried him then. Wasn't I digging spuds in the field?

There is a cycle in studying a play of this calibre. We may move from a full realization of the spine of the play as a whole to that of the spine of the characterizations, and from this to the point of the lines of dialogue; or we may reverse the procedure, in so far as this is possible, by studying the "texture" of the writing. The resulting understanding of the play may be the same. But in staging it, we must start with an over-all understanding of the work, regardless of how we first arrived at it. If the spine has not been first thoroughly discovered by the director and his cast, the lines will be inadequately rendered. Points will be blurred and either underplayed or overstressed. In other words, if the spine of the play is missed, the texture will be lost. And if the weave of the dialogue is poorly conveyed, then, of course, the spine will be lost, too. In either case, the play will be killed or lamed.

Like Shaw's Mrs. Warren's Profession, *first produced five years before, Synge's play gave rise to scandals that for a time obscured its real contribution to the modern theatre. The disturbances that attended the initial Dublin production (1907) and the subsequent American tour (1911–12) are vividly described in the following excerpt from F. L. Lucas's study of the play.*

[THE *PLAYBOY* RIOTS]
F. L. Lucas

. . . This hostility of the countryfolk to the law was common enough in Western Ireland, where the arm of justice was associated with the hated English oppressor. But still more, Synge thought, these primitive souls regarded crime as simply a sudden madness, which a man's own conscience would punish enough in the end, without need for police or magistrates.

Ironically enough, however, when *The Playboy* came to be performed, this lawless hero of a Nationalist poet had to be protected from the Irish audience by England's cruel police. For not even the plot of *The Playboy* was to prove so fantastic a farce as its stage-history. Originally I had meant to discuss the play before discussing its reception; but the play itself may mean more to the reader if he first realizes its extraordinary effect on its earliest Irish audiences.

From the outset, William Fay foresaw trouble; but the trouble he foresaw was nothing to what actually came. Fay had a shrewd theory about drama in general, that anger and savagery on the stage are infectious, and risk provoking a mood of anger and savagery in the audience also. So he and his brother begged Synge at least to make Pegeen a decent, likeable country-girl; and to cut out that final scene where she so brutally lassoes her own lover, and burns his leg with a glowing turf. But here the gentle Synge remained inflexible. Only a few specially dangerous phrases would he cut.

On the opening night (a Saturday) the audience, though quiet through the first two Acts, burst into hisses and cat-calls half-way through Act III at the words "all bloody fools"; and when it came to the mention of the unmentionable word "shift"—"a drift of chosen females standing in their shifts itself"—the howls rose to pandemonium. Fighting, it is said, broke out in the stalls, and it looked as if the stage would be stormed. Indeed the call-boy seized an axe from the boiler-room, and swore by all the saints to decapitate the first man across the footlights.

On the Monday night a riot was deliberately organized; some forty youths in front of the pit shouted, stamped, and blew trumpets; most of the piece had to be played in dumb-show. And night after night these tumults continued, despite the police, and the padding of the floor with felt to deaden the stamping.

On the last (Saturday) evening, it is reported, there were five hundred police keeping order in the theatre and its neighbourhood—police lining the walls, police sitting in a row along the center of the pit. To crown the farce, these pillars of the law found

From F. L. Lucas, *"The Playboy of the Western World,"* in his *The Drama of Chekhov, Synge, Yeats, and Pirandello* (London: Cassell, 1963), pp. 201–224. © F. L. Lucas, 1963. Reprinted by permission of Cassell & Company Ltd.

it impossible to keep their impassive dignity through the humours of Synge's dialogue, and finally collapsed with laughter at Michael Flaherty's speech—"the peelers in this place is decent, drouthy poor fellows wouldn't touch a cur dog." But for weeks afterwards the Abbey had audiences so scanty that Willie Fay would invite them to gather forward in the stalls. Not till a couple of months later, in March, did Lady Gregory's *Rising of the Moon* do something to appease the patriots.

There is a further account by George Moore in *Vale,* derived from the Irish dramatist, Edward Martyn, who was present. After the passage about "shifts" the crowded pit kept shouting "Lower the bloody curtain, and give us something we bloody well want"—a pleasing slogan, if true, for men shocked by crude language. Martyn, a devout Catholic, was himself pained by the play's irreverence. He disapproved, indeed, of rowdily interrupting performances; "but," he said, "Yeats shouldn't have called in the police. A Nationalist should never call for the police." Asked by George Moore whether, by parity of logic, he would refuse to call the police even if his own house were burgled, Martyn took refuge in casuistical distinctions between the rights of property and the rights of free speech. Such distinctions seem to me spider-webs.

Synge himself sat with a white face through the tumult. But the tension did serious harm to his health; as the failure of *The Seagull* to the health of Chekhov. Ibsen perhaps was tougher; but he watched from a greater distance the rage aroused by *Ghosts.*

Lady Gregory took a more active part than Synge, herself calling in the police (though she seems afterwards to have asked them to withdraw), and getting a nephew at Trinity, Dublin, to bring some fellow-undergraduates as supporters of the play. Unfortunately these young men still further inflamed political passions by singing "God save the King."

Reactions outside the theatre were equally grotesque. William Boyle withdrew his three plays from the Abbey. Arthur Griffith denounced it as an anti-Irish institution, financed by English gold. *The Playboy,* he thundered, was "a vile and inhuman story told in the foulest language we have ever listened to from a public platform." (Which suggests that Arthur Griffith must have passed his life in surroundings singularly pure.) And the *Freeman's Journal* echoed: "The hideous caricature would be slanderous of a Kaffir kraal."

Among the maunderings of the press appeared also a letter signed "A Girl from the West," lamenting that "Miss Allgood . . . is forced to use a word indicating an essential item of female attire which the lady would probably never utter in ordinary circumstances even to herself." Did Irish ladies, one begins to wonder, when they bought the things in shops, do it in dumb-show? Such prim cant only demonstrates anew how admirably true to life was Ibsen's *Enemy of the People.*

Yeats was away lecturing in Scotland, as the guest of Sir Herbert Grierson, when Lady Gregory wired news of the disturbances. At once he rushed back to Dublin, and showed himself at his best by refusing to yield an inch to the rabble, and holding a public debate in the theatre on the Monday after the last performance. Synge was ill and absent; but Yeats, in full evening-dress, together with his father, defended the play to an audience of workmen, students, and citizens, who now cheered, now howled him down. Mary Colum, who was present as a girl-student, has written—"I never witnessed a human being fight as Yeats fought that night, nor knew another with so many weapons in his armoury." That was brave. It reveals Yeats at his finest.

The American tour of the Abbey Players four years later, in 1911–12, let loose fresh frenzies. By now Synge was cold in Mount Jerome cemetery; but the Irish-American press still gabbled with hysteria. *"The Playboy* must be squelched," wrote *The Gaelic American,* "and a lesson taught to Mr Yeats and his fellow-agents in England." And again—"we pledge ourselves as one man to drive the vile thing from the stage . . . and we ask the aid in this work of every decent Irish man and woman and of the Catholic Church, whose doctrines and devotional practices are held up to scorn and ridicule in Synge's monstrosity."

At the New York performance there were showers of potatoes and vegetables, followed by cubic capsules of asafoetida, a resinous gum with a strong stench of garlic. (Art and science combined!) However, police dealt with the roughs; and Theodore Roosevelt both went to the theatre and published in his paper a warm tribute to the play. In Philadelphia arrest-warrants were issued for the company, under a bye-law forbidding "immoral and indecent plays"; which had been enacted for the benefit of Sarah Bernhardt on her visit of 1910.

In Chicago the City Council vainly directed the Mayor to ban the play; the Mayor, however, "instead of finding anything immoral . . . found the whole thing was wonderfully stupid." In Chicago also, Lady Gregory received a letter illustrated with pistol, coffin, hammer, and nails, beginning:

> "Lady Gregory . . . ha, ha. Foster-mother of the funny play boy.
> this is to console you from the dread that may fill your grizzly breast after you have read the contents of this note. *Your fate is sealed.* never again shall you gase *(sic)* on the barren hilltops of Connemara
> *Your doom is sealed"*

But Lady Gregory, judging from the drawing of the pistol that the author knew little of firearms, calmly ignored him. And despite these patriotic audacities the American tour became an artistic and financial triumph. Today, so one hears, Dubliners applaud *The Playboy* as an Irish classic, that does honour to the Eire which produced it. . . .

Mrs Warren's Profession

Much of the critical controversy surrounding Mrs. Warren's Profession *emerged at the time of its first productions in London and New York. The play was criticized, first of all, for the "immorality" of its subject. Here are some typical comments from the New York papers, 1905.*

THE LIMIT OF STAGE INDECENCY: SHAW'S *MRS. WARREN'S PROFESSION*

The New York Herald

"The lid" was lifted by Mr. Arnold Daly and "the limit" of stage indecency reached last night in the Garrick Theatre in the performance of one of Mr. George Bernard Shaw's "unpleasant comedies" called *Mrs. Warren's Profession.*

"The limit of indecency" may seem pretty strong words, but they are justified by the fact that the play is morally rotten. It makes no difference that some of the lines may have been omitted and others toned down; there was superabundance of foulness left. The whole story of the play, the atmosphere surrounding it, the incidents, the personalities of the characters are wholly immoral and degenerate. The only way successfully to expurgate *Mrs. Warren's Profession* is to cut the whole play out. You cannot have a clean pig stye. The play is an insult to decency because—

It defends immorality.

It glorifies debauchery.

It besmirches the sacredness of a clergyman's calling.

It pictures children and parents living in calm observance of most unholy relations.

And, worst of all, it countenances the most revolting form of degeneracy, by flippantly discussing the marriage of brother and sister, father and daughter, and makes the one supposedly moral character of the play, a young girl, declare that choice of shame, instead of poverty is eminently right.

These things cannot be denied. They are the main factors of the story. Without them there would be no play. It is vileness and degeneracy brazenly considered. If New York's sense of shame is not aroused to hot indignation at this theatrical insult, it is indeed in a sad plight.

This is an outline, or, rather, a suggestion of the story that Mr. Arnold Daly saw fit to enact in the Garrick Theatre last night before a morbidly curious audience that packed the theatre to suffocation, and doubtless will continue to do so as long as the play is permitted to be given.

Mrs. Warren, a child of the slums, has become a courtesan and is the mistress of several disreputable houses in Brussels, Berlin, Vienna and Budapest. Her profession has brought her wealth. She has a daughter, Vivian, educated in England in ignorance of her mother's real character, and who has achieved fame in college as a mathe-

"The Limit of Stage Indecency: Shaw's *Mrs Warren's Profession* [Review from *The New York Herald*, October 31, 1905]," reprinted in Montrose J. Moses and John Mason Brown, eds., *The American Theatre As Seen by Its Critics, 1752–1934* (New York: Cooper Square, 1967), pp. 163–166; the supplementary paragraph (in brackets) is from the same collection, pp. 166–167.

matician. This clever young daughter of a vile mother is in love with and is beloved by Frank, the flippant, good for nothing son of a prominent clergyman.

The mother goes to England to visit Vivian, and with her are two men, Praed, a mooning artist, with weak morals, and Crofts, a dissolute baronet, with no morals whatever. Crofts is the business partner of Mrs. Warren in her "profession." He is the capitalist who put up the money for her to start with.

Crofts would like to marry Vivian, but is in doubt about her parentage. He is not sure but that she is his own daughter. Nevertheless, he presses his suit through three acts. Possibly it is Praed, thinks Crofts, but Praed is quite sure that he (Praed) is not her father. They discuss the matter at length. As Crofts says, "It's very awkward to be uncertain about it"; that is, it is an awkward thing to marry your own child.

Then it develops that the clergyman was a former intimate of Mrs. Warren, and Crofts asserts that he must be Vivian's father. When the girl rejects his suit in favor of Frank he blocks the match by telling the young couple they are brother and sister, Frank's father, the clergyman, having been the girl's parent.

Mrs. Warren tells her daughter all the revolting details of her life of shame, and glories in it, as it saved her and "Liz," her sister, the drudgery of menial labor.

You may think that the pure and clever daughter is shocked, but forgives and tries to reclaim her mother. Not a bit of it. Her views coincide with those of her shameless parent, and Vivian admits that in the circumstances she herself would have considered licentiousness and sin quite the better choice. She almost envies the career of her aunt, who became rich through the ill gotten gains of the "profession" of shame and is posing now as the social leader in a cathedral town and the chaperon of young girls.

The clergyman, who, mind you, is not made by Mr. Shaw a deposed or unfrocked clergyman, but the spiritual and religious head of a large and prominent church, confesses himself to be a debauchee and a rake—a subject which father and son familiarly discuss and laugh over. The clergyman sits up all night with Crofts and becomes bestially intoxicated; then he starts in to write his sermon for the following day.

Frank, in love with Vivian, makes advances to Vivian's mother, whom he knows to be a lewd woman, and suggests that they go to the Continent together. And so on through the revolting story, until Vivian goes away to London to earn her own living and the other characters sink into obscurity in their old moral degradation.

Does not this literary muck leave a bad taste in the mouth? Does it not insult the moral intelligence of New York theatre-goers and outrage the decency of the New York stage?

There was not one redeeming feature about it last night, not one ray of sunshine, of cleanliness, to lighten up the moral darkness of situation and dialogue; not the semblance of a moral lesson pointed. As Letchmere says of his family in *Letty*, "We are rotten to the core," and the same might be said of the characters in *Mrs. Warren's Profession*.

The play was well acted from a technical standpoint by Mr. Daly as Frank, Miss Shaw as Mrs. Warren, and others of the cast; but while that is ordinarily cause for praise in a performance, it constituted an added sin to last night's production, for the better it was acted the more the impurity and degeneracy of the characters, the situations and the lines were made apparent. There were a few slight excisions made in the play as written, but what was left filled the house with the ill odor of evil suggestion, where it was not blatantly immoral.

After the third act Mr. Daly came before the curtain and made a speech in which he rather floundered as though he had forgotten what was committed to memory. He said that the play should only be seen by grown up people who could not be corrupted. Children might be kept to the old fashioned moral illusions, including Santa Claus and Washington.

"We have many theatres," he went on, "devoted to plays appealing to the romanticist or child—New York has even provided a hippodrome for such. But surely there should be room in New York for at least one theatre devoted to truth, however disagreeable truth may appear.

"This play is not presented as an entertainment, but as a dramatic sermon and an exposé of a social condition and an evil, which our purists attempt to ignore, and by ignoring, allow it to gain its strength. If Mr. Comstock devoted half the energy and time to providing soft beds, sweet food and clean linen to the poor of New York that he does to suppression of postal cards, we would have less immorality, for the logical reason that virtue would be robbing vice of its strongest features and attractiveness—comfort and health.

"It is a strange but true thing that everybody who has written to the newspapers, asking that this play be suppressed, has concluded the letter with the quaint statement, 'I know the play should be suppressed, although, of course, I have not read the book.' God has gifted these mortals with strange powers, indeed.

"If public opinion forces this theatre to close and this play to be withdrawn, it will be a sad commentary indeed upon twentieth century so-called civilization and our enlightened new country."

Then Mr. Daly retired amid vociferous applause from the double distilled Shawites present and the speculators who had tickets for sale for tonight—if there is to be any tonight for the play.

[Said the *Sun* for the same day, "If Mr. Daly had held to his original intention of playing the piece at a few matinees to invited guests, there might be some excuse for its production, but to throw so vile and unnecessary a concoction in the teeth of the public violates all canons of good art and common decency. . . . The play, in a word, smells to heaven. It is a dramatized stench." The *Times* observed: "Arnold Daly has made a serious mistake. *Mrs. Warren's Profession*, whatever its merits or demerits as a play for the closet, has absolutely no place in a theatre before a mixed assembly such as witnessed it at the Garrick last night. . . . Mr. Shaw takes a subject, decaying and reeking, and analyzes it for the edification of those whose unhealthy tastes find satisfaction in morbific suggestion." The *Evening Post* remarked, "There is nothing that is so offensive to the normal, clean and healthy mind as the affectation of a lofty motive in the commission of a mean and dirty action, and there was no more exasperating feature of the performance of Bernard Shaw's *Mrs. Warren's Profession* at the Garrick Theatre last evening than the false pretense, at once contemptible and abominable, which clothed the whole undertaking as a garment. . . . *Mrs. Warren's Profession* is one of those half-truths, which are ever the basest of lies—a composition primarily designed for mere sensation, in which all sense of veracity is lost in the mass of crude exaggeration and specious misrepresentation."]

J. T. Grein's review of the 1902 London production is considerably less heated and more objective, although he too finds the play morally offensive—especially for women. He also suggests that the problem Shaw was addressing is not an important one. But his chief objection to Mrs. Warren's Profession *is that the subject demanded a tragic treatment, and that Shaw nevertheless treated it in a purely intellectual way, thus falsifying reality.*

[THE FIRST PRODUCTION OF *MRS. WARREN'S PROFESSION*]
J. T. Grein

It was an exceedingly uncomfortable afternoon. For there was a majority of women to listen to that which could only be understood by a minority of men. Nor was the play fit for women's ears. By all means let us initiate our daughters before they cross the threshold of womanhood into those duties and functions of life which are vital in matrimony and maternity. But there is a boundary line, and its transgression means peril—the peril of destroying ideals. I go further. Even men need not know all the ugliness that lies below the surface of everyday life. To some male minds too much knowledge of the seamy side is poisonous, for it leads to pessimism, that pioneer of insanity and suicide. And, sure as I feel that most of the women, and a good many of the men, who were present at the production of *Mrs. Warren's Profession* by the Stage Society, did not at first know, and finally merely guessed, what was the woman's trade, I cannot withhold the opinion that the representation was unnecessary and painful. It is mainly for these reasons that, in spite of my great admiration for Bernard Shaw, the play was not brought out by the late Independent Theatre. As a "straight talk to men only" it is not sufficiently true to life to be productive of an educational effect. As a drama it is unsatisfactory, because the characters have no inner life, but merely echo certain views of the author. As literature, however, the merits of *Mrs. Warren's Profession* are considerable, and its true place is in the study.

Mrs. Warren's Profession is a "problem play" in the fullest sense of the word. Mr. Shaw will probably deny it, and claim that it is ordinary actable drama, but the text will give evidence in my favour. We hear Mr. Shaw all the time, and whatever vitality the characters possess is not their own, but Mr. Shaw's. They own also much of his contradictory elements—his depth of observation and thought and his extraordinary "cussedness." Here, as in most of G. B. S.'s work, the sublime is constantly spoilt by the ridiculous. It is the author's manner, and his way to express his contempt for the public. But that is a mere side issue. The main point is whether the problem is worth discussing and whether it has been dealt with in an adequate, convincing manner. I say no on both counts. The problem is neither vital nor important. It has none of the *raison d'être* of *Le Fils de Coralie* by Delpit, of *La Dame aux Camelias,* or of *Ghosts.* The case of Mrs. Warren has been invented with such ingenuity and surrounded by such impossibilities that it produces revolt instead of reasoning. For Mr. Shaw has made the great mistake of painting all the male characters with a streak of a demoralised tar brush; he has created a cold-blooded, almost sexless daughter as the sympathetic element: and he has built the unspeakable Mrs. Warren of such motley material that in

From J. T. Grein, *"Mrs Warren's Profession* [Review, January 12, 1902]," in his *Dramatic Criticism 1902–1903* (reprinted New York: Benjamin Blom, Inc., 1971), pp. 7–10.

our own mind pity and disgust for the woman are constantly at loggerheads. If the theme was worth treating at all the human conflict was the tragedy of the daughter through the infamy of the mother. Instead of that we get long arguments—spiced with platform oratory and invective—between a mother really utterly degraded, but here and there whitewashed with sentimental effusions, and a daughter so un-English in her knowledge of the world, so cold of heart, and "beyond human power" in reasoning that we end up hating both; the one who deserves it, as well as the other who is a victim of circumstances. Thus there are false notes all the time, and apart from a passing interest in a few scenes, saved by the author's cleverness, the play causes only pain and bewilderment, while it should have shaken our soul to its innermost chords.

It is not so easy to explain this singular effect, or, rather, it would be easy if it did not behove us to touch this work—in a newspaper—with kid-gloved fingers. Mr. Shaw, in his attempt to portray a woman of Mrs. Warren's type, either lacked the courage to play misère-ouverte, or, what is more likely, he had not sufficient knowledge of the monstrosity of such beings. His Mrs. Warren is a black soul with spots of human feeling dotted on in whitish chalk. But the real Mrs. Warren is the most abject creature in all humanity. I cannot say more. I can but refer Mr. Shaw to Parent-Duchatel, to Yves Guyot, to Dr. Commange, to Leo Taxil's "Corruption Fin de Siècle"—to a whole library on the colossal subject of human debasement. If Mr. Shaw had fully known the nature of Mrs. Warren's profession he would have left the play unwritten, or produced a tragedy of heartrending power. Now he has merely philandered around a dangerous subject; he has treated it half in earnest, half in that peculiar jesting manner which is all his own. He has given free rein to his brain and silenced his heart. He has, therefore, produced a play of a needlessly "unpleasant" understructure to no useful end. A play that interests in part, repels in others; a drama that plays fast and loose with our emotions, and will in some awaken a curiosity which had better been left in slumber. . . .

Max Beerbohm wrote two critiques of Mrs. Warren's Profession, *the first in 1898 when the play was first published and the second in 1902 when it was first performed. Beerbohm was not entirely negative in his assessment of the play: he admired its sincerity and fearlessness and found its stagecraft acceptable. But he considered* Mrs. Warren *a failure, mainly because it was a thesis play in which Shaw constantly intruded with his own ideas while failing to create real characters. Beerbohm detected signs that Shaw was attempting to treat Mrs. Warren as a tragic figure; but in his estimation the playwright failed because of his "profound ignorance of human nature."*

[IDEAS AND CHARACTERS IN *MRS. WARREN'S PROFESSION*]
Max Beerbohm

. . . "Mrs. Warren" is a powerful and stimulating, even an ennobling, piece of work—a great failure, if you like, but also a failure with elements of greatness in it. It is decried as unpleasant by those who cannot bear to be told publicly about things

Excerpted from Max Beerbohm, "Mr. Shaw's Profession [Reviews, May 14 and 21, 1898]," in his *More Theatres, 1898–1903* (New York: Taplinger, 1969), pp. 21–26; and from "Mr. Shaw's Tragedy [Review, February 1, 1902]," in his *Around Theatres* (New York: Simon and Schuster, 1954), pp. 191–195.

which in private they can discuss, and even tolerate, without a qualm. Such people are the majority. For me, I confess, a play with an unpleasant subject, written sincerely and fearlessly by a man who has a keenly active brain and a keenly active interest in the life around him, is much less unpleasant than that milk-and-water romance (brewed of skimmed milk and stale water) which is the fare commonly provided for me in the theatre. It seems to me not only less unpleasant, but also less unwholesome. I am thankful for it. . . .

I think it was Mr. Street who propounded an ingenious theory that the invention of printing had made serious and philosophical plays unnecessary, that one could learn far better from books than from the stage, and that the best thing for the stage to do was to be merely comic. But I hold that there is still some justification and some use for the dramatist-with-a-purpose. Though he may no longer be able to tell us what we did not know before, he can yet impress our knowledge in us more effectively than can any mere bookman; he can make us see our knowledge at new angles, and under new and more vivid lights. Nor is direct moral purpose always a fatal obstacle, but sometimes a very valuable incentive to dramatic art. In writing *Widowers' Houses, The Philanderer,* and *Mrs. Warren's Profession,* Mr. Shaw was, as he admits, impelled by a direct moral purpose. *A priori,* there is no harm in that. Whether the purpose that impelled him was morally sound is not a question which I have time to discuss. Whether it was quite genuine to him is a far more important point, and I am sure that Mr. Shaw is honestly firm in his convictions. Whether his convictions have helped him to write good plays, or have hindered him from doing so, is the point which most interests me and with which I propose to deal, taking *Mrs. Warren's Profession* as the test case, inasmuch as I think it to be the most considerable of the three works. Mr. William Archer has given us, through the *Daily Chronicle,* a long poem in which he declares this drama to be "intellectually and dramatically one of the most remarkable plays of the age," and Mr. Cunninghame Graham, coming upon us, rather suddenly, in the character of old play-goer, vows that in his opinion it is "the best play which has been written in the English language in this generation." But, as I have already suggested in these columns, there are some critics so advanced as to hold that a bad play is necessarily a good play, that (need I amplify the phrase?) there must be something very fine about a dramatist who defies the canons of dramatic art. There are also those who, confounding subject with treatment, and drama itself with the Sidney Webbs, believe that a serious theme is a touchstone of dramatic ability. An unpleasant theme, seriously treated, sends them into transports. Drag in the divorce-court, and they will solemnly credit you with immense talent for the stage. Drag in a brothel, and they will never have seen so great a play as yours. Mr. Shaw does not merely drag a brothel into his play, but makes it the play's basis. Let us be calm. Let us not be swept away on the strong wave of a genuine, but possibly mistaken, enthusiasm. My friends, let us consider the play as in itself it is. . . .

I know well that, in giving a mere sketch of a play which one does not like, one is bound to do the play some injustice. I do not think that I have done any considerable injustice to *Mrs. Warren's Profession,* but I should like to say at once that the play is well and forcibly written, that the idea of it is firmly gripped, and that, obviously, the scenes are ordered by one who has some instinct for stagecraft. But no amount of stagecraft, and good dialogue and philosophic grip will enable a man to write a serious play that can be anything but ridiculous, unless the man can also draw human characters. If Mr. Shaw had been able to draw Vivie as a real girl, Mrs. Warren as a real woman, and Frank as a real young man, he might have produced a play which would have justified even the superlatives of Mr. Archer and the reminiscences of Mr. Cunninghame Graham. "No conflict: no drama," as he himself says in one of his excellent prefaces. To this formula I would add "No sympathy: no conflict." Conflict of a kind there is between Vivie and her mother, but as no one could feel any sympathy for the mother, even were she real and not a mere secretion of Shawism, nor for the daughter who is a mere secretion of Shawism and more utterly unreal than the most romantic heroine across the bridges, the conflict is not of that kind which makes a play effective, but is rather such a shindy as might be waged between a phantom pot and an imaginary kettle. Maupassant's Yvette was a tragic and moving figure because she was a real girl, to whom the discovery of her mother's shame was really horrible. Mr. Shaw has declared that he thinks the scene in the second act between Vivie and her mother "tremendously effective." To whom, I wonder? As a matter of fact, it is not a scene at all. It is a fragment of a well-written pamphlet. Yvette tried to poison herself. "That," Mr. Shaw would say, "was very silly and romantic of her. My Vivie goes out into the world to make a living for herself." But that was the intention of Mr. Shaw's Vivie from the first rise of the curtain. The last fall of the curtain leaves her exactly as she was discovered. Nothing has been developed in her by the action of the play. Nothing has been developed in Mrs. Warren, nothing in Frank Gardner, nothing in any of the characters. Even unreal characters *can* be developed in a play. Even real characters *must* be developed; no development: no drama. Unreal characters, undeveloped, are no good at all. . . .

My readers may remember that I laid stress on the unrealness of the chief characters in his most ambitious play, *Mrs. Warren's Profession.* Well, I cannot admit that the chief characters in his other plays are one whit more real than Vivie Warren and her friends. They are, indeed, of precisely the same type. The men are all disputative machines, ingeniously constructed, and the women, who, almost without exception, belong to the strange cult of the fountain-pen, are, if anything, rather more self-conscious than the men. I am aware that there are inhuman persons in the world, here and there. One or two inhuman characters would not be amiss in a play. But the play that is monopolised by them can never be taken seriously. Does Mr. Shaw, like Mr. W. S. Gilbert, wish that any of his plays shall be seriously taken? For some of them, undoubtedly, that is his ardent wish, but, until he has been re-incarnated and has thoroughly re-written them, it will not be gratified. Moral purpose is all very well for a dramatist who, like Ibsen, can express it through the tragic or comic evolutions of realised human character. To a dramatist who cannot do that, moral purpose is a disaster; it forces him to burden himself and his puppets with a load which they cannot bear, a load without which they might be quite agile, effective and amusing. Mr. Shaw is not, as the truly serious dramatist must be, one who loves to study and depict men and women for their own sake, with or without moral purpose. When Mr. Shaw is not morally purposeful, he is fantastic and frivolous, and it is then that his plays are good. In farce, psychological reality is not wanted—it would be out of place, and *Arms and*

the Man, and *You Never Can Tell* lose nothing and gain much, whilst *Widowers' Houses*
and *Mrs. Warren's Profession* are ruined by the absurdity of their characters and situations. No one admires more heartily than I the keenness of Mr. Shaw's intellect and
the absolute sincerity with which Mr. Shaw maintains and lives up to his convictions.
Nor would any one be more heartily glad than I to see more intellectual force and
more moral earnestness in the serious plays that are written for the English stage. But
these qualities, without that human sympathy to which in the best dramatist they are
always subordinate, are thrown utterly away on serious play-writing. Mr. Shaw's penetrating eye is of great use to him in satire or in criticism. He is one of those gifted ob-
servers who can always see through a brick wall. But the very fact that a man can see
through a brick wall means that he cannot see the brick wall. It is because flesh and
blood make no impression on the X-rays that Herr Röntgen is able to show us our
bones and any latch-keys that we may have swallowed, or fish-hooks that may have
entered into our hands. Flesh and blood are quite invisible to Mr. Shaw. He thinks
that because he cannot see them they do not exist, and that he is to be accepted as
a realist. I need hardly point out to my readers that he is mistaken. To those who have
read his plays I need hardly point out that, to all intents and purposes, his serious
characters are just so many skeletons, which do but dance and grin and rattle their
bones. I can hardly wonder that Mr. Shaw has so often hesitated about allowing this
or that theatrical manager to produce one of his serious plays. To produce one of them
really well would be almost impossible at any ordinary theatre. There is, however, one
management which might attempt and be able to achieve the task. I refer to Messrs.
Maskelyne and Cook. . . .

The play is in Mr. Shaw's earlier manner—his 'prentice manner. It was written in
the period when he had not yet found the proper form for expressing himself in
drama. He has found that form now. He has come through experiment to the loose
form of "Caesar and Cleopatra," of "The Devil's Disciple"—that large and variegated
form wherein there is elbow-room for all his irresponsible complexities. In "Mrs. Warren" he was still making tentative steps along the strait and narrow way of Ibsen.
To exhaust a theme in four single acts requires tremendous artistic concentration.
When the acts are split up loosely in scenes the author may divagate with impunity.
But in four single acts there is no room for anything that is not strictly to the point.
Any irrelevancy offends us. And irrelevancy is of the essence of Mr. Shaw's genius. Try
as he would, in admiration of his master, he could not keep himself relevant to Mrs.
Warren. We find him bobbing up at intervals throughout the play, and then bobbing
down again, quickly, ashamed of himself. In the loose form which he has now found
for himself he can bob up as often as he likes, and always we are overjoyed to see him.
But in the old constricted form we frown at him. We frown not merely at the waste
of time, but also as at a breach of good taste. Mr. Shaw is a comedic person, Mrs.
Warren a tragic. The Restoration is over, and no dramatist could treat her from any
but a tragic standpoint. It is from this standpoint, of course, that Mr. Shaw has treated
her. And thus we are jarred by the involuntary intrusions of Mr. Shaw's self. They give
a painful effect of levity, though we know well that nothing can be further from levity
than the spirit in which Mr. Shaw regards his theme. Theme, spirit: that brings us to
the root of the matter. The main secret of the play's failure is that we have a come-

dian trying to be tragic. To create a tragedy, you must have a sense of that pity and terror which—"Agreed," Mr. Shaw will interrupt "and I have nothing if not that sense. If you don't find it in this play of mine, you must be blind." "Agreed," I rejoin. But I proceed to suggest that a man may be more than a comedian in himself, yet fail to be tragic in dramaturgy, and that Mr. Shaw does not feel the pity and terror of life in the way that a tragic dramatist must feel it. His sense of it is a sincere and fine one. But it is the satirist's sense. He is sorry for things as they are, and afraid of things as they are, and angry that they are not otherwise, and laudably anxious to reform them. His is a fine civic ardour, which I should be the last to disparage. But it does not constitute him a tragic dramatist. The tragic dramatist must feel pity and terror in a certain specific way. It is through the hearts of men and women that he must feel them. He must be able to see into their hearts, and show us what he has seen there. He must be able to create human beings. Comedy's main appeal is to the head, tragedy's to the heart. We can be intellectually interested in figures that do not illude us as real, but we cannot feel for such figures. Thus in comedy a subjectively created figure will do well enough, but in tragedy it is useless. Mr. Shaw cannot create a figure objectively, and thus he cannot communicate to us through drama a tragic emotion. Tragedy, of course, can appeal not only to the heart, but also, incidentally, to the head. From the intellectual point of view, "Mrs. Warren" is, as I have said, a most stimulating affair. We admire the writer's grip of his subject. We cordially agree with his views. We praise the trenchancy of his expression. A remarkable little pamphlet! We really must have it bound! . . . With a start, we realise that this is not a pamphlet whose leaves we are turning, but a play which is being acted. . . . Our mistake was rather a stupid one. For if this play had been a pamphlet, it would have been appealing to our hearts and our heads simultaneously. The fact that it appealed (despite its theme) only to our heads ought to have reminded us that it was an ill-created tragedy. So tragic a theme could not otherwise have failed to touch us.

In order to rouse public opinion against those economic conditions by which a Mrs. Warren is produced, Mr. Shaw, as dramatist, could not have chosen a better means than that of juxtaposing Mrs. Warren with a grown-up daughter who is ignorant of her mother's history and occupation. There you have the makings of a fine tragic conflict. Only it is necessary that the daughter should be of flesh and blood. And there you are bumped up against one of the limitations in Mr. Shaw's genius. Doubtless, Mr. Shaw will say that Vivie is of authentic flesh and blood. I am ready to believe that there may be, here and there, a well-brought-up girl who would behave as (admirably, if Mr. Shaw likes) Vivie behaves. Only, such girls are very rare, very abnormal; and, in any case, Mr. Shaw has not succeeded in making this one seem like anything but a figment created by him to show how, in his opinion, a girl in such circumstances ought to behave. But even if he had made her real, that would not be enough. The tragic dramatist must not only be able to make a character real: he must also be able to select the kind of character that is right for his purpose. In "Mrs. Warren," obviously, the character of the daughter ought to be normal. Were she a normal girl, the situation would stir us to pity and awe. As she is but an unsympathetic figment dangled before our eyes, we are merely interested. The whole play becomes a mere academic debate. Mr. Shaw has called attention to certain things, and has moved

a resolution, and we have all voted for the resolution, and there is an end of the matter. Perhaps I go too far. The moving of a resolution does give a kind of artistic finish
to a debate. But there is no kind of art in the conclusion of Mr. Shaw's play. We leave
Vivie Warren precisely the same as we found her. She has passed through her ordeal
without turning a hair. At any rate, any hair that may have turned has been pressed
back severely into its place. The girl is not at all to be pitied, and since we cannot pity
her, we lose all the emotion that the play might have given us. As an acute critic, Mr.
Shaw must have known that it was essential to his play that Vivie should be made
human. The fact that he did not make her so proves that he could not. The fact that
he could not puts him out of court as a tragic dramatist. . . .

Of Mr. Shaw's philosophy I need merely say that it rests, like Plato's *Republic*, on
a profound ignorance of human nature. Just as the great idealist of Athens imagined
that the equality of man to man, and of woman to man, would one day be not merely
recognised but also established, so does our idealist of London believe that the tactics
of Fabius are the one thing needed to ensure Socialism, Women's Rights and all the
rest of his touching propaganda. Let him continue to believe so, by all means. But let
him not imagine that, by writing dramatic representations of men and women as (perhaps) they ought to be, he is so far advancing his cause as to make any one believe in
the possibility of his characters. In a word, let him write no more plays-with-a-purpose.

Shaw wrote an extensive preface to Mrs. Warren's Profession, *in which he defended himself
against criticisms such as the foregoing, inveighed against the censorship that had suppressed* Mrs.
Warren, *and restated in his own words some of the basic theses of the play. The following excerpts
cover most of Shaw's main points, although the reader who wishes to get the full flavor of Shaw's
attack on censorship will want to read the preface in its entirety.*

PREFACE TO *MRS WARREN'S PROFESSION*
George Bernard Shaw

[The aim of the play is to analyze and criticize the economic origins of
prostitution]

Mrs Warren's Profession was written in 1894 to draw attention to the truth that
prostitution is caused, not by female depravity and male licentiousness, but simply by
underpaying, undervaluing, and overworking women so shamefully that the poorest of
them are forced to resort to prostitution to keep body and soul together. Indeed all at-

Excerpted from *The Bodley Head Bernard Shaw: Collected Plays With Their Prefaces*, ed. Dan H. Laurence
(London: Bodley Head, 1970), Volume 1, pp. 231, 234–235, 236–238, 241–243, 251–257, 262–264. Reprinted
by permission of The Society of Authors on behalf of the Bernard Shaw Estate.

tractive unpropertied women lose money by being infallibly virtuous or contracting marriages that are not more or less venal. If on the large social scale we get what we call vice instead of what we call virtue it is simply because we are paying more for it. No normal woman would be a professional prostitute if she could better herself by being respectable, nor marry for money if she could afford to marry for love.

Also I desired to expose the fact that prostitution is not only carried on without organization by individual enterprise in the lodgings of solitary women, each her own mistress as well as every customer's mistress, but organized and exploited as a big international commerce for the profit of capitalists like any other commerce, and very lucrative to great city estates, including Church estates, through the rents of the houses in which it is practised. . . .

[True Christian moralists would approve of the play's indictment of society]

Do not suppose, however, that the consternation of the Press reflects any consternation among the general public. Anybody can upset the theatre critics, in a turn of the wrist, by substituting for the romantic commonplaces of the stage the moral commonplaces of the pulpit, the platform, or the library. Play Mrs Warren's Profession to an audience of clerical members of the Christian Social Union and of women well experienced in Rescue, Temperance, and Girls' Club work, and no moral panic will arise: every man and woman present will know that as long as poverty makes virtue hideous and the spare pocket-money of rich bachelordom makes vice dazzling, their daily hand-to-hand fight against prostitution with prayer and persuasion, shelters and scanty alms, will be a losing one. There was a time when they were able to urge that though "the white-lead factory where Anne Jane was poisoned" may be a far more terrible place than Mrs Warren's house, yet hell is still more dreadful. Nowadays they no longer believe in hell; and the girls among whom they are working know that they do not believe in it, and would laugh at them if they did. So well have the rescuers learnt that Mrs Warren's defence of herself and indictment of society is the thing that most needs saying, that those who know me personally reproach me, not for writing this play, but for wasting my energies on "pleasant plays" for the amusement of frivolous people, when I can build up such excellent stage sermons on their own work. Mrs Warren's Profession is the one play of mine which I could submit to a censorship without doubt of the result; only, it must not be the censorship of the minor theatre critic, nor of an innocent court official like the Lord Chamberlain's Examiner, much less of people who consciously profit by Mrs Warren's profession, or who personally make use of it, or who hold the widely whispered view that it is an indispensable safety-valve for the protection of domestic virtue, or, above all, who are smitten with a sentimental affection for our fallen sister, and would "take her up tenderly, lift her with care, fashioned so slenderly, young, and so fair." Nor am I prepared to accept the verdict of the medical gentlemen who would compulsorily examine and register Mrs Warren, whilst leaving Mrs Warren's patrons, especially her military patrons, free to destroy her health and anybody else's without fear of reprisals. But I should be quite content to have my play judged by, say, a joint committee of the Central Vigilance Society and the Salvation Army. And the sterner moralists the members of the committee were, the better. . . .

[The Censorship will allow prostitutes to be represented on stage only if they are sentimentalized]

Now let us consider how such recruiting can be encouraged by the theatre. Nothing is easier. Let the Lord Chamberlain's Examiner of Plays, backed by the Press, make an unwritten but perfectly well understood regulation that members of Mrs Warren's profession shall be tolerated on the stage only when they are beautiful, exquisitely dressed, and sumptuously lodged and fed; also that they shall, at the end of the play, die of consumption to the sympathetic tears of the whole audience, or step into the next room to commit suicide, or at least be turned out by their protectors and passed on to be "redeemed" by old and faithful lovers who have adored them in spite of all their levities. Naturally the poorer girls in the gallery will believe in the beauty, in the exquisite dresses, and the luxurious living, and will see that there is no real necessity for the consumption, the suicide, or the ejectment: mere pious forms, all of them, to save the Censor's face. Even if these purely official catastrophes carried any conviction, the majority of English girls remain so poor, so dependent, so well aware that the drudgeries of such honest work as is within their reach are likely enough to lead them eventually to lung disease, premature death, and domestic desertion or brutality, that they would still see reason to prefer the primrose path to the stony way of virtue, since both, vice at worst and virtue at best, lead to the same end in poverty and overwork. It is true that the Elementary School mistress will tell you that only girls of a certain kind will reason in this way. But alas! that certain kind turns out on inquiry to be simply the pretty, dainty kind: that is, the only kind that gets the chance of acting on such reasoning. Read the first report of the Commission on the Housing of the Working Classes [Bluebook C 4402, 1889]; read the Report on Home Industries (sacred word, Home!) issued by the Women's Industrial Council [Home Industries of Women in London, 1897, 1s.]; and ask yourself whether, if the lot in life therein described were your lot in life, you would not rather be a jewelled Vamp. If you can go deep enough into things to be able to say no, how many ignorant half-starved girls will believe you are speaking sincerely? To them the lot of the stage courtesan is heavenly in comparison with their own. Yet the Lord Chamberlain's Examiner, being an officer of the Royal Household, places the King in the position of saying to the dramatist "Thus, and thus only, shall you present Mrs Warren's profession on the stage, or you shall starve. Witness Shaw, who told the untempting truth about it, and whom We, by the Grace of God, accordingly disallow and suppress, and do what in Us lies to silence." Fortunately, Shaw cannot be silenced. "The harlot's cry from street to street" is louder than the voices of all the kings. I am not dependent on the theatre, and cannot be starved into making my play a standing advertisement of the attractive side of Mrs Warren's business. . . .

[It was not the sex in Shaw's play that led to its suppression; it was the serious treatment of the social problems created by sex]

. . . Further, it is not true that the Censorship, though it certainly suppresses Ibsen and Tolstoy, and would suppress Shakespear but for the absurd rule that a play once licensed is always licensed (so that Wycherly is permitted and Shelley prohibited), also suppresses unscrupulous playrights. I challenge the Examiner to mention any extremity of sexual misconduct which any manager in his senses would risk presenting on the London stage that has not been presented under his license and that of his predecessor. The compromise, in fact, works out in practice in favor of loose plays as against earnest ones.

To carry conviction on this point, I will take the extreme course of narrating the plots of two plays witnessed within the last ten years by myself at London West End theatres, one licensed under Queen Victoria, the other under her successor. Both plots conform to the strictest rules of the period when La Dame aux Camellias was still a forbidden play, and when The Second Mrs Tanqueray would have been tolerated only on condition that she carefully explained to the audience that when she met Captain Ardale she sinned "but in intention."

Play number one. A prince is compelled by his parents to marry the daughter of a neighboring king, but loves another maiden. The scene represents a hall in the king's palace at night. The wedding has taken place that day; and the closed door of the nuptial chamber is in view of the audience. Inside, the princess awaits her bridegroom. A duenna is in attendance. The bridegroom enters. His sole desire is to escape from a marriage which is hateful to him. A means occurs to him. He will assault the duenna, and be ignominiously expelled from the palace by his indignant father-in-law. To his horror, when he proceeds to carry out this stratagem, the duenna, far from raising an alarm, is flattered, delighted, and compliant. The assaulter becomes the assaulted. He flings her angrily to the ground, where she remains placidly. He flies. The father enters; dismisses the duenna; and listens at the keyhole of his daughter's nuptial chamber, uttering various pleasantries, and declaring, with a shiver, that a sound of kissing, which he supposes to proceed from within, makes him feel young again.

Story number two. A German officer finds himself in an inn with a French lady who has wounded his national vanity. He resolves to humble her by committing a rape upon her. He announces his purpose. She remonstrates, implores, flies to the doors and finds them locked, calls for help and finds none at hand, runs screaming from side to side, and, after a harrowing scene, is overpowered and faints. Nothing further being possible on the stage without actual felony, the officer then relents and leaves her. When she recovers, she believes that he has carried out his threat; and during the rest of the play she is represented as vainly vowing vengeance upon him, whilst she is really falling in love with him under the influence of his imaginary crime against her. Finally she consents to marry him; and the curtain falls on their happiness.

The story was certified by the Examiner, acting for the Lord Chamberlain, as void in its general tendency of "anything immoral or otherwise improper for the stage." But let nobody conclude therefore that the Examiner is a monster, whose policy it is to deprave the theatre. As a matter of fact, both the above stories are strictly in order from the official point of view. The incidents of sex which they contain, though carried in both to the extreme point at which another step would be dealt with, not by the Examiner, but by the police, do not involve adultery, nor any allusion to Mrs Warren's profession, nor to the fact that the children of any polyandrous group will, when they grow up, inevitably be confronted, as those of Mrs Warren's group are in my play, with the insoluble problem of their own possible consanguinity. In short, by depending wholly on the coarse humors and the physical fascination of sex, they comply with all the formulable requirements of the Censorship, whereas plays in which these humors and fascinations are discarded, and the social problems created by sex seriously faced and dealt with, inevitably ignore the official formula and are suppressed. . . .

[The characters in the play behave with the passion and irrationality of real human beings]

. . . Mrs Warren's Profession is no mere theorem, but a play of instincts and temperaments in conflict with each other and with a flinty social problem that never yields an inch to mere sentiment.

I go further than this. I declare that the real secret of the cynicism and inhumanity of which shallower critics accuse me is the unexpectedness with which my characters behave like human beings, instead of conforming to the romantic logic of the stage. The axioms and postulates of that dreary mimanthropometry are so well known that it is almost impossible for its slaves to write tolerable last acts to their plays, so conventionally do their conclusions follow from their premises. Because I have thrown this logic ruthlessly overboard, I am accused of ignoring, not stage logic, but, of all things, human feeling. People with completely theatrified imaginations tell me that no girl would treat her mother as Vivie Warren does, meaning that no stage heroine would in a popular sentimental play. They say this just as they might say that no two straight lines would enclose a space. They do not see how completely inverted their vision has become even when I throw its preposterousness in their faces, as I repeatedly do in this very play. Praed, the sentimental artist (fool that I was not to make him a theatre critic instead of an architect!) burlesques them by expecting all through the piece that the feelings of the others will be logically deducible from their family relationships and from his "conventionally unconventional" social code. The sarcasm is lost on the critics: they, saturated with the same logic, only think him the sole sensible person on the stage. Thus it comes about that the more completely the dramatist is emancipated from the illusion that men and women are primarily reasonable beings, and the more powerfully he insists on the ruthless indifference of their great dramatic antagonist, the external world, to their whims and emotions, the surer he is to be denounced as blind to the very distinction on which his whole work is built. Far from ignoring idiosyncrasy, will, passion, impulse, whim, as factors in human action, I have placed them so nakedly on the stage that the elderly citizen, accustomed to see them clothed with the veil of manufactured logic about duty, and to disguise even his own impulses from himself in this way, finds the picture as unnatural as Carlyle's suggested painting of parliament sitting without its clothes.

[*Mrs. Warren's Profession* is a play for women]

I now come to those critics who, intellectually baffled by the problem in Mrs Warren's Profession, have made a virtue of running away from it on the gentlemanly ground that the theatre is frequented by women as well as by men, and that such problems should not be discussed or even mentioned in the presence of women. With that sort of chivalry I cannot argue: I simply affirm that Mrs Warren's Profession is a play for women; that it was written for women; that is has been performed and produced mainly through the determination of women that it should be performed and produced; that the enthusiasm of women made its first performance excitingly successful; and that not one of these women had any inducement to support it except their belief in the timeliness and the power of the lesson the play teaches. Those who were "surprised to see ladies present" were men; and when they proceeded to explain that the journals they represented could not possibly demoralize the public by describing such a play, their editors cruelly devoted the space saved by their delicacy to reporting at unusual length an exceptionally abominable police case.

[The reason Shaw does not portray Mrs. Warren as fiendishly wicked is that not she but society is guilty]

My old Independent Theatre manager, Mr Grein, besides that reproach to me for shattering his ideals, complains that Mrs Warren is not wicked enough, and names several romancers who would have clothed her black soul with all the terrors of tragedy. I have no doubt they would; but that is just what I did not want to do. Nothing would please our sanctimonious British public more than to throw the whole guilt of Mrs Warren's profession on Mrs Warren herself. Now the whole aim of my play is to throw that guilt on the British public itself. Mr Grein may remember that when he produced my first play, Widowers' Houses, exactly the same misunderstanding arose. When the virtuous young gentleman rose up in wrath against the slum landlord, the slum landlord very effectually shewed him that slums are the product, not of individual Harpagons, but of the indifference of virtuous young gentlemen to the condition of the city they live in, provided they live at the west end of it on money earned by somebody else's labor. The notion that prostitution is created by the wickedness of Mrs Warren is as silly as the notion—prevalent, nevertheless, to some extent in Temperance circles—that drunkenness is created by the wickedness of the publican. Mrs Warren is not a whit a worse woman than the reputable daughter who cannot endure her. Her indifference to the ultimate social consequences of her means of making money, and her discovery of that means by the ordinary method of taking the line of least resistance to getting it, are too common in English society to call for any special remark. Her vitality, her thrift, her energy, her outspokenness, her wise care of her daughter, and the managing capacity which has enabled her and her sister to climb from the fried fish shop down by the Mint to the establishments of which she boasts, are all high English social virtues. Her defence of herself is so overwhelming that it provokes the St James's Gazette to declare that "the tendency of the play is wholly evil" because "it contains one of the boldest and most specious defences of an immoral life for poor women that has ever been penned." Happily the St James's Gazette here speaks in haste. Mrs Warren's defence of herself is not only bold and specious, but valid and unanswerable. But it is no defence at all of the vice which she organizes. It is no defence of an immoral life to say that the alternative offered by society collectively to poor women is a miserable life, starved, overworked, fetid, ailing, ugly. Though it is quite natural and *right* for Mrs Warren to choose what is, according to her lights, the least immoral alternative, it is none the less infamous of society to offer such alternatives. For the alternatives offered are not morality and immorality, but two sorts of immorality. The man who cannot see that starvation, overwork, dirt, and disease are as anti-social as prostitution—that they are the vices and crimes of a nation, and not merely its misfortunes—is (to put it as politely as possible) a hopelessly Private Person.

The notion that Mrs Warren must be a fiend is only an example of the violence and passion which the slightest reference to sex rouses in undisciplined minds, and which makes it seem natural to our lawgivers to punish silly and negligible indecencies with a ferocity unknown in dealing with, for example, ruinous financial swindling. Had my play been entitled Mr Warren's Profession, and Mr Warren been a bookmaker, nobody would have expected me to make him a villain as well. Yet gambling is a vice, and bookmaking an institution, for which there is absolutely nothing to be said. The moral and economic evil done by trying to get other people's money without working for it (and this is the essence of gambling) is not only enormous but uncompensated. There are no two sides to the question of gambling, no circumstances which force us to tolerate it lest its suppression lead to worse things, no consensus of opinion among responsible classes, such as magistrates and military commanders, that it is a necessity, no Athenian records of gambling made splendid by the talents of its professors, no contention that instead of violating morals it only violates a legal institution which is in many respects oppressive and unnatural, no possible plea that the instinct on which it is founded is a vital one. Prostitution can confuse the issue with all these excuses: gambling has none of them. Consequently, if Mrs Warren must needs be a demon, a bookmaker must be a cacodemon. Well, does anybody who knows the sporting world really believe that bookmakers are worse than their neighbors? On the contrary, they have to be a good deal better; for in that world nearly everybody whose social rank does not exclude such an occupation would be a bookmaker if he could; but the strength of character required for handling large sums of money and for strict settlements and unflinching payment of losses is so rare that successful bookmakers are rare too. It may seem that at least public spirit cannot be one of a bookmaker's virtues; but I can testify from personal experience that excellent public work is done with money subscribed by bookmakers. It is true that there are abysses in bookmaking: for example, welshing. Mr Grein hints that there are abysses in Mrs Warren's profession also. So there are in every profession: the error lies in supposing that every member of them sounds these depths. I sit on a public body which prosecutes Mrs Warren zealously; and I can assure Mr Grein that she is often leniently dealt with because she has conducted her business "respectably" and held herself above its vilest branches. The degrees in infamy are as numerous and as scrupulously observed as the degrees in the peerage: the moralist's notion that there are depths at which the moral atmosphere ceases is as delusive as the rich man's notion that there are no social jealousies or snobberies among the very poor. No: had I drawn Mrs Warren as a fiend in human form, the very people who now rebuke me for flattering her would probably be the first to deride me for deducing character logically from occupation instead of observing it accurately in society. . . .

> [The opposition to *Mrs. Warren's Profession* comes from businessmen and officials who share in the profits from prostitution]

Many people have been puzzled by the fact that whilst stage entertainments which are frankly meant to act on the spectators as aphrodisiacs are everywhere tolerated, plays which have an almost horrifying contrary effect are fiercely attacked by persons and papers notoriously indifferent to public morals on all other occasions. The explanation is very simple. The profits of Mrs Warren's profession are shared not only by Mrs Warren and Sir George Crofts, but by the landlords of their houses, the newspapers which advertize them, the restaurants which cater for them, and, in short, all the trades to which they are good customers, not to mention the public officials and representatives whom they silence by complicity, corruption, or blackmail. Add to these the employers who profit by cheap female labor, and the shareholders whose dividends depend on it (you find such people everywhere, even on the judicial bench and in the highest places in Church and State) and you get a large and powerful class with a strong pecuniary incentive to protect Mrs Warren's profession, and a correspondingly strong incentive to conceal, from their own consciences no less than from the world, the real sources of their gain. These are the people who declare that it is feminine vice and not poverty that drives women to the streets, as if vicious women with independent incomes ever went there. These are the people who, indulgent or indifferent to aphrodisiac plays, raise the moral hue and cry against performances of Mrs Warren's Profession, and drag actresses to the police court to be insulted, bullied, and threatened for fulfilling their engagements. For please observe that the judicial decision in New York State in favor of the play did not end the matter. In Kansas City, for instance, the municipality, finding itself restrained by the courts from preventing the performance, fell back on a local bye-law against indecency. It summoned the actress who impersonated Mrs Warren to the police court, and offered her and her colleagues the alternative of leaving the city or being prosecuted under this bye-law.

Now nothing is more possible than that the city councillors who suddenly displayed such concern for the morals of the theatre were either Mrs Warren's landlords, or employers of women at starvation wages, or restaurant keepers, or newspaper proprietors, or in some other more or less direct way sharers of the profits of her trade. No doubt it is equally possible that they were simply stupid men who thought that indecency consists, not in evil, but in mentioning it. I have, however, been myself a member of a municipal council, and have not found municipal councillors quite so simple and inexperienced as this. At all events I do not propose to give the Kansas councillors the benefit of the doubt. I therefore advise the public at large, which will finally decide the matter, to keep a vigilant eye on gentlemen who will stand anything at the theatre except a performance of Mrs Warren's Profession, and who assert in the same breath that (a) the play is too loathsome to be bearable by civilized people, and (b) that unless its performance is prohibited the whole town will throng to see it. They may be merely excited and foolish; but I am bound to warn the public that it is equally likely that they may be collected and knavish.

At all events, to prohibit the play is to protect the evil which the play exposes; and in view of that fact, I see no reason for assuming that the prohibitionists are disinterested moralists, and that the author, the managers, and the performers, who depend for their livelihood on their personal reputations and not on rents, advertisements, or dividends, are grossly inferior to them in moral sense and public responsibility.

It is true that in Mrs Warren's Profession, Society, and not any individual, is the villain of the piece; but it does not follow that the people who take offence at it are all champions of society. Their credentials cannot be too carefully examined.

In a searching re-evaluation of Shaw's plays, the modern critic Eric Bentley finds the emotional center of Mrs. Warren's Profession *to be something quite different from the criticism of society Shaw insisted his real aim was. For Bentley, the main emotional concern in* Mrs. Warren, *as in other Shaw plays, is sex, and at a much deeper level than the playwright himself realized.*

[EMOTIONAL SUBSTANCE IN *MRS. WARREN'S PROFESSION*]
Eric Bentley

. . . If Shaw's plays are, or begin by being, a parody of the more conventional drama of his time, that parody is by no means confined to the form. We have already seen that the themes, too, tend to get turned around: these compositions not only do the opposite, as it were, but also say the opposite.

What of the emotions? Whatever the ultimate purpose of drama, its immediate impact is a strongly emotional one, and one cannot conceive of a story having an emotional effect upon an audience unless it is an emotional story and has a certain emotional structure. I may be forgiven for stating so rudimentary a principle because the Shavian drama presents us with a paradox: it has flooded a thousand theatres with emotion and yet has often been held to be emotionless.

Of course, this common opinion is absurd, bolstered though it can be with remarks of Shaw's own about being a mere "work machine" and the like. What we confront here is originality. Shaw may not have been an original thinker: he tried, rather, to make a synthesis of what certain others had thought. But he was an original person. What fitted him so well for the role of the enemy of convention was that his natural responses were not those of other people but all his own. His emotional constitution was a peculiar one, and that peculiarity is reflected in his plays.

Sex is, without doubt, the crucial issue. Comedy remains fertility worship, however sublimated, and it is fair enough to ask what Bernard Shaw made of the old sexual rigmarole—courtship and the barriers thereto. It is even fair to use any facts about Shaw himself that are a matter of public record.

On the other hand, one is not honor-bound to side with "modern" opinion against "Victorian" as to what is good and bad. The very "modern" Dr. Kinsey implied that human vitality could be measured in statistics on orgasms. Our subject Bernard Shaw will not pass into any Kinseyite paradise. Though he lived to be ninety-four, he seems to have experienced sexual intercourse only between the ages of twenty-nine and forty-three. "I lived a continent virgin . . . until I was 29. . . . During the fourteen years before my marriage at 43 there was always some lady in the case. . . . As man and wife we found a new relation in which sex had no part. It ended the old gallantries, flirtations, and philanderings for both of us." This quotation is from the letter to Frank Harris, who, as a Kinseyite before Kinsey, wrote:

> Compare his [Shaw's] private life with Shakespeare's. While Mary Fitton was banished from London Shakespeare could write nothing but tragedies.

Excerpted from Eric Bentley, "Bernard Shaw," in his *Theatre of War* (New York: Viking Press, 1972), pp. 12–19. Copyright © 1960 by Eric Bentley. Reprinted by permission of Viking Press, Inc.

That went on for five years. When the Queen died and Shakespeare's Dark Lady returned, he wrote *Antony and Cleopatra,* his greatest love story. As nothing like that happened in Shaw's life we can only get a text-booky, sexless type of play.

A remarkable blend of ignorance, invention, and arbitrary assumption! For actually Shaw concealed from Harris most of his private life; nothing much is known about Shakespeare's feelings for any woman; and no critic or psychologist of repute has ever argued that a man's writing has to be "text-booky" and "sexless" unless he is carrying on an adulterous romance; a more familiar argument would be that precisely the abstinent man's imagination might well be crammed with sex. But there is no settling the question a priori.

William Archer declared that Shaw's plays reeked with sex. It is a more suggestive declaration than Harris's. It reminds us that Shaw was able to re-create the sexual charm of both men and women to a degree unequaled by any English dramatist except Shakespeare. To be sure, he doesn't need bedroom scenes to do this. Morell has only to talk and we understand "Prossy's complaint." Undershaft has only to talk and we understand why he is a problem to his daughter. To say nothing of the long line of sirens from Candida to Orinthia! Few of the "sexy" ladies of Restoration comedy, by contrast, have any sex appeal at all. One thing Archer is sure to have had in mind is that the women in Shaw pursue a sexual purpose in a way absolutely unknown to Victorian literature. Of all the reversals in Shavian drama this is inevitably the most famous: the reversal in the roles of the sexes. Shaw once committed himself to the view that all superior women are masculine and all superior men are feminine. In his comedies, most often, the woman is active, the man passive. Perhaps by 1960 the theme has been restated *ad nauseam;* to Archer it was startling. As was Shaw's determination to rub the sore places of the sexual morality of his time. *Mrs. Warren's Profession* was for many years too "raw" a play for production in London, and it created a memorable scandal when it was produced in New Haven and New York in 1905. Like most of the major modern dramatists and novelists, Shaw mentioned the unmentionable. He even claimed to have "put the physical act of sexual intercourse on the stage" (in *Overruled*). Archer may well have felt that Shaw could not give the subject of sex a rest: he may not always have been at the center of it, but he was forever touching the fringes.

Here Frank Harris would have interjected, "He was always *avoiding* the center of it." And the interjection is called for. The impression that a man is unemotional in general and sexless in particular does not come from nowhere, nor are the kinds of sex I have been noting what the average spectator is looking for if he demands a "sexy" show. *Overruled* does not really "put the physical act of sexual intercourse on the stage," and, even if it did, it would do so comically, depriving the act of precisely that element which people miss in Shaw, which is not sex in general but the torridity of sexual romance. At that, if this element were simply absent, Shaw might very well have got away with the omission. But it is explicitly rejected. It is not that a Shavian couple cannot end up in bed but, rather, that they are likely to contemplate the idea—and reject it. If the characteristic act of the French drama of the period was the plunge into bed, that of the Shavian drama is the precipitate retreat from the bedroom door.

Harris would be right in reminding us that such was Bernard Shaw's emotional constitution. What other writer has ever created all the normal expectations in a scene between a king and his mistress *(The Apple Cart)* only to reveal later that their relationship is purely platonic? *Captain Brassbound's Conversion* shows the Shavian pattern to perfection. Is there sexual feeling in the play? There is. The process by which Brassbound and Lady Cicely are brought closer and closer is positively titillating. After which, what happens? They are parted. The play has a superb final curtain. "How marvellous!" says Lady Cicely, "how marvellous!" Then with one of those quick changes of tone that mark the Shavian dialogue: "And what an escape!" Is this unemotional? No. But the emotion is not erotic: it is relief at a release from the erotic. Such is the emotional content of this particular Shavian anticlimax.

As far as conscious intention goes, all Shaw's plays might bear the title he gave to three of them—plays for puritans—for that intention is to show romance transcended by a higher-than-erotic purpose. It is a classic intention, an application, really, of the traditional conflict of love and honor, with honor winning hands down, as it did in Corneille and even in one masterpiece of Racine's, *Bérénice*. We are concerned here not with philosophic intention but psychological substance. Where the philosopher insists that Shaw does not cross the threshold of the bedroom, the psychologist asks: Why does he hover at the bedroom door?

We know from the correspondence with Mrs. Pat Campbell that Shaw liked to play with fire. Even the correspondence with Ellen Terry entailed a playfulness not quite devoid of "danger." The boy Shaw had been witness to an odd household arrangement whereby his mother's music teacher contrived to be (it would seem) almost but not quite her lover. A slightly older Shaw has recently been portrayed as the intruder into a friend's marriage like his own Eugene Marchbanks: this is speculation. Let us look at the play *Candida*, which is a fact.

It has a notable Big Scene at the end, which is characterized by an equally notable improbability. A comfortable, sensible, parson's wife doesn't let herself get jockeyed into "choosing" between her husband and an almost total stranger. People—such people at least—don't do such things. A respectable woman's choice was made before the bans were read.

Perhaps Candida is not really respectable? That is the line of interpretation taken by Beatrice Webb, who declared her a prostitute. Will the play, taken as a play, bear this interpretation out? A dramatist's license to have the truth turn out different from the impression given to the audience is very limited, for it is to a large extent by giving impressions that he creates characters. Shaw has given the impression that Candida is *not* a prostitute.

Against this it can be urged that Shaw himself took Beatrice Webb's side and attacked Candida—in remarks he made about her in letters to James Huneker, Richard Burton, and others. True, but was that legitimate? He himself admitted that he had no more right to say what his plays meant than any other critic. One might add that he may have had less, for, when an author intervenes to correct our impressions of his work, he is often intervening to change or misinterpret that work.

Outside the play, Shaw is against Candida. Inside it, he is both for and against her, but he is for her effectually, and against her ineffectually, because the direct impression is favorable, while it is only by throwing logic back into the story when it is over that you can reach an unfavorable judgment. This means, I should think, that, though Shaw's intellect is against Candida, his emotions are for her.

What is it that this play has always projected in the theatre, and can always be counted on to project again? The charm of Candida. This is a reality so immediate and all-pervasive that it is hard for any other element in the play to make headway against it. Leading actresses know this and, hearing their director speak of Candida's essential badness, can afford to smile a Candida-smile, strong in the knowledge that there is nothing a director can do about this badness, once that smile has been displayed on stage as well as off.

I would say that it is a confusing play but that the confusion goes unnoticed because of Candida's charm and may even be the cause of a degree of emotional tension unusual in a Shaw play. Candida is made out of a Shavian ambivalence: he would like to reject this kind of woman, but actually he dotes on her. One quickly senses that he "is" Marchbanks. One also finds he protests (too much) that he is *not* Marchbanks. "I had in mind De Quincey's account of his adolescence in his Confessions,"* he wrote. "I certainly never thought of myself as a model." From the pretense of being De Quincey, no doubt, comes a certain unreality in some of the lines. As a character, Marchbanks seems to me not altogether a success because Shaw was hiding. What better image to hide behind than that of the kind of writer he himself was not—a romantic poet? Especially if De Quincey would do the job for him?

It didn't work perfectly except as pure histrionics. (Marchbanks, though a dubiously drawn character, is always an effective stage role, and still seems to correspond to the actors' idea of a poet.) But if no one in the play can reject Candida, there is a noteworthy niche in it for the man whom she will reject. This niche Marchbanks can fill nobly, and has his dramatic moment as he marches into it. His final exit is a magnificent piece of action. Possibly everything before that in this role is just as improvisation. Shaw could not make us believe in the poet's poetry. He does make us believe in his pain and his nobility, for at these points he could identify himself with Eugene completely without having to "think of himself as a model."

Dramatists usually speak of their characters individually, and that could be regarded as strange, because the drama, all through the centuries, has done much less with separate persons than with relationships. The traditional characters are, if you will, simplified to the point of crudity. What is not crude, as treated by the old dramatists, is the interaction of these characters. The dynamics of human relations are fully rendered. If what you do not get is the detailed psychological biography, what you do get is the essence of such relations as parent and child, boy and girl, man and wife.

Now modern playwrights, happily, have not departed from the classic patterns as much as they are supposed to have, and what rings true, emotionally, in *Candida* corresponds to Shaw's ability to find and recreate some of these elemental relationships. An inner obstacle, I tend to think, hampered him somewhat when he tried to "do" the Marchbanks-Candida relationship, but the Morell-Candida relation is both clear and challenging. It is, as Shaw himself said, the relationship of Nora and Torvald Helmer

---

*I think this is a slip and that Shaw did not mean *Confessions of an English Opium Eater* but the chapter "Premature Manhood" in *Autobiographic Sketches.*

turned around. In Shaw's play the man is the doll. But where Ibsen tells the story of a doll who finally comes to life, Shaw tells the story of a seemingly living person who turns out to have been a doll all along. (In other words, the relation of Shaw to Ibsen, instead of being direct, as it might seem, is an inverse one, exactly like the relation of Shaw to other nineteenth-century drama.) Into Morell Shaw can put that part of himself (a child) which finds Candida irresistible, just as into Candida he can put that part of Woman which he finds irresistible—the Mother in her. One would have to be as naïve a psychologist as Frank Harris to consider the mother-and-child relation less emotional than that of lovers.

Or less dramatic. Relationships become dramatic not in the degree of their eroticism but to the extent that they contain conflict. Pure love would not be a dramatic subject at all. Love becomes dramatic when it is *im*pure—when the loving element is submerged in a struggle for power. The axis about which *Candida* revolves is that of strength and weakness, not love and hate, and if one knows Shaw's views on the topic of the "weaker sex" in general the conclusion of *Candida* follows naturally. Instead of the little woman reaching up toward the arms of the strong man, we have the strong woman reaching down to pick up her child. It is remarkable how far Shaw's thought is from the standard "advanced thinking" of his generation with its facile assumptions about equality and comradeship. He is closer to Nietzsche.

Of the ending of *A Doll's House* it has been said: perhaps Nora has walked out in a mere tantrum and will be back in the morning. How much more savage is the ending of *Candida!* Only Strindberg could have written a sequel to it. The cruelty of the heroine, merely implicit in the present play, would have to come to the surface in any continuation of the story. Candida has chosen to let her husband discover his shame. She, as well as he, will have to take the consequences. Let the stage manager hold razors and strait jackets in readiness!

One reason why Shaw got so little credit for his treatment of the emotions is that the emotions he treats are not the ones people expect. The very fact that his favorite device is anticlimax should tell us that what he most insistently feels is "letdown." It may be retorted that, on the contrary, Bernard Shaw was the most buoyant and vivacious of men. That is also true. The axis "strength-weakness" is not more important to Shaw's content than the axis "elation-depression" is to his form. The dialogue ripples gaily along; then comes the sudden letdown. The circus has familiarized us with the pattern. It is the light of heart who take the pratfall. Even as the fool pops up in Shavian comedy in the highly intellectualized shape of a Jack Tanner, so the pratfall is transmuted into an anticlimax that has a climactic force. It has been customary to take these anticlimaxes as expressions of an idea, the idea of disenchantment. It is *the* idea of modern literature, and it is inseparable from an emotion far commoner and far more influential than romantic excitement. There seems to be no name for this emotion, and that too is significant. Let us call it desolation.

You cannot be disenchanted without having been enchanted. One is sometimes tempted to believe that our human desolation might have been avoided if only we had not started out so undesolate. It is not the fact that we don't have things that worries us but that we have lost them—or rather, been deprived of them. Desolation is the feeling of having been driven from paradise.

A friend of Bernard Shaw's said that when he saw *The Wild Duck* the bottom dropped out of the universe. One difference between Ibsen and Shaw is that the former produced this effect on the audience, whereas the latter produced it on the characters in a play. Just as a character in a melodrama loses a fortune, so a character in a Shaw play loses a universe. The experience may be given a playful treatment, as with Raina and Sergius. In the case of Morell, the treatment is only partly playful. It gets more serious as the play *Candida* proceeds. Morell finally loses his image of his wife and of himself. The curtain has to be rung down to save us from the Strindberg play that would have to follow.

What of *Mrs. Warren's Profession?* The starting point was a treatment by Maupassant of the theme of a girl finding out that her mother is a courtesan. In an early version of the tale Maupassant had the girl kill herself. In the later and better-known text (*Yvette*), he saves her to engineer for himself an ironic-poignant ending: she becomes a kept woman like her mother before her. Curtain! That is the kind of inversion of a suicidal ending which Shaw did *not* go in for. Or not any more. If Shaw had shown a "surrender to the system" (in comical fashion) in the ending to *Widowers' Houses,* he was now intent on showing a rejection of the system. In the first instance, Vivie Warren's revolt represents Shaw's rational rejection of capitalism, but the play culminates in a scene that has no necessary connection with economics, a scene of family crisis, a scene in which a daughter rejects her mother. Which after all is archetypal Shaw. Instead of the emotions of lover and mistress, he renders the emotions of parents and children, and particularly the emotion of the child rejecting the parent. *Major Barbara* is perhaps the grandest example of this archetype. The great last act of *Pygmalion* is the same thing in disguise, for Henry Higgins is the progenitor of the new Eliza, and that is why she must break free of him. Shaw's Joan has a father too—in heaven—and she comes at times almost to the point of breaking with Him. That she does not quite do so is the upshot of a play which, while it shows Joan's isolation from men, ends with a stretching of arms toward the heavenly father. . . . Vivie Warren is already a Saint Joan in that the experience Shaw gives her is that of being desolated. It is the experience he felt most deeply—presumably because it was the experience he had most deeply experienced. In any event, the two long scenes between Vivie and Mrs. Warren are playwriting of a standard England had not reached for a couple of centuries.

The background, however, is blurred. A Scribean climax is arranged to provide *élan* for the announcement that Vivie's romance is incestuous:

> CROFTS. . . . Allow me, Mister Frank, to introduce you to your half-sister, the eldest daughter of the Reverend Samuel Gardner. Miss Vivie: your half-brother. Good morning.
>
> FRANK (. . . *raising the rifle*). You'll testify before the coroner that it's an accident, Viv. (*He takes aim at the retreating figure of Crofts. Vivie seizes the muzzle and pulls it round against her breast.*)
>
> VIVIE. Fire now. You may.

Direct climax (as against anticlimax) was not really in Shaw's line, and in failing to parody Scribe here, Shaw has himself tumbled into the ridiculous. Perhaps the following act was bound to be an anticlimax in a way not intended—a mere disappointment.

Yet, it is hard to believe that the particular disappointments it brings are simply the result of a technical miscalculation. Rather, they involve hesitations about the subject. After so strongly creating the impression of incest, Shaw shuffles the notion off in the next act in a surprisingly ambiguous way. It would be easy enough, from a technical viewpoint, to make clear that no incest had been committed. Why did Shaw leave the situation doubtful? So that Vivie could dismiss the issue as irrelevant? In that case, what is relevant? Why is she giving Frank up? One can think of possible reasons, but what reason is one *supposed* to think of?

Unclarity in the work of so careful a craftsman, a writer, moreover, who has more than once been accused of excessive clarity, surely bears witness to inner uncertainty and conflict. To think of *Mrs. Warren's Profession* in this personal way is to realize what powerful aggressions it embodies. Shaw combined the themes of prostitution and incest in order to make quite a rational point: our mad society draws back in horror from incest, which is certainly not a pressing menace and perhaps not even a bad thing, while it encourages prostitution, which is a virulent social pestilence. But both themes have a resonance far beyond the bounds of intellect. It is as if they proved more than Shaw had bargained for. The incest theme is sounded—all too boldly. Then the young dramatist has no idea what to do with it. He takes it back. Only it is too late. So he half takes it back. After all, what is troubling Vivie does go beyond the rationally established causes. . . . Deep water! And Shaw flounders in it. Which has some interest for the student of the emotions. Even where Shaw's plays are faulty, they are not unemotional. On the contrary, it is because of a certain emotional involvement in the material, not because of incapacity for such involvement, that Shaw was not able to resolve certain problems and truly finish certain plays. *Candida* and *Mrs. Warren's Profession* could be cited in evidence. There is material in both which was not successfully worked through. . . .

From Script to Production *has continually focused on the transformation of the printed play into a living performance, on stage, screen, or television. It is therefore only proper that this anthology conclude with a review of a recent production of* Mrs. Warren's Profession *in which the critic's interest is divided equally between the play and its players. In reading the review, one wonders to what extent Stanley Price's rather negative opinion of* Mrs. Warren *is Shaw's fault, and to what extent it is conditioned by the way certain actors and a certain director have chosen to interpret the author's written signals. It is the playgoer's perpetual dilemma. Indeed, an appreciation of the inextricable relationship between script and production is perhaps the major lesson to be learned from a course such as the one which, with these discussions of* Mrs. Warren's Profession, *now comes to an end.*

[*MRS. WARREN'S PROFESSION* IN A 1971 PRODUCTION]
Stanley Price

"I think a really good performance of *Mrs. Warren's Profession* would keep its audience out of the hands of the women of the street for a fortnight at least." This hopeful sentiment was expressed by Shaw in one of the numerous statements he made about the play that was banned in this country for 30 years. If Shaw was right, however, and his play the moral prophylactic he intended, I must sadly report that current National Theatre audiences, far from eschewing commercial intercourse for the requisite fortnight, will be out on the street in droves seeking that now rare commodity, the strolling tart. This should read as an aspersion on the National's production and choice of play, rather than the morality of its audiences.

No doubt the National felt that *Mrs. Warren's Profession* had a renewed relevance in view of contemporary militancy over women's rights. To underline this their theatre programme contains a long piece by Germaine Greer, author of *The Female Eunuch,* entitled "A Whore in Every Home," a somewhat spectacular title reminiscent of the recent Marty Feldman film *Every Home Should Have One.* Yet far from stressing the contemporary relevance of Shaw's play to Women's Lib, Miss Greer's piece attacks Shaw for pussyfooting round the whole problem of prostitution, and for failing to grasp the nettle of women's rights and role with any genuine insight or conviction. Miss Greer concludes her piece with sentiments worthy of a Shavian preface: "The ambiguity of the apportionment of blame in *Mrs. Warren's Profession* does leave us however with an inkling of the truth, that prostitution is universal in a capitalist society in that all talent, all energy, all power is a commodity with a cash value. All contributions, material or spiritual or carnal, are marketable and will be marketed willy-nilly. Artists, teachers, craftsmen, lovers all hope to keep their faculties separate from the marketing of them, and none of them has more than Mrs. Warren's chance."

In fact I found Miss Greer's article more stimulating and provocative than the play presented to us, but it is not the business of the critic to deal with the programme notes rather than the programme itself. Thematically *Mrs. Warren's Profession* is of a piece with the two other recent Shaw revivals, the Aldwych's *Major Barbara* and Mi-

Stanley Price, *"Mrs. Warren's Profession* [Review]," *Plays and Players,* vol. 18, no. 5 (February 1971), pp. 42 and 45. Reprinted by permission of the author.

chael Blakemore's excellent production of *Widowers' Houses* at the Royal Court. It again illustrates Shaw's preoccupation with the wages of sin, and the effect of ill-gotten gain on the succeeding generation. *Mrs. Warren's Profession* is however the least dramatically satisfying of the three. Whereas *Major Barbara* and *Widowers' Houses* progress with character development and dialectical turn-about, the action and characters of *Mrs. Warren's Profession* remain static. Ronald Eyre's production only serves to emphasise this, as though, misled about the play's contemporary relevance, the message of the piece must be allowed to speak for itself. Thus, whenever the two principals, Coral Browne as Mrs. Warren and Sarah Badel as her daughter, Vivie, settle down to argue out the wages of prostitution they settle down with a vengeance, and a peculiar flatness descends on the proceedings. When all's said and done there is basically very little dramatic content to these mother-daughter exchanges.

Understandably Vivie is shocked that she has become a mathematical wrangler at Newnham on the proceeds of an international chain of brothels, and even more shocked that Mum has no intention of giving up her stock-holdings. On the other hand Mrs. Warren has paid scant maternal attention to her daughter for twenty odd years, so there is no great drama involved when her belated attempts to reclaim her maternal rights are abortive.

The part of Vivie is certainly no plum for an actress, and Sarah Badel tackles the part manfully. I use the adverb advisedly as there is a near-total lack of femininity about Shaw's drawing of the character. Starting off as a Cantabrigian prig Vivie ends up chastened, but with the same qualifications. Even the denouement of her romantic interest in the irresponsible, gold-digging Frank is blurred by Shaw. One is unsure whether Vivie's choice of emancipated spinsterhood is dictated by her realisation of Frank's intellectual inferiority, his gold-digging, or the possibilities of consanguinity. In addition it is scarcely dramatic for a woman who is ostensibly sexless to choose to renounce sex.

As Mrs. Warren, Coral Browne is a sad, but not totally unexpected disappointment. Miss Browne's effervescent theatricality has been seen at its best in Wilde and the last Joe Orton play. One has longed to see her tackle some of the Restoration parts, but as Mrs. Warren she abandons all zest and playfulness, and puts little in their place. She comes on as a gruff old cockney battleaxe and rings few changes. Shaw makes Mrs. Warren admit that she was "always a bit of a vulgarian," who could never have kept up appearances as her ex-madame sister has done as one of the most respectable women in the precincts of Winchester Cathedral. On the other hand Mrs. Warren also admits to enjoying a cosmopolitan society life among the pick of Europe's manhood. Thus one longed to see a little of Coral Browne's natural airs and graces with the h's dropped only when emotionally necessary. Instead one felt this Mrs. Warren had made her fortune out of the cockles and whelks concession at Brighton Racecourse rather than out of the ornate bordellos of that old common market.

But the evening is not without its pleasures. Alan Tagg, again designing as he did with the RSC's *London Assurance* under Ronald Eyre's direction, is among them. And a witty, sprightly performance as Frank from Ronald Pickup again shows the aptness of this actor's name. Everything literally seems to pick up when he is on stage. His movement and delivery are models of upbeat playing. Paul Curran as his hangdog clerical

father imparts a melancholy comedy to the one-time rake immured in a decrepit vic-
arage. Edward Hardwicke plays the sympathetic artist with warmth and simplicity,
and Bill Fraser follows his Boss Mangan in Chichester's *Heartbreak House* with yet another strong portrait of Shaw's capitalist villains who expose, out of their own mouths,
the iniquities of the capitalist system. As Sir George Crofts illustrates in his villainy,
Shaw's concern is with politics and economics rather than the new sociology or the new
Woman. As Miss Greer points out it is the profits of prostitution that concern Shaw,
not the evil itself. It is only a peg on which to hang a dramatic hat, and Shaw is less
at ease with it than he is with armaments manufacture or rack-renting.

The National, in their attempt to scour relevance out of old pans, might have
done better to consider the late and lamented Giles Cooper's *Everything in the Garden*, a
play that has never been produced successfully but which has some far more topical
and astringent things to say about prostitution and the woman's role in our society.